EDMUND BURKE AND THE ART OF RHETORIC

PADDY BULLARD

CAMBRIDGE
UNIVERSITY PRESS

CAMBRIDGE UNIVERSITY PRESS
Cambridge, New York, Melbourne, Madrid, Cape Town, Singapore,
São Paulo, Delhi, Dubai, Tokyo, Mexico City

Cambridge University Press
The Edinburgh Building, Cambridge CB2 8RU, UK

Published in the United States of America by Cambridge University Press, New York

www.cambridge.org
Information on this title: www.cambridge.org/9781107006577

First published 2011

Printed in the United Kingdom at the University Press, Cambridge

A catalogue record for this publication is available from the British Library

Library of Congress Cataloging-in-Publication Data

Bullard, Paddy, 1973–
Edmund Burke and the Art of Rhetoric / Paddy Bullard.
p. cm
Includes bibliographical references and index.
ISBN 978-1-107-00657-7
1. Burke, Edmund, 1729–1797. 2. Political oratory–Great Britain–History–18th century.
3. English language–18th century–Rhetoric. I. Title.
PR3334.B4Z58 2011
808.5′1–dc22
2010045700

ISBN 978-1-107-00657-7 Hardback

EDMUND BURKE AND THE ART OF RHETORIC

Edmund Burke ranks among the most accomplished orators ever to debate in the British Parliament. But often his eloquence has been seen to compromise his achievements as a political thinker. In the first full-length account of Burke's rhetoric, Paddy Bullard argues that Burke's ideas about civil society – and, particularly, about the process of political deliberation – are, for better or worse, shaped by the expressiveness of his language. Above all, Burke's eloquence is designed to express ethos or character. This rhetorical imperative is itself informed by Burke's argument that the competency of every political system can be judged by the ethical knowledge that the governors have both of the people that they govern, and of themselves. Bullard finds the intellectual roots of Burke's 'rhetoric of character' in early modern moral and aesthetic philosophy. He traces its development through Burke's parliamentary career to its culmination in his masterpiece, *Reflections on the Revolution in France.*

PADDY BULLARD is Lecturer in Eighteenth-Century Studies at the University of Kent, Canterbury, and a lecturer in English at St Catherine's College, Oxford. He is a former AHRC Research Fellow attached to the Cambridge Edition of the Works of Jonathan Swift, and Rank Junior Research Fellow at St Catherine's. He is co-editor of the online Jonathan Swift Archive.

to Rebecca

Contents

Acknowledgements

The late Christopher Lloyd, gardening correspondent for *The Guardian* and castellan of Great Dixter, maintained that the point of growing one's own vegetables – especially the sort of root crops with which Edmund Burke experimented at his farm near Beaconsfield – is to bring them on slowly in relatively uncultivated soil. This makes them far more delicious than the super-fertilized, shop-bought alternative. *Edmund Burke and the Art of Rhetoric* has been a long time growing, and hopefully its flavour is the better for it. But the analogy is a bad one, because the book could hardly have been planted in richer or sweeter soil. The President and fellows of St John's College, Oxford elected me to a Lamb and Flag Senior Scholarship in 1997, providing a home in which to complete the doctoral thesis from which this book germinated. Isabel Rivers and Nicholas Phillipson were scrupulous D.Phil. examiners. They have continued to offer me much-valued advice and encouragement, and to write me references, for which I cannot thank them enough. While writing the book I held posts at three Oxford colleges. My chief friend and colleague at each must stand in for many others in these acknowledgements: Ros Ballaster at Mansfield; Tom Keymer while he was at St Anne's; and Bart van Es at St Catz. I am particularly indebted to the Master and fellows of St Catherine's for electing me to the Rank Junior Research Fellowship in 2005, and for extending their wonderful generosity with a Research Associateship in 2008–9. It was at St Catz that this book took root and ripened. At the University of Kent, Jennie Batchelor, Bernhard Klein, Donna Landry and many other kind new colleagues have welcomed me warmly, ahead of harvest home.

David Womersley was the most patient and husbandmanlike of doctoral supervisors. His friendship and scholarly example, from which I continued to benefit at St Catherine's, lie behind all that is good in this book. I am deeply indebted to Jim McLaverty, David's fellow principal investigator at the AHRC Jonathan Swift Archive, for his generous support while I was a research fellow on that project, and since that time too. It is my constant study to imitate Jim's tact – intellectual and personal – and to give him fewer occasions for using it in its latter form. Among my other Swiftian colleagues, Adam Rounce and Daniel Cook have been great friends and co-conspirators.

The 'Restoration to Reform' seminar at Oxford University has been my scholarly seedbed for the last decade, and it was a privilege to act as co-convenor with Abigail Williams and Rebecca Bullard in 2006–9. Among the many friends I have learned from and argued with there, I would particularly like to thank Marilyn Butler, Luisa Calé, Liam Condon, Faramerz Dabhoiwala, Robert DeMaria, Rosemary Dixon, Markman Ellis, Stuart Gillespie, Kathryn Gleadle, Mina Gorji, Felicity James, Roger Lonsdale, Kate Loveman, Patrick Mackie, Jon Mee, Claude Rawson, Michael F. Suarez SJ, Kathryn Sutherland, Alexis Tadié, Kate Tunstall, Marcus Walsh, Sean Walsh and Susan Wyman. The international community of scholars working on Burke has been very supportive. I have benefited especially from Fred Lock's unrivalled knowledge of the subject. I first became interested in Edmund Burke as an undergraduate when I read the chapter on Hazlitt and Burke in David Bromwich's *Hazlitt: The Mind of a Critic*, so I am particularly grateful for his correspondence on matters Burkean. In June 2007 Fred, David and many other eminent Burke scholars presented their work at a conference I organized in Oxford, 'Edmund Burke and the Business of Affection'. I am grateful to the English and History Faculties at Oxford University for their generous support of that event. At this and other conferences I have gained many insights from talking to Eric Baker, Michael Brown, J.C. D. Clark, Claire Connolly, Ian Crowe, Frans de Bruyn, Michael Funk Deckard, Sean Patrick Donlan, David Dwan, Luke Gibbons, Ryan Hanley, Ian Harris, James Harris, Tony Howe, Jeremy Jennings, Robert Jones, Karen O'Brien, Joseph L. Pappin, Seamus Perry, Jennifer Pitts, Matthew Scott, Brian Young and many others.

Six colleagues took time out of their busy schedules to read parts of the manuscript: this book has been improved immeasurably by the expertise of Richard Bourke, Rebecca Bullard, Daniel Carey, Sean Connolly, Rhodri Lewis and Christopher Reid. I cannot thank them enough for their help. I must also thank my two anonymous readers at Cambridge University Press for their meticulous and generous treatment of the original manuscript. Working with Linda Bree, my exemplary editor at Cambridge University Press, has been a privilege, not least because this book shares her protection (and therefore has a sort of vicarious association) with so much that is excellent in recent eighteenth-century studies. The vigilant solicitude of Maartje Scheltens, who saw the book through the press, and of Damian Love, who copy-edited the manuscript, has improved the finished product immeasurably.

Clement Bullard and Louis Bullard concentrated my mind on the task at hand, while putting it all into perspective. Without the unstinting generosity of Anne and Frank Rees I doubt that the book would ever have reached completion. Diana Bullard and Elizabeth Bullard have been a constant source of love and support. This book is dedicated to Rebecca, with devoted love.

Abbreviations

Corr.	*The Correspondence of Edmund Burke*, ed. Thomas W. Copeland, 10 vols. (Cambridge University Press, 1958–78)
CW	*The Collected Writings of Rousseau*, gen. ed. Roger Masters and Christopher Kelly, 13 vols. (Hanover, NH: University Press of New England for Dartmouth College, 1990–)
EB	F.P. Lock, *Edmund Burke*, 2 vols. (Oxford: Clarendon Press, 1998–2006)
LRBL	Adam Smith, *Lectures on Rhetoric and Belles Lettres*, ed. J.C. Bryce (Oxford: Clarendon Press, 1983)
OC	Jean-Jacques Rousseau, *Œuvres complètes*, ed. B. Gagnebin and M. Raymond, Bibliothèque de la Pléiade, 5 vols. (Paris: Gallimard, 1959–95)
OED	*Oxford English Dictionary*
PE	Edmund Burke, *A Philosophical Enquiry into the Origin of our Ideas of the Sublime and Beautiful*, ed. J.T. Boulton (London: Routledge, 1958)
PW	*The Prose Works of Jonathan Swift*, ed. Herbert Davis, 16 vols. (Oxford: Blackwell, 1939–74)
TMS	Adam Smith, *The Theory of Moral Sentiments*, ed. D.D. Raphael and A.L. Macfie (Oxford University Press, 1979)
WS	Edmund Burke, *The Writings and Speeches of Edmund Burke*, gen. ed. Paul Langford, 9 vols. (Oxford: Clarendon Press, 1981–2000)

Introduction: Burke, rhetoric and ethics

William Wordsworth finished his studies at Cambridge University in January 1791, and spent the next four months kicking his heels in London, 'whirled about by the vortex of its *strenua inertia*', as he wrote to a friend.[1] In contemporary letters and later memoirs we see him making his first contact with the radical dissenting circles that would welcome him as an active member in 1793 – but he keeps an eye on mainstream politics as well.[2] He pores over the 'master pamphlets of the day', and attends debates at the House of Commons.[3] One 'tongue-favoured' orator in particular sets his heart racing with excitement during a visit to the strangers' gallery, as he later recalls in Book VII of *The Prelude*:

> This is no trifler, no short-flighted wit,
> No stammerer of a minute, painfully
> Delivered, No! the Orator hath yoked
> The Hours, like young Aurora, to his Car:
> Thrice welcome Presence! how can patience e'er
> Grow weary of attending on a track
> That kindles with such glory! All are charmed,
> Astonished; like a Hero in Romance,
> He winds away his never-ending horn;
> Words follow words, sense seems to follow sense;
> What memory and what logic! till the Strain
> Transcendent, superhuman as it seemed,
> Grows tedious even in a young Man's ear.[4]

Editorial tradition has it that this is a portrait of William Pitt the younger, probably on account of some earlier references Wordsworth makes to the familiarity of the Pitt family name. But the unnamed orator is far more likely to be Edmund Burke. Burke was admired and feared in almost equal measure for the brilliance and long-windedness of his parliamentary speeches, and the eulogistic apostrophe to the 'Genius of Burke' that Wordsworth inserts after this passage in his revisions of 1832 is framed as an apology for his satire of 1804.[5] But it is the details of Wordsworth's language here that confirm he has Burke in mind.

Wordsworth's lines resonate with little echoes from the master pamphlet of 1790, *Reflections on the Revolution in France.* Interestingly, it is Burke's satire on the rhetoric of the revolutionary radicals that seems to play most insistently through his memory. The poet's elusive image of the orator's speech as a 'track | That kindles with such glory' transfigures Burke's caricature of the leading radical Dr Richard Price, imagined warming himself up to deliver a political sermon: 'His enthusiasm kindles as he advances; and when he arrives at his peroration, it is in a full blaze.'[6] Burke the orator appears to Wordsworth as a marvellous 'Hero in Romance', a glowing personal presence that charms and astonishes. Earlier in *The Prelude* Wordsworth writes warmly of those endless 'Tales that charm away the wakeful night | In Araby, – romances, legends penned | For solace', so there is some reason to find temper in the satire here.[7] Except that Wordsworth's simile brings together romance and eloquence in a way that evokes another precedent from the *Reflections.* Burke makes the same connection in his attack on Jean-Jacques Rousseau as antecedent of the French Revolution (Wordsworth is thought to have been reading Rousseau, doubtless with enthusiasm, during 1791).[8] In the *Reflections* Burke alleges that Rousseau revealed to a mutual acquaintance how he set out to animate his own writings, if not exactly with 'fairies, and heroes of romance', then with 'that species of the marvellous, which might still be produced . . . the marvellous in life, in manners, in characters, and in extraordinary situations, giving rise to new and unlooked-for strokes in politics and morals'.[9] Correspondingly, Wordsworth imagines Burke as at once hero and narrator of a new kind of political and moral romance, rather as Burke had cast Rousseau in the same double, and ultimately Quixotic, role.[10]

Whether or not these correspondences are coincidences, they can help us to place Edmund Burke – and, more particularly, Edmund Burke the rhetorician – in a larger literary and intellectual landscape than he usually occupies. Either by means of serendipity or of very intelligent instinct, Wordsworth's recollections of Parliament in the spring of 1791 touch upon a quality that is essential to Burke's art of rhetoric. The impression received by the poet is that of having encountered a 'species of the marvellous' in human form, a person who is marked out even among his fellow parliamentarians by his extraordinary accomplishment as a speaker. And yet Burke is not proud: he seems somehow innocent of his distinction. In his way, the orator is one of that select Wordsworthian company engaged in a work of love, 'Who care not, know not, think not what they do'.[11] The poet is impressed enough by the orator's inartificial proofs ('What memory'), struggles to follow his reasoning ('what logic!'), and feels moved by his emotional appeals ('charmed, | Astonished'). But without doubt it is the character of the orator, his ethos, that strikes home. Wordsworth hardly notices whether the orator has managed to move the audience, or to win its assent through reasoned argument. The presence of the speaker, his talent and capacity as manifested by sheer personal charisma, are all his concern. In short, the rhetoric that Wordsworth witnesses is a rhetoric of character.

My business in the following pages is to explain how the combination of these two terms, 'rhetoric' and 'character', can help us describe the function and the beauty of Burke's writings. Burke is acknowledged to have been the most eloquent writer and speaker of his age, even by doubters like the young Wordsworth. His accomplishment both as a literary artist and as a political thinker is linked at the deepest level with contemporary conceptions of what it means to deliberate well in matters of state. This book is the first full-length study to give an account of these links: it proposes a theory of Burke's rhetoric. While outlining this theory I want to keep the term 'rhetoric' available for use in a relatively informal way, to denote various qualities of artfulness, dynamism and spontaneity in Burke's published works. These qualities were associated by Burke's contemporaries with his skill as a parliamentary speaker, and have been analysed ever since according to the systems of eloquence developed by theorists of the art in fourth-century Athens, first-century Rome and early modern Europe. A problem here is that the classical and humanist tradition of rhetoric, which seems indispensable as a contextual source for Burke's art, is systematic to its core. Rhetoric's claims to the dignity of being an art, rather than a mere knack, depend upon the rational way it accounts for all those persuasive irregularities of expression that lift language above grammar. But a systematic description of Burke's writings and speeches is quite inappropriate to the expansive and associative way in which he worked. Rhetoric is a system, but Burke is not a systematic thinker. The very idea of 'Burkean rhetoric' implies an awkward methodological contradiction: I shall try to plot a way through that contradiction in a moment.

It is no coincidence (as we shall see in this book's first chapter) that the 'character' component of Burke's 'rhetoric of character' poses similar problems. 'Character' is a descriptive word, referring to the general impression given by the manners, habits, social status and moral qualities of persons (or collections of persons). But to give the 'character' of a person is not only to describe – it is to evaluate morally. Even during the early eighteenth century, when the descriptive sense of the word 'character' predominated in common usage, having no character at all was a bad thing.[12] At the same time, those with too much character risked being satirized in Theophrastan caricature, or captured by stage typology. During the late eighteenth and early nineteenth centuries, the evaluative senses of 'character' took over, and they became positive, often in a strenuous sort of way. 'Character' came to stand for qualities of moral strength, perseverance, dutifulness, uprightness, and so on: this is the 'elevation of character' that Samuel Smiles, in *Self-Help* (1859), would present as the precondition and the end of getting on.[13] When John Stuart Mill denounced this sort of 'pinched and hidebound type of human character' in *On Liberty* (1859), critics responded by attacking his own vision of progressive human individuality as a system of enfeebling selfishness, quite incompatible with the prerogatives of social duty.[14] Burke's use of the term 'character' is rooted, as we shall see, in an early modern literary way of writing about human personalities that can seem strange to twenty-first-century sensibilities. It is defined by the early modern assurance that something definitive can be said about someone's morality and disposition in the space of a few paragraphs or sentences, or even within the compass of a well-turned paradox – that the complexity of human personality is somehow best served by extreme economy of description. But Burke also expends a great deal of rhetorical energy on presenting himself as something rather like a prototypical Smilesian hero: as unbendingly and unselfishly industrious, as a striving and dutiful new man. What removes Burke so far from the world of the mid-Victorian Liberals, of course, is his conception of his own vigorous character as a necessary, if minor supplement to the public characters of the landowning, aristocratic ruling classes – characters that he values precisely because they are 'sluggish, inert and timid' in their dominance, and therefore capable of representing the settled property of the nation.[15]

It is this conception that Burke has of his own public character as being at once expressive of personality, and meaningful only in the context of other, rather different kinds of character, that is so crucial to his rhetoric. If rhetoric is the art of finding the means of persuasion best suited to any given argument, Burke believes that the most truly political way to those means is through the display of one's own good political character, the rhetoric of ethos. And this rhetorical ideal feeds back into Burke's idea of good political character. It is manifested above all in a statesman's real knowledge of (or capacity to represent in some other way) the characters of those to whom (and of whom, and for whom) he speaks. The ethical principles here involve at once a theory about effective deliberation, a mechanism for political representation, and a vision of good government. Because these functions are inseparable in Burke's writings and speeches, the proper study of his rhetoric must focus on the terms of its referential purpose. To put it another way, the subject of his rhetoric (who is addressing whom, on behalf of whom?) is the pressing problem, to which the object of his rhetoric (argumentative persuasion) is subordinate.[16] We can begin to unfold this principle of Burke's rhetoric of character by looking at a few of his very rare direct statements about the nature of political eloquence.

MAKING DISCOURSE ETHICAL

Burke left behind only a very few direct comments on the art of political rhetoric. Perhaps his most revealing remark on the subject is preserved by James Boswell in the *Life of Johnson* (1789), a book that Burke himself enjoyed but rather disapproved of.[17] Boswell records a conversation at The Club led by Burke and Richard Brinsley Sheridan from 1778, two years before the start of the latter's parliamentary career. Sheridan had an envious interest in Burke's published speeches, and on this occasion he wondered (repeating a favourite observation of Oliver Goldsmith) what posterity would make of those speeches having been made so well, though 'not one vote would be gained by it'.[18] Burke replied candidly

> that it is very well worth while for a man to take pains to speak well in Parliament. A man, who has vanity, speaks to display his talents; and if a man speaks well, he gradually establishes a certain reputation and consequence in general opinion, which sooner or later will have its political reward. Besides, though not one vote is gained, a good speech has its effect. Though an act which has been ably opposed passes into a law, yet in its progress it is modelled, it is softened in such a manner, that we see plainly the Minister has been told, that the Members attached to him are so sensible of its injustice or absurdity from what they have heard, that it must be altered . . . There are many honest well-meaning country gentlemen who are in parliament only to keep up the consequence of their families. Upon most of these a good speech will have influence.[19]

Boswell captures a characteristic note in Burke's voice here, a touch of bitterness held back behind the tone of reasonable pragmatism. Eloquence is merely a consolation for the lack of influence, and flourishes in the absence of real power. Burke writes something similar eight years earlier in

Thoughts on the Present Discontents (1770) while lamenting the decline of independent MPs in the House of Commons. For a non-partisan country gentleman, ruining himself to get elected and then losing influence among the parliamentary placemen is bad enough. But 'if he has not the talent of elocution', reckons Burke, 'which is the case of many as wise and knowing men as any in the House, he is liable to all these inconveniencies, without the eclat which attends upon any tolerably successful exertion of eloquence. Can we conceive a more discouraging post of duty than this?'[20]

The striking thing in both passages is the easiness with which Burke allows Parliament to be largely dysfunctional as a deliberative institution, or even as a bulwark between equity and the 'injustice and absurdity' of ministers. These are large concessions to the cynicism of his non-parliamentary friends, and they are made for a particular rhetorical effect. They allow Burke to place a particular emphasis on the ethical function of parliamentary eloquence. The éclat of a 'tolerably successful' speech is enough to make good an opposition politician's entanglement with the whole system of parliamentary obstruction. It is as though the jobbery of Lord North's ministry and the dullness of the country gentlemen exist solely as a foil for the brilliance of the opposition talents.[21] Burke proposes that the only honest redress for MPs, and the most likely chance (small as it is) of averting a constant round of legislative catastrophe, is through the display of extraordinary eloquence. Mere good counsel is not enough – the speaker must make an impact, and the energy for that comes from self-directed motives.[22] The appetite for gaining 'a certain reputation and consequence in general opinion' is one; simple 'vanity' is another. Burke names the vice self-deprecatingly, and perhaps it is magnanimity that he really has in mind, the 'wild stock of pride' as he would later call it, referring to his friend Admiral Keppel, 'on which the tenderest of all hearts graft[s] the milder virtues'.[23] Winning the honourable character of an orator is a sufficient motive for undertaking the labours of parliamentary business. Correspondingly, the persuadable part of the Commons, the independent members, are there to keep up characters of their own. It is on this mutual ground for the estimation and assertion of character, this ethical medium, that good speaking can have a real political effect, says Burke – where it has any effect at all.

Another of Burke's rare moments of rhetorical self-reflection occurs in his *Appeal from the New to the Old Whigs*. It is found in a passage of self-vindication from the charges of inconsistency that he faced in 1790 after his change of position from conciliator of the American revolutionaries to opponent of the French revolutionaries. Burke defends himself by describing the difference between the emphatic rhetorical mode in which he writes and the kind of 'academic' discourse in which all possible considerations of a question must be weighed equally. 'A man who, among various objects of his equal regard, is secure of some, and full of anxiety for the fate of others', Burke writes,

> ... is apt to go to much greater lengths in his preference of the objects of immediate solicitude than Mr. Burke has ever done. A man so circumstanced often seems to undervalue, to vilify, almost to reprobate and disown, those that are out of danger. This is the voice of nature and truth, and not of inconsistency and false pretence.[24]

Burke describes how the speaker depends on the generosity of the audience to distinguish his general good intentions (which can only be taken on trust) from the exigencies of his argument. His point here is about the need for freedom, weight and energy in argument, and the peculiar relationships of trust that these qualities require. He is also making a claim about his own political character. Evidently Burke has none of the ballast of wealth or rank that his contemporaries recognize as legitimate tokens of authority. But the very fact of his participation in legislative debate – the fact that he is a speaker in Parliament, not merely a silent voter or backstairs bureaucrat – implies a concession on the part of those who do have this sort of authority that Burke speaks, at very least, with the weight of an honourable character. So long as the audience attends to Burke's 'reputation and consequence' as an orator, that audience has no reason to expect that Burke will make comprehensive, balanced, 'academic' arguments, rather than personal, partial and moral ones. It can require no tribute of reticence or deference from him. Neither does it have the right to charge him with hypocrisy or inconsistency when his polemics fall short of academic completeness and metaphysical truth. To whatever extent it is ethical, his oratory must necessarily be partial.

It is the relationship between the characters of speaker and audience that Burke takes as his fundamental concern in each of these remarks about rhetoric. The external objects of discourse (persuasive argument, or informative communication) are of secondary importance: the subjective part of discourse, the reputation of the speaker and the opinion of the persons to whom he is speaking, are what capture his attention. Burke may not be a systematic thinker, but the remarks show that he was in the habit of thinking critically about how character functions in rhetoric. We see this in the carefulness of his ethical discriminations. In the passage from Boswell's *Life* where he is talking about the parliamentary reception of oratory, Burke's immediate instinct is to distinguish between the audience broadly conceived (which confers 'a certain reputation and consequence in general opinion') and the part of the audience that is actually receptive to his rhetoric (the 'honest well-meaning country gentlemen'). The audience broadly conceived may be the body of the House of Commons, or the wider readership of his printed speeches. But both are distinct from the particular audience whose character it is to be persuaded by good speeches.[25] What interests Burke is the complex involvement of one kind of audience with another. The persuadability of the receptive part of the audience itself depends on the speaker attaining a 'reputation and consequence in general opinion' that only the general audience can confer. Burke's casual analysis of voting patterns in the Commons looks rather unsophisticated by the standards of modern empirical historiography, perhaps. But it shows that what he sacrificed in accuracy was made up for in the critical intelligence of his thought about political audiences.

There is consistency among these scattered remarks on eloquence, and, as we shall see, they correspond with certain rhetorical practices and preoccupations that recur throughout Burke's writings and speeches. When Burke thinks about the art of persuasion his instinct is to cut through all the peripheral questions of style, delivery and political culture that occupied his rhetorically minded contemporaries, and to go to the core of the art. Burke's interest is in the business of persuasion and proof – what Aristotle calls *pistis*, a term signifying both the state of conviction that occurs when somebody accepts an argument, and the process that brings about that state of assent.[26] According to Aristotle's description, the arguments of working politicians are likely to combine external proofs (statistics, information, legal precedents) with artistic proofs, such as rational argumentation (logos) and appeals to the audience's emotions (pathos). But it is a third kind of artistic proof – proof by means of establishing the character and credibility of a speaker (ethos) – that Burke takes as the organizing principle for the kind of political arguments he makes.

We do not know whether Burke ever read Aristotle's *Rhetoric*, but his comments agree with the Aristotelian dictum that moral character constitutes the most effective means of proof, and that ethos is the principle to which the other kinds of proof must refer.[27] The 'body' of rhetorical proof, according to Aristotle, is built up from logical arguments based on general maxims and common beliefs, or 'enthymemes'. But the problem with logical arguments is that their persuasiveness does not increase in proportion with their logicality. In the rough and tumble of civic dispute there is no correlation between a speaker's cogency and the effectiveness of their discourse. On the contrary, the most persuasive speakers do not use enthymemes when they move or reassure their audience.[28] Proofs based on the character of the speaker, however, are more persuasive the more ethical they are made: 'for we feel confidence in a greater degree', says Aristotle, 'and more readily in persons of worth in regard to everything in general, but where there is no certainty and there is room for doubt, our confidence is absolute'.[29] In a different sense, the ability of speakers to persuade by pathos is determined by their knowledge of ethos, because the emotions are rooted in that irrational part of the soul that everyone understands in terms of moral character: 'when describing a man's moral character we do not say that he is wise or intelligent, but gentle and temperate; but a wise man also is praised for his disposition, and praiseworthy dispositions we term virtues'.[30] The catalogue of emotions in the second book of the *Rhetoric*, which Aristotle provides as a guide to the passional dispositions found in all audiences, is presented as a counterpart to and extension of his account of ethos.[31]

For Burke, who tends to identify serious parliamentary eloquence with oppositional politics, winning the reputation of eloquence provides consolation for those who lack real power, and keeps alive the promise of a deferred 'political reward'. More importantly, it puts the speaker into a sphere of trust that allows him to make more emphatically rhetorical speeches, safe in the knowledge that his audience will grant him latitude to weigh the most pressing aspects of any given question. For 'if by a fair, by an indulgent, by a gentlemanly behaviour to our representatives', Burke warns, 'we do not give confidence to their minds, and a liberal scope to their understandings; if we do not permit our members to act on a *very* enlarged view of things; we shall at length infallibly degrade our national representation into a confused and scuffling bustle of local agency'.[32] A well-established ethos gives a speaker licence to be urgent, to abjure false delicacy, and to resist neutrality, and it allows him to do all this without renouncing the claims of equity. There is a point in the *Reflections* when Burke has a moment of self-consciousness about his reckless veneration of aristocracy, and he turns on the reader to reaffirm this ethical function in his writing:

> I do not, my dear Sir, conceive you to be of that sophistical, captious spirit, or of that uncandid dulness, as to require, for every general observation or sentiment, an explicit detail of the correctives and exceptions which reason will presume to

be included in all the general propositions which come from reasonable men. You do not imagine that I wish to confine power, authority, and distinction to blood and names and titles. No, Sir. There is no qualification for government but virtue and wisdom, actual or presumptive.[33]

The tone here is coercive, although Burke is appealing once again to the special latitude of political discourse. The pun of 'reason' against 'reasonable', a favourite of Burke's, shows a touch of Augustan wit.[34] It provides the vehicle for his most characteristic argument about political discourse: that at moments of crisis the habits and instincts of 'reasonable men' are more reliable guides for action than the control (the 'correctives and exceptions') of purely rational deliberation. Character supersedes ratiocination, dispositional reasonableness precedes the act of reasoning, ethos takes priority over logos. In so far as Burke thinks technically about rhetoric, this is his artistic principle: to secure as firm a bond as possible of common sense and shared reasonableness between artist and audience, so that the greatest latitude of thought and expression can be taken by the speaker without breaking the faith of the listener. The eccentric energy of the argument is balanced against the ethical ballast of the readership. Burke's art of rhetoric is an art of moral equipoise.

The orientation of Burke's rhetoric towards ethos obliges us to go beyond the common conception of the art as an instrument of persuasion. In Burke's hands, rhetoric is both something less and something more than a technology for interfering with the convictions of others. It is his theory of government that indicates the most appropriate way of understanding the sorts of comprehensive strategies we find in Burke's writings and speeches. From the very start of his political career Burke argues that it is the first duty of all legislators to attune themselves to the character and disposition of the political nation for whom they legislate. His experience of American colonial politics – his early realization that it would always be impossible to compel or impose upon the Americans – is the defining one here. 'People must be governed in a manner agreeable to their temper and disposition', he writes in *Observations on a Late State of the Nation* (1769), his first major pamphlet, 'and men of free character and spirit must be ruled with, at least, some condescension to this spirit and this character.'[35] 'The temper and character which prevail in our Colonies', he reiterates in his *Speech on Conciliation with America* (1775), 'are, I am afraid, unalterable by any human art. We cannot ... persuade them that they are not sprung from a nation, in whose veins the blood of freedom circulates. The language in which they would hear you tell them this tale, would detect the imposition; your speech would betray you.'[36]

The retort of rhetorical language back upon the ethos of the persuader defines the limit of its instrumentality.

It also points the way towards a more positive purpose for civil deliberation, based on knowledge of those tempers and dispositions. 'In effect, to follow, not to force the publick inclination', writes Burke at the end of his American engagement, 'to give a direction, a form, a technical dress and a specifick sanction, to the general sense of the community, is the true end of legislature.'[37] The relevance of this American insight to Burke's domestic politics was always explicit: 'The temper of the people amongst whom he presides ought therefore to be the first study of the Statesman', he asserts in *Thoughts on the Present Discontents* (1770).[38] In the *Speech on Economical Reform* (1780) Burke talks of the importance of parliamentary petitions as guides to this temper ('I would turn my eyes to the very quarter to which theirs are directed'), and uses the image of Abraham walking before God to suggest the delicate commixture of direction and supplication that he is trying to describe: 'We ought to walk before them with purity, plainness, and integrity of heart ... I cannot indeed take upon me to say I have the honour to *follow* the sense of the people. The truth is, *I met it on the way*, while I was pursuing their interest according to my own ideas.'[39] By the time of *Reflections on the Revolution in France* (1790) this art of political sympathy refers not only to the opinions, but to the capacities of the governed: 'In all bodies, those who will lead, must also, in a considerable degree, follow. They must conform their propositions to the taste, talent, and disposition of those whom they wish to conduct.'[40] Taste, talent and disposition, traditionally the prerogatives of the orator, have become somehow imprinted on the character of the audience. As a model for legitimate political representation, this principle of Burke's is likely to be nugatory to his modern readers. But as an ethics of deliberation it offers a key to understanding the integrity of his political thought, and to the art of his rhetoric.

BURKE'S ELOQUENCE

Burke's way of thinking about the business of political deliberation is basically ethical: his great concern is with the decorum of the relationship between the individual speaker and the other individuals, parties or institutions that the speaker is addressing. But it hardly seems right to let Burke have the last word on the matter. What specifically rhetorical qualities in his writings and speeches would we be ignoring, were we to read his writings and speeches purely in terms of the orator's character, and its relationship with the character of his audience? The most immediate contemporary responses to his oratory offer a way into this question. I want to consider two related points of similarity between Wordsworth's portrait of 1804 and some earlier descriptions of the orator in action. First is a common sense of the natural integrity of Burke's rhetoric – of its self-connectedness, as it were; and second is a sense of dissatisfaction at the spoken medium – an irritated feeling of missing something that might have been comprehensible in print.

On the positive side, Burke's eloquence strikes both Wordsworth and the earlier witnesses with an impression of organic unity, of life and growth and movement in his language and thought. They find a kind of living phenomenality in his speaking. Fanny Burney's memoir on the second day of Burke's speech at the opening of the impeachment of Warren Hastings in February 1788 is a typical example: 'When he narrated', she writes in her journal,

> he was easy, flowing, and natural; when he declaimed, energetic, warm and brilliant. The sentiments he interspersed were as nobly conceived as they were highly coloured; his satire had a poignancy of wit that made it as entertaining as it was penetrating; his allusions and quotations, as far as they were English and within my reach, were apt and ingenious; and the wild and sudden flights of his fancy, bursting forth from his creative imagination in language fluent, forcible, and varied, had a charm for my ear and my attention wholly new and perfectly irresistible.[41]

Burney's generous, if slightly box-ticking appreciation (she was a Hastings supporter) conveys her grudging sense of the totality of Burke's performance. Other common manifestations of this impression of organic wholeness are metaphors of flowering or fruiting. Burke's auditors were astonished at the superabundance of his invention: 'He was like a man in an Orchard', writes James Boswell after hearing Burke speak for the first time, 'where boughs loaded with fruit hung around him, and he pulled apples as fast as he pleased and pelted the ministry.'[42] Boswell wants to evoke the copious spontaneity of Burke's imagination – elsewhere he compares its variety to that of 'animated nature' – but ends up describing something wasteful (and something bruising) instead. The memoirist Nathaniel Wraxall recalled how Burke seemed always 'to be oppressed under the load and variety of his intellectual treasures; of which he frequently scattered portions with a lavish hand, to inattentive, impatient, hungry, and sleepy hearers, undeserving of such presents'.[43] Again, embarrassment and discomfort were common responses to the abundance of his gift.

A second recurring theme that seems implicit in Wordsworth's account is the idea that Burke's speeches really belonged to the printed page. Witnesses often described – hesitating between praise and blame – a peculiarly literary quality in his eloquence. Even his admirers found him 'abstracted and subtile', and too ready to refer particular issues to general principles: 'perhaps it is true', Burke admitted to Charles O'Hara in 1766, 'I myself dont know it; but think, if I had not been known to be the Author of a Book somewhat metaphysical, the objections against my mode of Argument would be of another nature.'[44] Burke is referring to *A Philosophical Enquiry into the Sublime and Beautiful*, the treatise on aesthetics that he had published anonymously in 1757. He must also have had in mind the recent report of a friend, the Dublin lawyer John Ridge, about some overheard comments on another debate: 'One called his speech "an Essay on Government"; Another said ... "that it was in short *The sublime and beautiful*". But this last', Ridge added, feeling the double edge of the compliment, 'was an admirer and not a malignant.'[45] And neither would Burke have missed the undertone of these apparently flattering reports. It was easy to associate literary people with unstatesmanly moral qualities: with a mean dependency on the praise of others, with the narrowness of retired pursuits, or simply with the poverty of the garret. Burke would do as much himself in *Reflections on the Revolution in France*.[46] The comments foreshadow a criticism that became increasingly common as his career progressed: that the analytical éclat of his speeches was precisely what made them unconvincing in debate. 'He is always brilliant in an uncommon degree', noticed his friend the Irish politician Henry Flood, 'and yet I believe it would be better he were less so ... I sincerely think it interrupts him so much in argument, that the house are never sensible that he argues as well as he does.'[47] Longinus suggests that sublime rhetoric should dazzle its audience so as to render the orator's artifice invisible. The brilliance of Burke's invention has the less useful consequence of obstructing its own polemical force.

Another aspect of these criticisms is that many observers felt his oratorical genius needed to be completed or fulfilled by the process of transcription and publication. Burke had an anxious sense that MPs who made well-structured, simple speeches, such as his colleague Charles James Fox, often appeared to advantage in the newspapers, while his more spontaneous and subtle performances were garbled by the reporters.[48] On the other hand, MPs who read well in the newspapers often appeared stiff and prosy when their speeches were carefully transcribed and published as stand-alone books – as the comparison between Burke and Richard Brinsley Sheridan proves.[49] Sheridan's set-piece orations, such as his celebrated speech at the Hastings trial on the Begums of Oudh (7 February 1787), were pointed, aphoristic performances, finely constructed and meticulously rehearsed.[50] But their grand simplicity seems lifeless on the page. Sheridan never published them in the sort of authorized edition produced by Burke.[51] The conversational syntax and rough transitions of Burke's speeches could baffle an audience, and yet set the printed page alight. Their verbal spontaneity is an unexpected condition of their effectiveness as literary prose. The jurist Thomas Erskine once made a furtive exit from Parliament halfway through what seemed to him an especially boring speech of Burke's on Indian affairs. Looking through the published copy later on, he found it 'so very beautiful that I actually wore it to pieces reading it'.[52] Burke's writings and speeches never quite fit into their proper medium – they have an awkward energy that seems always to be straining out of itself into a different form.

While Burke's friends noticed the overcharged literariness of his speeches, his detractors found his printed works full of redundant oratoricality. Reading the *Reflections*, Mary Wollstonecraft detects a reason perverted by 'the instantaneous applause which his eloquence extorts', and now unable to stem the 'torrent of shining sentences' produced by old parliamentary habits.[53] Typically, in some of the last publications of the Hastings impeachment Burke absorbs these sorts of criticism, and accuses Hastings's defence team of adopting a viciously polite and 'blandishing' rhetoric in order to extenuate their master's attrocities.[54] Radical readers often complain of a shifting, evasive, elusive quality in Burke's written treatises which they link instinctively with facility in speech. When Thomas Paine reads the *Reflections* he hears 'music in the ear, and nothing in the heart', while James Mackintosh, using a typically Burkean military metaphor, describes Burke's verbal excesses as a sort of discursive dirty warfare: 'He can cover the most ignominious retreat by a brilliant allusion … He can escape from an untenable position into a splendid declamation.'[55] The anonymous author of *Political Correspondence* (1793), who dedicates his second letter to a history of contemporary parliamentary eloquence, decides that the *Reflections* has earned Burke retrospective disqualification from the ranks of the great speakers – even though 'the pamphlet in question ought rather to be considered as a fine piece of declamatory composition and impassioned eloquence, than as a useful vehicle of solid instruction'.[56] The author has a keen sense of the unsettled way that Burke occupies his linguistic media: his written prose produces an effect of spontaneous eloquence, while his public speech gives an impression of literary density. Both properties draw attention to aspects of Burke's performances that function beyond the text. They encourage readers and auditors to make inferences about the personality of the author, to render themselves guardedly receptive or stubbornly resistant to his emotional appeals, and to pay critical attention to the form and force of his arguments.

APPROACHES TO THE PROBLEM OF BURKE'S RHETORIC

In so far as these properties of ethical, emotional and argumentative dynamism obtrude, they encourage all Burke's readers, whether hostile or sympathetic, to approach his writings and speeches as rhetoric. 'Rhetoric' will of course mean different things to different readers. To some, rhetoric is merely a kind of suspect language use, necessarily at cross-purposes with the discovery of truth because of its narrow designs upon an audience. To others, rhetoric has specific cultural or historical connotations, associated with the customs of political performance and debate common to the ancient democracies of Greece and Rome. These associations, which often lead to condemnation of the art for its insidiousness or parochialism, are themselves ancient. But they have never quite stuck. This is because rhetoric also has a relatively neutral and descriptive core. Rhetoric is by its proper definition an artistic discourse: it is the art of persuasion, according to the basic Aristotelian formula, based on the systematic analysis of natural (or non-artistic) eloquence.[57]

Burke's writings and speeches make a uniquely compelling subject in the history of the art of rhetoric for a combination of reasons. First, they display the sort of powerful, sometimes eccentric, and apparently spontaneous inventiveness that traditional rhetoricians call 'natural'. This is a dubious ascription, but it refers conveniently to qualities of creative unruliness that confound critical preconceptions, or, at least, that demand analysis on their own terms.[58] Second, and supplementing this 'naturalness', Burke's writings and speeches are accomplished and critically sophisticated in a way that suggests a considerable underlying artfulness, and an acquaintance with the pedagogical tradition of rhetorical training that formed part of the old *studia humanitatis*.[59] As we have seen, his admirers saw his eloquence as a talent so profoundly cultivated that it functioned for him as a second nature.[60] They felt that it had evolved above its immediate political function into something beautiful in its own right – in Aristotelian terms, into a fully artistic practice. But what ties these two reasons together is Burke's habit of thinking about the larger business of politics in terms of this same development of art out of nature. 'The people are the masters', he says in the *Speech on Economical Reform* (1780), 'they have only to express their wants at large and in gross. We [in Parliament] are the expert artists; we are the skilful workmen, to shape their desires into perfect form, and to fit the utensil to the use.'[61] In his most expansive moments Burke describes the use of reason in parliamentary deliberation as a sort of perfection of human nature: 'for man is by nature reasonable, and he is never in his natural state, but when he is placed where reason may best be cultivated, and most predominates. Art is man's nature.'[62] Of course the art of rhetoric is very far from comprehending the business of politics as Burke understood it, but it is clear that he considers the process of deliberation as being at once its highest and its most useful expression.[63] If politicians are philosophers in action, as Burke claims, then it is through the medium of rhetoric that their actions are manifested as art.

Burke's eloquence is central to his permanent achievement as a writer and thinker. For better or for worse, his most influential ideas about the conduct of human beings in civil society – about the conflict between local political prudence and the theoretical discourse of rights and natural law, and about the constitutional peculiarities of Great Britain, Ireland, America and India – are shaped by the expressiveness of the language in which they are framed. Moreover, many of the themes that occupy Burke fall within the pale of rhetorical theory: how do we know which citizens speak with authority on affairs of state? How can a legislator's knowledge of individuals help him to manage assemblies of men, or to understand the characters of whole nations? Should the topics of political debate be drawn from common maxims and prejudices, or from ideal discourses of justice and right? Burke's familiarity with ancient rhetorical theory extends beyond the digests and lectures from which it was commonly taught. His occasional quotations from classical rhetoricians – which include references to Isocrates' oration against the Sophists, Tacitus' *Dialogus de oratoribus* and Quintilian's *Institutio oratoria* – suggest that he had a broad knowledge of texts in the tradition.[64] The 'Book somewhat metaphysical' that he published in 1757, the *Philosophical Enquiry*, belongs to a line of commentaries on literary grandeur that begins with the widely read treatise on the sublime (*Peri hypsous*) attributed to Longinus.[65] Burke's particular affinity with the writings and career of Cicero, the academically inclined *novos homo* who made his reputation speaking against the corruption of provincial governors, was a preoccupation throughout his career.[66] Burke never made a sustained commentary on the art of rhetoric, but there is evidence everywhere of his having a sophisticated critical understanding of the art, an understanding that corresponds closely with his achievements as a writer and speaker.

Given the centrality of eloquence to his literary and political life, there is a conspicuous gap in the library of Burke criticism. Heretofore no full-length study has been dedicated to the subject of Burke's rhetoric. Why has it proved so difficult to give a general account of the artfulness with which Burke spoke and wrote? Burke's rhetoric is in fact a subject bedevilled with methodological problems. Inherent in his ideas and persuasive practices are certain properties that frustrate, or at least limit the scope of, attempts to define them artistically as a system of 'speculative principles'. These properties have proved unavailing to recent criticism, despite continuing scholarly interest in the principles of Burke's rhetorical art.[67] They permeate every level of our knowledge of Burke's eloquence: the meagre record of his oratorical performances, the unstable texts transcribed from them, their fraught political contexts, and the rhetorical theories that might help to describe them. Iain Hampsher-Monk has given a sharp analysis of the central problem, which he ascribes equally to the practices of literary critics and to those of political scientists who write on Burke. Both ignore the conceptual content of the rhetorical tradition, he argues: the critics refer to rhetoric only as a repository of literary figures and devices, while the politicians dismiss it as a flaw or excrescence in Burke's theory of government.[68] The basic principle of Burke's thought is that civil societies are constituted by the opinion of the political community.[69] Even if an abstract theory of government were to secure that community's sudden assent, Burke maintains, it could not have the deep correspondence with the dispositions and beliefs of its citizens provided by an immanent constitutional establishment.[70] In Hampsher-Monk's account, Burke exemplifies a method for ensuring that communities stay persuaded of this correspondence. He does so by confining political discourse to the sort of shared but unexamined premises that Aristotle prescribes for oratorical use in his *Rhetoric*: 'commonplaces and generalizations ... unsupported moral maxims ... the rhetorical flotsam and jetsam of philosophers' arguments as they appear in the mainstream of public life'.[71] By educing the customary workings of the prejudices and habits of the British and French political classes, Burke builds up a pragmatic account of authority and assent in these neighbouring states, one for which Aristotle's rhetoric provides an important precedent.

F.P. Lock, whose writings on Burke pay close attention to the figural texture of his prose, agrees that Burkean eloquence can best be explained in Aristotelian terms, as a structure of rational appeals to the received axioms of a given political culture.[72] Lock gives a different explanation for the problem of Burke's rhetoric, however. It is difficult to produce a coherent account of the subject, he suggests, because Burke's only critical work, the *Philosophical Enquiry into the Sublime and Beautiful*, does so little to illuminate his later political writings.[73] Indeed, every historian of Burke's eloquence faces the discouraging task of explaining why the *Philosophical Enquiry* is not a manual of political rhetoric.[74] Some of its themes do resurface in the later writings, such as the moral psychology of tragic pathos, and the salutary effects of obscurity. Burke has passages of grandeur and grandiloquence in many of his parliamentary speeches. But his critical thought on these subjects draws conventionally on the canons of neoclassical criticism, and shows little sign of having developed after 1759. More broadly speaking, the *Philosophical Enquiry* is concerned with the primary passions of pain, pleasure and delight, of terror and sociability, while his political writings tend to deal with the sort of passions that Samuel Johnson called 'adscititious': with friendship, pride, envy and indignation.[75] The lack of conceptual continuity makes it difficult to formulate a unified theory for Burke's rhetoric.

Indeed, Burke's rhetoric is much involved with technical complications. A properly artistic account of his eloquence would need to discover an underlying principle, a coherent structure for the relationship between Burke's critical ideas, his textual productions and his oratorical practices. Ideally the principle would have analogies in classical rhetoric while remaining true to the eighteenth-century intellectual background. And even before the rhetorical tradition is ransacked to find a valid set of contexts for the writings and speeches, there must be some evidence of the author's intention to think technically about the way that he wrote and spoke. In the cases of Bacon, Hobbes and Pascal that kind of evidence is readily available in their critical writings, and in critical literature that demonstrates their continuing interest in rhetoric as a pedagogic system based in living traditions of learning. As we shall see in Chapter 2, there are good grounds for concluding that the whole tradition of rhetoric was in irreversible academic decline by the time Burke encountered it as an undergraduate in the 1740s. He received it as a tired, etiolated inheritance.[76] The rhetorical concepts drawn from the undefiled wells of Aristotle by Hampsher-Monk and Lock provide useful theories with which to interpret Burke's rhetoric. But in the absence of firm evidence that Burke knew the *Techne Rhetorike*, it is important that we treat Aristotle as an part of the intellectual background, not as a direct context for Burke's thinking about argumentative practices.[77]

Moreover, Burke was not a systematic thinker, and Aristotelian rhetoric is a systematic art, or it is nothing.[78] As soon as it loses the completeness of its structure, it forfeits much of its explanatory power for the intellectual historian. The rhetorical tradition may remain useful as a source of descriptions for local linguistic effects and strategies – as the 'grammar' of irregularities it was taken to be by Burke's friend Adam Smith – but it no longer allows comparison and inference between its various systematic parts, its methodical branches, its practical applications and institutional settings.[79] As we shall see, the meagreness of its lingering manifestations in the literary culture of the mid eighteenth century seems to have discouraged Burke, with his generous intellectual temperament, from studying the art very closely. Given this fragmentation of contexts, the search for the underlying principle of Edmund Burke's rhetoric must begin with the internal evidence of his writings and speeches.

But the writings and speeches present some interesting textual challenges of their own.[80] In the first place, only a small proportion of the hundreds of speeches that Burke is known to have made in Parliament was recorded with any real care for accuracy.[81] In his lifetime Burke authorized (and probably oversaw) the publication of eight of his Commons speeches.[82] To these can be added Burke's published speeches delivered outside the Commons at the Bristol elections of 1774 and 1780, at the trial of Admiral Keppel in 1779, and during the impeachment of Warren Hastings.[83] There is evidence among Burke's papers to suggest that he made aborted efforts to publish some of his speeches before 1775.[84] Documents relating to three addresses on clerical subscription and the toleration of Dissenters that he made in 1772–3 were prepared for that end, as were a set of speeches on Indian affairs made in April and December 1772.[85] These early efforts seem to have been the result of indignation at the inaccuracy of the parliamentary reports that appeared in newspapers. Burke told Charles O'Hara in January 1771 that he was less concerned when the press attributed completely fabricated speeches to him (which at least tended to make sense), but 'when they are nearest to what I said, it is then the worst ... I never knew them in one instance, when they have remembered any thing of mine, that they did not totally misconceive the drift of it, and render it utterly ridiculous.'[86] The basic vitiation of the public record means that critics who want to deal closely with his language must confine themselves to a tiny part of Burke's known oratorical output. To do otherwise is to ignore Burke's most fundamental objection to the unofficial reporting of speeches in the press: that the reporters' failure to capture the stylistic detail of his speeches falsifies the whole decorum of their effect:

> the newspapers break not only the rules of decorum in real life, but even the dramatick decorum, when they personate great men, and, like bad poets, make the heroes of the piece talk more like us Grub-street scribblers, than in a style consonant to persons of gravity and importance in the State.[87]

They must also address the problem of whether to treat the eight polished, published speeches as different kinds of texts from the less polished trial transcriptions, or from the large-scale manifestos and polemics (such as *Thoughts on the Cause of the Present Discontents*, or *Reflections on the Revolution in France*) that Burke prepared for the press with comparable care. And they have to consider whether their standards of textual accuracy oblige them to overlook the inadequacy of the printed speeches as documents of the event of eloquence. A fully artistic rhetoric should include, after all, a theory of expressive gesture and a method of memorization, and needs to give some perspective on the dramatic interaction of audience and orator.

The historical record for the performative part of Burke's oratory is as tantalizing as the unauthorized reports of his spoken words.[88] Burke's speeches were sometimes highly theatrical, but his most dramatic gestures seem to have been isolated or impulsive, and it is difficult to build up a general description of his performance practice from the reports of casual witnesses. This is frustrating, because recent work by historians of Parliament such as Christopher Reid has given an increasingly fine account of the conventions that shaped Burke's oratorical practices in St Stephen's Chapel.[89] The sort of evidence that can be drawn from parliamentary diaries and reports, such as those of Matthew Brickdale, James Harris and Nathaniel Wraxall, suggests how Burke fits into the bigger picture, but allows us to form only the most impressionistic conclusions about his habits of gesture and elocution.[90] Burke's early fondness for the technique of aposiopesis, where speech is broken off to suggest overwhelming emotion in the speaker, developed during the 1780s into the fainting fits that interrupted several of the managers' speeches during the impeachment of Warren Hastings.[91] The extravagant theatrical gimmicks that Burke employed during the 1780s and 1790s were made famous in satirical prints and caricatures, but, again, they were not regular features of his speeches.[92] The most celebrated incident occurred on 28 December 1792, when Burke threw a dagger, a sample of weapons ordered by the French government from a Birmingham manufacturer, onto the floor of the Commons: 'this', he declaimed, 'is what you are to gain by alliance with France' – meaning blood, betrayal, murder.[93] 'Where's the fork?' wondered Richard Brinsley Sheridan. The incident brought much publicity to the debate, and it allowed Gillray and Cruikshank (among others) to portray a real heroism in Burke's outlandishness, where usually he appeared as a mere Quixote.[94] Gillray's 'The Dagger Scene' portrays Burke in what seems to have been his characteristic oratorical posture. It involves a sort of high-elbowed downward thrusting of the arm, as though he were punching or grinding home his point.[95] As Burke grew older his speeches seem to have become more intensely physical, even somewhat thuggish in their energy.[96] But there is no systematic way to link the linguistic effects recorded in the parliamentary transcriptions with the scattered information we have about Burke's performances. The printed speeches do not encourage the reader to imagine the speaker's physical presence. After all, it would be surprising if Burke had reproduced his parliamentary orations by re-enacting them in theatres or assembly rooms, rather than by writing them out and sending them to the press.

The tasks of reconstructing Burke's oratorical performances and of assessing the authority of the transcriptions of the public speeches are involved with formidable, if not intractable difficulties. They lie beyond the scope of this study – pressing as they are. Once these difficulties are acknowledged, however, the outline of a practicable method for describing Burke's rhetoric becomes traceable. The question of the artfulness with which Burke wrote and spoke is the subject of investigation here. In terms of textual criticism, that question focuses on the fine detail of Burke's language as well as on the larger form of his arguments. So my inquiry confines itself to the relatively small number of treatises and speeches that Burke authorized as his own (either through publication or private endorsement), while the texts of his publicly reported speeches are treated with caution.

In terms of critical methodology, the main problem is that of determining which aspects of the art of rhetoric can be used as valid intellectual contexts for Burke's writings and speeches, rather than as tools for the description of persuasive effects. It is clear that a technical treatment of the subject will require a theoretical framework, and that the framework ought to be constructed from materials that Burke himself would recognize and understand. Of course the very word 'theory' is a rare one in Burke criticism, for the obvious reason that Burke hardly ever used it without some terrible epithet: 'barren theory', 'mischievous theory', 'absurd theory', the best of the French National Assembly were 'only men of theory'.[97] But Burke's campaign of harassment against those who use metaphysical principles in legislative deliberation should not preclude technical criticism of his writings. 'I do not vilify theory and speculation [as such]', he insists, '– no, because that would be to vilify reason itself. *Neque decipitur ratio, neque decipit unquam.* No; whenever I speak against theory, I mean always a weak, erroneous, fallacious, unfounded, imperfect theory.'[98] It is easy to mistake Burke's suspicion of theoretical specialization in public actors (and especially in politicians with legal backgrounds) for a more principled aversion to methodical thought in general. In fact Burke was making a crucial distinction between the kinds of knowledgeability that are appropriate to different characters of men in political life. As we shall see, this sort of ethical distinction is characteristic of the habits of mind that shape Burke's rhetorical art. To equip ourselves for political deliberation, 'we ought rather to be learned *about* Sciences than *in* them', he writes in his 1751 *Note-Book*: 'By these means we can extend our views much more considerably; we keep our minds open, and prevent that littleness and narrowness that almost inevitably attends a confined commerce with any Art or Science however noble in itself.'[99] Discourses like the art of rhetoric are not only directed towards external, practical ends: they need internal standards of perfection and completion if they are to develop technically, and Burke affirms that the rational pursuit of their improvement is good and necessary. His only caveat is that internal guiding ends tend to seduce people into too narrow an interest in a single art. It is possible to write cogently about Edmund Burke's art of rhetoric, so long as its relation to the greater ecology of arts and sciences is always kept in mind.

The first chapter of this book establishes the intellectual context for Burke's thinking about rhetoric. As we have seen, certain comments that Burke makes about oratory suggest that he regards it as an art of proof, and believes that the mastery of it brings valuable indirect rewards to the speaker, regardless of immediate political ends. The most important sorts of proof for Burke are ethical: he regards rhetoric as an art of moral equipoise between the characters of speaker and audience. This sort of ethical approach to rhetoric is associated in early modern thought with Aristotle. At the beginning of the seventeenth century Francis Bacon predicted that a new science of practical ethics would grow up next to the well-cultivated art of rhetoric, involving the study of human character and the anatomization of the passions. This confluence of rhetoric with practical moral thought does indeed occur during the seventeenth century, in the fields of historiography, theories of the passions, Theophrastan character-writing and pulpit oratory. Later, Adam Smith synthesizes several aspects of rhetoric's ethical turn in his influential *Lectures on Rhetoric and Belles Lettres.*

In the second chapter I argue that this sort of practical, ethical thinking about rhetoric took on a particular form in Ireland during the years of Burke's childhood, university education and early employment. Throughout this period the client status of Ireland's legislature caused much resentment among the Irish political classes. From the 1690s a patriot programme of education in eloquence was proposed to remedy the perceived incompetence of Irish statesmen: the Irish would shake off their chains, if only they could speak well. These proposals bore fruit within the University of Ireland, where the professorship of rhetoric enjoyed a mid-century revival, and outside the academy, where Thomas Sheridan offered popular programmes of education in the art of elocution. It was amidst this culture of rhetorical reform that Edmund Burke received his academic and political education.

The philosophical treatise that Burke wrote during these early years, his *Philosophical Enquiry into the Origin of our Ideas of the Sublime and Beautiful,* is not exactly a rhetorical handbook. But it has much to say about what Burke calls 'the business of affecting the passions', and about the relationship between aesthetic responses and the social impulses that determine the psychology of moral obligation. The third chapter of this book shows how Burke's ideas about moral obligation are shaped by his reading in two branches of the Epicurean tradition: one is modern, centring on the Lockean moral philosophy of an important group of philosophers based in eighteenth-century Cambridge; the other is ancient, involving Lucretius' didactic poem *De rerum natura.* Only through these Epicurean contexts can the rhetorical and philosophical character of Burke's treatise be properly understood.

The fourth chapter describes how the ethical component in Burke's rhetoric deepens in scope during his years as a member of the British House of Commons. Burke makes political ethics one of his great themes from the very beginning of his career as a parliamentary orator. During the 1770s his concern is with the institutional character of the British Parliament, and with the personalities of leading statesmen within that institutional context. As his career progresses, the larger constitutional aspects of these concerns begin to supersede personal ethics in Burke's mind. He comes to think of the characters of statesmen as keys by which to turn the locks of institutional change. The process of parliamentary impeachment is essential to this broadening of Burke's political ethics, not least because the special legal status of its proceedings has the potential to confer a permanent authority on forensic oratory.

The fifth and sixth chapters focus on the final development of Burke's ethicized rhetoric in *Reflections on the Revolution in France* (1789). In *Reflections*, written as his career in Parliament draws to its close, Burke's ideas about discursive decorum and effective deliberation are most intricately involved with his theory of government. Burke argues that the consummation of the legislator's art lies in the 'description' of citizens. For a state to be properly balanced, politicians must have the expertise to distinguish the various 'moral denominations' that their laws will put in equipoise. Burke believes that the language and rhetoric of his opponents prove them incapable of this sort of complex social analysis. In defiance of their attenuated idea of selfhood, Burke adumbrates a conception of political character intended to be realistic, historically dynamic and fully adapted for the business of deliberation.

CHAPTER 1

The ethical turn in early modern rhetoric, 1600–1760

ETHOS IN EARLY MODERN RHETORIC

Surveying the landscape of the sciences in the second book of *The Advancement of Learning* (1605), Francis Bacon notices a conspicuously neglected field of knowledge, an area of study apparently left derelict by the learned. It is the ground of the science 'which co*n*sidereth of the APPETITE and WILL OF Man', and it lies right next to the well-cultivated gardens of rhetoric (so 'excellent, and excellently well laboured'). The ground is derelict, he conjectures, because learned people 'have despised to be conuersant in ordinary and common matters' such as practical ethics.[1] Eloquence itself, and the pride of learned ambition, has drawn intellectuals away from the sort of inquiry that would be most useful to their public discourses, and from the sort of prudential morality based on the empirical or historical study of human behaviour. As a first step towards restoring the science of the 'Culture and Cure of the Mynde of Man', Bacon isolates two factors that are beyond the command of the subject: points of fortune (the basis of which is inscrutable) and 'Poyntes of Nature' – that is, 'the seueral characters & tempers of mens Natures and dispositions specially hauing regard to those differences which are most radicall in being the fountayns and Causes of the rest'.[2] He calls for a systematic categorization of the varieties of human disposition, and the only precedent he can think of for this kind of anatomy of character is the treatment of ethos 'by *Aristotle* as in passage in his Rhetoricks'. At a practical level, civil history is the best source for this kind of knowledge, and when Bacon revises this passage for the *De augmentis* he mentions the histories of Livy, Tacitus, Herodian, de Comines and Guicciardini as further models: 'for a character so worked into the narrative gives a better idea of the man, than any formal criticism and review can'.[3] The necessary supplement to the knowledge drawn from these sources will be an account of the human passions or 'perturbations and distempers of the affections', along with a prescription for their cure. Solon compared the people to the sea and the orators to the winds, because each would be quiet if the other did not trouble it; and similarly, the mind would be temperate if the affections 'did not put it into tumulte and perturbation'.[4] Again, Bacon's principal example of such an investigation of the passions is the second book of Aristotle's *Rhetoric*, and he acknowledges that even there the nature of the affections is considered collaterally to the art of moving them in other people.[5]

Bacon's concern for the relationship between the art of eloquence and the everyday business of moral psychology, and his sense that Aristotle should be the starting point for thinking about it, anticipate an important new direction that rhetoric takes during the seventeenth and eighteenth centuries.[6] Bacon's pragmatic approach to the subject represents a break with the cautious deductions of his humanist predecessors, as a comparison with John Rainolds's pioneering series of lectures on Aristotle's *Rhetoric* at Oxford during the 1570s makes clear. Aristotle included a catalogue of the passions in his rhetoric because it is important for speakers (especially forensic orators) to understand the dispositions of their audiences, and to anticipate how their emotions might affect their judgments.[7] But Rainolds cannot countenance the idea that different kinds of speech might be adjustable to different audiences, and he ignores the material that appears in Book II of the *Rhetoric*. This is because the ultimate intention for all language is divine truth, and that intention is single and immutable.[8] For Bacon, by contrast, rhetoric is the technique of applying '*Reason to Imagination*, for the better moouing of the will', and as such it is especially close to the 'parte of knowledge touching the seuerall Characters of [human] Natures and dispositions'.[9] Both belong to that characteristically Baconian enterprise, the 'pressing of a man's fortune' as he makes his way through the world.[10] And both refer to individual persons, so they cannot be taught denotatively: 'Not however that I would have these characters presented in ethics (as we find them in history or poetry or even in common discourse), in the shape of complete individual portraits, but rather [by] the several features and simple lineaments of which they are composed.'[11] The rules for attaining ethical knowledge are, however, formulable, and Bacon organizes them under a single principle. The inner motives for a person's actions are almost always revealed by facial expressions, particular deeds and unguarded words, or by character and motive more generally, and the real challenge is to work out what single ruling inclination these symptoms refer to: 'Neyther is it sufficient to infourme our selues in mens endes and natures of the variety of them onely, but also of the predominancy what humour reigneth most, and what end is principally sought.'[12] From the context it seems that Bacon's use of the word 'humour' here has little to do with the bodily humours of Galenic medicine. It is a psychological term, referring to the Montaignean idea (later to become a heavy commonplace in the satire of Pope) that even the most variable characters are controlled by a single 'ruling passion'.[13]

An obvious problem presents itself to those who would apply this ethical knowledge to the art of rhetoric. How can this basic theorizing about the psychology of individuals be relevant to the art of addressing assemblies and audiences? Since psychology is a science of particularities and diversities, is it not categorically incompatible with the business of societies and states? Bacon was writing after the Ramist academic reforms had done much to reduce rhetoric to a system of academic or courtly exercises, and he may have Ramus in mind when he complains that even good speakers neglect the ethical dimension of their art:

> if a Man should speake of the same thing to seuerall persons: he should speake to them all respectiuely and seuerall wayes: though this *Politique part of Eloquence in priuate Speech*, it is easie for the greatest Orators to want: whilest by the obseruing their well graced fourmes of speech, they leese the volubilitie of Application.

This does not solve the problem of how to address many persons at once, but it does indicate some of the qualities that the ethically alert speaker should cultivate. Bacon makes play between the literal sense of 'volubility' as 'aptness to turn from one thing to another' (he writes of the 'volubility' of 'serpentine wisedom' in a later discussion of Machiavelli) and the word's more figural sense of a 'ready flow of speech' (as in Puttenham's 'flowing of wordes with much volubilitie').[14] His pun suggests that eloquence itself has no function without its '*Politique part*', the versatility of adaptation to the 'seuerall persons' of an audience, or to several different kinds of audience. Bacon emphasizes precisely the part of Aristotelian rhetoric that Rainolds found most embarrassing. For the modern orator, audiences are as likely to be small and private as public and general. In either case, there can be no practical art of persuasion without knowledge of the various characters of men. As Ronald S. Crane pointed out long ago, the eighteen new pieces Bacon wrote for the 1625 edition of his *Essayes or Counsels* represent an unfinished attempt at this fledgling moral science.[15] At least four of the new additions (on 'Revenge', 'Envy', 'Boldness' and 'Anger') draw material from the second book of Aristotle's *Rhetoric*.[16] The essay 'Of Anger' is particularly clear about the proper application of its method. 'We will first speake', Bacon writes, 'How the Naturall Inclination, and Habit, *To be Angry*, may be attempred, and calmed. Secondly, How the Particular Motions of *Anger*, may be repressed . . . Thirdly, How to raise *Anger*, or appease *Anger*, in Another.'[17] There is a steady movement from the culture of personal disposition, through the cure of public self-presentation, to the instrumental stirring or placating of emotion in other people. The art of persuasion is a natural complement to the knowledge of self, and of the characters of others.

There was, as Bacon predicted, an ethical turn in writing about rhetoric during the seventeenth century, and it is seldom discussed by historians of criticism.[18] The grand surveyors who dominated twentieth-century study of rhetoric tended to limit their readings to books that dealt prima facie with rhetoric and logic – as to some extent they were obliged to do, given that the humanistic tradition of rhetorical manual-writing is so broad, so continuous and so well defined by its institutional settings in educational curricula.[19] This meant that they underestimated the porousness of rhetorical theory, and its tendency to leak concepts and vocabulary into what Bacon figured as adjacent fields, including those of psychology or practical morals. The following chapter covers a long historical stretch, from the publication of the *Advancement of Learning* in 1605 through to the early eighteenth century, when the young Edmund Burke became intellectually active. It looks at works by a broad range of rhetorical theorists, *moralistes*, essayists and literary critics for signs of progress in Bacon's programme for the parallel cultivation of the art of rhetoric and the knowledge of social character. I have tried to resist the temptation of presenting a smooth narrative of conceptual change, or of pervasive Aristotelian or Baconian influence, and I do not argue that Burke drew directly from the books that I discuss – although many of them appear in the sale catalogue of his library, or in the index to his published correspondence.

This chapter has a more modest purpose: to show that the ethical bias of Burke's thought about rhetoric has precedents in early modern literature. Its focus is upon classical, seventeenth-century and contemporary writers who explored the idea that is at the heart of Burke's rhetoric of character: that orators are best able to secure a good moral character in the minds of their audience by demonstrating their understanding of what moral character is. Several early modern commentators dwelt on the Roman conception that this sort of knowledge is best displayed by the incorporation of character portraits into rhetorical texts. Writing and speaking about characters is linked closely to the business of writing and speaking with character. The relevance of this theme to the literary criticism of Burke's day is confirmed by Adam Smith, whose widely influential lectures on rhetoric and belles-lettres present a contemporary synthesis of many of the texts and ideas that I discuss below. As we shall see, Burke inherits this interest in the rhetoric of character, and concern about the compatibility of eloquence with modesty, in his turn. In the background of this narrative of ideas there is, of course, a classical inheritance of writing about rhetorical ethics, upon which the writers I discuss constantly draw. Before beginning the narrative, it will be useful to give a sketch of this tradition.

Bacon's conclusion about the science of human 'characters & tempers' is that even the scant attention it has received from the learned has been accidental, the knock-on effect of the super-cultivation of a neighbouring field, that of rhetoric. Aristotle only discusses these topics in practical morality, it seems, because they touch on his art of eloquence. But practical morality, and especially the idea of character, is more deeply involved with the Aristotelian theory of rhetoric than Bacon's georgic imagery implies. Aristotle imagines the art of rhetoric not as a neighbouring plot to the moral sciences, but as a side-shoot or sucker (*paraphues*) that has grown up in political science between dialectic and ethics – he also calls rhetoric the counterpart (*antistrophos*) of dialectic.[20] Just as the matter of dialectic is made up of syllogistic arguments, says Aristotle, so the body (*soma*) of rhetorical proof is made up of enthymemes, or abbreviated syllogisms.[21] But there is more to the art of rhetoric than the method for inventing good logical enthymemes.[22] The body of the argument needs an animating principle – it needs, as Aristotle puts it, to be made ethical ('ethikous gar poiei tous logos') – and similarly, in order to be truly artistic, rhetorical ethos should be expressed through the logos itself, rather than through an audience's externally conceived idea of the speaker's character.[23] For Aristotle, ethos is the very spirit of rhetoric, and he considers it more persuasive ('kuriotaten . . . pistin') than the other two kinds of artificial proof, those that work through pathos and logos.[24]

The idea that study, cultivation and a degree of artfulness are necessary for those who would express a public moral character is fundamental to the *Rhetoric*. Concerning the three ethical qualities necessary for the securing of conviction (good sense, virtue and good will towards the audience), Aristotle writes that 'the means whereby [the orator] may appear sensible and good must be inferred from the classification of the virtues; for to make himself appear such he would employ the same means as he would if he were presenting others'.[25] Artful rhetoricians express their ethos through discourse, and in doing so they use the same sorts of signs (*semeion*) that poets, for example, would use to represent persons in their writings.[26] The signs that do this best are ones that indicate a person's principles through moral choice (*proairesis*), and ones that represent a person's moral habits (*hexeis*), especially through the use of decorum in rhetorical style: 'if then anyone uses the language appropriate to each habit, he will represent [*poiesei*] the character'.[27] Aristotle is relatively unconcerned about the connection between these outward signs of character and the speaker's inner state of moral being, because he understands that in the political arena one cannot expect ethos to function in anything more than this artistic way. With the expression of pathos audiences are always in danger of forming wrong conclusions (*paralogizatai*), because sympathetic emotion gives people the impression they are hearing truth.[28] But orators who speak ethically offer conviction in a limited and calculable way, and politicians neither can nor should be trusted any further than that.

Aristotle's theory of rhetorical ethos translates awkwardly into Roman and humanist thought, not least because, as Quintilian points out, there is no term in the Latin language directly equivalent to ethos.[29] The concept of *conciliare* or the securing of good will (made much of by Antonius in Cicero's *De oratore*) is more the external end of ethos than a constituent principle, while *ingenium* or natural talent (emphasized by Crassus in the same work) is the opposite of an artistic attainment.[30] But Aristotle's central idea of the artistic, discursive nature of rhetorical ethos, and his sense that an orator should express his own moral character with the same kinds of signs that a poet would use to depict a literary character, emerges distinctly enough in Roman rhetorical theory. In *De oratore* Antonius describes how forensic orators should paint in words the characters of people they would defend ('exprimere mores oratione'). If this character-drawing is done with taste, each virtue they describe will be like a brushstroke painting the speaker's own ethos ('quasi mores oratoris effingat oratio').[31] Quintilian agrees that, in so far as ethos denotes moral character, the portrayal of people who have what the audience perceives to be good character necessarily reflects ethos on the portraitist.[32] In both rhetoricians there is a sense of the orator's character emerging from a series of discrete negotiations with other public characters, and with the collective character of the audience itself. Persuasion through ethos is gentle and insinuating, but it is more likely to create an enduring impression (*perpetuum*) than the violent, immediate (*temperale*) movements of pathos.[33]

Later in the classical period Aristotle's discursive model of ethos is developed further in Letters XCIV and XCV of Seneca's *Epistulae morales.* Seneca criticizes earlier Stoics for maintaining that a purely dogmatic philosophy, made up of general rules intended for universal application, is sufficient to guide people towards wisdom. Instead he advocates the gathering together of *praecepti* (guidelines suitable to each particular habit of life), *decreti* (firm doctrines that make the mind unswervingly decisive), and a third unit of ethical knowledge for which he finds no Latin term, but which is recognizable as character-writing: 'this science [the Rhodean historian] Posidonius calls *ethologian*, while others call it *characterismon.* It gives the signs and marks that belong to each virtue and vice, so that distinctions may be drawn between like things. Its function is the same as that of the precept.'[34] Seneca's own take on the organic image of rhetoric is that these characters are the foliage that grows upon the bare branch of moral doctrine. Seneca is establishing rules for the implementation of preceptive philosophy as part of a personal regime of moral discipline, so the practical context here is slightly different from the political scene of Aristotle's *Rhetoric.* But the basic ingredient of Aristotelian rhetorical ethos – the artistic representation of authorial character through writing about character – is also combined in the Senecan idea of character-making.

The classical tradition sees rhetorical ethos as producing deep, durable and subtle effects of persuasion. But this is not to say that the concept works always at cross-purposes with more immediately persuasive strategies of rhetoric. Quintilian in particular sees a sliding scale of forcefulness determined by the level of abstraction involved in the mimesis of character. One of the *schemata sententiae* or figures associated with Grand Style, which both ancient and early modern rhetoricians considered to be of irresistible emotional force when employed properly, is prosopopoeia, or 'person-making'.[35] This important figure involves the lending of a voice to any abstraction, person or thing that is readily distinguishable from the speaker or writer. A famous modern example is spoken by Shakespeare's Antony, who in *Julius Caesar* imagines Caesar's corpse rising again to 'Cry "Havoc!" and let slip the dogs of war', and only just stops short of putting 'a tongue | In every wound of Caesar that should move | The stones of Rome to rise and mutiny'.[36] This kind of striking, dramatic representation of speech has as one of its subsets the figure ethopoeia or 'character description', which by Quintilian's definition involves only the representation of human voices, not of persons as such. It is interesting that he places ethopoeia at the gentler end of the emotional scale ('leniores adfectus') because of its tendency to humour, whereas the figure of *hypotyposis*, which involves the description of a person or thing's outward actions (not words), is classified alongside the powerful visual effects of *enargeia*. Similarly, apostrophe, where the person or thing is only described in so far as it is addressed by the orator, is an even more bold and distracting figure of this kind.[37]

Quintilian's account of these figures resolves itself into an interesting observation about their effects on audiences. In proportion as the information conveyed is ethically complex, and penetrates to the inner life of the character represented, it appears to be slower to move the listener. The outward representation of a person in words is more striking than the inward representation of their thoughts. Quintilian offers no psychological speculation about all this, but one explanation would be that the dynamic of sympathy between speaker and audience is temporarily disrupted when a third person obtrudes too far onto the rhetorical scene. The figure of prosopopoeia and its nearly-related tropes suggest that it is precisely the mediation of voice or character through representation, with whatever levels of shading or obscuration that involves, which lends it real rhetorical force. As we shall see, this is an insight that greatly interested Adam Smith and Edmund Burke in their turns.

WRITING ABOUT THE CHARACTERS OF OTHERS: RHETORIC AND THE 'KNOWLEDGE OF MEN'

The new methods for discussing the knowledge of human character that emerge during the seventeenth century often have a rhetorical bias: they return to the question of how best to use the knowledge of character in writing and speech.[38] The aim of asserting an orator's personal ethos is no longer paramount, however. Instead, knowledge of character is rededicated to two closely connected ends: first, that of providing writers with the kind of moral information they can deploy through powerful figures of description or ekphrasis, such as *enargeia*, *ethopoeia*, topography and narration; and second, that of accompanying these figures with what Marc Fumaroli calls 'a sort of soundtrack that lends a voice to the things or persons described: dialectic, dialogue, personification'.[39] The business of knowing and writing about character leads the writer towards literary forms in which the author's voice or style is mediated, and secondary voices are imagined. As

Fumaroli explains, ekphrasis is the figure par excellence of the courtly Jesuits whose writings dominate European rhetorical theory during the first half of the seventeenth century – among them Louis Richeome, Nicolas Caussin and (writing about the passions for a polite readership in French, not Latin) Pierre Le Moyne.[40] In his *Peintures morales* (1640–3), Le Moyne presents a 'gallery' of dialogues, historical tableaux and *charactères*, representing the passions through 'les techniques du roman appliquées à la parénèse morale' – this is French ethical rhetoric in its quintessential form.[41] It is hard to tell whether Jesuit rhetoricians like Le Moyne have much direct impact in Britain, but they form a deep contextual background for the writers discussed later in this chapter, especially Shaftesbury and Adam Smith.

When rhetoric enters the sphere of practical morality, the authority of the second book of Aristotle's *Rhetoric* is never far away. Once again, it is European academics such as Gérard Vossius, a Dutch humanist with particularly close contacts in England, who do most to reintroduce Aristotle into the technical discussion of rhetoric at the start of the century.[42] The English epitome or *Briefe* (1637) of Aristotle's rhetoric that was once attributed to Thomas Hobbes indicates its rising profile in Britain.[43] Turning to a French critic well known among British readers, René Rapin in his *Discours sur la comparaison de l'eloquence de Demosthene et de Ciceron* (1670) judges Aristotle to be 'the only one, that knew well how to penetrate into the Heart of Man, the most impenetrable thing in the whole World ... 'Tis to him we are indebted, for teaching us how to keep secret Intelligence with the Soul by the Assistance of the Passions.'[44] There is a characteristic ambiguity in this comment: the soul with which Aristotle's reader is taught to keep up a secret intelligence could be her own, or could be another's. The passions are reason's spies, it seems, in the foreign territory of the soul, where self-analysis and social observation are bound together as sources of moral intelligence.

Bacon's original association of Aristotle's rhetoric with practical morality is perhaps at the back of John Locke's mind when he dictates a concise reading list of modern books on this ill-defined subject to the clergyman and pamphleteer Samuel Bolde:

To fit a Gentleman for the conduct of himself whether as a private man, or as interested in the government of his Countrey, nothing can be more necessary, than the knowledge of Men; which tho it be to <be> had chiefly from experience, and next to that, from a judicious reading of History, yet there are books which of purpose treat of Humane Nature, which help to give an insight into it. Such are those that treat of the passions and how they are moved, whereof Aristotle in his second book of Rhethorick has admirably treated, and that in little compass ... La Bruyer's Characters are also an admirable piece of painting ...[45]

In the closing sections of *Some Thoughts Concerning Education* (1693) Locke had prescribed foreign travel as the great source of experience, since it allows conversation with 'People of Tempers, Customs, and Ways of living, different from one another'.[46] But he is talking about a more general and social kind of 'knowledge of Men' here, and one with several literary manifestations. As ever, the second book of Aristotle's *Rhetoric* is Locke's authority for a subject that spreads across three fields: first, historiography; second, guides to the passions; and third, character-writing, this last category now represented by the French *moraliste* Jean de la Bruyère.[47] And of course Locke had already thought deeply about the metaphysics of personal identity while preparing the 1694 second edition of *An Essay Concerning Human Understanding*.[48] 'Person', he writes in a new section dedicated to the subject, 'is a forensic term', and should be used only to signify those parts of conscious selfhood that mark out the legal and moral responsibilities of free, rational agents, as distinct from identity of body or of soul.[49] Locke is looking backwards here to the Roman category of *personae*, by which Cicero expresses the different kinds of role or character with which nature has clothed us ('nos a natura indutos'), and with which we dress ourselves for civic life.[50] The new theory of personality that Locke develops in 1694 allows him to consider whether one individual man or woman could be two distinct persons (in the narrow, 'forensic' sense of that word) at two different points of time: for 'if it be possible for the same Man to have distinct incommunicable consciousness at different times, it is past doubt the same Man would at different times make different Persons'.[51] The congruence between Locke's technical and moralistic treatments of personal identity indicates that there were favourable intellectual circumstances for rhetorical ethics at the start of the eighteenth century.

Locke's informal reading list offers a useful framework for the subject, because it suggests how for early modern theorists of 'the knowledge of Men' there is no real dividing line between rhetorical instruction, psychological speculation, prudential advice and social description. Historians of selfhood sometimes identify John Locke as the philosopher who provides the socially attenuated or 'thin' metaphysics of personal identity that underwrites the whole universalizing liberal discourse of rights.[52] He is not thought of as a thinker much concerned with the vulgar complexities of morality as shaped by the contingencies of experience or community. But his remarks to Bolde and the passages from *Some Thoughts Concerning Education* show that even he continued to recognize the need for practical and socially versatile methods for conceptualizing the modern self. A closer look at each of the three genres mentioned by Locke – historiography, psychology and character-writing – shows how intimately the knowledge of passions and characters is involved with the rhetorical question of how writers should go about representing human personalities.

In Locke's opinion the primary source for the 'knowledge of Men' is books of history, and in this he agrees with Bacon (among many others). Seventeenth-century historiographers are often concerned with the theory of representing historical characters, a topic that tends also to involve discussions of style and rhetoric. Thucydides and Sallust provide the best models for vivid historical portraiture, and these two ancient historians are typically linked, because their prose styles share a certain quality of laconic density.[53] Thomas Hobbes brought the issues into focus in the critical conspectus that introduces his translation of Thucydides' *Eight Bookes of the Peloponnesian Warre* (1629). The key to Thucydides' art, according to Hobbes, is the skill with which he integrates into the bare narrative of his history the sort of moral or political analysis that lesser historians treat in 'discourses inserted', or in 'subtile coniectures, at the secret aymes, and inward cogitations of such as fall vnder their Penne'.[54] This observation is consistent with the austere historical style recommended by Quintilian, and associated by French historiographers of the seventeenth century with the *imperatori brevitas*, the language of princes, soldiers and statesmen.[55] Hobbes likes the modesty of Thucydides' integrated style, the way it avoids showy digressions or portraits, but he also appreciates how it deepens the reader's response to his dense, rapid prose. Defending Thucydides against the long-standing charge of obscurity, Hobbes judges that 'in the Characters of mens humours and manners, and applying them to affaires of consequence, it is impossible not to be obscure to ordinary capacities ... the obscurity that is, proceedeth from the profoundnesse of the Sentences, containing contemplations of humane passions'.[56] The quality that Hobbes connects with good writing on the human character is depth, and he associates the expression of depth in Thucydides with his aphoristic, somewhat esoteric style.[57]

Towards the end of his life Hobbes becomes cautious about exporting these insights into the passions from the realm of the personal and particular to the realm of political philosophy. Twenty-six years after the publication of the *Peloponnesian Warre*, he writes in *De corpore politico*

(1655) about the most frequently discussed passage of Sallust's *Bellum Catilinarum*, the climax of the character of Catiline:

> [Catiline's] mind was daring, crafty, fickle, capable of the most profound dissimulation, and of acting any part whatever; covetous of the property of others, lavish with his own [*alieni appetens, sui profusus*]; extremely eager in the gratification of desires; eloquence enough he had, but little wisdom [*eloquentiae satis, sapientiae parvum*].[58]

Hobbes is dissatisfied with Sallust's final epigram on the conspirator's eloquence: 'And perhaps this was said of *Catiline*, as he was *Catiline*', he stipulates. 'But it was true of him as an Author of Sedition. For the Conjunction of these two Qualities made him not *Catiline*, but Seditious.'[59] The implied point here is obviously anti-rhetorical.[60] Eloquence should not be dignified by association with psychological complexity, Hobbes thinks, and so what Sallust presents as a paradoxical antithesis ought really to have been framed as a causal consequence: there is a necessary connection between seditious eloquence and diminished wisdom. Contrary to his earlier association of discursive depth with 'contemplations of humane passions', Hobbes now asserts that it is characteristic of seditious, foolish people to name passions, not things, in their speeches. But he is kicking against Sallust's generally high reputation here. One of Hobbes's most sympathetic readers, Charles de Saint-Évremond, described the same passage on Catiline as proof of Sallust's 'true knowledge of Men', and particularly his insight into how a character can 'seem to be opposite to himself' while remaining distinct.[61] Where other historians (Saint-Évremond has Tacitus in mind) overshoot the mark by being too subtle in their tracing of events to the ingenious policy of a few individuals, Sallust reveals the 'Genius of Men, and afterwards Affairs come as naturally, by the Actions of those Persons whom he hath describ'd, which are never far-fetched'.[62] Insights that are made irrelevant for Hobbes by political reasoning, and for Tacitus by political fact, become for Saint-Évremond the essence of good historical writing. He shows how in Sallust they combine into a rich effect of narrative decorum and psychological probability. These historiographers are as much concerned with demonstrating how to think about human character – deeply, slowly, with an openness to paradox – as they are with the historical information that their characters contain.

Locke's second category of books that deal in the 'knowledge of Men' covers treatments 'of the passions and how they are moved', a genre that he identifies closely with the second book of Aristotle's *Rhetoric*. Again, Hobbes provides the best English example of such a treatment: the first part of his *Elements of Law*, titled *Human Nature* (1640), is based around a catalogue of the passions in Aristotelian form.[63] Hobbes's descriptive analysis of the catalogue is more radical than Aristotle's, however. Rather than treating the passions as motive forces circumscribed by the rational and moral conduct of life, Hobbes sees them as simple, natural, morally neutral impulses that inform all human action. As such he removes the passions from their specifically rhetorical, social context, rejecting it for an ego-centred account of the pursuit of felicity and power.[64] But among Hobbes's less philosophical Continental contemporaries, several were producing prudential guides to the passions that fit Locke's description more closely: for example, Marin Cureau de la Chambre's *Charactères des passions* (1640, English trans. 1650), is a well-known taxonomy of emotions designed to show what his English translator calls 'The art to know Men'.[65] This phrase from his English translator's preface accurately anticipates the title of de la Chambre's treatise on *L'Art de connoistre les hommes* (1759–60), another work in which self-understanding and the knowledge of the passions of others are presented as inseparable from one another.[66] The basically Stoic character of these preoccupations, which is particularly evident in Pierre Charron's *De la sagesse* (1701), sometimes reveals an underlying scepticism about the reliability of the passions as signs of human character. Charron would not have understood, for example, David Hume's description of personal character in terms of semi-permanent patterns of passions.[67] Like many of the later Stoic prudentialists, Charron figures the passions as like 'the *Mobb*', set on by the imagination (that 'perfect Incendiary in the State') to 'set all in an uproar and confusion', or as mutineers in the army of the soul: 'They mutinie without our leave', agrees the Belgian theologian Jean-François Senault, 'and by an Impression which they make in our countenance, they teach our enemies all that lies within our hearts.'[68] These metaphors of insurrection imply that, for the Stoic prudentialists, the passions play a regular but highly unstable part in the constitution of personality. They make up the body of character, as it were, but they often turn the order of the body upside-down.[69]

This is not quite the view, however, of the moderate Presbyterian churchman Edward Reynolds, whose *Treatise of the Passions and Faculties of the Soule of Man* (1640) makes the most substantial British intervention on the subject. Reynolds pays the common tribute of praise to the 'learned and excellent discourse of Aristotle, in the second Booke of his Rhetoricks', which he reads as a treatment of the passions in 'their Civill respects'.[70] What seems strange to Reynolds is that Aristotle passes over the 'Nature, Essence, Operation and Properties' of the passions in *De anima*, and fails to treat of their corruption in his ethics.[71] It is this double omission that Reynolds sets out to supply in the *Treatise of the Passions.* He describes the passions conventionally, as characters or impressions made by the soul on the outward form of the body. In so far as these 'Motions' tend to the advancement of the natures of God's creatures, and in so far as their 'inward Root and Principles' are in reason rather than the sense, he considers them providential and essentially good, if prone to corruption when they are controlled only by their own laws.[72] One consequence of this account is Reynolds's very optimistic view of how the passions determine the 'force & power of Speech upon the minds of men'. Among the 'Vertues of Speech' he mentions its grammatical, rhetorical and logical qualities. But by far the most important of its virtues are 'Morall, as Gravity, Truth, Seriousnesse, Integrity, Authority; When mans Speech is better beleeved for his Life than for his Learning'.[73] For Reynolds the ethical character of the speaker is essential to rhetoric, a view he illustrates with the story of the Spartan princes who, on hearing an opinion they approved from a man of suspect morals, 'required another man of reputation to propose it: That the prejudice of the person might not procure a rejection of his Iudgement'.[74] Reynolds's *Treatise* is almost exactly contemporary with Senault's *De l'usage des passions,* which contains a similarly positive treatment of ethos in rhetoric (as might be expected from the General of the Paris Oratory). Senault finds the orators 'more blameless than the poets' because their chief end is to preserve truth against the passions of their audiences: 'By this harmless cunning', he continues, 'they formed Towns, governed Commonwealths, and for a long time commanded Monarchies; for they studied their inclinations, and did so handsomely handle them . . . that Monarchy was become a slave to Eloquence.'[75] The danger, according to Senault, is that eloquence can only drive the monarch's passions up and down, rather than stabilize them – 'policy' alone can do that.

In place of the third category, character-writing, Locke names a specific text as though it were *sui generis*: 'La Bruyer's Characters are also an admirable piece of painting'. La Bruyère's *Caractères* does not really belong to a class by itself, though. Locke passes over the earlier seventeenth-century tradition of satirical and moralistic character-writing in English by writers like Joseph Hall, John Earle and the literary circle of Sir Thomas Overbury, despite its common roots with La Bruyère's in the *Characters* of Theophrastus.[76] Stylistically, both British and French character-writing shares with the historiographical character-writing discussed above a tendency to witty brevity. As Richard Flecknoe explains in his *Collection of the Choicest Epigrams and Characters* (1673), Theophrastan characters should be like maxims, since 'they discourse not, but give you onely the heads of things in general, and that so briefly, as every Line is a Sentence, and every two a *Period*'.[77] Accordingly, seventeenth-century 'characters' adopt a rhetorical posture of resolution, generality and summary within a literary structure that suggests fragmentation, particularity and occlusion. This formal paradox is particularly pointed in La Bruyère, because the greater part of the *Caractères* is made up of Rochefoucauld-style maxims that relate only tangentially to the verbal portraits scattered among them.[78] The 'knowledge of Men' that Theophrastan characters purport to embody is distributed uncertainly between personified example and generalized definition. So La Bruyère's form casts the whole prudential enterprise of character-writing in an ironic light.

Perhaps Locke passes over the British Theophrastans in favour of La Bruyère because he admires the Frenchman's subtle scepticism about the metaphysical underpinnings of human personality:

> Men have no characters, or at any rate none that shows any consistency, that does not contradict itself, and through which they may be recognized ... They have opposing passions and contradictory weaknesses; they find it easier to make extremes meet than to follow a line of conduct that is all of a piece.[79]

The radical inconstancy of human actions is a familiar topic in Montaigne and his followers, but La Bruyère goes some way beyond them: first, by suggesting that the perversity of the human will makes any real act of 'recognition' impossible; and, second, by directing his attention towards the anatomization of the inconsistencies themselves. 'Restlessness of mind,' he writes, 'unevenness of temper, inconstancy of heart, uncertainty of behaviour: these are all vices of man's soul, but they are different from one another, and though they seem related they do not invariably imply one another in a single individual.'[80] La Bruyère's most celebrated illustration of this principle of temperamental indeterminacy is his character of Ménalque, a distracted aristocrat who blunders about Paris, bewildered by the responses of strangers to his profound absence of mind.[81] The character of Ménalque is an essay in what consciousness, with its discontinuities and moments of self-forgetfulness, looks like from the outside. La Bruyère is as much interested in the disjunctions as in the connections between personality and consciousness, and his characters depict the comic struggle of French society to live up to its aristocratic principles.[82] But there is a positive element to La Bruyère's satire, and he writes hopefully about the discipline and intelligence with which a true *honnête homme* can learn to control the deceitful tendency of his own passions:

How much art it takes to retrieve the ease of nature! how much time, how many rules, what attention and what labour are needed to dance with the same freedom and grace as one walks; to sing as one speaks; to speak and express oneself as one thinks; to infuse as much strength and vivacity, passion and persuasiveness into a prepared speech, delivered in public, as one sometimes shows naturally and spontaneously in familiar conversation![83]

Where he touches upon rhetoric La Bruyère makes it a profoundly ethical business: the artful expression of personality is itself as close as one can get to the essence of *honnêteté* and reasonable action.[84]

If we compare these three literary sources mentioned by Locke for the knowledge of the characters of men – historiographical, psychological and Theophrastan – several distinct notions of its practical applications emerge, especially with regard to the business of writing and speaking persuasively. Above all, it is clear that ethical expertise itself confers ethos on the writing and speaking of a moral agent. Or, to look at the question in a less rhetorical way, it is assumed that anybody who can display ethical expertise must have gathered much experience of the world, thought deeply about it, and learned to master their own passions while doing so. To command this assumption is to have great power over the moral preconceptions of others. In the case of the historiographers, this is one aspect of the Tacitean commonplace that only veterans of high office have the authority to write histories of states. Putting the familiar dictum in less exclusive terms, Joseph Addison later warns in *The Freeholder*, no. 35 (20 April 1716) that only writers who 'have themselves been versed in publick Business, and thereby acquired a thorough Knowledge of Men and Things' have a right to try their hands at writing the characters of statesmen.[85] In the case of the theorists of the passions, the highly ethicized conception of rhetoric educed by Senault and Reynolds paints a picture of morally conspicuous people funnelling the passions of their publics towards the truth, by dint of their own 'Gravity, Truth, Seriousnesse, Integrity, Authority'. In the case of Theophrastan La Bruyère, it is only by the laborious study of inconstant human hearts that a person can hope to recapture 'natural' gracefulness and ease from the hobbling influence of the passions. In each of these cases we see the basic Aristotelian aim of 'making one's discourse ethical' developed in ways that are less straightforwardly artistic, more oblique and discreet.

Another point of comparison is that each of the sources is concerned with finding a literary style for discussing character. A certain dense, rapid, aphoristic style is peculiarly appropriate, it seems, to prudential moralism. Although the knowledge of men is an everyday kind of wisdom, it has a peculiar complexity and density that tends to stagger expression. Unsurprisingly, there is an underlying assumption that this complexity is more suited to literary than to oratorical forms. Hobbes notices at once the incompatibility of the style with spoken oratory in his comments on the rhetoric of Thucydides: 'For words that passe away (as in publike Orations they must) without pause, ought to be vnderstood with ease, and are lost else; though words that remaine in writing for the Reader to meditate on, ought rather to be pithy, and full.'[86] The more rich an expression is in ethical information, the more it inclines towards the realm of written literature. Saint-Évremond describes the peculiar quality of attention that the character-writing of Sallust and Tacitus, with its dense, non-declamatory style, requires of the reader: we are obliged 'diligently to scan every word in an abrupt Style, when the words will admit of a various construction, lest we should lose ourselves in too general Considerations'.[87]

On the other hand, the density of character-writing is favourable to some highly portable forms of expression, such as maxims, aphorisms, paradoxes and apothegms. The association of character-writing with the coining of maxims is common in early eighteenth-century political writing and historiography. 'Characters' and maxims were understood to convey the same sort of information: subjective, experiential, practical, and yet generalized and generally recognizable. René Rapin connects Thucydides' penetrating knowledge of 'the most imperceptible *Movements* of the secretest Passions that set Mankind on work' with his aphoristic style: ''Twas through the Shrewdness of his *View*, that he stor'd his Mind with those grand Maxims of the *publick Good*, and all those *political* Considerations wherewith his *History* abounds.'[88] To take a more worldly example, Robert Molesworth complains in a passage from the preface to his *Account of Denmark* (one that may owe something to the close of Locke's *Some Thoughts Concerning Education*) that schoolmaster grammarians take no pains with their pupils 'to inculcate the good Maxims, and recommend the noble Characters the old Historians are so full of'.[89] Maxims and characters together epitomize the knowledge that can be drawn from history. In his *Proposal for Correcting the English Tongue* (1712) Swift warns of the 'excessive fear of pedantry' that drives young university wits into writing Grub-Street imitations of the French *moraliste* mode: 'This they call *knowing the World*, and *reading Men and Manners.*'[90] Yet throughout his life Swift experimented with the Rochefoucauldian maxim, and its presence here as an object of his satire shows how high a cultural profile it had at the beginning of the eighteenth century.[91] All of these are important examples to remember when reading the printed speeches of Burke. To speak about the particularities of human character, as Burke does most famously in the *Speech on American Taxation* (1774), is to risk overcharging an oration with ethical information. It is also to leave the writer or speaker unusually exposed to the disagreement, indifference or misunderstanding of the public, since character is a delicate issue, about which everybody feels qualified to form an opinion.

ADAM SMITH'S SYNTHESIS

This chapter has traced how the rhetorical category of ethos returned to relevance during the seventeenth century as part of a popularized prudential moralism. But the revived Aristotelian model flourished in another form during the same period: it guided new ideas about how the *ars dicendi* could be adapted to the ends of Christian evangelism. Sixteenth-century academic reforms had shaped the rhetorical syllabus into a powerful and scientific system. But in the process persuasion had been stripped away from rhetoric, leaving only ornamentation to do its work.[92] The humanists had little use for ethos – indeed, a common purpose was to exclude the vagaries of personal communication and the influence of the individual voice from the discovery of arguments and the ordering of things. Their reforms tended to reduce public rhetoric to narrow exercises in academic display, useful enough for the courts of Renaissance princes but inadequate to most other public purposes. So the seventeenth-century writers on rhetoric who followed them began responding to the growing need for a modern system of persuasion, for a rhetoric that was at once more moving and less antagonistic to the Christian virtues of humbleness and charity. Only a few scraps of Roman authority were available for this task. Quintilian, for example, had made the association of Aristotelian ethos with mild and conciliating emotions ('mites atque compositos'), and with a style from which all traces of pride, elevation and sublimity ('elatum, saltem ac sublime') have been removed.[93]

A more immediate source was the medieval tradition of pulpit eloquence derived from patristic texts, and especially from Augustine's *De doctrina Christiana*, the fourth book of which concludes with a startling discussion of ethos and persuasiveness. There should be nothing to stop a bad, eloquent person composing a sermon, and that sermon being delivered by a good but uneloquent person, according to Augustine, so long as the sermon is true to God's word: 'when this happens, one person transfers from himself what is not his own, and one receives from the other what is his own'.[94] Augustine severs the yoke of decorum with which Cicero had bound together the levels of style ('humile, temperatum, grave'), the weightiness of the subject discussed ('parva, modica, magna'), and the rank, character or duties of the orator.[95] For the Christian, even the most lowly themes (and, by the Evangelical example, the most lowly speakers) are made sublime by the redemptive ends of pulpit eloquence. This is what Erich Auerbach calls the 'lowliness of the sublime' exemplified in Augustine's own *sermo humilis*.[96] In treatises on homiletics written during the seventeenth century one often finds aspects of Aristotelian rhetoric magnified, as it were, through the lens of Augustine's evangelical humility. The French Jesuit Nicolas Caussin's *Eloquentia sacrae et humanae parellela* (1619), for example, is now recognized as a particularly erudite synthesis of the pagan and patristic traditions, and the first modern rhetoric to speak at length about passions and characters.[97] Caussin goes further than Augustine in his rejection of Ciceronian decorum, however, arguing that Christian humility is itself the most sublime of human characters, and as such the most appropriate to a grand and majestic style.[98] These concerns are also prevalent in discussions of sacred eloquence by Joseph Glanvill, Bernard Lamy, Blaise Pascal and François de la Mothe-Fénelon, to name only the most conspicuous theorists of the age.[99]

This conjunction of a revived interest in rhetorical ethos with the Counter-Reformation's urge for eloquent humility leaves a deep mark on secular theories of rhetoric at the beginning of the eighteenth century. It is particularly notable in the criticism of Anthony Ashley Cooper, third Earl of Shaftesbury, and of his fiercest eighteenth-century critic, Adam Smith. Shaftesbury had an abiding conviction that moral writing is defined by its rhetorical function, and that this obliged authors to think deeply about their own moral characters. The paradox of Shaftesbury's rhetorical theory is that it is essentially ethical, but that its principal technique involves the concealment of authorial character. The paradox is explored most deeply in section I.iii of 'Advice to an Author', the third of the treatises collected in *Characteristicks* (1711). Here Shaftesbury makes a complicated analogy between the characters of Plato's dialogues and the conflicting passions or opinions found by the philosopher in his or her own breast. The characters of dialogue are produced by meditation on the passions: 'by a certain powerful figure of inward Rhetoric, the Mind [of the philosopher] *apostrophizes* its own FANCYS, raises 'em in their proper Shapes and Personages, and addresses 'em familiarly'.[100] Shaftesbury departs from Plato when he argues that, if a dialogue is in the first instance morally imitative, any incidental representation of imperfect social characters will support the representation of virtue. The various 'personages' summoned from the philosopher's mind, he argues, are the same in kind as the characters found in the dialogues of Plato and Xenophon:

> 'Twas not enough that these Pieces treated fundamentally of *Morals*, and in consequence pointed out *real Characters* and *Manners*: They exhibited 'em *alive*, and set the Countenances and Complexions of Men plainly in view. And by this means they not only taught Us to know *Others*; but, what was principal and of highest virtue in 'em, they taught us to know *Our-selves*.[101]

Shaftesbury proposes (following a similar recommendation from Horace, later discussed by Burke in the *Philosophical Enquiry*) that readers of Plato's dialogues should use the text as a sort of mirror, in which the minor (or 'second') characters reflect different aspects of their own passions or imaginations. To one side of the reader's self-image, he or she will perceive in this mirror the shadowy figure of Socrates, conceived by Plato as 'in himself *a perfect Character*; yet, in some respects, so veil'd, and in a Cloud, that to the unattentive Surveyor he seem'd often to be very different from what he really was'.[102] The clouding and cloaking metaphors that Shaftesbury uses here are his way of describing the effect of Socratic irony – 'the same involution, shadow, curtain, the same soft irony', as he calls it in his manuscript *Askemata* or philosophical regimen.[103] Even though the '*perfect Character*' is concealed behind a screen of 'refined raillery', apprentice philosophers must somehow mend their own characters to conform with this occluded model. As is so often the case in the *Characteristicks*, Shaftesbury's tendency to obscurity and paradox hides the coherence of his thinking on questions of selfhood and authorship. To Shaftesbury's mind the external knowledge of the characters of men and the internal knowledge of the self are inextricably involved with one another, and 'he who deals in *Characters* must of necessity know *his own*, or he will know nothing'.[104] There is more than a touch of metaphysical wit to this aphorism. The word '*Characters*' can be taken to mean either representations, impressions and abstractions in their most general sense – ideas, one might say – or human personalities in the senses mentioned above. It is common enough to say, like Charron or Cureau de la Chambre, that the knowledge of others depends upon self-knowledge, but Shaftesbury suggests that it is a precondition of all philosophical expression. Self-knowledge is essential to the writer who would follow in the literary path of Plato and Xenophon, because an author cannot produce writings in which readers will see their own selves reflected without understanding the snares of *amour propre*, and the necessity of keeping one's own '*Author-Character*' out of view.

For Adam Smith, Shaftesbury's remarks on ethos and style present a uniquely problematic case. In the first ten of his thirty *Lectures on Rhetoric and Belles Lettres* (first given in 1746) Smith surveys the post-Restoration literary scene, and picks out four representative cases of modern literary decorum: the simple style of Sir William Temple, the plain style of Jonathan Swift, and the modest style of Joseph Addison; the third Earl of Shaftesbury is the fourth writer, and the crucial exception to Smith's rule of Augustan stylistic propriety. For Smith, Shaftesbury's literary style is interesting because it is basically dysfunctional. It is symptomatic of some simple moral failings in the author himself that have the effect of short-circuiting his whole system of soliloquy, self-veiling and character-writing.[105] What Smith admires most in the writings of Temple, Swift and Addison is an apparently Shaftesburian quality, however: their stubborn consistency of character, their refusal to concede anything to the reader's admiration. He relishes the undistinguished uniformity of their prose, because in each case that uniformity guarantees the correspondence between their style and their general character: 'These authors did not attempt what they thought was the greatest perfection of stile', Smith explains, 'but that perfection which they thought most suitable to their genius and temper.'[106] Smith contrasts the integrity of their prose with what he perceives to be the exemplary failure of Shaftesbury as an author. Shaftesbury's great error was that he 'formed to himself', according to Smith, 'an idea of beauty of Stile abstracted from his own character, by which he proposed to regulate his Stile'.[107] The causes and consequences of this abstraction make up a Scriblerian comedy of literary feebleness:

> [Shaftesbury's] weakly state of body as it prevented the violence of his passions, did not incline him greatly to be of any particular temper to any great height. His Stile therefore would not be naturally more of one Sort than another. As therefore he was not lead to have any particular Stile, by the prevalence of any particular inclination, it was natural for him to form some Model or Idea of perfection which he should always have in view . . . Polite dignity is the character he aimed at, and as this seems to be best supported by a grand and pompous diction that was the Stile he made choise of.[108]

Shaftesbury, it is clear, has no character at all. Unlike the clubbable Scriblerians he is by upbringing and education unattached to any particular set of men or opinions (respectively the faults of his grandfather the first Earl and his tutor Locke). The Socratic 'perfect character' or 'idea of perfection' that he keeps always in view is barely adequate to the purposes of solitary writing, but it contrasts sadly with the robustly socialized characters of his Augustan contemporaries. Smith points out that it would be untenable among the accidents of common life.[109]

Smith's attack on Shaftesbury is an expression of the central idea of the *Lectures on Rhetoric and Belles Lettres*: that ethos is at the root of all other questions in the science of rhetoric. Style always refers to characters before it refers to particular passions. In Lecture 6 Smith suggests that rhetoric was the unnecessary invention of obtuse grammarians who were embarrassed by the irreducibility of language to their systems, and who instead promoted the idea that figures and tropes have some sort of occult emotional weight latent within them.[110] In fact, Smith reasons, figurative language has no magical power to influence the passions:

> When the sentiment of the speaker is expressed in a neat, clear, plain and clever manner, and the passion or affection he is poss<ess>ed of and intends, *by sympathy*, to communicate to his hearer, is plainly and cleverly hit off, then and then only the expression has all the force and beauty that language can give it.[111]

The style most suitable to a particular sentiment is determined not by the 'affection' itself, but by the relation of that affection to the character of the speaker. In other words, it is meaningless for a rhetorician to make abstract prescriptions about the correct figure or style for particular sentiments, since styles always refer to characters first. 'When all other circumstances are alike', he argues in Lecture 8, 'the character of the author must make the style different.'[112] Authorial characters are morally neutral in the same way that figures and tropes are rhetorically neutral, and accordingly it is their relations that Smith emphasizes: 'There are variety of characters which we may equally admire, as equally go<o>d and amiable', he observes in Lecture 7, 'and yet these may be very different ... The consideration of this variety of characters affords us often no small entertainment, it forms one of the chief pleasures of a sociall life, and few are so foolish as to blame it or consider it as any defect.'[113] It is this point that Smith's meticulous distinctions between the simplicity of Temple, the plainness of Swift and the modesty of Addison, three styles that are superficially similar in their sophisticated uniformity, go on to illustrate.

In Lecture 15 Smith broaches an important problem in the theory of character, the question of how one's understanding of authorial character is developed by the practice of character-writing. He divides *ethologia* into two main categories, the direct and the indirect, and he observes that direct descriptions of the 'mixture of each particular passion or turn of mind there is in the person' require the most acute and perspicacious observation. His examples of the direct mode are Sallust's character of Catiline and Tacitus' character of Agricola. Modern ethologists such as Cardinal de Retz, Lord Clarendon and Bishop Burnet are concerned less with the proportions of passions than with 'the Peculiar Tinges which these may Receive from the other Ingredients of their Character', and their characters are complex and direct.[114] But the most sophisticated kinds of character portrait make direct reference neither to the inward passions nor to the metaphysics of identity. They restrict themselves to the description of a person's outward behaviour, so the virtues and passions that make up that character are described indirectly. Smith distinguishes the 'general' indirect manner of La Bruyère, whose striking, compacted sketches capture the 'air' of a person with ostentatious economy, from the more ample 'particular' indirect manner of Theophrastus. Theophrastus had the 'most agreeable' method of all, but Smith thought that La Bruyère's characters had the greatest elegance and rhetorical power. His ordering of these different kinds of character-writing is counter-intuitive because the most accomplished examples of all (those of Sallust and Tacitus) are the least sophisticated stylistically, while the most impressionistic examples (those of La Bruyère) display the greatest stylistic complexity: 'There is a Certain order and arrangement in the Pictures exhibited by Bruyere', Smith notes, 'which the least alteration of any member would destroy.'[115] But this complexity is not to be confused with delicacy. The point of Smith's hierarchy is to distinguish La Bruyère's character-writing as 'most proper for those who would Study the Rhetorical art', because it is the most powerful example of the mode.[116]

So why are La Bruyère's characters, with their indirection, their gaps of information, their sense of human representation as a fundamental absence to the spectator, so much the most powerful example of character-writing? There is no record of Smith offering an explanation for La Bruyère's effectiveness, although he does suggest that they strike a perfect balance between the tedious particularity of Theophrastus and the impressionistic generality that he associates with the celebrated character of Falkland in Clarendon's *History of the Great Rebellion*.[117] But there does seem to be a connection between Smith's assertion of the superiority of Swift, Temple and Addison's literary characters over that of Shaftesbury (as discussed in Lectures 6–11) and the superiority of La Bruyère's indirect character portraits over the direct ethological mode of Sallust and Tacitus (as discussed in Lecture 15). Smith would appear to think that La Bruyère's minimalism and indirection somehow cause his rhetorical power. Where Sallust and the historians conduct the charge of moral energy invested by the reader too efficiently, La Bruyère allows that charge to build up, to play across the gaps and absences of his characters. Unlike Shaftesbury's 'perfect' character, the Augustans make no imposition upon the moral taste of others. They recognize implicitly that all character is morally neutral, and that it would be, as Smith says, 'very absurd to blame that of a good-natured man because he wanted the severity of a more rigid one'.[118] La Bruyère reflects the moral neutrality of character by what he leaves out. In Lecture 15 Smith observes that it would be easy to rewrite a character of Theophrastus in the style of La Bruyère, since the particular circumstances described by the former imply the sort of general character described by the latter. But it would be impossible to rewrite La Bruyère in the style of Theophrastus. There is an irreducible integrity to the characters of the modern ethologist. What Smith does not explain in these lectures is why that irreducibility, or the moral neutrality of the three Augustans, gives a certain moral or rhetorical power to their characteristic styles of writing. Does Smith have a coherent theory of the rhetorical power of character? The answer is: yes, but it is not complete in his lectures on rhetoric – for the core of his thinking about character, we must go to *The Theory of Moral Sentiments* (1759).

Throughout *The Theory of Moral Sentiments* Smith's thought is turned towards this question of the power of the moral sentiments. As a conjectural history of morality, the *Theory* is bound to explain the efficiency with which conscience and sympathy direct human conduct, when there are so many more turbulent and attractive appetites at play upon our bodies and minds. Francis Hutcheson and David Hume constructed their moral systems on the sentiments of benevolence and humanity, but Smith argues that conscience has a firmer foundation in the human frame:

> It is not the soft power of humanity, it is not that feeble spark of benevolence which Nature has lighted up in the human heart, that is thus capable of counteracting the strongest impulses of self-love. It is a stronger power, a more forcible motive, which exerts itself upon such occasions. It is reason, principle, conscience, the inhabitant of the breast, the man within, the great judge and arbiter of our conduct. It is he who, whenever we are about to act so as to affect the happiness of others, calls to us, with a voice capable of astonishing the most

presumptuous of our passions, that we are but one of the multitude, in no respect better than any other in it ... It is a stronger love, a more powerful affection, which generally takes place on such occasions; the love of what is honourable and noble, of the grandeur, and dignity, and superiority of our own characters.[119]

The textual evidence for Smith's revisions of *The Theory of Moral Sentiments* (most notably the final pre-publication draft of 1759 and the substantial alterations he made to the sixth edition of 1790) indicates that he worked hard to amplify such highly rhetorical passages, the ones that both describe and evoke the force of moral sentiments.[120] For a theoretical treatise the language is overwhelmingly strenuous, heaving with impulses, forcible motives, exertions and astonishments – it is striking that Smith allows so much bluster into his prose at such an important textual crux.[121] It exemplifies the sort of writing that Smith had in mind when he wrote in Chapter 7 of the *Theory*, on the history of ethical writing, about the efforts of the ancient moralists 'to characterize the sentiment of the heart, upon which each particular virtue is founded ... It is of all other [sciences] the most susceptible to the embellishments of eloquence.'[122]

But when Smith has made his grand stylistic gestures the question remains, *how* is it that the 'inhabitant of the breast' transforms the moral passions into characters that are so much more effective than the 'feeble spark of benevolence'? In the famous passage quoted above there is a vacillation between modest supplication ('we are but one of the multitude') and exaltation in the 'grandeur, and dignity, and superiority of our own characters'. These two impulses of pride and modesty, of energy and containment, exist together within the human breast because both of them refer to characters, to representations of the self, before they refer to actual passions or affections. Viewed from the outside as 'characters of virtue', pride and modesty seem to be most perfectly balanced in the character of magnanimity. According to Smith, the virtue of magnanimity has a particularly strong command on our sympathies because the brave concealer of his misfortunes does nothing directly to disturb our basic emotional neutrality: 'We are amazed to find that he can command himself so entirely. His firmness, at the same time, perfectly coincides with our insensibility.'[123] If Smith's reduction of the moral sentiments to principles of sympathy seems at first to be excessively optimistic, one gains confidence from ironic shadings like these. Even when Smith's rhetoric of morality is at its most sublime, it does not betray the reader into expecting sentimental warmth at such heights of virtuous elevation.

Smith's explanation of sympathy hinges upon a paradox, one that he conceals behind the concept of 'propriety'. According to the rule of propriety, imaginative representations or characterizations of other people's feelings are so much more powerful than direct affections (such as the 'feeble spark of benevolence') not because they amplify the corresponding passions, but because they depress them. In order to make the insensible spectator 'go along' with one's emotions, the primary colours of sentiment need dimming and shadowing. The passionate sufferer longs for the 'sole consolation' of sharing his 'violent and disagreeable passions' with others, but 'he must flatten, if I may be allowed to say so, the sharpness of his natural tone, in order to reduce it to harmony and concord with the emotions of those who are about him'.[124] Sentimental communication depends upon the rounding of the passions, the smoothing of their natural edges, so that they fit with propriety into the world of sympathy. The process of 'flattening' tempers and darkens the natural tone of the emotions, although in terms of their communicability it does not necessarily mute them. If simple emotions must be 'flattened' so as to become communicable, complex actions must be set in relief in order to gain the spectator's sympathy. As Smith writes in the chapter on 'the sense of Merit and Demerit', the affections that underpin our moral judgments seem 'to be a compounded sentiment, and to be made up of two distinct emotions; a direct sympathy with the sentiments of the agent, and an indirect sympathy with the gratitude of those who receive the benefit of his actions'.[125] Our judgments of other people involve a sort of stereoscopic doubling of the characters of those with whom we exchange our moral sentiments, and as our sentiments are compounded, as they take on extra dimensions through sympathetic exchange, they also increase in their power to affect.

When it is our own characters and conduct that we are judging, the situation is even more complicated, and the force of our moral sentiments is potentially more powerful. This is where the impartial spectator enters into Smith's system: 'When I endeavour to examine my own conduct ... I divide myself, as it were, into two persons; and that I, the examiner and judge, represents a different character from that other I, the person whose conduct is examined into and judged of.'[126] This model of self-division into different characters is Shaftesburian in origin, but Smith frees the discussion of character from Shaftesbury's Stoic anxiety about moral self-sufficiency by showing how all the energy of moral sentiments is derived from the external judgments of other people, or rather, by the subject's own characterization of those judgments. People desire 'not only praise', writes Smith, 'but praiseworthiness; or to be that thing which, though it should be praised by nobody, is, however, the natural and proper object of praise'.[127] The extensive revisions that Smith made to the sixth edition of the *Theory* in 1790, including the completely new sixth chapter 'Of the Character of Virtue', are largely amplifications of this central thesis: that our moral sentiments become multi-dimensional and powerful through the process of representation. So Smith's theory of propriety in *The Theory of Moral Sentiments* suggests by analogy how a character – such as the literary character of Temple, Swift or Addison – can be at once flattened or morally neutral, and rhetorically impressive or sympathetic. More generally, Adam Smith's synthesis of the various strands of early modern thought about persuasiveness in ethical writing brings the Aristotelian inheritance of an ethicized rhetoric into the sphere of Smith's admiring friend and reader, Edmund Burke.[128]

CHAPTER 2

Rhetoric in Ireland, 1693–1765

Adam Smith is one of a generation of Scottish philosophers, critics and lecturers on rhetoric who create a new academic discipline during the mid eighteenth century: the study of literature in modern vernacular languages. The peculiarly Scottish character of this innovation has been much remarked upon, and the originality and influence of the Scottish belletrists – Smith, Hugh Blair, Lord Kames and George Campbell among them – is much admired.[1] But there are several important respects in which the Irish, rather than the Scots, should be seen as the real pioneers of this new development in the art of rhetoric.

Historians of the rise of English studies sometimes notice that two Protestant Irish academics, John Lawson and Thomas Leland, published books on eloquence in 1758 and 1764, several years before Blair or Campbell sent their rhetorics to the press.[2] Lawson and Leland were professors of oratory at Trinity College, Dublin, and their treatises are elaborations of their lectures. But these two important rhetoricians are dismissed as being neither engaged with the modern, practical applications of the oratorical arts, nor capable of the theoretical self-reflection with which Smith, Blair and company raise the 'New Rhetoric' into a new discipline.[3] This unsatisfactory assessment does justice neither to the strengths of their published writings, nor to the local context of Lawson and Leland's work. While an important motivation for the Scottish belletrists is their nostalgia for the eloquence of the national parliament lost at the union of 1707, the Irish rhetoricians are moved by a more immediate concern. A few yards from the front gates of Trinity College, Dublin stands Sir Edward Lovett Pearce's Parliament Building, completed in 1735 by Arthur Dobbs. A long line of patriotic Irishmen had complained that the members of this parliament were incapable of defending the interests of the people they represented, because they lacked both the education and the civic principles that are the necessary qualifications of effective commonwealthsmen. Lawson and Leland are responding to a series of proposals that Trinity College should provide practical training in the use of the English vernacular for the purposes of political deliberation, legal representation and religious instruction. In this they complement the work of (among several others) Leland's associate Thomas Sheridan, an actor and educationalist who lectured outside the academy in Dublin, throughout England and in Scotland on the public utility of proper training in elocution. The distinctive urgency with which Irish commentators promote the renewal of national eloquence has several other corollaries. It foreshadows the increasing eloquence and confidence of the 'Patriot' group in the Irish parliament after the Money Bill Dispute of 1753. It whets the public appetite for reports and publications of speeches from the lower house after 1763. And it informs the ambitions of Edmund Burke, a graduate of Trinity College, Dublin and friend of Leland, who begins his extraordinary oratorical career in the English House of Commons in 1765. The Irish export their rhetorical arts before the Scots do theirs.

The history of the resurgence of rhetoric in mid-century Ireland is less straightforward than all this implies. The connections between texts, institutions and practices are cultural and personal, and as such they can only be inferred from the surviving documents. There is much revisionist scepticism about the very existence of a coherent Irish Patriot politics at this time, so to attribute to its supposed ideologues a body of theoretical opinion about rhetoric is a hazardous move.[4] Even as literary history the narrative is shot through with perplexities. One source of these is the inheritance of Jonathan Swift, whose spirit hangs like a cormorant over the garden of Irish eloquence. Swift is remembered as an honoured precursor by the writers and politicians discussed in this chapter, but he proves to be an ungrateful antecedent. The Dean of St Patrick's is supremely artful in his avoidance of the arts of eloquence, as Adam Smith notices when defining his 'plain style' (as opposed to Sir William Temple's more conciliatory 'simple style'): 'Swift never gives any reason for his opinions but affirms them boldly without the least hesitation … He is so far from studying the ornaments of language that he affects to leave them out even when naturall.'[5] More strikingly, beneath his precise, unyielding style there is a vein of virulently anti-rhetorical sentiment, and Swift reserves for the orators of the Irish parliament a particularly brutal contempt. So the Irish critics and patriots of the mid century must treat their harbinger with caution. When Thomas Leland makes an innocuous reference to Swift's Anglo-Latin travesties in a passage on the semantic function of idiom, for example, his English controversial opponent Richard Hurd replies with a sneer about the indecency of 'your countryman, Swift, in his dotages'.[6] Leland's friend Edmund Burke is an attentive student of Swift's complicated legacy at this time. As Swift's previously unpublished historical memoirs appear during the 1760s in the Faulkner and Hawkesworth editions of his *Works*, Burke uses them to refine his evolving thought about political ethics, and takes them as an important warning about the corruption of party allegiance.

JONATHAN SWIFT'S ANTIPATHY TO ELOQUENCE

A great commonplace about the history of early modern education is that rhetoric is central to the *studia humanitatis* at the start of the seventeenth century, and that by the century's close it is a discipline in irreversible decline. Old rhetoric gets elbowed aside by new science: the Royal Society of London celebrates the succession with a 'constant Resolution', as Bishop Sprat describes it, 'to reject all the amplifications, digressions, and swellings of style: to return back to the primitive purity, and shortness, when men deliever'd so many *things*, almost in an equal number of *words*'.[7] In 1690 John Locke reckons it 'evident how much Men love to deceive, and be deceived, since the great Art of Deceit and Errour, Rhetorick I mean, has its established Professors, is publickly taught, and has always been had in great Reputation'.[8] Locke is perhaps overestimating rhetoric's reputation: within two years of publication his *Essay* would itself be on the curriculum at Trinity College, Dublin, and professors of rhetoric found themselves an endangered species.[9] The seventeenth-century revolution in method does much to drive rhetoric off the educational agenda, but it would be a mistake to think that the modernists have a monopoly on anti-rhetorical sentiment.

In fact, the supremely post-rhetorical mind of the age belongs to their most belligerent enemy, Jonathan Swift. The evidence of his writings shows that Swift had a lifelong aversion to orators and their art – to parliamentarians, enthusiastic preachers and obtrusive talkers of all kinds. So it is a peculiar historical irony that, after his death, Swift was read as an authority on political eloquence by a later generation of patriot Irishmen. Swift famously satirizes the language-planning to which Sprat alludes with the image of men carrying around sacks of '*things*' to brandish at one another instead of '*words*'.[10] His distaste for all kinds of false refinement in language is more extreme than the ordinary dissatisfaction with rhetoric of the empiricist or sceptic, because it springs from a profound moral compulsion about the business of persuasion. It combines a grim estimation of human recalcitrance with a ferocious recruitment of that recalcitrance against the forces of modernism, enthusiasm and faction, the objects of his own indignant eloquence. As one would expect, this compulsion has a defining effect on the way that Swift writes. Sprat prefers the language of artisans, countrymen and merchants to that of scholars and wits, and Swift is similarly sensitive to the dignity of common usages and understandings.[11] But more than Sprat, Swift considers real simplicity to be the high and elusive end of literary refinement, and as such supremely appropriate to his own self-styling as a scholar-wit.[12] As a writer, Swift demands that the world stay still while he lashes it – but 'Still to lash, and lashing smile | Ill befits a lofty style.'[13] So his own rules of propriety lead him to a characteristically sleek levelness of expression: 'Proper Words in proper Places, makes the true Definition of a Stile', he tells a young clergyman in 1720, but to define that style 'would require too ample a Disquisition'.[14] Although Swift never wrote such a disquisition, eloquence is a topic that he comments on directly in his writings. Gathered together, these remarks help shed light on the most pressing problem with his views on eloquence: how the artfulness of his writing can be reconciled with his intensely anti-rhetorical agenda. Several twentieth-century commentators, Martin Price, F.P. Lock and Robert Phiddian among them, have described the acuity of Swift's satirical and political strategies.[15] But it is possible to approach Swift's rhetoric in a way that is at once more oblique and more simple than theirs (and as such more true to Swift's disposition). The first step is to recognize the compulsiveness of Swift's aversion to rhetoric: his dislike of eloquence is a moral prejudice before it is a critical principle. The second is to see it as a prejudice that intensifies over Swift's life, and that finds its supreme expression in his late writings on Irish political culture.

In each of his three most important literary roles – as churchman, satirist and back-room politician – Swift behaves as though the whole business of persuasion were a farce. His contempt for rhetoric takes its clearest form in his scattered remarks on pulpit eloquence. The heart of the problem is the dependence of the *ars praedicandi* upon the compliance of an audience: 'the Preaching of Divines helps to preserve well-inclined Men in the Course of Virtue', he observes, 'but seldom or never reclaims the Vicious'.[16] Any preaching that pretends to effect durable transformations in the opinions of an audience is necessarily untrue to the recalcitrance of fallen man. Swift's opinions are in line here with the Augustinian rhetoric of the French Jansenist *moralistes*. In the Port-Royal *Logic*, in Bernard Lamy's *De l'art de parler* and most famously in Pascal's

Pensées, the Jansenists evoke a true eloquence that rises above the traditional prescriptive rhetorics taught by their Jesuit opponents: 'le vrai éloquence se moque de l'éloquence', writes Pascal.[17] The Jansenists celebrated the *esprit de finesse* or intuitive mind that picks its way instinctively through the fallen realm of judgment and sentiment.[18] Swift shares some of the Jansenists' opinions, but he is more radically pessimistic about the involvement of eloquence with human will and appetite. He thinks of the Ciceronian pathetic style as useless for religious exhortation, because it is designed only to secure the immediate temporary assent of debaters or voters. The human will is always at the mercy of a digestive tract, he warns the young clergyman, 'at least in these Northern Climates; where, I am confident, the strongest Eloquence of that [moving] Kind will leave few Impressions upon any of our Spirits, deep enough to last until the next Morning, or rather to the next Meal'.[19] Note the complicity with which Swift specifies '*our* spirits': he writes as one of the unpersuaded. Correspondingly, in 'The Mechanical Operation of the Spirit' eloquence is associated with the faulty digestion of the enthusiastic preacher – 'Hawking, Spitting, and Belching, the Defects of other Mens Rhetorick, are the Flowers, and Figures, and Ornaments of his.'[20] These tokens of an inarticulate, flatulent oratory are reduced further to the level of purely mechanical eloquence elsewhere in Swift's satire, and particularly in *A Tale of a Tub.*

So if Swift doubts that eloquence ever alters conviction, what does he think it is for? The simple answer is that eloquence is the means by which proud and impertinent people obtrude their opinions upon others: Swift hates rhetoric, because he hates pride more than any other moral quality.[21] But there is more to Swift's aversion than that. He is contemptuous of rhetoricians because, in order to impose upon others, they must first be imposed upon themselves. Eloquence is a gesture of domination, thinks Swift, that hides a mean submission. In *Thoughts on Various Subjects* he writes: 'Positiveness is a good Quality for Preachers and Orators; because whoever would obtrude his Thoughts and Reasons upon a Multitude, will convince others the more, as he appears convinced himself.'[22] This aphorism is based on a Ciceronian commonplace about the persuasiveness of sincerity, but Swift darkens it with irony.[23] Any integrity the speaker's 'Thoughts and Reasons' might have is lost behind the lust to obtrude, the fussy vice of positiveness, and the pantomime of feigned conviction. Ethical cost vastly outweighs argumentative benefit.

Swift lays open this paradox of the aggressive orator's fundamental passivity in *A Tale of a Tub*. The *Tale* begins with a disquisition upon the various 'Oratorical Receptacles or Machines' by which those who 'desire to talk much without Interruption' have squeezed and thrust themselves into a position of rhetorical eminence: they are the hangman's ladder, the popular stage and the preacher's pulpit.[24] The pulpit is represented both as a 'machine' or tool for dispensing oratory and as a vessel for catching inspiration. Swift's scheme of wit develops this ambiguity between eloquence as manipulative action and as inert reception, often on a scale of minute verbal detail. The oratorical machines represent a culture locked into diminishing cycles of self-consumption: 'Nature it self hath instructed the Hearers, to stand with their Mouths open', writes Swift, and their slack-jawed posture corresponds obscurely with the gaping, capacious emptiness of the preacher's tub. Their meta-type, of course, is the spider of the *Battel of the Books*, with its '*over-weening Pride, which feeding and engendering on it self, turns all into Excrement and Venom*'.[25] They also foreshadow the scenes of purposeless, entropic eloquence one finds in Swift's later satire. There is bemused Gulliver, tied to the ground, watching a preening Lilliputian dignitary mount a tiny rostrum and go through 'every part of an Orator ... many Periods of Threatenings, and others of Promises, Pity and Kindness'. There is Gulliver himself wishing for the 'Tongue of *Demosthenes* or *Cicero*' before delivering to the King of Brobdingnag his constitutional history of Britain – which turns out to be 'an Heap of Conspiracies, Rebellions, Murders, [and] Massacres'. Most troublingly, there are the Houyhnhnms in their senate, incapable of the corruptions that give rise to human rhetoric, and yet stuck in a perpetual round of mutual 'exhortation' about the mooted Yahoo genocide.[26] The topic of their debate is vexing enough, without the aggravation of their perplexed and recirculating deliberations. In Pascal's terms, the Houyhnhnms are possessed so entirely by the morality of the mind and of knowledge that they lack the capacity for the morality of judgment, the *esprit de finesse* which requires sentiment and intuition, and which characterizes the dynamism of true eloquence.

During Swift's later years he found in the Irish parliament the perfect object for his anti-rhetorical compulsions. 'The Parliament here are as mad as you could desire them', he reported to Knightley Chetwood in 1715; 'all of different parties are used like Jacobites and dogs'.[27] In Ireland Swift sees a political culture twisted by factional hatred, and yet incapable of factional energy. In his fifth letter the Drapier even feels himself obliged to explain his un-Irish 'Habit of Writing and Discoursing, wherein I unfortunately differ from *almost* the whole Kingdom', by attributing it to an apprenticeship spent in London.[28] In his old age

Swift's contempt for the Irish parliament is animated by a personal enmity. Its focus is Joshua, Viscount Allen, an erstwhile friend who opposed the campaign to grant Swift the freedom of the City of Dublin in 1730. In *A Vindication of Lord Carteret* (1730) Swift conjectures that Allen has betrayed their friendship because he wants to prove his eloquence in a cause he is known to oppose, and thus 'gain the Reputation of the first *Orator* in the kingdom'.[29] This is Swift at his most bluntly ironic, as is evident from a contemporary poem about Allen called 'Traulus' (or 'Lisper'). Here Swift lingers cruelly over Allen's disadvantages as a parliamentary rhetorician:

> And though you hear him stut-tut-tut-ter,
> He barks as fast as he can utter.
> He prates in spite of all impediment
> While none believes that what he said he meant ...
> For let him sputter through a session,
> It never makes the least impression.
> Whate'er he speaks for madness goes,
> With no effect on friends or foes.[30]

The three-toed Hudibrastic rhyme of 'impediment' with 'said he meant' is a particularly infantile enactment of Allen's speech disability. It also suggests the sedimentary sinking of his silty eloquence through the indifference of friends and foes. In *Thoughts on Various Subjects* Swift notes an aphorism of Hippocrates, that 'stuttering People are always subject to Looseness'. He comments: 'I wish Physicians had Power to remove the Profusion of Words in many People to the inferior Parts.'[31] In 'Traulus' Allen's defective oratory is excrementalized once more, and flushed towards oblivion.

The wild round of insanity, copromania and demonic possession in 'Traulus' anticipates Swift's culminating satire on Irish eloquence, 'A Character of the Legion Club' (1736). Swift had often described the Irish Senate as a club – that is, as trifling, self-selecting, inward-looking.[32] But the 'Legion Club' goes a little further, populating the half-completed new Parliament Building at College Green, Dublin, with ghouls, wild beasts and madmen. All join in a roaring cacophony of unattended, recirculating oratory:

> While they sit a-picking straws
> Let them rave of making laws;
> While they never hold their tongue,
> Let them dabble in their dung ...
> We may, while they strain their throats,
> Wipe our arses with their votes.[33]

Insanity, copromania and the oratorical urge connect once again, as Swift connected them in 1704. In section IX of *A Tale of a Tub*, Swift's narrator proved how prosperous the inmates of a Bedlam would be if allowed out to Court, to the bar or to Parliament. The inmates of the 'Legion Club', however, are confined forever to their hellish Irish madhouse.

Even this selection of Swift's anti-rhetorical remarks shows that the business of eloquence is something more than a casual object of his indignation. Swift is in fact compulsive in his distaste for rhetoric. His aversion to oratory perhaps sublimates a frustrated desire for the truly public life from which he was excluded by temperament and circumstance. But it also involves a sort of cruel and anxious exuberance at his own rhetorical power, an exuberance to which his admirers among the Irish Patriots perhaps responded. This excitement often manifests itself in images of incision, of stripping and cutting. There is the flayed woman and anatomized beau of *A Tale of a Tub* section IX, of course. There is also Swift's description of himself in the *Vindication of Carteret* as 'an incensed political *Surgeon* ... Who, without waiting for [his enemy's] Death, will *flay*, and *dissect* him alive'.[34] Swift tries the keenness of his scalpel wit in another aphorism from *Thoughts on Various Subjects*: 'Eloquence smooth and cutting, is like a Razor whetted with Oil.'[35] This looks like a generalized remark about the effect of rhetorical acuity, but the aphorism must also be a sensual reimagining of his own writing style. The blandness of the razor's polished, lubricious plane and the extreme sharpness of its edge are apprehensions of sense that Swift evokes with great economy, by their connotation with one another, not by description. And yet Swift's razor of eloquence does not seem to be doing anything here – it is an object of latent menace, just as the bland surface belies the cutting edge. Swift's caution about the sharpness of his own satirical talent underlies the modesty of his account in 1715 of why the Tory ministry chose him to be its chief propagandist four years earlier. Robert Harley had wanted 'some good pen, to keep up the spirit raised in the people, to assert the principles, and justify the proceedings of the new ministers'.[36] None of these actions – rousing, asserting or justifying – has much to do with the more incisive, instrumental ends of persuasion. They are more suited to a readership among a metropolitan political class that, for all its turbulence, is largely settled in its allegiances, and that looks to the press to supply arguments that support those allegiances: 'the generality of the People know not how to *Talk* or *Think*', Swift observed in *The Examiner*, no. 16, "till they have read their *Lesson* in the Papers of the Week'.[37] As we shall see, Swift's settled contempt for the parliament at College Green as he knew it is not incompatible with the project of the Irish Patriots, which was to create almost from scratch a civic culture of eloquence, rather than to reform an existing one. The kinds of exhortatory rhetoric that Swift recognized as politically valid were of much use to the Patriots, who understood their cause to be an embattled and emerging one, rather than a mature, settled militancy. They also responded warmly to the commonwealthsman and Old Whig elements of Swift's own complex political identity.

ELOQUENCE AND THE IRISH PATRIOTS

But to what extent do Swift's violently anti-rhetorical views correspond with the opinions of his Irish contemporaries? Many educated Protestant Irishmen of the early eighteenth century display a degree of Swift's indignation and despair at the proceedings of the Irish parliaments. Unlike Swift, however, some believe that the parliament at College Green is small enough, and sufficiently uncertain of its own character, still to be transformed into the model of a virtuous senate. A new generation of patriot orators would spring up, if only a truly liberal classical education, with proper emphasis on the art of rhetoric, were available in Ireland. The reform of university curricula to this end was a favourite project of the political circle of Robert, Viscount Molesworth, the Dublin landowner and 'Real Whig' politician to whom Swift dedicated his fifth *Drapier's Letter* in December 1724.[38] In his *Account of Denmark* (1692) Molesworth argues that liberty, honour and political commitment can be supplied only by certain kinds of public education. Like his hero Locke, Molesworth is jealous of the success with which the seventeenth-century French rhetoricians (both Jesuit and Jansenist) promoted their national language, but he believes that the English-speaking nations could easily supersede them, if only classical educational practices were adopted in the British universities.[39] The philosophical academies of the ancient democracies, unlike their modern scholastic counterparts, did not confine themselves to philology or sophistic 'wrangling', Molesworth observes. Their students learned 'how and when to speak pertinently, how to act like a Man, to subdue the Passions, to be publick-spirited' – all essential attainments, writes Molesworth, to students preparing for careers in public deliberation and arbitration.[40]

Molesworth's conception of rhetorical education is essentially ethical: he follows the Ciceronian dictum that good speaking is always an expression of personal *vírtu.* During the 1720s Molesworth becomes increasingly concerned with how the want of liberal education is making the Irish political classes slaves to the English interest. Many Irish parliamentarians are obliged to manage their own estates, for fear of bad tenants ruining their land. This in turn forces them into

> low Employments and mean Company, to frequent Fairs and Markets ... they degenerate by degrees; the best Education of many of their Sons, reaching no higher, than to know how to make the most of a Piece of Land. How can the Business of Parliament, the Duty owing to ones Country, and the Value of Publick Liberty, be sufficiently understood, under such cramp'd, and low Education, help'd by little or no reading?[41]

Swift makes similar warnings about the illiteracy of Ireland's political classes during the 1720s.[42] He seems also to have been aware (and uncharacteristically tolerant) of the patriotic anti-clericalism of the Molesworth circle.[43]

Molesworth's vision of a civic education for patriot orators was sharpened in the minds of his friends John Toland and Matthew Tindal, whose hostility to the dominance of Tory clerics over the British universities is evident in many of their pamphlets from this period.[44] In 1722 Molesworth himself became the natural ally of a group of students at Glasgow University who were campaigning for the restoration of their suspended right to elect a rector – a post that Burke himself was to hold many years later.[45] When James Arbuckle, the leader of the group, left Glasgow for Dublin in 1724, Molesworth helped him to set up a new *Dublin Weekly Journal*, in which the campaign for rhetorical education continued.[46] Another young acolyte in the Molesworth circle was the clergyman and philanthropist Samuel Madden.[47] In his *Reflections and Resolutions Proper for the Gentlemen of Ireland* (1738) Madden brought Molesworth's project for civic education home to the world of Trinity College, complaining that the university failed to instruct the sons of Irish gentlemen 'in the great Art of speaking well and properly before a publick Audience'.[48] The cure that he prescribed for the endemic bashfulness of the Protestant ruling classes was that they should be made

> to pronounce some of the best Orations in the Classicks, and above all, some of our best *English* Speeches, that are to be found in the Histories of our Parliamentary Affairs and Debates there, and to deliver them with due Emphasis and Action, with proper Motion and Cadence of Voice, and a full Sense of the Subject they speak on.[49]

There was no native culture of eloquence in the Irish houses of parliament to compare with that at Westminster, and Madden's pronouns ('our ... there') enforce the comparison. But there was a gathering consensus that there ought to be. By the 1750s this widely held opinion stimulated a general appetite for civic education with a rhetorical emphasis. The fourth Earl of Chesterfield, who came to Dublin as Lord Lieutenant in 1745, wrote to Madden on the subject of rhetorical training in 1749. Chesterfield considered Trinity College greatly superior to the English universities, but thought that 'the purity and elegance of the English language ought to be particularly attended to, for there you are apt to fail in Ireland'.[50] The letters that Chesterfield wrote to his son around this time return continually to the importance of cultivating habits of elocution: 'as a speaker, you will be ranked only according to your eloquence, and by no means according to your matter ... your sole business now, is to shine, not to weigh'.[51] His grimly cosmetic attitude to political deliberation seems to have struck a chord in mid-century Dublin. George Berkeley, another friend of Madden, wondered in *The Querist* whether 'half the Learning and Study of these Kingdoms is not useless, for want of proper Delivery and Pronunciation being taught in our Schools and Colleges'.[52] It is also worth noting that Burke discussed Madden's writings with his contemporaries while he was at Trinity College: on 21 March 1747 he writes to Richard Shackleton that he cannot lend his copy of the *Reflections and Resolutions* because another friend has misplaced it.[53]

The mid-century project for cultivating parliamentary eloquence in Ireland must also be understood in its own institutional contexts: what sort of assembly would these imagined Irish orators be addressing? Before 1689 the Irish political classes had seldom enjoyed the security to worry about such matters. But even as they grew confident of their domestic power after the Glorious Revolution, the constitutional status of their parliament within the British Crown became increasingly uncertain. This was a problem that afflicted the emergent Irish Protestant Patriot movement in particular. A small but vocal tradition of texts, to which Molesworth's *Account of Denmark* gained a sort of retrospective admission after 1720, argued in Lockean fashion that Irish citizens had a claim on certain ancient parliamentary liberties. William Molyneux's *Case of Ireland Stated* (1698) demonstrated that these liberties had been ratified by a series of legal precedents going back to the Middle Ages, and which reflected inter alia the 'reason and common rights of all mankind'.[54] Molyneux's reasoning led him to the conclusion that the Irish parliament had an equal authority under the British constitution with the Parliament at Westminster.[55] But he made this assertion tentatively, and eighteenth-century Irish Patriots who followed him found that it was not an easy claim to substantiate.[56] In 1719–20 the Sunderland administration passed the Declaratory Act through the British Parliament, which affirmed its power to make laws sufficient to bind the people of Ireland. It also took away from the Irish House of Lords the right to affirm or reverse judgments made in the Irish courts, leaving it with little more authority than a grand jury.[57] The difficulty faced by the Irish opponents to this act was that their assertions of Irish parliamentary independence under the British Crown assumed that the British legislature and judicature remained correspondingly subordinate to the King-in-Parliament. But it was clear that in the balance of real power the Westminster Parliament now had considerably more weight than the Crown.

This uncomfortable fact obliged the Irish Patriots to fall back on some rather abstract reasoning about the character of their parliament. Swift, who observed the passing of the bill in a state of despairing listlessness, eventually resorted to a display of rhetorical foot-stamping: 'Were not the People of *Ireland* born as *free* as those of *England*? How have they forfeited their Freedom? Is not their *Parliament* as fair a *Representative* of the *People*, as that of *England*?'[58] The author of *A Letter of a Member of the House of Commons in Ireland* (1720) is forced to argue by analogy that if 'both *Legislature* and *Judicature* belong to the very *Institution* and *End* of the *English* Parliament, the same must in the like manner belong to the parliament in Ireland'.[59] From the Molesworth camp, John Toland is careful in his *Reasons Most Humbly Offer'd* (1720) not to question the '*Arcana Imperii*' that necessitate the binding of Irish people to English laws. His objection to the bill is that it will give the British House of Lords a quasi-legislative power that must upset the delicate constitutional balance of the British constitution's executive, legislative and deliberative parts: and there is, after all, 'a vast difference between *Ireland*'s being annext to the Crown of *Great-Britain*, and being subject to the Lords of *Great-Britain*'.[60] This sort of reasoning has less power in 1720 than it had in 1698. The Irish Patriots place a high value on the institution of parliament, and imagine it as the proper scene for their political endeavours. But as parliamentary orators they remain vulnerable to charges of absurdity while the constitutional foundation of their assembly is so unsteady. From the mid 1720s the British Parliament in fact left the Irish political classes to rule in Ireland more or less as they pleased. And yet it was not until the mid century that Irish Patriot orators gained sufficient confidence to mount a forceful opposition against English influence and executive mismanagement. Only then did the Moleswort hian project for cultivating Irish eloquence begin to make practical sense.

THOMAS SHERIDAN AND BRITISH EDUCATION

In 1756 the movement for the civic reform of Irish education found an unlikely publicist, the actor Thomas Sheridan. Sheridan's attempts as a theatre manager to bring a degree of politeness to the Irish stage – which were supported in 1747–8 by a young Edmund Burke – had ended in 1754 with a riot that destroyed his theatre in Smock Alley.[61] After an unsuccessful attempt to revive his fortunes at Covent Garden during the 1754/5 season, Sheridan began a parallel career as an academic reformer and lecturer. In *British Education* (1756) Sheridan proposed his peculiar vision of a patriotic educational system based on the 'art of elocution' – by which he meant little more than the 'graceful management of the voice, countenance, and gesture'.[62] The book is dedicated to Chesterfield, and in its preface he indicates that the hint for his elocutionary plan came from a conversation they had in 1746.[63] Elsewhere Sheridan traces the project to a remark made to him in 1735 by his father's friend Jonathan Swift. When the young Sheridan, who had just entered Trinity College, Dublin, described his course of reading, Swift asked: 'Do they teach you English? No. Do they teach you how to speak? No. Then, said he, they teach you *Nothing*.'[64] The anecdote is consistent with Swift's complaint to the young clergyman about how the Irish neglect to study the English language.[65] Although Sheridan's general thesis is unpromising, the detail of his argument is rather original, and the personal eloquence that attracted large audiences to his lectures also invigorates his prose. He inherits from the Molesworth circle an idea of the primarily civic function of education, and a sense that modern scholastic curricula fail to prepare the university student for public life: 'it would be hard to say what one duty of society, or what one office as a citizen, he is qualified to discharge, or sustain after his close application of so many years'.[66] But the anticlerical animus of Molesworth is transformed in Sheridan's work by a radical reimagination of the clergy's role in civic education. Enlarging upon a hint that he finds in Swift's *Proposal for Correcting the English Tongue* (1712), Sheridan argues that only the continual public usage of clergymen in divine service can fix and purify the English language through time.[67]

Sheridan presents his project as a response to a peculiarly British problem. In the ancient republics, he proposes, private virtue was taken to be a sufficient guarantee for the defence of constitutional liberty. In a modern commonwealth such as the one united under the British Crown, by contrast, the complex balancing of powers between the King, lords and commons, and the ever-present threat of corruption through luxury, require a principle of moral obligation that is of a superior force to the rather abstract duties of personal virtue. Only the dispensation of divine rewards and punishments, underwritten by a corresponding system of natural and civil laws, has enough moral purchase on human passions to keep liberty alive in a monarchy like Britain. It follows from this that the real bulwarks of the British constitution are the preachers and pulpit orators who make sense of the law to the general populace by promulgating the Christian precepts of charity and faith: 'to persuade men to practise them, it is necessary that they should be forcibly inculcated, and frequent impressions made till practice ripens into habit'.[68] Sheridan's rather intricate argument leads him to the conclusion that it is only through religious eloquence that the British constitution can be adequately defended. In a strikingly rhapsodic passage Sheridan describes spoken oratory as

> the immediate gift of God, who has annexed to it (when cultivated by man) powers almost miraculous, and an energy nearly divine ... Persuasion is ever it's attendant, and the passions own it for a master.[69]

Written or printed eloquence, on the other hand, is 'the invention of man, a mere work of art, and therefore can contain no natural power'. By using this dichotomy of speech and writing to educe the 'vast superiority' of the former, Sheridan allows himself to dismiss the whole business of the invention and arrangement of arguments from his rhetoric. When a speaker's tone of voice comes sincerely 'from the heart, accompanied by corresponding looks, and gestures', only then will conviction be won.[70] Language in its disembodied, written form, stripped of this personal index, is the mere 'handmaid' of speech.[71]

Sheridan's treatise had an extraordinary impact on local opinion. Towards the end of *British Education* its author hints that he has plans for the institution of his educational ideas, and on 6 December 1757 he put his project for a new kind of endowed academy before an invited audience of Dublin worthies at the Music Hall in Fishamble Street. It is a mark of Sheridan's persuasiveness that part of the audience formed itself into the 'Hibernian Society' soon afterwards, and that 'upwards of one Hundred and fifty Names' were subscribed towards the foundation of a school based on his singular proposals.[72] As the project gained momentum a barrage of attacks on Sheridan began to appear in the pamphlet shops, especially from clergymen stung by the imputation that their lack of sincerity as preachers was the direct cause of declining public morals. The third meeting of the project's committee was interrupted by an unnamed young man (sometimes identified as Edmund Burke's close friend William Dennis), who later printed his intervention as *A Second Oration to the Hibernian Society* (1758). Using a favourite image of Swift's, he warned: 'We are beginning at the Tail of Things, planning an *Attick* Story, before we fix the Foundation; laying Scheme of Oratory, before we have made Men, "*rational* Creatures;" talking loudly of *Taste* and *polite Arts*, but not a Word of *Virtue*, the *primary End*, at which all Education should aim.'[73] This would seem to be the voice of commonwealthsman principle demanding the restoration of Irish educational reform to its original civic ends. But the list of committee members printed in *The Proceedings of the Hibernian Society* (1758) includes Molesworthian educationalists like Samuel Madden and the physician Francis Hutcheson, whose father the philosopher had been another member of the Molesworth circle. There seems to have been a consensus that Sheridan's initiative was 'of such Consequence, that any reasonable Prospect of succeeding in it is enough to awaken and rouse a generous Mind'.[74] Also involved were Patriot politicians such as the Earl of Charlemont and Henry Flood, as well as Edmund Burke's friend Thomas Leland, a follower of Charlemont and fellow of Trinity College. Leland would become the prime mover in the establishment of the academy over the following years (Sheridan was never to teach at the academy himself); he was elected Professor of Oratory at Trinity College in 1762, and he published his own lectures on eloquence two years later.[75]

The Hibernian project was always a tendentious one, and people responded to it with extremes of commitment and opposition. But these strong responses prove that Sheridan's book gave voice to a widely held idea. Many educated Dubliners believed that Irish public life needed to be invigorated by a revived civic eloquence. For better or worse, the most fervently anti-rhetorical writer of the age, Jonathan Swift, stood as a sort of presiding spirit over the Irish movement for the reform of rhetorical education. In fact his contempt for all sorts of cultivators of oratorical technique is the direct progenitor of Sheridan's minimalist reduction of the art to a system of gesture and elocution. Sheridan, who does not seem to have been aware of this irony, tapped into a national fascination with rhetorical performance – even his opponents responded to him by delivering set-piece orations. The generation with whom Edmund Burke studied at Trinity College felt keenly this frustrated enthusiasm for oratory. The debating club or 'Academy of Belles Lettres' that Burke and William Dennis ran between April and July 1744, with its rehearsals of celebrated orations and mock-parliamentary skirmishes, was an earlier student-led initiative to supply opportunities for practising vernacular rhetoric.[76] But what remains of academic instruction in rhetoric were available to Burke and his contemporaries at Trinity College? And what changes were afoot?

THE EDUCATION OF AN ORATOR AT TRINITY COLLEGE, DUBLIN

As far as the curriculum at Trinity College during the first half of the eighteenth century was concerned, there were some vestiges of ancient rhetorical method that survived in Archbishop Laud's restored scholastic curriculum. But for the most part Molesworth (who matriculated into the college in 1675) and Madden (who matriculated in 1705) were right to complain of its absence. The old scholastic practice of forcing students to make Latin declamations ended shortly before Burke arrived at Trinity.[77] He may already have encountered the classical rhetoricians at Abraham Shackleton's school in Ballatore, where he gained a good enough grounding in the classics to be judged 'more fit for the Colledge than three parts of my Class'.[78] In the absence of any positive evidence, however, Shackleton's Quakerism gives cause for doubting that his pupils would have spent much time on rhetoric.[79] Shackleton was something different from John Locke's 'learned country School-master (who has all the Tropes and Figures in *Farnaby*'s *Rhetorick* at his Fingers ends)' – but who does not consider it his business 'to teach his Scholar to express himself handsomely in *English*'.[80] In any case, Burke was well prepared for his first few months at Trinity, which were occupied with the *Institutionum logicarum libri duo* of the scholastic systematician Franco Burgersdijck. His letters from this period to Shackleton's son Richard are full of sarcasms against 'that Sprightly Dutch author'.[81] In the second book of the *Institutionum* Burke would have encountered terse summaries of the parts of rhetoric that early modern logicians had absorbed into their art: the construction of rhetorical arguments from induction, enthymeme and example; the invention of arguments from commonplace topics; and the methodical arrangement of arguments by natural or arbitrary order.[82] This is the only evidence we have of Burke reading a technical discussion of rhetoric at Trinity College – albeit one that was stripped of the ethical and political contexts that fleshed out its ancient original, Aristotle's *Art of Rhetoric*.[83] It is clear, moreover, that even the fifteen-year-old Burke was aware of the polite disdain in which the sophistic part of undergraduate studies was held: 'be sure not to let your Son be bred up in the Art and Formality of Disputing', advised Locke, 'unless instead of an able Man, you desire to have an insignificant Wrangler, Opinionater in Discourse, and priding himself in contradicting others'.[84] This common contempt resurfaces as a lively satirical theme in Burke's later political writings.

Burke's reading of Burgersdijck represents the preliminary stage of the philosophical (or 'scientific') half of his studies at Trinity College. A contemporary booklist preserved in the senior lecturer's ledger for 1736 suggests the similarly scholastic character of the rest of his course.[85] Our knowledge of the literary side of the Trinity College curriculum in Burke's day is slightly more accurate, but such evidence as we have gives very little indication of the Roman orators or rhetoricians being studied – only some unspecified part of Cicero could be read as an alternative to Livy.[86] The dialogues of Lucian, the speeches of Demosthenes and the treatise on the sublime attributed to Longinus were among the prescribed Greek texts, although Burke's heart seems always to have been with the Latin authors. The 1736 and 1743 booklists may be deceptively limited guides to Burke's undergraduate reading, however. We know that courses of study at Oxford and Cambridge in this period were much more adventurous, and less rigidly scholastic and Aristotelian, than the official statutes and curricula suggest.[87] If we make a similar allowance for Trinity College, it is worth looking to the English universities for hints of what else Burke might have been reading during the 1740s. Evidence of study in rhetorical theory is rare, but not unavailable. Burke's connections with Christ Church College in Oxford were especially strong, and it fits the college's political character that Cicero was the most popular author there after 1730, his *De officiis* featuring in the 'collection books' more often than any other text (*De oratore, Orator* and *Brutus* also appeared frequently).[88] But there is little comparable evidence of rhetorical theory being read in the more clerical colleges.[89] At Trinity College in Cambridge, on the other hand, Daniel Waterland told students preparing for the ministry how to model their academic orations 'on one of *Tully*'s on a similar Subject'. In *Advice to a Young Student* (written 1710; pirated edn 1730; corrected 2nd edn 1755) he sketched a method for imitating classical speeches:

> Consider the argumentative Part by itself, which *Freigius*'s Analytical Notes will assist you in; and then you will best distinguish the Ornaments which Oratory adds, and the Art of ranging and managing each Topick, and become able to imitate him, allowing for the Difference of the Subject. However, the bare reading of his Compositions will make your Thoughts more free, and more just than otherwise.[90]

It is the stages of Waterland's system of imitation that reveal most about his idea of rhetoric. He expects the student to make a topical abstract of the given oration, and this 'argumentative Part' belongs to to its own stage of analytic activity.[91] The second stage, the actual business of imitation, involves not only the ornamental embellishments of elocution but also the dispositional 'art of ranging and managing each Topick', an art that he seems to think of (contrary to fashionable thinking) as more rhetorical than argumentative. Waterland's methodical separation of logic from rhetoric is designed to encourage intellectual grace and freedom – Jonathan Swift would doubtless have approved. He is not so much prescribing an academic exercise as outlining good discipline for reading and preparation. There is no evidence to suggest that Burke's tutor at Trinity College, Dublin (an academic placeman called John Pellissier) gave such thoughtful advice. But Waterland's comments at least give an idea of current best practice, and a hint of what might have been going on behind the bare Trinity curriculum lists.

A better indication of the general enthusiasm for rhetoric at Trinity College in this period is the rapid expansion of the university's provision of rhetorical training during the years immediately following Burke's own spell as an undergraduate. In 1753, five years after Burke graduated, John Lawson was elected to the college's Professorship of Oratory and History, a chair founded in 1724 and first occupied by Swift's friend Patrick Delaney. Lawson was an unusual tenant of the chair, first because he chose to emphasize the teaching of rhetoric rather than of history, and second because his lectures merited publication. The posthumous edition of his *Lectures Concerning Oratory* (1758) shows how sympathetic Lawson was both to the civic agenda of Molesworth and Madden, and to the concern of Swift and Sheridan for the cultivation of spoken vernacular English in Ireland:

> The end now proposed is Improvement in Eloquence; And how is this Eloquence to be exerted? In our own Tongue. Thus it is, we are to speak at the Bar, in the Senate, in the Pulpit. To it therefore must our Rules principally relate, and from those who have written in it, we must draw Citations and Examples: Which we cannot perform properly in a learned Language . . . General Precepts avail little to this End, without Experience; their Use lieth in the practical Application, in frequent Trials . . .[92]

Lawson takes pains to explain the institutional setting of his lectures, and notes that 'the chief Design proposed in the Establishment of the present Lecture, was to teach the Art of Speaking, the Rules of distinct, proper, graceful Pronunciation'.[93] This sounds like a response to Sheridan's claim that Trinity fails to provide practical tuition in oratory. The lectures are only part of the total education in rhetoric that Lawson provided at Trinity:

he describes how the 'perpetual discourses' printed in his book are designed to supplement the 'laborious' exercise of textual analysis and oral disputation undertaken by his pupils.[94] One indication of the rising profile of rhetoric at Trinity after Lawson's tenure is that in 1762 the foundation of his professorship was altered so that it became a chair in oratory alone.

Lawson's successor as Professor of Oratory was Burke's friend Thomas Leland, whose commitment to the subject had been proved by his efforts in support of Sheridan's Hibernian Academy. Following Lawson, Leland published his lectures in 1764 as *A Dissertation on the Principles of Human Eloquence.*[95] Fénelon's *Dialogues* are the presiding influence here, and Leland takes from them his characteristic blend of psychological naturalism and intelligent piety.[96] Like Fénelon or Sheridan, Leland presents his work as a general literary theory of rhetoric written from a preacher's perspective, but he is less willing than Sheridan to consider eloquence as a direct gift of the holy spirit. This is largely because of the polemical context of the *Dissertation.* It is a response to the theory of biblical inspiration outlined by Bishop William Warburton in *The Doctrine of Grace* (1763), a notoriously vituperative and doctrinally eccentric treatise on miracles and Methodism. Leland's willingness to take on the contemporary Goliath of British religious controversy is itself a mark of the intellectual confidence of Trinity College in 1764. Warburton argues that, since the standard of rhetorical excellence varies between countries and times, its principles must be arbitrary, except in so far as they support the external ends of stifling reason and inflaming the passions.[97] Leland responds by demonstrating that the tropes and figures of rhetoric 'are in themselves the *real, natural,* and *necessary* result of *real* passion and emotion', though like any other sign they may be simulated by deceit.[98] The Apostles were not inspired to write in perfectly modulated Ciceronian periods, writes Leland, because a refined style would have been entirely unsuited to their original readers, and to their own character and condition.[99] Instead, the New Testament is written with just that 'plainness and ingenuous simplicity, that language of noble sentiments and unspotted integrity', that the rules of decorum mark out as 'indications of exalted manners, and clear and noble conceptions'.[100] Leland's work is much more discursive and original than his predecessor's rather conventional lectures. It is less anxious about absorbing Sheridan's challenge to academic rhetoric, and yet it also reflects more of what was distinctive about the rhetorical culture in Ireland at the time: its pragmatism, its willingness to develop or break from classical prescriptions, and its peculiar combination of a civic, patriotic rhetoric and underlying religious agenda.

Another less obvious set of contexts for Leland's *Dissertation* can be found in the treatise on the sublime and beautiful published by his friend Edmund Burke seven years earlier. Leland and Burke share a distinctive theory of the imagination, both arguing, against the accepted wisdom of the time, that descriptive language in poetry evokes no vivid mental image in the mind of the reader.[101] The *Dissertation* and the *Philosophical Enquiry* also have a common methodological grounding in the Lockean psychology of sensation, and they both derive from it a conviction that standards of aesthetic taste are based on real, universal principles, even if the manifestations of those principles vary through history and across cultures.[102] Above all, Burke and Leland both apply the theory of these principles and variations to the category of the sublime. Leland is more willing than Burke to denote his debts to the French neoclassical debate on the subject: he acknowledges the influence of Boileau on his description of the sublime as an effect upon human sentiment, rather than as a metaphysical quality that inheres in certain objects.[103] He also lacks Burke's reticence about describing the ethical sublime, using the 'noble pathos' one feels for persons of great virtue as an example of sublime sentiments functioning without the mediation of visual images (Warburton, by contrast, limited the sublime to the visual imagination).[104] Despite these small differences it is clear that Burke and Leland come from the same intellectual milieu. Both men discuss topics in rhetorical criticism using a cautious Lockean epistemology, which they combine with the sort of pragmatic moral realism more often associated with their countryman Bishop Berkeley.[105] When seen against the background of the Irish Patriots' campaign for a revived civic oratory, and of the relatively progressive curriculum on offer at Trinity College, it seems reasonable to conclude that this common milieu is distinctively Irish, and distinctively of its time. It may be significant that Burke was resident in Dublin during the winter of 1763/4, just as Leland was preparing his lectures on eloquence for the press – the two friends must surely have discussed their critical work. But on this occasion Burke was not in Ireland on literary business.

IRISH PATRIOT ELOQUENCE IN 1763

In December 1762 Burke had told his friend Charles O'Hara that he expected the next meeting of the biennial Irish parliament to be 'sufficiently animated if I am not mistaken', and when the new session opened he travelled to Dublin among the vice-regal party to play his small part in it, as private secretary to the new Chancellor of the Irish Exchequer, William Gerard Hamilton.[106] Hamilton obtained his patent in April 1763, and Burke was rewarded at the same time with a pension of £300 per annum on the Irish civil list. But as the earlier letter to O'Hara makes clear, Burke was well aware of how 'odious and unpopular' such grants had become in Ireland. Indeed, the chief business of the small but noisy Irish Patriot opposition of 1763–4 was to harass the Dublin Castle administration into measures that would limit the liability of the Irish establishment for expensive English pensions like Burke's. Particularly effective in this respect was a young Irish parliamentarian of Burke's acquaintance who was previously involved with Leland in Sheridan's Hibernian Academy, Henry Flood. Flood had only recently aligned himself with the opposition group, but he took an early opportunity to grab attention with an aggressively patriotic oration during the second day's debate on the address to the King. Having protested at how 'those who distinguish themselves by the independence, disinterestedness and public spirit . . . are too often branded by the name of *faction*', he taunted his fellow parliamentarians with an accusation previously levelled at them by Robert Molesworth: that they did not even have the excuse of selling their independence at a high price; that most of them were corrupted by no more than 'a familiar and a gracious Smile, or a Squeeze of the Hand' from a ministerial undertaker.[107] He concluded with a motion demanding information about the enrolment of further pensions, a move that would pave the way for a debate on the circumstances of Hamilton's appointment as Chancellor of the Exchequer. Burke had come to witness a parliamentary storm, and he quickly found himself near the centre of it.

What did Burke make of the Irish political scene in 1763–4? The new session of the Irish parliament was relatively uneventful in constitutional terms. The Dublin Castle administration allowed Edmond Sexton Pery, Flood, Charles Lucas and their Patriot associates occasional small victories on pet issues, such as limitations of the duration of parliament, but guarded the progress of their own money and supply bills with vigilance. And yet the session is important to the history of the Irish parliament, because it marks the emergence in the lower house of a credible (if as yet ineffective) opposition group, and the first serious steps of that group towards the institutional self-confidence that would lead to their securing of the parliament's legislative independence twenty years later in 1782.[108] Only a handful of Irish MPs were consistent supporters of the Patriots, but the lack of any larger party organization amongst the loyal majority meant that a larger section of parliament could often be brought around to support patriotic measures, as was evident from the rejected money bills of the early 1750s. As such, oratory had an important role at the College Green assembly. This was the first parliamentary session since the conclusion of the Seven Years' War, and the first opportunity in over a decade to debate such important issues as the grant of pensions on the Irish civil list, or the extent of the military establishment that list should support during a time of peace. As Burke must have seen, the Irish political classes had at last a working deliberative forum. This was, to an extent, the moment that Molesworth and Molyneux had looked forward to at the start of the century. Patriotic oratory moved to the heart of a campaign to oppose British corruption of the Irish parliament, and to stir up the 'silent and implicit acquiescence in the grievance', as Flood put it, 'which is universally allowed to accrue from pensions, [and which] is a prostitution of our character and a breach of our trust'.[109]

Flood figures conspicuously in the most important document of general public interest in the new Irish Patriot eloquence, James Caldwell's two volumes of *Debates Relative to the Affairs of Ireland in the years 1763 and 1764*. This book is the first attempt to record and publish speeches from the Irish parliament, a practice that was increasingly common at Westminster.[110] Indeed, the most productive parliamentary diarist of the 1770s, Henry Cavendish, cut his teeth as a transcriber of oratory in the Irish parliament: in 1774 he gave invaluable assistance to Burke at Westminster, providing the transcript of what would become the printed text of his *Speech on American Taxation*.[111] Caldwell acknowledges that the parliament's lack of constitutional independence curtails the scope of its debates, but insists that 'they afford a sufficient field for the Patriot and the Orator' – indeed, the provincialism of the assembly does even more credit to the spirit of its members, which is perhaps why 'there is scarce one Native of this Country in the Parliament of *England* that is not a speaker of some distinction'.[112] Burke's employer, William Gerard Hamilton, certainly distinguished himself in this respect – Henry Flood admitted that it was Hamilton who gave him 'the highest idea of the power of eloquence' at this time – but his success as an orator was due largely to the meticulous preparations that Burke made for him each time he spoke.[113] For his own part Burke increasingly regarded his work for Hamilton and his Irish pension as a kind of slavery.

One indication of Burke's real political sympathies during this period is that nearly all of his surviving correspondence with Irish politicians from the mid 1760s is addressed to Patriot members, with the exception of his letters to Hamilton and his associate John Hely Hutchinson. When he broke from Hamilton in 1765, it was to the Patriots Henry Flood and John Monck Mason, both contemporaries of his at Trinity College, that he turned for reassurance.[114] His long-running friendships with Hercules Langrishe, Lucius O'Brien and James Caulfield, Earl of Charlemont, also date from this time.[115] Burke seems to have felt more at home among these opposition figures than he did among the pensioners of Dublin Castle, and evidently he shared their ambition, inculcated by generations of patriotic commentators on Irish affairs, of participating in a virtuous political assembly shaped by the deliberations of independent orators. But whatever Burke had in common with the Irish Patriots culturally, he had already progressed beyond their relatively unsophisticated politics. The great weakness of their position was that it depended on an uncompromising appeal to natural and ancient rights, quite unsupported by any history of pragmatic political customs or prescribed forms for the distribution of power. By the end of the 1760s Burke had made the business of synthesizing such customs and forms central to his own principles. In terms of models for their conduct, several of the Patriots, particularly Charlemont and Flood, looked to William Pitt the elder and his associate Charles Townshend.[116] Even before he entered Parliament himself, Burke knew too much about Westminster politics to feel uncritical admiration for these men: in a letter to Flood of May 1765 he reports sceptically that 'nothing but an intractable Temper in your friend Pitt' can prevent a lasting ministry being put together by George Grenville, 'and the Crisis will shew whether Pride or Patriotism be predominant in his Character'.[117] Burke anticipated correctly that pride, Pitt's ruling passion, would come out on top.[118] His vision of British politics as a moral drama of isolated, self-motivated personalities remained the defining insight of his work for the next decade, and Pitt's pride was still a central theme in his *Speech on American Taxation* in 1765.

There is another hint in Burke's correspondence with Flood that he had become too much of a political realist to take much interest in the agenda of the Irish Patriots. Flood had asked him 'if any new book of merit comes out, or any old one comes to your memory that will be of use in my Hibernian labours pray hint it to me', and Burke had responded by sending him 'the new Edition of Swift's Posthumous Works'.[119] It is often assumed that Swift did not enter the pantheon of Irish Patriot heroes until the beginning of the nineteenth century, but there is in fact plenty of evidence that Edmond Sexton Pery, Charles Lucas and their opposition colleagues were speaking of him as a precursor by 1763.[120] By giving Flood the latest volumes of Hawkesworth's posthumous edition, Burke signals their shared interest in an effective, cosmopolitan and independent patriot of an earlier generation. But Burke also saw Swift's work as problematic, and it may be that he was as concerned to draw these problems to Flood's attention as he was to celebrate Swift's uniquely powerful application of his literary talent to politics.

Much can be inferred about the way Burke read Swift by his editing of Swiftiana for *The Annual Register*, the compendious periodical he founded in 1758 and continued to edit while working for Hamilton. In *The Annual Register for 1758* Burke had selected several passages from the newly published *Four Last Years of the Queen*, concentrating particularly on Swift's aggressive character portraits of Somers, Marlborough, Godolphin and the other lords of the Whig Junto. Burke often writes reverently of the Junto, and he resents Swift's satire on their personal failings: 'they may serve as a striking example of the melancholy effects of prejudice, and party zeal'. But he prints them nevertheless, and by doing so shows his fine appreciation of Swift's 'peculiar happiness', as he describes it, 'of putting those he would satirize in the most odious and contemptible light, without seeming directly to intend it'.[121] Burke's name appears in the list of subscribers to volumes XV and XVI of Hawkesworth's London edition of Swift's *Works* in 1765, and, since his publisher Robert Dodsley provided review copies for work on *The Annual Register*, it must be the spare that Burke gives to Henry Flood. In *The Annual Register for 1764* (published 1765) Burke published extensive extracts from these two new volumes. Once again it is Swift the Clarendonian character-writer that he selects for excerption, culling the four characters of Queen Anne, Ormond, Harley and Bolingbroke from *An Enquiry into the Behaviour of the Queen's Last Ministry*, now published for the first time.

The *Enquiry* is the most successful of the accounts Swift wrote of the Tory ministry of 1710–14, because it avoids the querulous and surly partiality of his other historical memoirs. The piece is structured around a self-deprecating joke. Swift describes how in 1711 he chose 'three Persons from among the rest of Mankind, on whose Friendship and Protection I might depend': James Butler, Duke of Ormonde, Robert Harley, Earl of Oxford and Henry St John, Viscount Bolingbroke, the three Tory grandees who took power after the collapse of the Godolphin–Marlborough ministry in 1710.[122] The joke is Swift's admission that at the time he quite misjudged both their ability to protect him (slight) and the nature of their friendship with one another (fragile) – an error 'much to the discredit of my sagacity'.[123] Swift's historiography rejects all affectation of Tacitean insight about high-political manoeuvrings, or 'refinements', as he calls them.[124]

Sallust is the model here, and with great economy Swift presents the characters of Harley and Bolingbroke as sufficiently complementary to explain their original alliance, and yet necessarily antagonistic in their final dispositions. Swift explains the political genius of Harley and Bolingbroke in terms of their characteristic magnanimity, and their fall as its necessary consequence. They have a common indifference to the 'little helps and little hindrances' offered by lesser men: Harley's contempt for the opinions of others manifests itself in an impenetrable reserve, Bolingbroke's in a reckless freedom of manners and indifference to common forms.[125] Harley is so consumed by politics that he is willing to 'personate' the faults of the Queen (irresolution, procrastination, wilfulness) as though they were his own, and so create an illusion of complete control. He does so at the expense of the loyalty of his fellow ministers. When Swift tries to restore some concord between Harley and Bolingbroke in 1712, he gets no help from their friends, who 'observed the common prudential Forms of *not caring to intermeddle*, which together with the Addition of a Shrug, was the constant Answer I received'.[126] The implicit contrast with their opponents, the Junto Whigs, is crucial here, and Burke's editing serves to bring it out. Sunderland and Somers have the knack of seeming to empty their hearts, while encouraging others to do the same. They lack the nobility of Harley and Bolingbroke, but their friendly, unprincipled characters create durable personal allegiances and organizations.

Burke's extraction of these character portraits from the historical narrative allows him to make a point that is perhaps only implicit in Swift's memoirs of 1715. The magnanimous 'genius' of Queen Anne's Tory ministers may be admirable, but its pragmatic limitations are obvious when viewed against the social sophistication of the Junto. Bolingbroke's eloquence and Harley's refined ministerial tactics are unavailing, because it is their character and political ethos that finally determine the fate of their ministry, not their will or reason. It is perhaps frivolous to speculate about whether Burke, when he sent these Swift volumes to Henry Flood, intended a coding warning to his Irish friend about the unreflectively magnanimous politics of the elder Pitt. Our knowledge of the gift does allow us to see an Irish dimension, however, in Burke's editorial attitude to Swift's political work. The Swiftian extracts that Burke selected are concerned with the opposed political forces of justified magnanimity and impertinent pride, and with the tendency of both moral qualities to delude and waylay the unreflective statesman. As we shall see, this basic Burkean insight into political ethics becomes crucial to his own portraits of Pitt and Townshend in the *Speech on American Taxation* (1775), to his response on British patriotic pride in *A Letter to the Sheriffs of Bristol* (1777), and to his attack on the political ethics of revolutionary Jacobinism more generally.

This chapter has focused on local and national contexts for the development of Burke's thinking about rhetoric. Burke was born in Dublin and educated in the Protestant milieu of Trinity College.[127] The peculiar features of mid-eighteenth-century Irish public life left a lasting impression on his political character. First is the memory of Jonathan Swift, an Irish writer whose unprecedented political effectiveness and rapid fall from influence was a vexing precedent for young Irishmen with cosmopolitan ambitions. Although Burke's own political loyalties lie with Swift's enemies – the family line of Court Whigs that runs from the Somers–Sunderland Junto through Walpole and Newcastle to the Rockingham connection – Swift's satire of Whig political argument anticipates and illuminates Burke's ethical critique of his opponents' rhetoric, as we shall see. A second Irish context is the distinctive academic milieu of Trinity College, and the eighteenth-century debate over what function the University of Ireland should serve in the education of the Irish political classes. The formal study of eloquence was limited in Burke's own day, but he was aware of the general opinion that this lack needed remedying, and his close friend Thomas Leland was among a new generation of academics who stepped forward during the 1750s and 1760s to do so. Connected with the Patriot debate about civic education is a third Irish context. One of its consequences outside the academy is the popularization of books on the practical side of public speaking that concentrate exclusively on the improvement of gesture, posture, action and pronunciation, and which sweep aside the bothersome business of logical argumentation, composition and style. The man responsible for this trend, the Irish actor and Swift biographer Thomas Sheridan, was familiar to Burke from his student years as a follower of the Irish stage, and the two would be reacquainted as members of Samuel Johnson's circle in London.

In all three of these Irish contexts the practical, personal and ethical aspect of rhetoric is predominant. As such they are consistent with several pieces of evidence that survive from Burke's student days that indicate the fundamentally ethical bias of his mind, even at this early stage. Among the records of the Academy of Belles-Lettres that he convened with his undergraduate friend William Dennis is the minute for a meeting of 8 May 1747 at which another member proposes a standing order 'to restrain us from throwing personal reflections on each other'. Burke's argument against the motion anticipates his protest to Markham: 'we act here not in our real but certain personated characters', he says, and 'any reflection on Mr. Buck [the proposer] of this Society does not hurt him as Mr. Buck of the — '.[128] The argument is significant because at several of the meetings Burke spoke in prescribed characters: as Brutus on the death of Lucretia, as Caesar before the expedition into Gaul, as a Roman senator opposing Regulus' return to Carthage, and so on. His reply to Mr Buck suggests that he understood these personated orations as extensions of a more subtle ethical licence that defined the spirit of the club, a licence to speak away from one's received social personality. The connection between, on the one hand, the artificial characters of drama or history and, on the other, the candid allowances of character that should be made in certain defined social situations, is one that Burke makes instinctively.

By the time of the *Note-Book* (*c.*1751) Burke's interest in questions of character is still more pronounced, and it has a tighter rhetorical focus. Of the twenty-four pieces copied into the notebook that Burke kept at the start of the 1750s, eight are character portraits in the Theophrastan style – short, generalized depictions of socio-moral types written in an epigrammatic style.[129] Burke's characters of 'a [F]ine Gentleman', 'a Wise Man' and 'a Good Man' are each prefaced by a brief critical comment on the Theophrastan mode. In '[F]ine Gentleman' Burke is concerned that 'a Character is too complete a thing to be drawn into a Definition' before it is viewed 'in as great a variety of Lights as the Subject will bear'; conversely, in 'Good Man' he is anxious that 'a Character [should be] in no danger of becoming declamatory or vague by expressing an abstract Quality'.[130] Between these opposite extremes of hasty denotation and diffuse generalization Burke looks for a medium, and hopes to achieve a special effect of moral realism when he hits it. His character of 'a Wise Man' has nothing to do with the semi-divine ideal of the Stoics, nor is it an allegorization of abstract prudence. Characteristics like wisdom, Burke writes, 'which appear to depend wholly on reason and prudence, have always some inferior supports in our passions; even reason and prudence themselves depend, if not for their substance, yet certainly for their colour and bent on our native constitution and complexions'.[131] These early remarks suggest that the young Burke has a self-consciously sophisticated attitude to the relationship between character and personal identity, and that he has inherited something of the Augustans' relaxed approach to the morality of hypocrisy. Above all, they show that he is thinking and writing about these issues from the beginning of his intellectual life.

CHAPTER 3

The Epicurean aesthetics of the Philosophical Enquiry

When one measures Edmund Burke's *Philosophical Enquiry into the Origin of Our Ideas of the Sublime and Beautiful* against the accumulated bulk of his surviving writings – the collected volumes of his correspondence, pamphlets and speeches, the twenty-five reels of microfilmed manuscripts among the Wentworth muniments alone, the twenty-six volumes of longhand transcript from the trial of Warren Hastings – it seems extraordinary that this small treatise could influence so decisively how the rest of his work is read and understood. The 1757 first edition of the *Philosophical Enquiry* was after all a lean sort of book: Burke was obliged to put a little more flesh on its argumentative bones (an 'Introduction on Taste', and several new passages and chapters) when he published the second edition in 1759, and he remained rather apologetic about it. From early in his parliamentary career he complained that the treatise had given him a reputation for being 'abstracted and subtile', and when in 1792 Edmund Malone encouraged him to return to it, he found that he had no appetite for the subject: 'The thread of speculative Science once broken is not easily spliced again.'[1] So if Burke himself felt that three decades of Westminster graft had extinguished his interest in speculative aesthetics, why do modern readers continue to search for connections between the *Philosophical Enquiry* and the larger body of his writings?

The obvious reason is that Burke's critics, from Paine and Wollstonecraft down to the Straussians, have always wanted to say something comprehensive about his intellectual character, and to connect his first with his last thoughts.[2] Burke's most characteristic thought (according to the Straussians) is his denial that reason is the best tool for constructing political constitutions, since 'good order or the rational is the result of forces which do not themselves tend towards the good order or the rational'.[3] Strauss argues that Burke's earliest move to emancipate sentiment and instinct from reason is made in the *Philosophical Enquiry*, where the young author rejects 'classical' attempts to understand visible or sensible beauty in the light of intellectual beauty.[4] So the hedonistic empiricism of the *Philosophical Enquiry* belongs to the same movement of thought which prompts its author, thirty years later, to denounce the 'metaphysical' perfection of Girondin political theory. This narrative of ideas lies behind many late twentieth-century attempts to sketch an intellectual biography for Burke. Its great disadvantage is that it distracts from the specific things that Burke had to say in 1757 about the experience of pleasure and pain, about the psychology of moral obligation, and about the art of moving the passions. These questions may have only a tangential relation to his later thought, but they have great potential for illuminating his political rhetoric.

Another reason for reading Burke's treatise on the sublime and beautiful alongside the later work is that so much of his life after 1765 was spent arguing, persuading and making speeches – and the *Philosophical Enquiry* is very easy to mistake for a handbook of rhetoric.[5] At the very beginning of the preface to the first edition Burke salutes 'Longinus' and his 'incomparable discourse on a part of this subject' (it is uncertain whether he means the aesthetic part or the rhetorical part). Clearly, he expects readers to approach the book as though it were a late development of the neoclassical rhetorical theories that derived from the treatise attributed to Longinus called *Peri hypsous*.[6] But the search for first principles that characterizes Burke's method quickly reveals that the *Philosophical Enquiry* is not in the business of rhetorical manual-making. Indeed, it has long been recognized that his focus on the psychological effects of sublime objects, rather than upon the nature of the objects themselves, represents the partial completion of a slow turn from rhetoric to subjectivity in Enlightenment aesthetics.[7]

There are, however, several features of the text of the *Philosophical Enquiry* that sit awkwardly with the received anti-rhetorical account. The first part of the treatise closes with Burke's pious and conventional anticipation that his research into the human body and mind will discover stronger traces of divine wisdom.[8] Yet soon a more practical, rhetorical imperative obtrudes for Burke: 'besides this great purpose, a consideration of the rationale of our passions seems to me very necessary for all who would affect them on solid and sure principles' (*PE*, I.xix.53). Again, the distinction between the sublime and beautiful is 'never to be forgotten by any whose business it is to affect the passions' (*PE*, III.xxvii.124). In the 1759 second edition Burke argues that there must be a universal standard of taste among men, because without it 'no hold could possibly be taken either on their reason or their passions' (*PE*, 11). A proper scientific understanding of the mechanics of the passions will give, Burke promises, 'a double strength and lustre to any rules we deliver on such matters' (*PE*, IV.xi.140). This mindfulness of 'business' and rhetorical instrumentality, this artist's attentiveness to different kinds of power and purchase on the human psyche, is characteristic of Burke's thinking throughout the *Philosophical Enquiry*.[9] It is comparable to the method that George Campbell and Joseph Priestley would later profess in their philosophical rhetorics of the later 1770s.[10] Certainly, Burke develops no prescriptive system of rules for employing his discoveries. But their practical, rhetorical ends are assumed everywhere.

My argument in this chapter is that the *Philosophical Enquiry*'s business-like approach to the human passions has some very deep roots in earlier eighteenth-century arguments about the psychological foundations of moral experience. In the standard modern accounts of these arguments, a broadly utilitarian, voluntarist, Epicurean or 'extrinsic' theory of morality is seen in sharp conflict with a Stoic theory of natural affection in humans and its harmony with a universal order.[11] The 'extrinsic' or hedonistic argument is generally associated with Thomas Hobbes, John Locke and other philosophers who argued that humans have no natural inclination to the good, the only source of which (as far as Locke is concerned) is the command of God. The 'intrinsic' argument, on the other hand, is drawn from the works of the third Earl of Shaftesbury, Francis Hutcheson and their Stoically inclined eighteenth-century followers, who find evidence for a strong bent towards the good at the heart of human moral experience. The *Philosophical Enquiry* is a treatise of aesthetics and literary analysis, but close attention to its critical idiom and method reveal the breadth of its engagement with the larger argument in moral philosophy. Burke holds very much to the Lockean, 'extrinsic' position in these debates, but he is also keen to absorb certain elements of the 'intrinsic' theory of moral sentiments into his neo-Epicurean theory. It is a telling historical coincidence that Adam Smith made a corresponding synthesis of arguments from the extrinsic camp into his own *Theory of Moral Sentiments*, published in the same year as the second edition of the *Philosophical Enquiry*. Before I turn to these larger contexts, however, I want to look further into what Burke's treatise can tell us about his rhetorical thought.

THE BUSINESS OF AFFECTING THE PASSIONS

The *Philosophical Enquiry* works from a rhetorical perspective in so far as it focuses on everyday evidence of how language moves and persuades people. Its concern is with the mechanics of human perception, in so far as they are revealed by our psychological experiences. Burke never rationalizes his technique for observing those mechanics, but the implied assumption is that human responses to literature and art are relatively uniform. This uniformity gives adequate grounds for inferring the psycho-physiological principles of emotional response from descriptions of how readers (especially the reader of the treatise itself) are affected by heightened literary language. So the *Philosophical Enquiry* is 'rhetorical' in so far as it focuses on everyday evidence of how language moves people. Once again, its approach is practical and utilitarian.

The greater part of Burke's empirical inductions (if they deserve that name) are made through the medium of poetry, and confirmed only through the reader's secondary recognition of their truth. Burke uses scenes from Lucretius, Milton and the Bible as a curious sort of secondary object world, an imagined ground for observing virtual experiments on the passions. What makes this literary empiricism all the more striking is Burke's insistence that language can have no properly mimetic function, and that it is absurd to think of it conjuring real images to the mind. The medium of literary *parole* through which he conducts his little thought-experiments on the passions is proved to be wholly ineffective when applied to the representation of sensible experience. According to Burke, ekphrastic description has no proper correspondence with the reader's visual perception. This argument appears to signal his complete rejection of Aristotle's poetics of *mimesis*, Quintilian's doctrine of *enargeia*, and with it the whole rhetoric of vividness and imaginative power constructed by the humanists.[12] But what looks like a sharp break with rhetorical tradition in fact leads to a revised account of language's emotive force. Poetry's inability to imitate sensible images corresponds directly, Burke argues, with its efficiency as a communicator of mental states: 'it is indeed an imitation in so far as it describes the manners and passions of men which their words can express; where *animi motus effert interprete lingua*'.[13] Passionate language moves its auditors so efficiently because it is purely customary, social and sympathetic. It need only refer to the reality of other human minds, without adverting to the nature of things. One of the main rhetorical functions of language is to reveal the impression of emotions upon dispositions, 'to display rather the effect of things upon the mind of the speaker, or of others, than to present a clear idea of the things themselves' (*PE*, v.v.172). It persuades by imitating not pictures of things, but the characters and qualities of minds – or, in Horace's terms, the 'natures' of other people.

Rather unexpectedly, Burke's argument about the empirical evidence of our responses to heightened language puts some important aspects of the

Longinian rhetorical sublime to one side. For the French neoclassical rhetoricians who discussed Longinus at the end of the seventeenth century, the *grande âme* of the orator or poet is an exemplary instance of the ravishing, astonishing sublime object, and one that guarantees the dominance of ethos over simple pathos.[14] Burke agrees that it is the nature of sublime objects to provoke astonishment and admiration, but he is sceptical about the effectiveness of sublimity in persons as a force in rhetorical performances. It is too blunt, too cumbersome a tool. In so far as the business of moving the passions is interpersonal, Burke argues, it belongs to the sphere of the beautiful. He makes this point clear in his discussion of a literary source that we investigated in Chapter 1, the character portraits in Sallust's *Bellum Catilinae*:

> It is worth observing, how we feel ourselves affected in reading the characters of Cæsar, and Cato, as they are so finely drawn and contrasted in Sallust. In one, the *ignoscendo, largiundo*; in the other, *nil largiundo*. In one, the *miseris perfugium*; in the other, *malis perniciem*. In the latter we have much to admire, much to reverence, and perhaps something to fear; we respect him, but we respect him at a distance. The former makes us familiar with him; we love him, and he leads us whither he pleases. (*PE*, III.x.111)

This is from 'How far the idea of BEAUTY may be applied to the qualities of the MIND', a chapter that has no corresponding section in the earlier discussion of sublime objects, unless one counts Job preparing his seat on the street in the section on power – '*the young men saw me, and hid themselves*' (*PE*, II.v.67). The admiration, reverence and fear elicited by the character of Sallust's Cato are in Burke's terms 'inferior effects' of the sublime. He judges sublimity of character to be an obvious hindrance to statesmanship, because it is a principle of astonishment, repulsion and division. But this is not to say that sublime characters always make ineffective politicians. In some later comments on the *Iliad*, Burke writes of the reader's continued affection for the Trojans, even though the unlovable Greeks are 'far their superiors in the politic and military virtues' (*PE*, IV.xxiv.158). The emotional component of public association, Burke seems to be saying, is an arbitrary principle in the practical world of politics, and it has no fixed political meaning. Still, suspicion of the sort of awe-inspiring rhetorical ethics associated with Demosthenes in *Peri hypsous* recurs, as we shall see, throughout Burke's political career.[15]

Burke offers a psychological explanation for the difference between, on the one hand, our responses to sublime or beautiful things and, on the other, our responses to sublime or beautiful persons or actions, in an important passage in the 'Introduction on Taste'. The shorter 1757 first edition of the treatise deals almost exclusively with the nature of instinctive non-judgmental responses to sensible experience. When Burke appends the essay on taste in 1759 he writes for the first time about their ethical, judgmental aspects. He does so, first, in order to excuse their absence from the body of the work; and, second, to explain his wish to avoid discussing the complex, intellectual processes of taste as though they were simple and instinctive, as the moral sense theorists tended to do. 'So far as the imagination and the passions are concerned, I believe it true, that the reason is little consulted', he concedes; 'but where disposition, where decorum, where congruity are concerned, in short wherever the best Taste differs from the worst, I am convinced that the understanding operates and nothing else' (*PE*, 26). Aesthetic judgment, in Burke's terms, involves the rational tempering of sensibility and imagination by experience and knowledge. This is the dominant process, says Burke, in our response to any work of the imagination that concerns itself with 'the manners, the characters, the actions and designs of men', rather than with the representation of sensible objects, or with the direct manipulation of emotion:

> All these [manners, characters, etc.] make a very considerable part of what are considered as objects of Taste; and Horace sends us to the schools of philosophy and the world for our instruction in them . . . Indeed it is for the most part in our skill in manners, and in the observances of time and place, and of decency in general, which is only to be learned in those schools to which Horace recommends us, that what is called Taste by way of distinction, consists; and which is in reality no other than a more refined judgment. (*PE*, 23)

We should take this passage as a warning against looking too hard in the *Philosophical Enquiry* for the source of Burke's ethicized rhetoric – although the treatise may help us to define its parameters. In the 1757 edition Burke writes about social experience in purely passional terms, but in the 1759 introduction he allows the final adjudication to 'judgment'. The point about Horace's 'schools' is that they represent the synthesis of rational inquiry with personal experience. In *De arte poetica*, lines 309–22, Horace recommends that the most copious source of eloquence is the sort of knowledge that understands personal characters in terms of their proper moral *gestalt*, and that allows a writer or orator to sketch those characters accordingly. These lines correspond with *De arte poetica*, lines 99–118, the section quoted by Burke in *PE*, v.vi.173 and again in the *Reflections*: both passages belong to the structuring sequence of comments on ethos that runs down the spine of *De arte poetica*.[16] At lines 108–11 Horace argues (following Lucretius) that the only way to hit upon a decorous emotional style in writing is to feel the appropriate passion oneself.[17] At lines 309–22 Horace's Epicurean emotional realism is externalized and ethicized as he directs the aspiring poet to 'the Socratic pages' ('Socraticae chartae') for subject matter, adding that the study of life and manners is another source of 'living words' ('vivas voces'). These passages had a complicated tradition of eighteenth-century commentary, the most important being the Earl of Shaftesbury's elaborate interpretation of Horace's 'schools' in Part III of *Characteristicks* (1711), 'Advice to an Author'. Shaftesbury reads the passage as a reference to the interlocutors or '*second Characters*' of Plato's Socratic dialogues, whose personalities 'shew'd human Nature more distinctly, and to the Life' – in contrast with the ironic elusiveness of the master-philosopher himself.[18] Burke touches on Horace more lightly, but with a similar purpose. When characters, manners and morals are up for discussion, he argues, the credibility of a critic's judgment can be assessed only against that critic's personal skill or experience of the world – that is, by criteria that bring the critic's own character into question.

Finally (and most problematically) the *Philosophical Enquiry* shows how Burke thinks about rhetoric through its concern with the loose and rhetorical nature of much apparently sound critical language. Burke's concern is with the confusingly figurative nature of some fashionable critical key terms that should properly refer, he believes, to the experiences of immediate sense perception. The declared purpose of the *Philosophical Enquiry* is to establish the true relationship between two 'frequently confounded' critical concepts, 'the sublime' and 'the beautiful'. According to Burke, sublimity and beauty 'stand on foundations so different, that it is hard, I had almost said impossible, to think of reconciling them in the same object' (*PE*, III.xiii.114). Nevertheless, both terms have been applied indiscriminately 'to things greatly differing, and sometimes to natures directly opposite', especially when a single object is described as at once sublime *and* beautiful.[19] Although Burke blames no particular writer for this notorious abuse of critical language, he is almost certainly thinking of the Earl of Shaftesbury, who uses the collocation 'sublime and beautiful' in an important passage from the fourth treatise of the *Characteristicks*, 'An Inquiry concerning Virtue and Merit'.[20] Shaftesbury introduces the phrase 'sublime and beautiful' as a sort of distilled translation of a set of keywords derived from certain Stoic themes in the moral philosophy of Cicero. In an influential passage from Book I of *De officiis*, Cicero describes the foundation of *honestum* or the 'moral good' in rational human nature by way of analogy between the aesthetic and moral senses: just as humans are the only animals to perceive beauty, loveliness and harmony ('pulchritudinem, venustatem, convenientiam') in the visible world, so they are the only animals with an instinct for the benefits of beauty, consistency and order ('pulchritudinem, constantiam, ordinem') in the moral sphere of thought and action.[21] Shaftesbury also makes direct reference to a parallel passage about the *honestum* from Cicero's treatise *De finibus*, in which the character 'Cicero' makes the same point about moral goodness being rooted in human nature.[22] 'Cicero' does so to refute his interlocutor Torquatus, an Epicurean who argues that all morality is mere convention, an efficient means of gaining the immediate simple pleasure that accompanies the experience of public respect.[23] When Burke attacks what he takes to be the tendentiously abstracting, idealizing thought that underlies Shaftesbury's analogy between aesthetic sublimity and moral beauty, he implicates himself in an ancient back-history of philosophical conflict. Part of Burke's purpose in the *Philosophical Enquiry* is to correct certain abuses of critical language that can be linked to the writings of Shaftesbury, and that have still more complicated implications (none of them referred to explicitly by Burke) beyond the Shaftesburian context.

A second set of Shaftesburian key terms comes under Burke's scrutiny in Part III of the *Philosophical Enquiry*, when he looks closely at the language used by Shaftesbury and his followers to discuss beauty, particularly the beauty of 'proportion' and its supposed opposite, 'deformity'.[24] Burke is especially impatient with writers who link beauty with proportion, a concept that he associates with 'number' and 'measurement' rather than with immediate sensation:

> But surely beauty is no idea belonging to mensuration; nor has it anything to do with calculation or geometry. If it had, we might then point out some certain measures which we could demonstrate to be beautiful, either as simply considered, or as related to others . . . [but] we have not this help. (*PE*, III.ii.93)

Once again, it is not easy to understand Burke's point here without referring to Shaftesbury's *Characteristicks* – and he gives no explicit indication that the reader should do so. Judging by his critique of the sublime/beautiful collocation, Burke correctly associated Shaftesbury with moral sense theorists like Francis Hutcheson, who ascribe moral and aesthetic experience to 'a separate faculty of mind, and distinct from the judgment and imagination; a species of instinct by which we are struck naturally, and at first glance' (*PE*, 26). But there is also suspicion here of the Stoic exercises that the author of the *Characteristicks* prescribes for cultivating these instincts: 'the Contemplation of those *Numbers*, that

Harmony, Proportion and *Concord*', as he puts it, 'which supports the universal Nature, and is essential in the Constitution and Form of every particular Species, or Order of Beings'; it is our 'Sense of *Order* and *Proportion*', according to Shaftesbury, that explains the 'Force of *Numbers*' on the human imagination.[25] Burke attacks this cosmic aesthetic from two angles. First, he denies that any kind of 'long attention and enquiry' or 'assistance from our reasoning' is involved in the appreciation of beauty – for judgment, as we remember from the introduction, is relevant only to representations of human manners and characters. Second, he argues that ideas of proportion cannot be 'sensed' directly, since 'they are discovered by mensuration, and ... are the objects of mathematical enquiry' (*PE*, III.ii.92). This is the most controversial part of his polemic: it was a tenet of the popular Shaftesburian aesthetics of Joseph Addison, for example, that 'we are struck, we know not how, with the Symmetry of any thing we see, and immediately assent to the Beauty of an Object, without enquiring into the particular Causes and Occasions of it'.[26] By contrast, Burke's own definition of beauty is severely (if rather whimsically) hypothetical, and confines itself to 'those qualities in bodies by which they cause love, or some passion similar to it' (*PE*, III.i.91). The periodical reviewers teased Burke for his exclusion of 'proportion' from the vocabulary of beauty, which suggests that even his better-informed contemporaries found it difficult to understand how narrowly he was aiming his critique of critical language at the Shaftesburians.

Burke inherited his censorious attitude to the accuracy of other writers' technical vocabularies either directly or indirectly from the French neoclassicists, who had a sort of ironic relish for the business of affixing definitions to obviously indefinable concepts like the *je-ne-sais-quoi* and the sublime.[27] When Joseph Addison imported this critical tick into English belles-lettres he smoothed away much of the playfulness with which La Bruyère had discussed the sublime, or Bouhours the *je-ne-sais-quoi* – and the immediate influence of John Locke and his strictures on the abuse of words was in the background here. What Burke adds to Addison's Lockean critical method is an interest in the specifically metaphorical nature of many aesthetic terms of art, and a slightly more relaxed attitude to their useful rhetorical function. The term 'taste', for example, is 'like all other figurative terms ... not extremely accurate', but it leads on to a series of more specific metaphors of sense in morality that everyone understands and consents to – a sour temper, a bitter curse, a bitter fate – notwithstanding the disagreements they might have about whether the sourness or bitterness in (say) tobacco or lemons is a pleasant or unpleasant thing (*PE*, 12, 14). This is the 'natural relish' that we distinguish instinctively from acquired and customary pleasures, and it gives Burke confidence that he can establish a universal 'standard of taste'.

So there are four ways in which the *Philosophical Enquiry* can be seen to comment on rhetorical issues: first, in the businesslike, 'empirical' account that it gives of the passions; second, in its turn from the Longinian idea of rhetorical sublimity towards the sympathetic persuasiveness of ethical beauty; third, in its contrast of the purely passional way that natural objects affect us with the extra dimension of reason that is added when we judge representations of human actions, manners or characters; and, finally, in its concern with correcting the evocative but inaccurate deployment of critical vocabularies. Utility, sympathy, reason, accuracy – these have never been the most popular critical categories in discussions of the *Philosophical Enquiry.* Indeed, it is difficult to argue that they represent Burke's true rhetorical concerns when the whole argumentative momentum of the treatise seems to stress the superb indifference of sublime objects to our uses or feelings, the very limited 'influence of reason in producing our passions', and the irresistible power of obscure ideas compared with the diminished force of clear ones.[28] The tensions between the *Philosophical Enquiry*'s lucid expository method and its occasionally dark and disorderly themes can be explained, however, if we look further into its contemporary intellectual contexts. In the following sections I argue that Burke's treatise is Epicurean in its intellectual character, and that this designation when applied properly can help us to understand some apparent inconsistencies in his approach to contemporary debates about the nature of moral obligation, its psychological principles, and its application to the business of moving the passions. The rhetorical implications of the *Philosophical Enquiry* are deeply involved with its Epicurean contexts.

THE 'PHILOSOPHICAL ENQUIRY' AND THE CHARACTER OF EPICUREANISM

He that can with *Epicurus* content his Ideas with the *Films* and *Images* that fly off upon his Senses from the *Superficies* of Things; Such a Man truly wise, creams off Nature, leaving the Sower and the Dregs, for Philosophy and Reason to lap up. This is the sublime and refined Point of Felicity, called, *the Possession of being well deceived* ...[29]

With these grave words the teller of Swift's *Tale of a Tub* concludes his report on a series of anatomical experiments he has witnessed over the preceding week. Having seen a woman flayed and the carcass of a fop dissected, he can at last assure his readers that the outside of 'most' corporeal beings 'is infinitely preferable to the *In*'. This is one of several moments in *A Tale of a Tub* at which Swift lends his sarcastic voice to a chorus of late seventeenth-century Anglican rationalist polemic written against the materialist systems of the modern Epicureans, and particularly against Gassendi and Hobbes.[30] The Epicureans wanted to root out Aristotelian ontology from its well-established position in university curricula, and to replace the old scholastic system of natures and essences, of matter and form, with a more vivid and simple model for scientific knowledge. The Epicurean model would indeed confine itself to the surfaces of things, acknowledging only the movement of corpuscular atoms through an empty void in its ontic scheme.[31] It would divert scholarly inquiry away from the moral, the miraculous, the eschatological and the incorporeal, towards the visible, physical world and its living inhabitants. Learned clerics would lose their control of the universities to querulous natural philosophers – not a happy prospect for Swift.[32] One of the slight confusions in Swift's satire, however, is that it has an Epicurean source. His patron Sir William Temple complained in his essay 'Upon the Gardens of Epicurus' of 'the Vanity of all that Mortal Men can ever attain to know of Nature, in its Originals or Operations', and he did so with the authority of Epicurus himself.[33] Temple's anti-scientific prejudice kindled a lifelong contempt for natural philosophy in the mind of his protégé. It also caused him a satirical indecision: which is more objectionable, Swift wonders, the false pride of Epicureans' innovating spirit, or the creeping modesty of their philosophical aims?

There is a hint of this same indecision (its Swiftian satirical dress replaced by a more pious shift) in Part III of Burke's *Philosophical Enquiry*. Surgical insides and outsides are the topic once again:

> How different is the satisfaction of an anatomist, who discovers the use of the muscles and of the skin, the excellent contrivance of the one for the various movements of the body, and the wonderful texture of the other . . . how different is this from the affection which possesses an ordinary man at the sight of a delicate smooth skin, and all the other parts of beauty which require no investigation to be perceived? In the former case, whilst we look up to the Maker with admiration and praise, the object which causes it may be odious and distasteful; the latter very often so touches us by its power on the imagination, that we examine but little into the artifice of its contrivance; and we have need of a strong effort of our reason to disentangle our minds from the allurements of the object to a consideration of that wisdom which invented so powerful a machine. (*PE*, III.vii.108)

Unlike Swift, Burke is willing to acknowledge how a bloody discourse of anatomy might be 'considered as an hymn to the Creator'.[34] But he cannot make up his mind about those alluring, Epicurean superficies. Burke identifies himself as one 'who works beyond the surface of things', in so far as he is concerned with the causes of 'the affections of the sublime and beautiful' (*PE*, I.xix.54). And yet, when the creator made humans capable of allurement and affection, 'he did not confide the execution of his design to the languid and precarious operation of our reason; but he endued it with powers and properties that prevent the understanding' (*PE*, III.vii.107). When we take pleasure from the delicate surface of human skin, are we fulfilling the design of our bodies and affections, or are we ignoring the ends and purposes that should be the only concerns of rational creatures? Burke thought it unreasonable to expect answers to a problem like that 'in an argument so light as this' – but, so long as we take the *Philosophical Enquiry* on its own modest terms, we can say that there is something characteristically Epicurean in the dilemma itself. As the parallel with Swift and Temple suggests, the seventeenth-century Epicurean inheritance was much divided by the disparate attempts of philosophers, natural historians, poets and moralists to assimilate whatever they could of its refreshing energy, and of its humane materialism, into the Christian realm of intellectual respectability. Burke was an assimilator as well, and he found particular parts of the Epicurean tradition more useful than others as he wrote the *Philosophical Enquiry.*

Three basic tenets of Epicureanism came down to the learned world of the seventeenth and eighteenth centuries through the historical summaries of Diogenes Laertius, the criticism of Cicero, and the didactic verse of Lucretius' *De rerum natura.*[35] The first, as we have seen, was that we live in a material universe of perpetual accumulation and dissolution, made up of randomly moving sub-visible atoms, uninformed by intellectual spirits or providential design.[36] The second was that the gods, if they exist as anything more than images of perfection in human dreams, are extraterrestrial beings that lack either the will or the ability to intervene in mundane affairs.[37] The third was that human motive is circumscribed by the urge to pursue pleasure and avoid pain, and that all doctrines of justice, duty and self-restraint are soon reduced to those simple realities. Burke does not presume to deal with ontology, and the theology of the *Philosophical Enquiry* (although minimalist and confined almost exclusively to the Judaic revelation) is framed in conventionally pious terms.[38] But the third, ethical strand of Epicureanism feeds into his thinking more directly. Burke assumes that our experiences of sublime and beautiful objects are for the most part made up of responses to immediate sense impressions, or to artificial strategies for affecting them. As such his book pays a great deal of attention to the natural, original dispositions of men and women, and very little to the cultivation of those dispositions through art or industry – nobody would mistake it for the work of a neo-Stoic. He never expects his readers to strain their faculties into a disciplined or sophisticated appreciation of an object, because any serious reflection on sublimity or beauty requires the closest attention to one's natural responses to those phenomena, and, as such, to one's own nature.

As we have seen, Burke's basic aim for the *Philosophical Enquiry* is to answer the Stoic moral sense theorists who argue 'as if the Taste were a separate faculty of the mind, and distinct from the judgment and imagination' (*PE*, 26). Burke thinks that our experiences of beauty and sublimity are simple, immediate apprehensions of sense. The nature of our capacity to form refined, complex judgments on those apprehensions is an entirely separate matter, and the moral sense theorists are wrong to confound the process of apprehension with the process of judgment. We can come at truths about the world (and about its supernatural design) all at once by attending to our senses; or we can go the long way around, via 'that noble and uncommon union of science and admiration, which a contemplation of the works of infinite wisdom alone can afford to a rational mind' (*PE*, I.xix.52). Burke insists that the integrity of the former approach should be maintained against the dignity of the latter.

This sort of emphasis on the functions of basic sensory inclination is distinctively Epicurean. For the Epicurean ethicist, all pleasure and aversion is determined by the physical disposition of the individual, not by reason, and relatively little can be done to modify the consequences of those determinations in moral judgment, since humans can only will what it pleases them to will. The controversial Epicurean moralist, Bernard Mandeville, makes a distinction between Christian Epicureans like Erasmus, Gassendi and Temple, who claim that piety and virtue are the only true sources of *voluptas*, and libertines such as Hobbes's follower Charles de Saint-Évremond, who associate it with more straightforwardly sensual pleasure.[39] Mandeville doubts that there is any real quarrel here, deciding

> that whether Men be good or bad, what they take delight in is their Pleasure, and not to look out any further Etymology from the learned Languages, I believe an *Englishman* may justly call everything a pleasure that pleases him, and according to this Definition we ought to dispute no more about Mens Pleasures than their Tastes: *Trahit sua quemque Voluptas.*[40]

In short, the core of Epicureanism is its doctrine concerning the ordering of pleasure, desire and volition in human experience: pleasure is always the first mover, and is as ineluctable as our tastes. Moralists or rhetoricians might dream of altering somebody's desires and by that change affecting their will, but it would take nature itself, or providence, or divine grace (depending on your creed) to exert that power.

This emphasis on the variety of human dispositions determines Epicureanism's relation to the other philosophical schools: it recognizes that different kinds of character are attracted to the Stoic, Pythagorean or Platonic systems, and does not press its own claims to universal validity. As a philosophy much concerned with human dispositions, it is self-conscious (and quite relaxed) about reflecting a certain disposition of character that is typical of its adherents. This is why David Hume placed his essay 'The Epicurean' (subtitled '*The man of elegance and pleasure*') at the head of the set of four 'philosophical characters' that he added to the 1742 edition of his *Essays*. Hume designed his characters of the Epicurean, the Stoic, the Platonist and the Sceptic 'not so much to explain accurately the sentiments of the ancient sects of philosophy, as to deliver the sentiments of the sects, that naturally form themselves in the world' – but, as the first essay suggests, this is itself an Epicurean distinction.[41] Above all, the Epicurean sage is a person of taste, dedicated to the refinement of his or her sensibility. Hume's Epicurean, like the young Burke, is a philosopher of sensation, dedicated to the study of an inward world of natural passions. He is fiercely opposed to the Stoic and the Platonist, and to all proud, severe philosophers who expose themselves to this characteristic rebuke:

> You pretend to make me happy by reason, and by rules of art. You must, then, create me anew by rules of art. For on my original frame does my happiness depend. But you want power to affect this; and skill too, I am afraid: Nor can I entertain a less opinion of nature's wisdom than of yours.[42]

The refinement of taste is linked closely with the Epicurean's sensitivity to his own constitutional make-up, and this sensitivity in turn makes him concerned with the variety and immutability of other human characters. Hume's concern here for the original constitution of the body corresponds with remarks on the human frame made by Lucretius in *De rerum natura*, the most widely read repository of Epicurean philosophy to survive from the ancient world. As we shall see, Burke was well acquainted with Lucretius' didactic poem, with its rationalist ethics and heterodox vision of an atomistic material universe. In a couplet that recurs throughout the poem, Lucretius warns that the power of every natural thing is contained by deeply fixed boundaries (both physical and temporal), and that it is the same with the race of men: although learning ('doctrina') brings a smooth external polish to some, it cannot eradicate the original traces of the character of each mind ('naturae cuiusque animi vestigia prima').[43] It seems Hume expects his readers to have formed their idea of Epicureanism through Lucretius, because he makes a direct reference to *De rerum natura* in the central apostrophe to a personified *'Pleasure'*.[44] The Epicurean describes how '*Virtue*' teaches him to moderate enjoyment so that '*Pleasure*' becomes a permanent companion.[45] Like the young Burke, Hume's Epicurean is concerned with the natural disposition of moral subjects – in short, with their basic characters – and with the determining effect of different kinds of pleasure on the will.

HUTCHESON AND LOCKE'S EPICUREANISM

The writer who brings these issues of taste and disposition into the contextual ambit of the *Philosophical Enquiry* is Francis Hutcheson. Hutcheson's two Dublin treatises, *An Inquiry into the Original of Our Ideas of Beauty and Virtue* (1725) and *An Essay on the Nature and Conduct of the Passions* (1728), deal with some problematic Epicurean elements in the philosophy of John Locke and his followers. When the *Philosophical Enquiry* appeared in 1757, the author's closest Irish friends, Richard Shackleton and William Dennis, assumed that its purpose was to refute Hutcheson's argument that our moral perceptions have the same simplicity and originality as our physical senses. According to Dennis, Burke felt that Hutcheson's foundation of his moral philosophy on an assumed natural sense of 'the Beauty, Order, fitness and Rectitude of Actions ... indirectly saps Religion by representing Virtue independent of it'.[46] In other words, Dennis took Burke to be a voluntarist in his theology. On the evidence of the *Philosophical Enquiry*, this assessment is fairly accurate, but not complete. Burke believes that our moral obligations derive from the commands of God, and that God intends humans to apprehend those commands either through the immediate experience of his terrifying power, or (for a lucky few) through the laborious process of reasoning upon the natural law. Nevertheless, in Part I of the *Philosophical Enquiry* Burke discusses three classes of 'social passions' that 'God has planted in man' in order to draw individuals into civil associations: sympathy, which binds and unites them; imitation, which gives rise to manners and other forms of social compliance; and ambition, which provides a motive for perfecting natural capacities. Burke is willing to acknowledge the power of these moral motives: sympathy, 'if turning on pain', may be a source of sublime affections, and ambition prompts us to be 'conversant with terrible objects', giving another route to the sublime.[47] What he disagrees with Hutcheson about is the validity of the Shaftesburian analogy between our experience of these social passions and our experience of aesthetic delight. It all comes down to the question of moral power. Burke, probably following Locke, doubts that beauty has sufficient force to work as a moral motive. 'The Philosophers indeed shewed the beauty of Virtue', admits Locke, 'But leaving her unendowed, very few were willing to espouse her ... But now there being put into the Scales, on her side, *An exceeding and immortal weight of Glory*; Interest is come about to her; And Virtue now is visibly the most enriching purchase, and by much the best bargain ... Upon this foundation, and upon this only, Morality stands firm, and may defy all competition.'[48] Burke is willing to discuss a natural human inclination to the social good, so long as the larger structure of human morality retains this firm voluntaristic foundation – indeed, Burke does his best to make it firmer still.

The *Philosophical Enquiry* also pursues Hutcheson at a more detailed argumentative level. Burke thinks Hutcheson's numbering of 'taste' among a multitude of internal faculties or senses to be 'useless, and unphilosophical too in a high degree', and again it seems he holds to this opinion out of allegiance to Locke (*PE*, 27). Hutcheson takes issue with Locke's well-known hedonistic account of how volition (in regard to action) is tied to a more or less simple sense of '*uneasiness*' or '*Desire*, which is an *uneasiness* of the mind for want of some absent good'.[49] For Locke, the good is apprehended through its capacity to produce pleasure, so our knowledge of it is developed from our experiences of pleasure and pain – this is the hedonistic principle that Locke seems to have taken from his reading of Gassendi.[50] In the second edition of the *Essay Concerning Human Understanding*, Locke refined his original account of motivation so that it describes better those occasions when the '*greater good*, though apprehended and acknowledged to be so', fails to move the will: volition and desire must be proportionable to one another before we are moved to act, he observes, and desire can be '*suspended*' and mitigated by reflection, though volition itself is evidently ineluctable.[51] In the *Essay on the Nature and Conduct of the Passions*, Hutcheson allows that the desire to perform benevolent actions may be accompanied, as Locke originally asserted, by a painful uneasiness before the performance and by a pleasurable joy afterwards, but insists that the desire itself is the precedent and cause of those sensations, not their consequence.[52] This observation cuts through Locke's efforts to find a place for 'suspension' and judgment in human motivation. Given its causal priority to the ideas of reward or punishment, the desire for the good of others must arise, according to Hutcheson, from a moral faculty that is quite removed from the simple experiences of pain and pleasure. Where Locke reduces the simple idea of desire to '*an uneasy Sensation in the absence of* Good', Hutcheson argues that desire is in fact 'as distinct from any *Sensation*, as the *Will* is from the *Understanding* or Senses'.[53] Although Burke has his own reservations about Locke's psychology of pleasure, he follows Locke's basic account of the relationship between sensation and motivation, and ignores Hutcheson's qualifications.[54]

Hutcheson wrote the 1728 *Essay* as a response to various criticisms of the moral sense theory first elaborated in his 1725 *Inquiry*.[55] The most irritating and persistent (if not the most formidable) of these criticisms came from a broad spectrum of opinion that he identified as 'Epicurean' – a category in which he includes contemporary English Lockeans, French Augustinians, anarchistic libertines and anybody else who argued that the foundational impulses of moral life are selfish rather than benevolent.[56] Hutcheson's keen nose for Epicurean ideas was noticed by the Church of Scotland theologian Archibald Campbell, who was moved to wonder '*Is a Thing false, because* Epicurus *maintain'd it? Or is a Thing true, because the late Earl of Shaftesbury (whose Principles Mr.* Hutcheson *professes to explain and defend) was pleased to declare for it?*'[57] Like Shaftesbury before him, Hutcheson was ready to acknowledge that some kinds of Epicurean were more philosophical (and less wicked) than others – 'Epicureans of the better sort' and 'Epicureans in their senses', like Gassendi, Charleton, Temple or Locke, must be distinguished from atheists and libertines like Hobbes and Mandeville.[58] The 'Epicurean' treatise that Hutcheson credits with first apprising him 'of the necessity of a farther illustration of *disinterested Affections*' is *The Foundation of Morality* (1726) by John Clarke, a schoolmaster from Hull. Clark made an early attempt to extend Locke's hedonistic account of the passions into a theory of moral sentiments, arguing from the principle that benevolence must be classified as a kind of desire, the desire to do good to others. But the 'Object and Cause of Desire', he points out, 'is Pleasure alone, or the supposed means of procuring it'.[59] Pleasure and self-love must therefore be at the root of morality.

Several 'Epicurean' lines of thinking proposed by John Clarke for countering Hutcheson's psychology of multiple senses are developed further by a group of English latitudinarian academics and divines working during the three or so decades before Burke's treatise appeared in 1757.[60] The group in question represents two generations of teachers and pupils at Cambridge University during its years of mid-century post-Newtonian Enlightenment.[61] This fenland coterie had a basic common purpose: to sharpen certain conceptual tools forged by Locke and Newton into a new set of philosophical instruments for examining practical ethics, and to fit those tools to a latitudinarian Anglican theology. The two senior members of this group, the theologian Edmund Law and the moral psychologist John Gay, were elected to college fellowships in the mid 1720s.[62] A second generation of writers who studied with them in Cambridge during the late 1720s and 1730s went on to acknowledge and disseminate their ideas in works of natural law, psychology and popular philosophy – it included the essayist Soame Jenyns, the psychologist David Hartley, the natural lawyer Thomas Rutherforth and the poet and pamphleteer John Brown.[63] The evidence of Burke's library catalogue suggests that he had a keen interest in several members of this group of 'Epicurean' thinkers during the early 1750s, and signs of their impact on his early thinking can be traced through the pages of the *Philosophical Enquiry*.[64]

Burke was particularly interested in the writings of the later generation, and in the *Philosophical Enquiry* he adopted several of their strategies for reconciling natural religion and experimental natural philosophy. He shares their impatience with abstract thought, their social pragmatism and their peculiar blend of ecclesiological conservatism with intellectual daring.[65] Moral sense theory is the common enemy of both because it grounds the ontology of moral goodness in human nature, rather than in the providence of an infinitely loving divinity, manifested in the dispensation of ultimate rewards and punishments. Accordingly they attack it with a similar pincer movement of empirical and theological arguments. The shared aim is to elucidate the connection between Locke's account of 'happiness' as the simple idea behind all human desire and motivation and his description of God's law (enforced by future rewards and punishments) as the ultimate criterion of happiness and misery – and thus 'the only true touchstone of *moral Rectitude*'.[66] Law, Gay, Thomas Johnson, Rutherforth and Brown all speak up in the eighteenth-century debate about moral obligation, and their accounts of the psychology of virtue share a distinctively anti-metaphysical character. Searching through the canon of classical ethics, Thomas Rutherforth finds no serious argument to challenge the Lockean synthesis: the ancient schools were in fact '*unanimous* in allowing *that every man's own happiness is the proper end of all his actions*'.[67] John Brown speaks for several of his Cambridge contemporaries when he concludes from this that 'the only *Reason* or

Motive, by which Individuals can possibly be *induced* or *obliged* to the Practice of Virtue, must be the *Feeling* immediate, or the *Prospect* of future *private Happiness*'.[68] At a time when neo-Stoic (Shaftesbury, Hutcheson) and rationalistic (Clarke) explanations for the human compulsion to moral goodness dominated British philosophy, the Cambridge moralists stuck to a steadily realistic hedonism, and in 1757 Burke channelled these principles into his moralistic treatise of aesthetics.

Of all the Cambridge moralists, John Brown seems to have had the most immediate impact on the *Philosophical Enquiry*. The importance of Brown's *Essays on the Characteristicks* (Burke owned a copy of the 1755 fourth edition) is that the experience of reading it seems to have sharpened the argumentative edges of Burke's thought. As we have seen, the principal argument of the *Philosophical Enquiry* is about the correct use of two terms of art in aesthetics, 'sublime' and 'beautiful'. These terms have of late been 'frequently confounded' by careless writers, Burke complains, even though the qualities of sublimity and beauty 'stand on foundations so different, that it is hard, I had almost said impossible, to think of reconciling them in the same subject'.[69] I have suggested that Burke has in mind a famous passage from Shaftesbury's *Characteristicks* as he writes this. The mind judges moral and aesthetic objects instantly and ineluctably, writes Shaftesbury: 'Nor can it withhold its *Admiration* and *Ecstacy*, its *Aversion* and *Scorn*, any more in what relates to one than to the other of these Subjects. So that to deny the common and natural Sense of a SUBLIME and BEAUTIFUL in Things, will appear an Affectation merely, to any-one who considers duly of this Affair.'[70] It is this same passage that John Brown extracts in his second critical essay on the *Characteristicks*, titled 'On the Motives to Virtue', to illustrate Shaftesbury's basic definition or 'Criterion of Virtue' (a phrase that John Gay also uses in his 'Preliminary Dissertation'), and also to illustrate the looseness and ambiguity of his philosophical language. Referring directly to the phrase 'natural Sense of a SUBLIME and BEAUTIFUL in Things', Brown asks:

> what new Idea do we gain from this pompous Definition? Have we not the same general Idea from the Word *Virtue*, as from the more diffused Expression of *the Sublime and Beautiful of Things*? ... They are all general Names, relative to something which is yet unknown, and which is no more explained by the pretended Definition, than by the Word which is attempted to be defined ... To say, therefore, that Virtue consists in acting according to the *fair*, the *handsome*, the *sublime*, the *beautiful*, the *decent*, the *moral Objects* of *Right* and *Wrong*, is really no more than ringing Changes upon Words.[71]

It is Brown's Lockean focus on linguistic hygiene that distinguishes him from earlier 'Epicurean' critics of Shaftesbury such as Bernard Mandeville, from whose arguments he takes pains to distance himself. Like Burke, Brown subscribes to Locke's dictum that 'the precise real Essence of the Things moral Words stand for, may be perfectly known', those essences having nothing external to the mind for archetypes. It is only through the 'Negligence or Perverseness of Mankind' that moral words are less precise than the terms of natural philosophy.[72] Burke's efforts to define the terms 'sublime' and 'beautiful' take up the terminological problem that Brown had left unresolved with Shaftesbury. Burke inherits this problem from Brown, and in doing so, the main controversial purpose of the *Philosophical Enquiry* is aligned with that of the succession of Lockean, 'Epicurean' critics of moral sense theory to which Brown himself belongs.

The imperative of defining our moral vocabulary shapes Burke's reading of another Cambridge student of Law and Gay: the physician and psychologist David Hartley, whose *Observations on Man* he owned in the 1749 first edition. It is sometimes assumed that Burke took against the *Observations*, because he appears to throw out Hartley's theory of the association of ideas from the *Philosophical Enquiry*.[73] At the beginning of the fourth section on 'the efficient causes of the Sublime and Beautiful', Burke acknowledges that many things do affect us through the ideas we associate with them rather than through innate qualities – dangerous objects being the example he uses. But he rejects as absurd Hartley's general argument, adapted from Gay's 'Preliminary Dissertation', that association underlies all our passional responses: 'some things', Burke argues, 'must have been originally and naturally agreeable or disagreeable, from which the others derive their associated powers; and it would be, I fancy, to little purpose to look for the cause of our passions in association, until we fail of it in the natural properties of things' (*PE*, IV.ii. 131). Despite this dismissive acknowledgement, there is good evidence in the text that Burke inherited fundamental methodological principles from Hartley's work.[74] Once again, Locke's *Essay* is the object of contention. It was Locke's opinion that ideas enter our minds from one of two sources, either through sensation, or through '*the internal Operations of our Minds, perceived and reflected on by our selves*', which he called 'reflection'. When Hartley defines his differences with Locke in Chapter 3, section ii of the *Observations*, it is principally this second category of ideas to which he objects. Lockean 'reflection', says Hartley, is nothing more than 'a Term of Art, denoting an unknown Quantity'.[75] Hartley is particularly impatient with Locke's examples of words that signify ideas drawn from this sort of reflection – '*Perception, Thinking, Doubting, Believing, Reasoning, Knowing, Willing*', etc. – because according to his own associationist theory of language, none of these words has an idea attached to it: they are words capable only of abstract definition.[76]

In short, Hartley's theory involves a radical reduction of ideas to their sources in physical sensation. It is this radical move that Burke absorbs into his own chaste sensationism: 'That great chain of causes', Burke maintains, 'which linking one to another even to the throne of God himself, can never be unravelled by any industry of ours. When we go but one step beyond the immediate sensible qualities of things, we go out of our depth' (*PE*, IV.i.129–30). The best evidence that Burke's sensationism evolved out of careful study of Hartley's work is a small but distinct borrowing that Burke makes from the *Observations*. When Hartley justifies his rather cavalier way with the sort of second-order ideas that Locke explains in terms of the mind's reflections on its own functions, he does so by comparing his own technical vocabulary with that of Sir Isaac Newton. Newton assigns the words 'æther' and 'attraction' to what are really unknown causes or qualities, Hartley observes, but he does so with no intention of 'resting' in the assignation, as the schoolmen did with their terms of art. These expressions are in fact arbitrary signs under which Newton 'treasure[s] up all that can be known of the unknown Cause', so that data may be compared, experiments attempted, and 'Laws of Action will, perhaps, be discovered hereafter; so that we may be able to predict the Phænomena.'[77] In the section that immediately precedes his rejection of Hartleyian associationism, Burke has an even larger epistemological short cut of his own to justify. Where Hartley proposes an elaborate physiological account of sensation, Burke denies that any such explanation is either possible or necessary. And, like Hartley, he does so by referring to Isaac Newton's usage of two technical terms, 'attraction' and 'æther'. Burke's interpretation is slightly different from Hartley's (indeed, it carries an implicit criticism of Hartley) because he considers Newton's account of the 'subtle elastic æther' to have been a step too far beyond 'this great man['s] usual cautious manner of philosophising'.[78] This querulous qualification of Hartley's argument shows that Burke was an attentive and critical reader of the *Observations*.

The thing I want to stress about Burke's conversation with Brown's *Essays* and Hartley's *Observations* is that the issues involved are fundamental to the methodology, the first principles and the philosophical character of the *Enquiry*. In both cases the correct employment of technical vocabulary in moral reasoning is a key issue, and as such they confirm the importance of the theory of language that takes up the fifth and final section of Burke's treatise. They also give context to his austere limitation of the examples from which he builds his arguments to the evidence of primary sense data. Indeed, they suggest that Burke's sensationism is extreme even by the standards of enlightened post-Lockean empiricism – although it stops short of the radical scepticism with which Hume treated these topics. Burke looks to the Bible, to the poets, to handbooks of aesthetics or to popular scientific treatises for the materials of his inductive reasoning, but it is to these Cambridge moralists that he turns for the principles that govern the reasoning itself. But Burke also had his own points to make on the questions of pleasure, pain and sensitive response which suggest that there was a more immediate Epicurean source for his thinking during the 1750s. That source was Lucretius' philosophical poem *De rerum natura.*

BURKE AND LUCRETIUS ON THE PSYCHOLOGY OF PLEASURE

Burke's *Philosophical Enquiry* inherits the hedonism of Locke's *Essay* in so far as both refer moral and aesthetic experience back to the indefinable ideas of pain and pleasure, and especially to pleasure. Burke's special interest in these indefinable ideas is with their mutual relation, and particularly with how certain modifications of pain, related to our experience of fear and terror, seem to function as a kind of 'relative pleasure'.[79] To this class of stimulating discomfort, which includes various feelings of astonishment, admiration and lingering horror, Burke assigns a new term of art: he calls it 'delight'. We sometimes seek out experiences of terrible, painful, sublime phenomena, says Burke, because they are 'delightful', rather than directly gratifying. The language with which he distinguishes delight from simple pleasure is forever folding in on itself and flirting with paradox, especially during his discussions of the efficient causes of sublimity in the fourth part of his treatise:

> As common labour, which is a mode of pain, is the exercise of the grosser, a mode of terror is the exercise of the finer parts of the [nervous] system ... if the pain and terror are so modified as not to be actually noxious; if the pain is not carried to violence, and the terror is not conversant about the present destruction of the person, as these emotions clear the parts, whether fine, or gross, of a dangerous and troublesome incumbrance, they are capable of producing delight; not pleasure, but a sort of delightful horror, a sort of tranquillity tinged with terror; which as it belongs to self-preservation is one of the strongest of all the passions. Its object is the sublime. (*PE*, IV.vii.136)

We know this is a crucial passage for Burke because he has used an almost identical idiom at I.iii.34 to describe the experience of escaping great danger, where the subject is left 'in a state of much sobriety, impressed with a sense of awe, in a sort of tranquillity shadowed with horror'.[80] The collocation 'delightful horror' has also appeared before, during Burke's discussion of infinity at II.viii.73. In the passage above there is tension between pain and delight, but Burke also requires us to conceive of a 'tranquillity' that involves the 'strongest of all passions'; and of almost violent motions operating upon the finest parts of our constitutions. Structurally, Burke ought to have matched these paradoxical discussions of 'delight' with a long chapter on the corresponding modifications of pleasure that we experience uneasily – such as 'grief', which is love modified by bereavement. But he omits to do so, and this suggests that the engaging, motivating forces of pleasure and delight are everywhere his primary concern. Burke's doubts about the mutual exclusivity of pain and pleasure prompt him to define a passional state that lies between those two simple sensations, and which is in physical terms neutral, tranquil, emotionally still, but which nevertheless has a sort of sensational colouring: it is a neutrality 'tinged' with terror, or just 'shadowed' with delight. In the *Philosophical Enquiry* Burke is much concerned with describing such states of neutrality and in-betweenness. He is interested in how the language of physical description, for example, remains visually neutral, and provokes no real imaginative response. His great objection to Locke is that the *Essay Concerning Human Understanding* describes no simple state of indifference, no neutral medium into which the contrasting experiences of pain and pleasure resolve themselves.

This idea of a 'sensible tranquillity' corresponds closely with one of the most fundamental conceptions of Epicureanism: that the end of true philosophy is to deliver the subject into a state of *voluptas*, or tranquillity of mind and body. Epicurus himself describes this ideal state in the most important surviving fragment of his ethical writings, the 'Letter to Menoeceus', and the true definition of *voluptas* remains a prominent theme in the summaries of his moral philosophy written by the seventeenth-century Epicureans.[81] There are two types of pleasure, says Epicurus: the first is characterized by stillness, by 'a constant placability, Calmnesse, and Vacuity or Immunity from all perturbation and dolour'; the second is characterized by dynamism: it is 'resident in motion; and so consisteth only in a certain sweet affectation or pleasant titillation of the sense, as may be exemplified in joy, hilarity, eating and drinking'.[82] The first he describes as a 'stable kind of pleasure', the second as 'Moveable pleasure'. Only *voluptas* can produce true 'happiness', which is the end of Epicurean morals. In a limited sense this doctrine resembles the Lockean argument that relief from discomfort is itself a source of pleasure, but when Epicureans write of *voluptas* they refer only to pleasure in this first, non-positive, stable sense. In Walter Charleton's paraphrase:

> When we are Exempted from pain, we join in that very Exemption and Vacuity from all molestation, and every thing wherein we joy, is a pleasure: as every thing wherewith we are offended, is a pain: therefore is the privation of all pain, by us [the Epicureans] rightly named a Pleasure.[83]

This is not to say with Locke that the cessation of pain is an efficient cause of pleasure, but rather that the absence of pain has its own delightful, pleasure-tinted aspect. In both Burke and Epicurus we encounter a problem of definition. The 'stable pleasure' of Epicurean *voluptas* corresponds with what Burke terms 'delight', while the 'Moveable pleasure' of sensory gratification matches what Burke understands as merely positive pleasure. The structures of these two double definitions map onto one another closely. The difference is that Burke is more interested in the lingering traces of past emotion, the nervous impression left by fading astonishment or terror, than in the quality of the calmness that their passing causes.

What confirms the connection between Burke's theory of delight and the Epicurean principle of *voluptas* is that phrase in IV.vii, 'not pleasure, but a sort of delightful horror, a sort of tranquillity tinged with terror'. It is there in the text of the 1757 first edition of the *Philosophical Enquiry*, as we have seen in the passage quoted above from I.iii, and Burke echoes it a fourth time in a passage introduced into the second edition of 1759, revealing as he does so its poetic origin. In the new chapter on 'Power' Burke writes:

> Lucretius is a poet not to be suspected of giving way to superstitious terrors; yet when he supposes the whole mechanism of nature laid open by the master of his philosophy, his transport on this magnificent view which he has represented in the colours of such bold and lively poetry, is overcast with a shade of secret dread and horror. (*PE*, II.v.69)

In each of these four passages Burke describes a distinctive combination of terror with delightful or tranquil 'transport'. In the excerpt above, Burke refers indirectly to the 'master' Epicurus, and shows how Lucretius' *esprit fort* is tempered by an exquisite receptivity to the sublime in nature. He quotes from the proem to *De rerum natura*, Book III, the poet's response to the 'master's' discoveries in natural philosophy: 'His ibi me rebus quaedam divina voluptas | percipit atque horror' ('Thereupon from all these things a sort of divine delight gets hold upon me and a terror').[84] With this quotation Burke reveals the source of his physiology of the sublime: it is not Longinus, but Epicurean Lucretius whose verse provides the model for Burke's locutions 'delightful horror' and 'tranquillity tinged with terror'.[85] Like Lucretius, Burke reserves this 'delightful terror' for describing a special kind of wonder experienced concomitantly with the acquisition of scientific understanding. Lucretius' poem helps stop the reader marvelling at many trivial things ('mirari multa relinquas'),[86] while promising a more intoxicating kind of wonderment at the void that lies behind them. Burke seems to relish the skill with which Lucretius turns his meaning across the line ending, from the pleasure of 'divina voluptas' into the trembling of 'horror' – a move consistent, after all, with the Epicurean psychology of pain turning into delight that he had expounded previously. In the *Philosophical Enquiry* Burke aims to develop an idea that works as a powerful poetic irony in *De rerum natura*, Book III: that the materialistic natural philosophy offered by the 'master' Epicurus as a cure to the anxieties of ignorance and superstition is itself a source of spiritual experience – divine ecstasies, tremblings and so on. These responses are the same in kind, Burke implies, as those of the Psalmist, who only differs from Lucretius in the superior degree of his ravishment: 'Tremble, thou earth! at the presence of the Lord; at the presence of the God of Jacob.' Burke's point is that Epicurean descriptions of the discomforts of religious experience are useful to the Christian apologist because they correspond so closely with the poet's own description of the delights of scientific understanding. Moreover, religious experience is more intensely, magnificently voluptuous, and as such it fulfils the body's capacity for sublime delight more completely than natural philosophy.

Like Epicurus in the 'Letter to Menoeceus', Lucretius locates this divine delight at the borders between pleasure and pain, and yet set apart from both extremes of sensation. Perhaps the most famous of all Epicurean passages is the proem to Book II of *De rerum natura*, a popular section for translation into English since 1557, and the source of Francis Bacon's Epicurean quotation in his 1625 essay 'Of Truth'. It plays a prominent part in Gassendian reconstructions of Epicureanism, and John Dryden selected it as one of the five passages from *De rerum* that he translated for his 1685 miscellany, *Sylvae*:

> 'TIS Pleasant, safely to behold from shore
> The rolling ship, and hear the tempest roar;
> Not that another's pain is our delight,

> But pains unfelt produce the pleasing sight . . .
> So little this corporeal frame requires,
> So bounded are our natural desires,
> That wanting all, and setting pain aside,
> With bare privation sense is satisfied.[87]

Dryden is careful here (offering a distinctive reading in the penultimate line) to clarify Epicurus' meaning on an important point: that the delight of the spectator is different from positive, moveable pleasure.[88] Dryden's Lucretian 'delight', rather like Burke's, is a grim sort of satisfaction that has been rescued from, or 'produced' from pain, but which exists aside from that sensation. This passage is concerned particularly with the vicarious, sympathetic sensations we experience when witnessing the pain of others. As such, it corresponds closely with some of Burke's later remarks on the experience of witnessing tragedy in a dramatic setting.

Burke makes two main points about tragedy: first, that tragedy affects us only in so far as it deceives us into thinking or feeling that we are witnessing a real event; and second, following on from the first, that the delight we derive from tragedy cannot be caused by our satisfaction at having escaped the pain we see on-stage ourselves:

> So it is certain that it is absolutely necessary my life should be out of any imminent hazard before I can take delight in the sufferings of others, real or imaginary, or indeed in any thing else whatsoever. But then it is a sophism to argue from thence, that this immunity is the cause of my delight either on these or on any occasions. No one can distinguish such a cause of satisfaction in his own mind I believe; nay when we do not suffer any very acute pain, nor are exposed to any imminent danger of our lives, we can feel for others, while we suffer ourselves; and often then most when we are softened by affliction; we see with pity even distresses which we would accept in the place of our own. (*PE*, I.xv.48)

The passage quoted above from *De rerum natura* anticipates not only the problem that Burke is posing here but the answer to the problem as well. The problem is why the avoidance of pain seems to create pleasure; the answer is that it is not actually pleasure that we feel in those situations, but a bare neutrality 'tinged with pain', and this we experience as though it were delight. For Burke, as for Dryden's Lucretius, it is only by distinguishing these classes of moral sensation that we can begin to describe our moral responses and motives. The separation of responsive delight from immediate sense experience also allows Burke to describe how relatively mild or artificial pity can overcome the positive experience of pleasure or pain. Delight expands the sphere of sympathy by creating a second sensitive nature for the subject.

There are several other themes and passages in the *Philosophical Enquiry* that indicate a strong Lucretian influence on Burke's early thought. The easy way that Burke has of switching between a pious wonderment at the marvels of nature, and a clear-eyed approach to the scientific observation and explanation of those marvels, is characteristically Lucretian. Like the Cambridge Epicureans Burke is careful to note the absurdity of discussing infinite objects in terms of our finite sense perceptions, and like Lucretius he is fascinated by the various forms of optical illusion and 'deception' that form artificial impressions such as that of infinity.[89] For both Burke and Lucretius the true sublime involves the discovery of real grandeur behind the simulacra of our sense impressions – although Burke is more confident than Lucretius that the simulacra can lead the subject on to an adequate understanding of the transcendent sublime.[90] Burke's account of the physiological effects of light on the human eye, of the immediate pain and pleasure that attend all visual experiences, has a distinctly atomistic character, and Burke relates it closely, again like Lucretius, to the sensual perception of rough and smooth objects by the feeling of touch.[91] Most significantly of all, Burke employs Lucretius as a witness to the special affinity that sublimity has with language. A second direct quotation from *De rerum natura*, added like the first to the 1759 edition, appears at v.v.172 of the *Philosophical Enquiry*. Its purpose is to illustrate Burke's argument that language has an emotional effect on readers even when there are no distinct images or even ideas attached to a writer's words:

The terrible picture which Lucretius has drawn of religion, in order to display the magnanimity of his philosophical hero in opposing her, is thought to be designed with great boldness and spirit.

> *Humana ante oculos fœdè cum vita jaceret,*
> *In terris, oppressa gravi sub religione,*
> *Quæ caput e cæli regionibus ostendebat*
> *Horribili desuper visu* [sic] *mortalibus instans . . .*

What idea do you derive from so excellent a picture? none at all most certainly; neither has the poet said a single word which might in the least serve to mark a single limb or feature of the phantom, which he intended to represent in all the horrors imagination can conceive.[92]

Like the earlier quotation from Lucretius, this one is concerned directly with the 'master' or 'philosophical hero' Epicurus, and describes a drama of philosophical dauntlessness before the terrors of superstition. The passage 'is thought to be designed with great boldness' by several latitudinarian apologists, but Burke may also have in mind David Hume's recent reference to it in his dissertation on *The Natural History of Religion*, published alongside his essay 'On the Standard of Taste' a few months before the *Philosophical Enquiry* in 1757.[93] In either case, it is a daring quotation for a sober work like the *Philosophical Enquiry*, and Burke seems to doubt how he should use it. The tone of his commentary hesitates between condemnation of its vague imaginative design and admiration of its pathetic force. Lucretius has succeeded in a poetic sleight of hand – the depiction of the phantom of a phantom where truth ought to be – and Burke is half-inclined to expose the trick as mere rhetoric, and half inclined to wonder what greater effect language could have. It is a striking quotation, one that sounds many echoes back through the treatise, and yet Burke allows himself only to be interested in it as poetry, as an almost abstracted instance of rhetoric. The power of the passage, he goes on, is 'to display rather the effect of things on the mind of the speaker, or of others, than to present a clear idea of the things themselves'. What it really conveys is the spirit of philosophical emulation with which Lucretius is inspired by the bold and magnanimous character of Epicurus, a sentiment that should be reproduced a second time as we read the extract – or a third time, if Burke too has been moved in his turn (which perhaps he affects not to have been). The horrible face of Superstition is beside the point here, since the precise persuasive effect of the passage is almost completely tangential to its apparent descriptive purpose.[94] What the effect finally resolves itself into is a set of comparisons between communicating personalities and dispositions. Meaning and emotion are fluid, but ethos is real and constant.

The *Philosophical Enquiry* is the most important document that we have for the first thirty years of Edmund Burke's intellectual development, and this is perhaps why Burke's commentators have played down its many contradictions of purpose. Although it is a short treatise, really little more than an essay, it claims to lay the foundations for a complete account of the emotions and the business of affecting them. It falls short of fulfilling this ambition. And although it presents itself as performing an Addisonian marriage of fine taste and respectable liberal piety, its emphasis on bodily sensation aligns it with a controversial tradition of hedonistic, 'Epicurean' ethics. But the most curious thing about the *Philosophical Enquiry* is the reticence of its author about its larger polemical agendas. The structure of Burke's argument, indeed the very title of the treatise, is involved in a critique of the aesthetic aspects of Shaftesbury's moral philosophy, and yet no direct reference is made to the *Characteristicks*, or to the works of his follower Francis Hutcheson. Although the *Philosophical Enquiry* is methodical and systematic, there is evidence that the author has had to pull his text back from the brink of an argumentative muddle, and that it was this anti-Shaftesburian context that had confused him. Perhaps Burke found that his underlying moral concerns were too urgent to pursue with the nice tools of literary analysis, or without resorting to the same miscegenation of aesthetics and ethics to which he objected in the *Characteristicks.* Perhaps he feared that an explicit critique of Shaftesbury would embroil him in some endless train of pedantic wrangling. Perhaps the treatise emerged from a real struggle over his religious faith. In any case, Burke felt unable to avow certain crucial aspects of his agenda. This is why the *Philosophical Enquiry* is a problematic, elusive book.

But if one looks more closely at what Burke is saying about the compulsive nature of human responses to sensible experience, there is also a deeper consistency between his moral theme and his reticent style. As he makes clear in the conclusion to Part I, he has well-defined motives for writing the book: first, because he is moved to admire the traces of providential wisdom left upon the human frame; and, second, because 'a consideration of the rationale of our passions seems to me very necessary for all who would affect them upon solid and sure principles' (*PE*, I.xix.53). Burke is digging himself double foundations for a comprehensive moral and rhetorical theory. The propensity of pain to motivate or compel us is straightforward, as he acknowledges at the beginning of the section on 'Power' – but pain always causes aversion as well. Pleasure, on the other hand, is a more complicated, less compulsive affair: 'for pleasure must be stolen', writes Burke, 'and not forced upon us; pleasure follows the will' (*PE*, II.v.65). This maxim, which resembles the Virgilian tag used by Mandeville in the passage quoted above ('each is led on by his own pleasure'), is in some respects the key to the *Philosophical Enquiry.* Burke sets out to establish how objects of sublimity or beauty ever manage to move human passions, given the deadening force of habit and the obstinacy of the will. He does so by demonstrating the surprisingly oblique impact of certain powerful impressions upon the sensorium. Burke's categories of the sublime and beautiful, although they represent the extremes of aesthetic experience, are both to some extent enervating.

The sublime staggers and astonishes, the beautiful melts and relaxes. Delight is a special kind of enervated feeling in which these experiences cross over and resolve themselves, and this effect depends on the idea of pain and danger becoming communicable, where normally it would drive the subject away. At the same time it functions as a kind of 'exercise of the finer parts of the system', tempering the will, and allowing it freedom to follow the idea of pain – even as it allows pleasure freedom to follow the will in its turn (*PE*, IV.vii.136). The *Philosophical Enquiry* proposes a finely woven theory of the relation between artistry, pleasure and compulsion, and Burke makes sure that there is decorum between his argument and his style. It would have been quite inappropriate to present so subtle a theory of the passions in a pedantic, denotative, polemical form. The Epicurean character of the treatise is crucial here, because it aligns Burke's psychological speculations with an idea of human nature that is deducible from first principles and realistic about motives. At the same time it traces a path of communication with a Godhead that is too sublime to mind the trivial actions of men and women. The *Philosophical Enquiry* describes obstinate, wilful subjects being moved by sublime, and possibly indifferent agents. It suggests that this exchange tells us something essential about the art of persuasion.

CHAPTER 4

Episodes in the evolution of Burke's eloquence

This chapter describes how the ethical component in Burke's rhetoric develops and deepens in scope during his years as a member of the British Parliament. In the process, it offers the barest sketch of his career as an orator. But my real subject here, as ever, is the rhetorical principles that lie behind Burke's writings and speeches, in so far as they can be inferred from his occasional remarks on matters of state, on parliamentary process and on public morality. The practical business of politics has its place in this account as well. During his first five years as an MP the general purpose of Burke's rhetoric is to explain the party principles of the Rockinghamite Whigs, and to assert his own qualifications as a parliamentarian. In *Thoughts on the Present Discontents* the commonplace moral topic of friendship proves especially apt for this dual task, since it serves both to express his party's distinctive codes of prudent allegiance, and to make his own membership of that aristocratic 'connexion' seem natural. But if true politics is morality writ large, friendship can only magnify the virtues of private affection up to the relatively small scale of party organization.

As Burke immerses himself deeper in the study of trade and empire after 1770, he feels a growing need to express the exponential enlargement of Britain's interests during the previous half-century. He begins to stress how important it is that statesmen have the capacity of mind that will allow them to comprehend their enormous duties. Burke's great speeches on American affairs of 1774–5 describe an imperial trade so expansive and vigorous that it staggers representation: 'when we speak of the commerce with our Colonies', he warns in the *Speech on Conciliation* (1775), 'fiction lags after truth; invention is unfruitful, and imagination cold and barren'.[1] From the mid 1770s onwards Burke endeavours to prescribe the kind of enlarged liberal intelligence that would qualify a politician to manage this massive political object: for 'magnanimity in politicks is not seldom the truest wisdom; and a great empire and little minds go ill together'.[2]

Encouraging the House of Commons to accept its own competence as a judge of complex Indian affairs during the *Speech on the Nabob of Arcot's Debts* (1785), Burke warns that 'if we make ourselves too little for the sphere of our duty; if, on the contrary, we do not stretch and expand our minds to the compass of their object, be well assured, that every thing about us will dwindle by degrees'.[3]

Corresponding with this enlargement of perspective, the scope of Burke's domestic politics also expands steadily through his mid-career. By 1774, Burke's early concern with the ethics of political allegiance has given way to a larger interest in political institutions. The characters of leading statesmen are now seen against the backdrop of a Parliament that has its own trans-historical character. Next, during the later 1770s Burke begins to talk of the character of Parliament itself as an expression of national opinions and dispositions: the scale of his main political object continues to increase. The question now is whether individual MPs should be said to represent their constituents, or some larger national interest. A further magnification of Burke's domestic politics happens during the 1780s. Burke adopts the tool of parliamentary impeachment against Warren Hastings, a colonial administrator whose engrossment of power in India becomes the synecdoche for an empire-wide system of abuse and exploitation.[4] While the scope of Burke's political objects steadily increases, he always refers his inquiries back to the human scale of morality – to questions of responsibility, individual agency and personal character – and that is how they stay connected with the ethical core of his rhetoric.

THE PROOFS OF FRIENDSHIP

In September 1793 Edmund Burke sends to the Duke of Portland the treatise we now know as *Observations on the Conduct of the Minority*, a damning memorandum about the conduct of the Foxite Whigs and their enthusiasm for the French Revolution. Burke suggests that the Duke should lock up the manuscript and read it after its author's death, which he anticipates shortly: 'Then remember, that your Grace had a true friend, who had, comparatively with men of your description, a very small Interest in opposing the modern System of morality and policy; but who under every discouragement was faithful to publick Duty and private friendship.'[5] This melodramatic declaration returns to two themes that Burke worries himself with at every stage of his political career: his motivations and his friendships. The problem, as he is the first to acknowledge, is that he simply does not look the part of the cool, conservative Whig. Something about his background and character does not add up. What possible reason could Burke have for informing himself so deeply on such a range of issues – American, Indian, legal, commercial – when he had no hope of a direct opportunity to influence their handling by government? At the time of Burke's *Speech on the Nabob of Arcot's Debts* (February 1785), his old Select Committee colleague Henry Dundas even alleges that the unaccountability of Burke's defending oppressed Indian interests is positive evidence of some secret corruption.[6] Anyone trying to infer motives from Burke's general opinions will mistake the man: 'I like parliamentary reforms', he confesses to Hercules Langrishe in 1795, 'as little as any man who has boroughs to sell for money, or for peerages, in Ireland.'[7] This is a basic difficulty, it seems, that his rhetoric must overcome. Burke acknowledges to Portland how hard it must be to square his declared political principles either with his energetic character, or with his obscure and unpropertied origins, or with his 'very small interest' in supporting the old oligarchic order of morality and policy. 'At every step of my progress in life (for in every step I have been opposed), and at every turnpike I met', he writes three years later in *A Letter to a Noble Lord*, 'I was obliged to shew my passport, and again and again to prove my sole title to the honour of being useful to my Country' – his knowledge of its laws.[8] In short, Edmund Burke needs to explain exactly what he, an Irish adventurer, is doing at Westminster. And while the need to explain becomes less pressing as his reputation grows, it never goes away. Burke can plead the talents and industry of the *novus homo* when challenged by his declared enemies, but when dealing with those who need to trust him, or to depend upon his word, the best proof of his good faith is the 'private friendship' that he avows here to the Duke.[9] From the beginning of his parliamentary career in 1765, his character is guaranteed in the House of Commons by the friendship and trust extended to him by a group of well-known public men, and particularly by the prime minister of the day, his patron the Marquis of Rockingham: 'My strength was always in those admirable Men', he writes in 1789, 'with whom I have been connected. Stripped of them I am nothing.'[10] One sign of the importance of friendship to Burke's moral imagination is the speed with which it evolves, between 1765 and 1770, from a matter of personal identification into a major principle in his politics.

Friendship becomes an important principle for the rhetoric of Burke's party in 1766, when Rockingham loses the treasury seals, and several of his ministerial colleagues choose to keep their places in government rather than return with him to opposition. Burke's early political writings and speeches return constantly to the theme of friendship betrayed, and to the 'broken, distracted councils, their public disagreements and private animosities' of the new Grafton–Pitt ministry.[11] The climax of *Observations on a Late State of the Nation* (1769), for example, is a set piece of close-range conjectural history, imagining the erosion of political trust if party allegiance continues to be loosened, 'from friendship to civility; from civility to enmity: few are the steps from dereliction to persecution'. The followers of the new ministry are finally 'turned out, emptied of all natural character, of all intrinsic worth, of all essential dignity, and deprived of every consolation of friendship'.[12] During the six months that separate the *Observations* from *Thoughts on the Causes of our Present Discontents* (1770), Burke's thinking about party allegiance becomes less fretful and more versatile. At the heart of the matter is the relationship between friendship as an essential component in the mechanics of parliamentary organization and friendship as an indispensable index of private moral consistency. Any statesman who believes sincerely in his political principles, Burke reasons, will look for a means of reducing them to practice. He will acknowledge the duty of getting men who share his opinions into positions of power, and of refusing to split that body of opinion for private considerations: 'Such a generous contention for power, on such manly and honourable maxims', he writes, 'will easily be distinguished from the mean and interested struggle for place and emolument. The very stile of such persons will serve to discriminate them . . .'.[13] Burke is talking about a mode of ethical proof here, a style that observers can judge and discriminate, and its value as a political sign is that it cannot be counterfeited or reduced to an art. 'The connexion and friendship of good men is their glory', he writes to a colleague the following year. 'It is a thing which bad men cannot long mimick; No wonder they should look upon it with malignity and envy.'[14] The tone of sanguine realism in these assertions is all the more striking because 'friendship' is the most common of commonplace topics in eighteenth-century practical morals, and several of Burke's contemporaries had recently voiced scepticism about its importance.

When considering the rhetorical texture of Burke's arguments about friendship, it is helpful to remember some of the common claims about its virtues that he declines to make. Burke does not claim that friendship transforms the inward moral state of those who experience it, or that it guarantees the sincerity of its participants when they talk or write to one another. Nothing that Burke says about friendship in *Thoughts on our Present Discontents* is falsified by Bernard Mandeville's insistence that friendship is rooted in self-interest and pride, or by Samuel Johnson's perception that friendship encourages insincerity because friends tend to indulge and palliate one another's vices.[15] David Hume points out the obvious fact that some people are fanatically loyal to their party, 'who, on other occasions, discover no great generosity of spirit, or are found to be easily transported by friendship beyond their own interest'.[16] But again, this is beside the point of the *Thoughts on our Present Discontents.* Burke is concerned with the simple fact of friendship, and with its general moral consequences (rather than its particular effects on a person's conscience). It is almost impossible to fake the fact of established friendship, Burke reckons. Moreover, there are ways of developing for pragmatic purposes one's disposition to friendship, and of reducing it to a kind of philosophical discipline. Burke uses a Baconian language of moral husbandry when he proposes at the end of the *Thoughts* that it is

> our business carefully to cultivate in our minds, to rear to the most perfect vigour and maturity, every sort of generous and honest feeling that belongs to our nature. To bring the dispositions that are lovely in private life into the service and conduct of the commonwealth; so to be patriots, as not to forget we are gentlemen. To cultivate friendships, and to incur enmities.[17]

Burke deploys the same word 'cultivate' to designate both the moral regimen of the mind and the social discipline of allegiance and opposition. The final proof of friendship as a political and moral sign is straightforwardly pragmatic. Responding to sharp criticism of his parliamentary manners from his friend Bishop William Markham later in 1771, Burke justifies his aggressive loyalty to the Rockingham connection: 'By arranging myself with them I trust I have given some sort of security to the publick for my good Behaviour. The versatility of those sudden evolutions which have something derogated from the credit of all publick professions are things not so easy in large Bodies, as when men act alone; or in light Squadrons.'[18] The proof of friendship, which underwrites its value as a political sign, is the practical and moral constraint it puts upon the individual politician's actions and opinions.

Burke claims the authority of two distinct historical precedents for this political system of friendship: the first is that of ancient Roman *amicitia*, the second that of the modern system of party developed by the Junto Whigs at the start of the eighteenth century. The source for the Roman precedent in *Thoughts* is Ciceronian:

> Some legislators went so far as to make neutrality in party a crime against the State. I do not know whether this might not have been rather to overstrain the principle. Certain it is, the best patriots in the greatest commonwealths have

always commended and promoted such connexions. *Idem sentire de republica*, was with them a principal ground of friendship and attachment; nor do I know any other capable of forming firmer, dearer, more pleasing, more honourable, and more virtuous habitudes ... This wise people was far from imagining that those connexions had no tie, and obliged to no duty; but that men might quit them without shame, upon every call of interest. They believed private honour to be the great foundation of public trust; that friendship was no mean step towards patriotism; that he who, in the common intercourse of life, shewed he regarded somebody besides himself, when he came to act in a public situation, might probably consult some other interest than his own.[19]

Burke's editors have had difficulty explaining the Ciceronian tag '*idem sentire de republica*', which means 'to think the same way about political matters'. It mangles a passage in Cicero's dialogue *De amicitia* where the character Laelius reports an argument *against* friendship once proposed to him by Scipio: that it tends to end acrimoniously when two people disagree about politics.[20] In fact the tag is lifted from Lord Bolingbroke's *Dissertation upon Parties* (1733): Burke duplicates exactly the misquotation of Laelius' words that Bolingbroke makes in the first 'Letter' of the *Dissertation*.[21] Although Burke had a habit of attacking Bolingroke in print, the *Thoughts* owes much to Bolingbroke's analysis of English political parties, and of the threatened resilience of the British constitution to their depredations.[22] Burke differs from Bolingbroke, and from their Roman forebears, with his more modern interest, probably inherited from the Scottish scientists of man, in how the social passions are modulated through public allegiances. The syntactical asymmetry of Burke's list of 'habitudes' in this passage ('firmer, dearer, more pleasing', etc.) imitates the clumsy growth of honourable dispositions from pleasing social ones, and of virtuous manners from honourable ones. His triplicated progression of clauses enacts rhetorically how private and public manners should be mutually supportive and coactive. The syntax is energetic, but it is also fumbling, almost tactile. Burke imagines friendships running through society like tendrils. They are at once exploratory and tentative, and the further they explore – 'through hard essays of practised friendship and experimented fidelity' – the more these soft sentiments are tempered and strengthened.[23]

What Burke has inherited from Cicero is the Roman's sense of *amicitia* as a very public relation.[24] Burke knew the treatise *De officiis*, where Cicero describes how anybody possessed of moral goodness (*honestum*) will be moved powerfully to friendship with any other person who demonstrates the same quality.[25] Although citizenship, kinship and patriotism are more natural ties, *amicitia* has a special power to illuminate a public life. The benefits that friendship confers upon the public man are intimate ones (advice, discussion, encouragement, comfort, even reproof) rather than open ones, but throughout this passage Cicero suggests the vicarious attractiveness of friendship to the outside observer. It is obvious how the right sort of friendships might shed light on the ethos of an orator, but for Cicero the influence of friendship on character is incandescent. In *De amicitia* he describes the friend as a glorious beacon of probity and virtue, one who shines flashes of hope into the future, and he gives an unexpected twist to this visual metaphor by adding that probity and virtue are so attractive that they draw us to people we have never even seen.[26] The two books that Cicero wrote on the subject of *gloria* have been lost, but it is clear from another passage in *De officiis* (in which he refers back to *De amicitia*) that he regards personal friendship as analogous to the sort of public glory to which the orator aspires, since both involve the good will, confidence, admiration and esteem of others – sentiments, Cicero points out, that are 'awakened in the masses in the same way as in individuals'.[27] This corresponds with Burke's assertion that the friendship of good men 'is their glory'. Aper, the lawyerly rhetorician of Tacitus' *Dialogus de oratoribus*, describes more pragmatically how eloquence allows you to make and keep friendships, form them into more extensive connections, and at last to 'embrace whole provinces' with your influence. But these are the benefits rather than the conditions of oratory.[28] There is something circular about the relationship between friendship and ethos for Tacitus as for Burke: they grow together slowly and strongly.

The second historical authority that Burke appeals to as support for his rhetoric of friendship is that of the Court Whig Junto, those ministers of the early years of Queen Anne's reign whose characters by Swift Burke had printed in *The Annual Register*. Burke names four Junto politicians as participants in an exemplary political association: Sunderland, Godolphin, Somers and Marlborough:

In one of the most fortunate periods of our history this country was governed by a *connexion*; I mean, the great connexion of Whigs in the reign of Queen Anne. They were complimented upon the principle of this connexion by a poet who was in high esteem with them. Addison, who knew their sentiments, could not praise them for what they considered as no proper subject of commendation. As a poet who knew his business, he could not applaud them for a thing which in general estimation was not highly reputable. Addressing himself to Britain,

Thy favourites grow not up by fortune's sport,
Or from the crimes or follies of a Court.
On the firm basis of desert they rise,
From long-try'd faith, and friendship's holy ties ...

They believed that no men could act with effect, who did not act in concert; that no men could act in concert, who did not act with confidence; that no men could act with confidence, who were not bound together by common opinions, common affections, and common interests.[29]

The last sentence contains another tricolonic figure, and once again the scheme of amplification fits precisely with the point that Burke is making: the gradations between pragmatic intention ('act with effect') and public bond ('act with confidence') consist of an accumulation of trust, and the dense accumulation of the syntax corresponds with this idea.[30] The verses that Burke quotes from Addison's panegyric to Marlborough, *The Campaign* (1704), refer originally to the ties of friendship that link Marlborough to the royal family – although there is some ambiguity in the lines that follow (since 'favourites' are in a generalized plural throughout) as to whether the 'Sovereign's well-distinguished smiles' are not 'shared' between the successful general and his wife Sarah Churchill, with whom Queen Anne's passion for friendship was so closely identified, rather than between Marlborough and his Whig political allies.[31] But the historical ambiguity of the original passage hardly matters to Burke – it is the fact of friendship that concerns him.

The other friendship on view here, of course, is the mutual affection between the four lords and Joseph Addison himself. Burke gives only a sketch of the historical situation, but it is enough to suggest how similar his own position is to that of Addison, another man of letters 'who knew his business' and who progressed eventually from patronized poet to secretary of state. It is a rather oblique kind of self-reference, but it is enough to connect his character as an author with a larger Whig tradition of amicable political allegiance. Just as Burke's reading of *The Campaign* fits imperfectly with the history of the Junto, there are some problems with his choice of Addison as the laureate of political friendship. Like Mr Spectator, Addison had a celebrated gift for intimacy – Swift's correspondence, for example, proves how he let 'Party give way to Friendship' after their deep political enmity – but he was cripplingly bashful among superiors and cold among strangers.[32] His character, much like Mr Spectator's in the closed circle of his club, suggested that the virtues of friendship more often fail to circulate, and that intimacy based on shared opinion works against all kinds of broader sociability.[33] But again, knowledge of these biographical inconsistencies only serves to highlight the compelling paradox that underlies Burke's point here: that public friendships between politicians are acts of social restriction that somehow produce expansions of social connection. David Hume writes something similar in his essay 'Of the Delicacy of Taste', where he observes that worldly people, 'whatever strong sense they may be endowed with, are [seldom] very nice in distinguishing characters', whereas people of relatively confined friendship carry their affections 'further, than if they were more general and undistinguished'.[34] This was an idea that Joseph Addison played with himself. His essay in *The Spectator*, no. 68 opens with a corresponding paradox: 'that Conversation is never so much streightened and confined as in numerous Assemblies'.[35] Discourse becomes more 'free and communicative' in clubs of acquaintances, he continues, but it is most 'open, instructive and unreserved' when restricted to two intimate friends.

The codes of friendship discussed by Burke in *Thoughts on our Present Discontents* are rhetorical in the simple sense that they demonstrate the good character of the author and his party – they are self-descriptive as well as being more generally normative. But they also give us the first instance of a problem that one encounters often when thinking about Burke's rhetoric. Burke regards friendship as a public sign, as a matter of personal style that expresses certain facts of allegiance, as well as certain moral dispositions in an individual or group. Its primary political function, according to Burke, is organizational, and crucial to that function is its persuasiveness: friendship helps to convince both participants within the virtuous 'connexion', and those who observe the connection from outside, that there is at least a minimum sufficiency of disinterested, public-spirited motivation involved in the group's counsels. The problem is that the value of friendship as a natural (and therefore unfalsifiable) sign precludes any association of it with the contrivances and techniques of traditional rhetoric. Friendship cannot be taken up as a political or rhetorical tool – it always has to exist already in the habits and manners of the connection. So friendship is a purely ethical proof, although it is defined by its prudential consequences. In the letter to Markham, Burke asserts that 'the principles of true politics are those of morality enlarged', and his passages on friendship elicit a corresponding magnification and projection of the ethical realm.[36] It becomes possible to talk about Burke as a rhetorical technician, I think, when this process of enlargement, together with whatever distortions or illuminations it involves, is taken as the object of investigation. In the case of friendship, Burke takes a half-exhausted, slightly unfashionable topic from the index of moral commonplaces, and uses its very weaknesses as a source of rhetorical energy. As we shall see, this is a technique that he pushed to a turbulent extreme in *Reflections on the Revolution in France.*

THE DEVELOPMENT OF BURKE'S POLITICAL ETHICS (I): BETWEEN WIND AND WATER

During the first decade or so of his parliamentary career, Burke attaches increasing importance to the idea that, when thinking about the morality of parliamentary conduct, one must consider how the votes and speeches of MPs are mediated through the larger, institutional identity of Parliament. In *Thoughts on the Present Discontents* he argues that the 'peculiar character of the House of Commons' is under attack. A group of obscure, backstairs politicians is conspiring to degrade the assembly from its proper dignity as a national council into a mere tool of Court. This conspiracy has thus far escaped detection, adds Burke, because the legislative machinery of government remains (as Bolingbroke predicted it would in the *Dissertation upon Parties*) fundamentally unaltered. One aim of the *Thoughts* is to draw attention away from this machinery towards the character of the House, 'not with regard to its legal form and power, but to its spirit' – for it is its spirit that is in danger.[37] The common consensus as Burke understands it is that the spirit of the House is manifested in its popular mandate. But this cannot be true, he writes, because the judiciary, the House of Lords and even the monarchy itself owe their authority as much to popular consent as does the unreformed House of Commons.

What distinguishes the character of the Commons is, first, its peculiar function of representing the opinions (which Burke distinguishes carefully from the direct will) of the political nation; and, second, the fluctuation of its membership, which is continually drawn up from and returned to the body of that nation. With regard to the first of these characteristics, 'general opinion is the vehicle, and organ of legislative omnipotence', as Burke writes in his *Letter to the Sheriffs of Bristol* (1777).[38] This is not an executive omnipotence that Burke is describing, but a negative omnipotence of limitation and circumscription: the House of Commons is 'not instituted to be a controul *upon* the people', he writes in 1770, 'it was designed as a controul *for* the people'.[39] The second 'characteristical distinction' of the House of Commons from the Crown and the judiciary is that the tenure of its individual members is temporary. This adds great complexity to the ethical makeup of the Commons, since each member retains the permanent character of an opinion-bearing citizen in addition to the fugitive character of a legislator:

> The capacity of a magistrate being transitory, and that of a citizen permanent, the latter capacity it was hoped would of course preponderate in all discussions, not only between the people and the standing authority of the Crown, but between the people and the fleeting authority of the House of Commons itself.[40]

But the sort of consistency of opinion that should be expected from a morally competent citizen is never as prevalent in Commons debates as one might expect it to be. In this passage from the *Speech on American Taxation*, Burke contrasts the 'fleeting authority' of the House of Commons with the characters of its individual citizen members, which he considers far more stable and permanent than the character of the institution they constitute.[41] 'It is impossible not to observe', he tells the Commons in 1774, 'that this house has a collective character of its own', but the fugitive nature of that character has a constant potential for variance with the opinions even of its individual members.[42] Above all the character and opinions of the House are much less stable and consistent than those of individual actors. A few months later, at the opening of his *Speech on Conciliation*, Burke laments that when legislating for the American colonies the House has made 'more changes to their sentiments and conduct, than could be justified in a particular person'.[43] Obviously, Burke is politely deflecting a charge of inconsistency from some of his fellow MPs here, but the contradistinction of personal and institutional ethos is still a real one. It is his sense of institutional changeability that prompts Burke's own efforts to stabilize his sentiments and conduct on the American question by hard study, 'in order, amidst so vast a fluctuation of passions and opinions, to concenter my thought; to ballast my conduct'. Burke is advertising the predominance of 'citizen' over 'magistrate' in his own parliamentary character here, and this claim is as much a rebuke to other orators as it is a boast about his own ethos.

These two basic conceptions of parliamentary character, citizen versus magistrate, underwrite Burke's critical position with regard to the conspicuous parliamentary personalities of his day. In the *Speech on American Taxation*, Burke draws the characters of the two most celebrated speakers of the previous decade, William Pitt the elder, Earl of Chatham, and his erstwhile Chancellor, Charles Townshend. This pair of set-piece portraits contains Burke's most direct commentary on the business of parliamentary eloquence, and as such it deserves special attention, both as criticism and as rhetorical example. Burke is self-conscious about using character portraiture as a device for structuring his speech: 'Great men', he explains, 'are the guide-posts and land-marks in the state.' This means that their individual characters can be used as indexes to the character of the institution to which they belong.[44] As Burke's heightening of the correspondences and contrasts between Pitt and Townshend suggests, the construction of character is also an imitative process: characters are 'instructive to those who wish to form themselves on whatever of excellence has gone before them'.[45] The retirement of Pitt in 1766 and the death of Townshend in 1767 are themselves tokens of how rapidly the House's cast of dominant personalities changes, but it is Pitt and Townshend's failure to stabilize the 'general opinion' represented by the House of Commons that betrays their deepest political weaknesses.

The character of Pitt the elder in the *Speech on American Taxation* seems to have been drafted by Burke for *Thoughts on our Present Discontents* four years earlier, but was left out so as not to antagonize Pitt's popular support.[46] 'The power of that gentleman', Burke had written of Pitt in 1770, 'was vast indeed and merited; but it was in a great degree personal, and therefore transient.'[47] In 1774 he expands greatly on this hint, tracing the principle of transience back into the core of Pitt's personal character, and then outwards again into the character of the administration he formed in 1766. The clue to that character is nothing so solid as a ruling passion or virtue. Burke draws Pitt's character by his hobby-horses – which is to say, by his rhetorical commonplaces:

> For a wise man, he seemed to me at that time, to be governed too much by general maxims. I speak with the freedom of history, and I hope without offence. One or two of these maxims, flowing from an opinion not the most indulgent to our unhappy species, and surely a little too general, led him into measures that were greatly mischievous to himself; and for that reason, among others, perhaps fatal to his country; measures, the effects of which, I am afraid, are for ever incurable. He made an administration, so checkered and speckled; he put together a piece of joinery, so crossly indented and whimsically dovetailed; a cabinet so variously inlaid; such a piece of diversified Mosaic; such a tessellated pavement without cement; here a bit of black stone, and there a bit of white; patriots and courtiers; kings friends and republicans; whigs and tories; treacherous friends and open enemies: that it was indeed a very curious show; but utterly unsafe to touch, and unsure to stand on.[48]

Poised for a moment between deference and censure, Burke moves at last into bathos. As Burke's friend Elizabeth Montagu noticed in 1762, 'a man of great wit might be a match for Mr. Pitt. Ridicule is the only weapon with which he can be subdued, false eloquence and fictitious patriotism are fine subjects for raillery.'[49] The licence with which Burke mocks the great commoner comes from a sense that, despite the 'vast space he fills in the eye of mankind', Pitt is too distant, too canonized and sanctified, for his character to be drawn.[50] Indeed, he wonders whether Pitt has any recognizable character at all, since his famous maxim that administration should concern itself with '*Not men, but measures*' tends (as Burke had argued in 1770) to 'destroy all test of character as deduced from conduct' – the word 'measures' is repeated significantly in the above passage.[51] Pitt is characterized instead by his absence and by his influence, an undirecting force of superintendence without which his Dunce-like ministers cannot move, and yet which has no power to execute Pitt's vaunted measures. Nautical metaphors often express the vast scale of imperial business in Burke's rhetoric: here Pitt's allies, deprived of his influence, are 'whirled about, the sport of every gust, and easily driven into any port'.[52] The failures of sentiment and intelligence that force Pitt the orator to rely on misanthropic 'general maxims' correspond with the weakness of his administration. The lack of connected thought in Pitt's oratory was often noticed: James Harris complained in his parliamentary diary that the absence of ordered argument in Pitt's speeches allowed him to record nothing but 'glowing scraps or splendid morsels' from them.[53] Burke develops this common observation by showing how the fragmented forms of Pitt's oratory manifest themselves in his disconnected political measures. His rhetoric stamps itself too truly onto government. Pitt's cabinet of state becomes some piece of eccentric domestic architecture from a Shandean country house, or a chequered pavement, trodden by the common foot but safe to nobody. Where Burke looks for Pitt's magnificence of character, he finds evidence only of whimsy and humour.[54]

The climax of the *Speech on American Taxation* is Burke's character of Charles Townshend, which follows immediately after the character of Pitt. For all his parliamentary predominance, Townshend is positioned in the speech as though he were a sort of erratic emanation of Pitt's declining influence.[55] Pitt is incapable of friendship because he is cold and misanthropic, Townshend because he wishes to please universally, and therefore cannot be constant.[56] Pitt is so peremptory that his followers dare to presume no opinions of their own; Townshend adjusts himself before the disposition of the House 'as at a looking glass'. Townshend's character is the positive impression taken from the hollow mould of Pitt's character, and yet it is entirely plastic to the inclinations of the parliamentary audience. It is evident that Burke considers Townshend to be somewhat Pitt's superior as a rhetorician, and his treatment of the younger man's brilliance in Parliament is an essay on the effect of extraordinary eloquence. And yet Townshend's example is pernicious. There is contrast with Pitt's failures in the character of Townshend as well as correspondence:

> Perhaps there never arose in this country, nor in any country, a man of a more pointed and finished wit; and (where his passions were not concerned) of a more refined, exquisite, and penetrating judgment. If [Townshend] had not so great a stock, as some have had who flourished formerly, of knowledge long treasured up, he knew better by far, than any man I ever was acquainted with, how to bring together within a short time, all that was necessary to establish, to illustrate, and to decorate that side of the question he supported. He stated his matter skilfully and powerfully. He particularly excelled in a most luminous explanation and display of his subject. His style of argument was neither trite and vulgar, nor subtle and abstruse. He hit the house just between wind and water. – And not being troubled with too anxious a zeal for any matter in question, he was never more tedious, or more earnest, than the pre-conceived opinions, and present temper of his hearers required; to whom he was always in perfect unison. He conformed exactly to the temper of the house; and he seemed to guide, because he was always sure to follow it.[57]

True to the tradition of Augustan eulogy, every compliment that Burke offers dissembles some serious condemnation. Townshend never built up much knowledge of business – but then his glibness and facility compensated for want of information. He excelled in the epideictic branch of rhetoric, 'display of his subject' – which in fact suggests that he was undistinguished in the truly political spheres of forensic and deliberative debate.[58] The three infinitives 'to establish, to illustrate, and to decorate' are honourable enough in themselves, but Burke groups them in a rhetorical triplication, switching the expected climax for a weakening progression: solidity declines into mere ornament. These ambiguities do not seem treacherous or vindictive, because they are so rhetorically efficient. They express the unsoundness of Townshend's character without moralizing. A comparison with Horace Walpole's assessment – that Townshend spoke only 'to show how well he could adorn a bad cause, or demolish a good one' – indicates the quality of Burke's restraint here.[59] The only quality of Townshend's mind untouched by Burkean irony is his exquisite acuity. 'He hit the house just between wind and water' says Burke, continuing the nautical metaphor from his character of Pitt. As his auditors list to the port side, Townshend's broadside hits them below the waterline, and as they list back to the starboard their hulls flood with the brine of their own passions and pre-conceived opinions. With one fragment of nautical idiom Burke describes Townshend's rhetoric all at once as precise, almost violently forceful and distinctly below-board.

Above all, Burke is concerned with how Townshend's character interacts dynamically with the collective character of the House of Commons. If Pitt is so truculent that his personality disappears from view, Townshend is so compliant that his character ceases to represent anything more than the immediate disposition of his audience. For both men, predominance leads to a sort of dissolution of character, and Burke always manages to persuade himself that this is a political disadvantage: 'If I had enjoyed a reputation of greater splendour', he wrote to the classicist Samuel Parr in 1787, 'I might have been more intent on what might nourish that reputation, than on those ends, for which alone a reputation ought to be cultivated.'[60] Townshend's case is particularly interesting in this respect, because his predominance in the Commons involves all the symptoms of a strong sentimental attachment – 'He was truly the child of the house', Burke writes, 'he never thought, did, or said any thing but with a view to you' – and yet it produces all the moral effects of petulance and inconstancy. Burke ascribes Townshend's political motives to a 'great and masculine' love of fame, 'a passion which is the instinct of all great souls', and yet the effects of this noble instinct are feminizing: 'he adapted himself to your disposition; and adjusted himself before it, as at a looking-glass'.[61] Townshend's private correspondence suggests how near this paradoxical assessment was to the truth.[62] Indifferent to personal rectitude, Townshend vacillates between popular independence and the most abject conformity. 'He was a candidate for contradictory honours', concludes Burke, 'and his great aim was to make those agree in admiration of him who never agreed in anything else.'[63] Charles Townshend was the rhetorician whom the House of Commons both desired and deserved, and yet his example as a parliamentary orator involves an unacceptable sacrifice of personal consistency. Pitt was the statesman whom the House most admired, and yet his personal style disqualified him from effective administration. These two highly effective parliamentary orators, both of whose work is portrayed as politically dysfunctional, allow Burke to chart a middle course for his own ethos between the extremes that their examples represent. His lifelong aversion to the kind of conspicuous parliamentary personalities that they embody would later precipitate his split with Charles James Fox and his break from the party he thought best adjusted to reconcile aristocratic pride with legislative modesty.[64]

THE DEVELOPMENT OF BURKE'S POLITICAL ETHICS (2): PUBLICITY AND REPRESENTATION

On the morning of 19 December 1774 a collection of speeches made by Edmund Burke during the recent parliamentary election in Bristol appeared in London bookshops.[65] Three weeks later, on 10 January 1775, his publisher James Dodsley issued an authorized edition of the *Speech on American Taxation*, with the character portraits of Pitt, Townshend, Greville and Conway that are discussed above. Burke had delivered the speech at the House of Commons to great acclaim on 19 April 1774. The rapid sale of this book was itself overtaken when the enormously popular *Speech on Conciliation with America* appeared on 22 May.[66] Content aside, the printed texts of these three speeches, issued in rapid succession, represent a remarkable innovation in political publishing. Burke had no obvious precedent for putting transcriptions of his oratory through the press in this way, and no other contemporary MP was engaged in comparable acts of publication.[67] By presenting his speeches to the public in a literary form, Burke was making a conspicuous assertion of their merit. It is true that unauthorized reports had been appearing regularly in London newspapers after the Middlesex election crisis of 1769, and sometimes transcriptions were supplied by the speakers themselves.[68] Nevertheless, the printing of speeches and debates from Westminster had constituted a statutory breach of privilege since 1642, when Bulstrode Whitlocke enforced its prohibition as a matter of security during the Civil War.[69] The privilege was often reasserted, mainly because it helped keep the acts and decisions of Parliament separate in the public mind from the deliberative process. Now, for the first time in over a century, a credible parliamentarian was authorizing the publication of his transcribed oratory in printed form. One could add more grandly that, since the days of the Roman orator-rhetoricians Cicero and Quintilian, no published speeches had claimed public attention for their literary excellence as much as for their political or forensic content.[70]

Burke's decision in 1775 to publish his own oratory was made practicable by a combination of historical and personal circumstances, and particularly by a change in his parliamentary status in the autumn of 1774. The attitude of Parliament towards the reporting of its debates had softened over the previous decade. Even the most punctilious defenders of privilege were yielding to the burgeoning of popular interest in its proceedings, and to the determination of newspaper men like William Woodfall to satisfy that interest with detailed reports. So there was a newly created market for Burke's speeches, and a political culture both inside and outside Westminster to make sense of them. Burke's act of publication was relatively unobjectionable to the ministry because it was unlikely to have any immediate effect on the legislature itself. Indeed, Burke was acutely aware that he was trusting his arguments to the most unpunctual of readerships. Writing to his Irish friend Sir Hercules Langrishe in 1795 about the speech on Irish parliamentary reform he had printed during the previous year, Burke lamented that it had not had the sort of instant effect it 'cannot possibly fail (though with less pleasant consequences) to produce hereafter': 'What a sad thing it is that the grand instructor, Time, has not yet been able to teach the grand lesson of his own value; and that, in every question of moral and political prudence, it is the choice of the moment which renders the measure serviceable or useless, noxious or salutary.'[71] Personally, Burke felt none of the common motives for holding aloof from the press. He held no public office that obliged him to secrecy, and he was born below the pride of rank. The Rockinghamites were stubbornly committed to parliamentary opposition during the 1770s.[72] If his ideas were to have any political consequence, they had to appeal to general opinion both in and out of doors. As a non-elite MP, Burke's acknowledged place in the House was that of a 'man of business'.[73] His job was to keep abreast of political information, and to present the connection's views to a wider public – work that was not expected of his more gentlemanly colleagues. However, Burke's subordinate status within the Rockingham party changes radically in November 1774, when the citizens of Bristol, the third largest electoral constituency in Britain, confer upon him the considerable dignity of election to Parliament by a popular mandate.[74] So at the start of 1775 he is an amphibious sort of politician: at once modest enough to stoop to the press, and famous enough to blazon his name across the title page of a book. Burke still lacks the acknowledged personal influence – what he later calls the 'weight of Opinion, natural or acquired' – to claim simple personal authority in political debate.[75] By his own account, he is just a parliamentary grafter. Burke's speeches of 1774–5 keep up the protests of resolute modesty, but they also display an increasing sense of the rhetorical opportunities opened up by his uncertain status.

Above all, Burke realizes that he has a liberty to make very close arguments, to ballast his speeches with information, to invest them with all the persuasive momentum of which they are capable – and that not all of his colleagues enjoy the same kind of freedom. Apologizing for the length of the *Speech on Conciliation*, Burke laments that such prolixity 'is the misfortune of those to whose influence nothing will be conceded, and who must win every inch of their ground by argument'.[76] He is conceding a weakness here, and asserting an unusual liberty to amplify his reasoning at the same time. Buoyed up by his recent acquisition of status, Burke presents his proposals in the *Speech on Conciliation* as ethically neutral, as a series of pure strands of rhetorical reasoning: 'being totally destitute of all shadow of influence, natural or adventitious, I was very sure, that, if my proposition were futile or dangerous; if it were weakly conceived, or improperly timed, there was nothing exterior to it, of power to awe, dazzle, or delude you'.[77] He is overplaying his modesty here, but there is certainly a pressing need for him to excuse his unconventional mode of address. In *Conciliation* Burke puts a general plan of administration to the House, despite his disconnection from and opposition to government – and he knows that he takes this freedom 'somewhat disreputably', because he can have no legitimate expectation that the House will even be 'properly disposed for [its] reception'.[78] For those who read the printed speech outside the house, the gap between the legislating posture of Burke's proposal and the diffusion of its perlocutionary force will be even more pronounced.

But Burke has a highly artistic strategy for naturalizing his incongruous mode of address. Its decorum is guaranteed because his proposal is one of concession, conciliation and salutary neglect, rather than of big government and coercive belligerence. The modesty of his plan is enacted through a rhetoric of controlled bathos. Burke excuses a passage of close statistical analysis by observing that 'generalities, which in all other cases are apt to heighten and raise the subject, have here a tendency to sink it'.[79] When contemplating American commerce, he feels 'all the pride of power sink, and all presumption in the wisdom of human contrivances melt, and die away within me'.[80] 'Instead of filling me with pride, I am exceedingly humbled by it', Burke says of Parliament's duty to judge colonial disputes.[81] The eloquence of the speech is set off against Burke's urge for silence and aposiopesis: 'a great flood stops me in my course', for example, as he considers the possibility of a colonial representation at Westminster.[82] Reflecting on the patched-up legal idiom in which he frames six legislative proposals at the end of the speech, he confesses that 'I was resolved not to be wise beyond what is written; I was resolved to use nothing else but the form of sound words, to let others abound in their own sense; and carefully to abstain from all expressions of my own. What the law has said, I say. In all things else I am silent.'[83] This sentence is a montage of received legal idioms and biblical snippets – the Clarendon editors catch two of them, missing only 'abound in their own sense' (from Romans 14.5).[84] The *Speech on Conciliation* lays claim to a special deliberative freedom, one that is given a 'parliamentary form' by Burke's rhetoric of decorous diffidence.

Liberty of argument becomes especially important to Burke after his election as one of the MPs for Bristol, because the larger municipal constituencies had begun to insist on their right to issue direct instructions to their representatives.[85] Burke takes the earliest safe opportunity – a meeting at the conclusion of the poll on 3 November 1774 – to assert his opposition to this sort of demand. In so far as politics is about direct will, Burke acknowledges, it should be the electors who dictate the course of legislation, if anybody. But for the most part matters of government 'are matters of reason and judgment, and not of inclination; and what sort of reason is that, in which the determination precedes the discussion; in which one set of men deliberate, and another decide?'[86] Burke now sees his own task of hard and detailed argument as more typical of the proper functions of Parliament – discussion, reason and judgment – than the simple assertion of interest and will, to which he made such concessions before. He gives a full account of this position in the manuscript draft of a speech on the duration of parliaments made in May 1780:

> Faithful watchmen we ought to be over the Rights and privileges of the people. But our Duty if we are qualified for it as we ought is to give them information and not to receive it from them[,] and [we] are not to go to School to them to learn the principles of Law and Government ... If I changed my Ground, cryd up or cryd down men, or things, or opinions[;] if I wagged and shifted about with every change ... Of all these things they are perfect sovereign Judges without appeal. But as to the detail of particular measures and or to any general Schemes of Policy. They have neither enough of Speculation in the Closet, nor of experience in business to decide upon it. They can well see whether we are tools of a Court or their honest Servants. Of that they can well judge, and I wish always exercised their Judgment[,] but of the particular merits of a measure I have other standards.[87]

Passages like this are a reminder of the continuing importance to Burke of the negative example of Charles Townshend, that most accomplished of waggers and shifters. Addressing his Bristol constituency prior to the election of September 1780, Burke puts the same point to them directly: 'you chose me, in my place, along with others, to be a pillar of the state, and not a weathercock on top of the edifice, exalted for my levity and versatility, and of no use but to indicate the shiftings of every fashionable gale'.[88] Having ascribed Townshend's oratorical success to his exquisite responsiveness, Burke is now demanding the approbation of his own audience for refusing to respond to their inclinations. The distinction between general opinion and free deliberation is crucial here, and his comments on representation during this period always valorize the business of reason in his own work. Burke has written a note on the margin of the draft quoted above: 'people are to be gratified in any Object of Government they have at heart – I say as an Object of *Interest.* But if they go upon Theory, all disputants equal.' What he means, of course, is that 'interest' relates to various quantities of wealth or power, and is subject to proportions and economies – whereas the theory of state is abstract and universal. Its contentiousness serves to emphasize its impersonality. Burke writes something analogous to this in the *Reflections* about the relation between his being much engaged with the reasoning of the National Assembly and quite indifferent to its authority.[89]

However, the ground that these arguments and interests are drawn against is not at all equal or universal: it is entirely moral and personal. Burke insists that electors take seriously their basic responsibility, which is to superintend the characters of their electors, and to arbitrate upon their consistency and independence. Again, at the election of September 1780 he puts this demand directly to his constituency: 'Look, Gentlemen, to the *whole tenour* of your member's conduct. Try whether his ambition or his avarice have justled him out of the straight line of his duty; or whether . . . a degenerate and inglorious sloth, hath made him flag and languish in his course? This is the object of your enquiry.'[90] Political character is the only valid criterion upon which representatives may be judged by their constituency.[91] Indeed, Burke considers the political rights of electors to be defined and limited by this duty of ethical superintendence. He expects them, implicitly, to make an ethical judgment about the capacity of their representatives as reasoners, while paying no attention to the actual arguments and reasonings their representatives make – reasonings which they have 'neither enough of Speculation in the Closet, nor of experience in business to decide upon'. This is all very hard to swallow, but perhaps it is consistent with the proceedings of an unreformed legislature that publishes only its votes and resolutions, not its debates.

IMPEACHMENT AND PARLIAMENTARY FORM

Burke is twenty years into his career as an MP when he hits upon a parliamentary method that is truly complementary to his ethical politics. On 17 February 1786 he moves that the correspondence between the former Governor General of Bengal, Warren Hastings, and the East India

Company's Court of Directors should be laid before the House of Commons.[92] This is his first official step towards the impeachment of Hastings, a process that dominates the remaining third of his public life. The charges Burke brings against Hastings are complicated, and they get much obscured by the process of trial. Of the twenty-two articles of impeachment that he prepares for discussion by committees of the whole House of Commons in 1786–7, only four ever go before the House of Lords for judgment: first, the allegation that Raja Chait Singh of Benares was driven to revolt by Hastings's persecution in 1781; second, that the deposition and confiscation of the income of the Begums (or Princesses) of Oudh was unusually cruel; third, that Hastings had received illegal presents from various Indian sources; and fourth, that corrupt and extortionate contracts had been awarded to Hastings's creatures.[93] The relation of these charges to Burke's broader conception of empire and international law is a subject of the greatest interest, but the rhetorical and ethical ideas that lie behind the prosecution are in more urgent need of scholarly attention. The Hastings impeachment is often thought of as a discrete episode in Burke's intellectual career, a transcontinental excursion into imperial bureaucracy and colonial abuse.[94] But there are striking continuities that I want to emphasize here between Burke's early work on parliamentary ethics and his final resort to the protracted public interrogation of a failed statesman. There are striking developments as well, particularly in Burke's anxiety that his work should have proper parliamentary validity, and that his remarkable writings and speeches should be given some sort of legislative authority. Accordingly, my main concern here is with the practical form of Burke's campaign of impeachment, more than with its content.

Impeachment gives Burke's ethicized rhetoric a venerable, and yet rather singular official form.[95] The essential structure of Burke's prosecution is derived from the oldest customs of the House of Commons, as he takes great pains to explain. Burke believes that impeachment is the process that embodies most substantially the 'ancient inquisitorial powers' of Parliament: it enacts the right of the Commons to try any statesman (excepting only the monarch) for treason or any other high political misdemeanour before the House of Lords.[96] Burke seems always to have been interested in impeachment as a neglected tool for guarding the purity of the constitution, and as a relic of a recent political past that was less formalized and lawyerly, more passionate and personal.[97] Impeachment offers him a recognized institutional form with which to shape those ethical-political principles that underlie his character portraits of Townshend and Pitt, and that compel him to justify his personal independence from his Bristol constituents. In terms of general civil improvement, Burke is attracted to impeachment because it helps remind Parliament that it is more than a talking shop for the approval of ministerial measures. Parliaments are also competent to accuse and to judge in more immediate ways. Impeachment is a grand and solemn procedure of justice, and yet the human scale of the impulses it contains allows it to function as a sort of socio-political 'cement', Burke thinks, one that 'binds [the constitution] together': 'This is the individuating principle that makes England what England is ... It is by this tribunal that Statesmen who abuse their power are tried before Statesmen and by Statesmen, upon solid principles of State morality.'[98] There is an almost Coleridgean apprehension of reconciled division and unity in this hasty expression of Burke's. The phrase 'individuating principle' is normally associated with the metaphysics of personal identity, whether it refers to the soul, to the body, to consciousness or to some combination of the three.[99] But Burke seems here to be thinking at once of the principles that distinguish the English constitution from other political systems, and those that keep statesmen distinct from statesmen. Impeachment reveals and distinguishes the character of statesmen in Parliament, in other words, and by doing so it reveals the genius of the nation and its constitution.

Impeachment is especially good because it does all of this before the superintending eye of a semi-public tribunal. All points of law at an impeachment are delivered by the judges '*upon the Record*', '*seriatim* and *in open Court*', as matters of opinion rather than decision. It is customary for them to be printed with all the other trial proceedings, including speeches by both prosecution and defence, in an authorized transcription of the trial after its conclusion.[100] In time, these published proceedings take on something of the constitutional authority of law reports, so a memorable impeachment promises its managers a kind of political and legal immortality.[101] The legislative measures of ministers are recorded in the parliamentary journals, but the managers of an impeachment get the very formulation of their arguments preserved for posterity – it is a way of publishing spoken eloquence that also guarantees its permanent preservation. It is only typical of Burke's bad luck that neither of these customs – publicity of legal process, and publication of proceedings – was observed at the impeachment of Hastings. And lastly, Burke likes impeachment because the prosecutors are so very nearly as much on trial as the delinquent: it is a supremely adversarial procedure. 'Every accuser was', Burke acknowledges, 'himself under accusation at the very time he accused another', and this perilous circumstance is an endless source of tension and vigour for his rhetoric.[102] Participation in the drama of impeachment puts him in the same sphere with some of his political heroes: with Lords Bacon, Clarendon and Macclesfield, with 'Lord Somers, Lord Halifax, and some of our best men', whose state trials he alludes to as though they were functions of their distinguished characters.[103] Burke the impeacher is much possessed by the manes of the Whig statesmen who dominated British politics during the first quarter of the eighteenth century, as he had been while writing *Thoughts on our Present Discontents*, and would be again while reviewing the impeachment of Sacheverell in *An Appeal from the New to the Old Whigs*. At the acquittal of Hastings in 1796, Burke feels that he and the Commons, in their failure to impeach, have been themselves convicted to posterity – as false accusers of an exonerated man.[104]

The impeachment is also characteristically parliamentary, Burke believes, because it is all about representation. The most important continuity between Burke's thinking about the ethics of parliamentary representation during the late 1770s and his management of the impeachment after 1786 is that both turn on the qualities that persons assume when they act as representatives – and particularly on the capacity of individuals to embody an institution, or a system, or a description of persons. In this sense the impeachment of Hastings is the ultimate political embodiment of Burke's ethicized rhetoric. When Burke opens the impeachment proceedings on 15 February 1788, he asks the Lords to imagine Hastings as 'one in whom all the frauds, all the peculations, all the violence, all the tyranny in India are embodied, disciplined and arrayed'.[105] Hastings is a sort of Leviathan of the British in India, an artificial person through whom all their abuses march in order. And Burke quite properly regards his own managerial role as that of embodying the inquisitorial power of the House of Commons.[106] In 1780 Burke wrote that parliamentary electors should consider the '*whole tenour*' of their representatives' conduct when they go to the polling booth, and this language of character continues to inform his direction of the impeachment five years later. The decorum of such grand political justice obliges Burke to prosecute what he calls the 'general tenour of [Hastings's] conduct', rather than his particular crimes. 'He is just in that situation in which he may well call witnesses to his character', he warns at the opening of the trial, 'but he will find himself utterly unable to justify his conduct.'[107] It is a higher, more public conception of character that he is trying to impress upon the Lords here. Burke anticipates that isolated failings, even criminal ones, will always be excused in people who hold very arduous stations: but 'of this I am certain, that *a general evil intention*, manifested through a long series and a great variety of acts, ought to have much greater weight with a *publick political* tribunal'.[108] It is this character of criminality that Burke is labouring to establish, because parliamentary impeachment must do much more than prove mere facts of misdemeanour. It is 'too great for trifling or petty causes' – and it is too great, in its way, for the prosecution of mere individual persons.[109] It must have its own expanded forensic scope, Burke thinks, so as 'to assign the criminality; to fix the *species* of that criminality; to mark its consequences'.[110] It must reveal how personal habits of abuse represent, sustain and inform whole systems of evil.

As parliamentary strategy, these ideas are a testimony to the moral ambition of Burke's campaign. In the event, however, there can be no doubt that he intellectualizes them too deeply, and finds it impossible to compromise when the Lords (and public opinion) fail to understand their expansive force. At some points in the impeachment Burke seems to be making inaccuracy a supreme point of principle, as it had once been the principle of his aesthetics. In his great essay on the legal thinking behind the prosecution, the *Report on the Lords' Journals* of 1794, for example, Burke makes much of how, in the impeachment of Henry Sacheverell for treason in 1710, no particular treasonous words are specified in the indictment – it is enough that Sacheverell's entire sermon on the perils of false brethren be admitted as evidence of treasonous intent.[111] This is an important example for Burke of how the 'Plainness and Simplicity of a Parliamentary Proceeding' contrasts with 'the technical Subtilties of the inferior Courts', which would never allow so woolly a formulation.[112] But technical subtleties were what the senior lawyers in the Lords had been demanding since 1786. Burke's principled attention to the character of Hastings and of his criminality, rather than to the establishment of his crimes as simple facts, leads to the failure of the impeachment. It also prompts some of Burke's most deeply considered reflections on the political applications of his moral thought.

Burke's thinking about the business of impeachment turns on a series of apparently contradictory political qualities that are reconciled, he believes, within the procedure itself. First and foremost, impeachment is an extraordinary method of parliamentary business, something 'not within the ordinary resort of the law'.[113] And yet despite its unfamiliarity, impeachment puts Parliament in touch with the origins of its constitution, and restores to it something essential in its institutional character: it reveals 'the known authentic sources of jurisprudence, the privileges of Parliament, the justice of the kingdom, the only securities of our constitution'.[114] The idea of impeachment as an old-fashioned mode that somehow refreshes and purifies the constitution also lies behind Burke's presentation of the process as rude and gothic, as well as capable of guaranteeing the civility of the wider community. At the opening of the trial Burke suggests that impeachment has fallen out of use since the trial of Macclesfield in 1725, because of 'the polish of our times, less fertile perhaps in great offences than those that have gone before us'.[115] This idea of its procedural rudeness in an age of politeness remains a rich source of irony for Burke throughout the trial, as he details the savagery of British rule in India, and the civil sophistication of the societies it has destroyed. Beginning the nine-day-long *Speech in Reply* (1794) that concludes his management of the impeachment, Burke is careful to present the style he has been using as rudely, and yet properly, *anti*-rhetorical:

> The commons of Great Britain are a rustic people. A tone of rusticity is the proper accent of those whom we represent. We are not acquainted with the urbanity and politeness of extortion and oppression. We know nothing of the sentimental delicacies of bribery and corruption. My lords, we speak the language of truth and we speak it in the plain language in which truth ought to be spoken.[116]

The underlying idea here – of a European civility that is really the mitigation of certain ferocious social impulses by codes of honour – anticipates Burke's famous statements on politeness and manners in the *Reflections* and the *First Letter on a Regicide Peace*.[117] It also has much in common with his attack on the sentimental egotism (and eloquence) of Rousseau in *A Letter to a Member of the National Assembly*.[118] Burke is trying to excuse himself here from the aggressively personal reflections for which his parliamentary speeches had become notorious since the mid 1780s.[119] But he is making a larger point about forensic decorum as he does so. Burke associates rhetoric as such with politeness, with 'blandishment', with what he calls the 'false candour' of Hastings's defence team. The 'rhetorical blandishments' with which Hastings's crimes have been excused and diminished 'are things which are ten times more at war with virtue ... than any real vice known by its name and distinguished by its proper character in the world'.[120] These blandishments are not so much about concealment, then, as they are about the redescription and effacement of crimes. In private society, Burke allows, 'every one knows that palliating names are given to vices' – an adulteress is called 'gallant', an adulterer 'a man of good fortune' – but parliamentarians have a positive duty to use a harsher, more public tone.[121] Real vice is at least distinct and personal, whereas Hastings has succeeded in presenting himself as an 'ambiguous animal', possessed of no moral character at all. Burke hopes that the impeachment proceedings have an innate formal tendency to distinguish the moral qualities of the defendant – as well as of the Parliament that accuses and judges him. He tries to convey how Parliament must embody both the rude revenging passion and the refined reason of the nation as a whole, while keeping these characteristics separate and intact: 'He that hath made us what we are, has made us at once resentful and reasonable' – especially, he argues, when we are prosecuting justice.[122] Parliament must represent both of these social impulses, and must fix them, so that they do not cancel one another out. The impeachment may be imprecise in terms of legal procedure, Burke avers, but it sharply distinguishes and defines everything that comes under its inquisitorial cognizance.

Rude simplicity is one token that Burke offers his audience to help it distinguish the moral truth of the prosecution's oratory from the rhetorical blandishments of the defence. But he also speaks of a more powerful touchstone for political judgment, one upon which the token of simplicity depends: the test of decorum. A certain crude rusticity of tone ensures the purposefulness of the impeachment, because it is the '*proper* accent of those whom we represent' – adopting the language in which 'truth ought to be spoken' guarantees the social and political integrity of the procedure. Similarly, the prosecutors of Lord Macclesfield attacked the defendant with indignant asperity in 1725 because this was 'the language that became them', a language 'proper to convey guilt'.[123] This emphasis on propriety (as opposed to punctiliousness) of form runs through all of Burke's Indian speeches. The rhetorical choice of a common decorum is, he believes, underwritten by the custom of the House with regard to the language of deliberation – which 'has always been *loquendum ut vulgus*'.[124] His declared principle in the *Speech on Fox's India Bill* (1785) is to ask himself 'what part it was *fit* for a member of parliament, who has . . . [wound] himself into the inmost recesses and labyrinths of the Indian detail, what part, I say, it *became* such a member of parliament to take'.[125] In terms of rhetoric, he decides that it would be wrong to describe the cruelties of the East India Company in emotional language, because it is improper to appeal for immediate sympathy with 'those whom we are used to consider as strangers'. Instead he bespeaks a cold, descriptive tone that he associates with Tacitus and Machiavelli, one 'very sparing of epithets either to persons or things', because to do so will be 'to modulate myself to this temper' of disengagement.[126] It is the orator, not the audience, who must adjust his sympathies, for the sake of sympathy itself.

Adam Smith's psychology of moral sentiment, which may be at the back of Burke's mind here, places great emphasis on the repulsiveness of extreme suffering to humanity's general sensibility, and describes how a sympathetic response requires a certain mitigation of its signs. Smith writes of this mitigation in terms of propriety.[127] Correspondingly, when Burke describes in the *Speech on the Nabob of Arcot's Debts* (1785) the devastation wreaked on the Carnatic region of India by Haidar Ali of Mysore in 1780, he finds himself 'unable to manage it with decorum; these details are of a species of horror so nauseating and disgusting . . . I find it more advisable to throw a pall over this hideous object, and to leave it to your general conceptions'.[128] Whenever Burke uses this sort of imagery of drapery or integument – and it is a recurring feature of his rhetoric in the *Reflections*, as we shall see – the veiled object is imagined obscured, but retains its placement in the audience's imagination. Burke's rule of propriety is such that it must leave the sufferings of India where they are. Their egregiousness tends to distract everyone from the fact that defendant, accuser and judges are all assembled together in Westminster, and the proper passions of the occasion concern the actions of these three parties alone.

This is not to deprecate the pathetic description of innocent and distant pain, as Burke emphasizes in the *Speech on Continuation of the Impeachment* in December 1790:

> by magic of eloquence, the remotest sufferings of mankind are thus brought home to our bosoms . . . But let us take care that our appeal to the passions is not rendered rather ridiculous than pathetic, by having no proper relation to the point in question. Nothing out of its place and season, is powerful or decent.[129]

What Burke has in mind here is the popular sympathy that Hastings has earned through his endurance of the impeachment. This sympathy is more strictly out of place in the trial, Burke suggests, than any of the people or events that lie removed from it by time or distance. Indeed, it is the defendant's defiant 'demeanour' that Burke singles out in the *Speech in Reply* as evidence that a consciousness of guilt has alienated Hastings from the real business of the trial:

> there is a behaviour which indicates a want of sense, a want of decorum, a want of attention to the local situation of human affairs, a demeanour which indicates not the firmness of conscious innocence, but the hardened audacity of long,

habitual, desperate, insolent guilt. My Lords, there is a nobleness in modesty. There is something in insolence that is always base and servile.[130]

This paradoxical point about Hastings's demeanour is the first of four topics into which Burke divides his summary of the whole prosecution, so it has great significance for him. Indeed, Hastings's 'proud defiance of public opinion' had been a theme in Burke's speeches on the first and third days of the opening of the impeachment eight years previously. When Hastings refuses to disclose his defence at the start of the trial, Burke comments that this might be 'a proper answer' in a private person 'who has no character to sustain; but is that a proper answer for a Governor accused of bribery?'[131] A person of high office does not have the luxury of despising vulgar calumny: charges of corruption must be refuted. By the end of the trial in 1794, Burke is drawing a more directly ethical conclusion from Hastings's proud demeanour – he suggests that it should be taken as a form of evidence. He proposes that Hastings's superiority to the scene of impeachment argues a character or habit of guilt that cannot be dissembled. The defendant has displaced himself away from the scene of justice, and cannot even imagine what would be proper to the character of innocence.

While the impeachment draws slowly to its conclusion during the mid 1790s, the issue of linguistic decorum takes on added urgency for Burke, as he begins to imagine how this great labour of his later years will be received by future generations. Burke had never expected to win a formal conviction against Hastings. His only business in the prosecution, he told Philip Francis in 1785, was to consider 'what will acquit and justify myself to those few persons and to those distant times, which may take a concern in these affairs and the Actors in them'.[132] But where would these distant readers be able to read the fruits of Burke's labour? Even before the impeachment, Burke had derived consolation for the way in which Fox's 1783 India Bill had been overturned in the House of Lords from the fact that its measures were preserved in the journals of the House of Commons (where it had been passed): 'May the day of that generous conflict', he declaimed in 1785, 'be stamped in characters never to be cancelled or worn out from the records of time.'[133] But as tightly as Burke clings on to these small consolations of a parliamentary career spent in opposition, even they slip away from him in the end. From the beginning of the trial, the Lords signal their opposition to the permanent publicity that Burke valued so highly in impeachments by letting their legal authorities, the senior lawyers among their members who sat in the inferior law courts, resolve their opinions on legal points in camera, rather than in open court.[134] In his *Report on the Lords' Journals* Burke insists upon what has been lost by this new procedure:

nothing better could be devised by Human Wisdom than argued Judgments publicly delivered for preserving unbroken the great traditionary Body of the Law ... and for enabling the Learned of the Bar and all intelligent Laymen to distinguish those Changes made for the Advancement of a more solid, equitable, and substantial Justice, according to the variable Nature of Human Affairs, progressive Experience, and the Improvement of Moral Philosophy, from these hazardous Changes in any of the ancient Opinions and Decisions ...[135]

Obviously, the Learned of the Bar are of less interest here to Burke than the future generations of intelligent laypersons, whose meditation on the law will encompass not only the advancement of equity, but also its application through the progressions of history, and the refinement of moral thought. So even at this late stage Burke believes that the decorum of his prosecution is generous enough to adjust itself to the unknowable moral exigencies of an unborn readership. But the most consoling promise of a future readership comes to Burke not from the self-regenerating body of traditionary law, but from the parliamentary institution that sits permanently above it. With the custom of impeachment, he argues in 1790, parliamentarians 'have on our side a system, clear and decisive, recognized as a principle of the constitution and adopted in practice. The right of impeachment never dies, but by judgement or derliction [*sic*], and the proceedings of the Commons are as immortal as their public capacity.'[136] The fugitive, deathless continuity of the House of Commons distinguishes it both from the moribund permanence of the peerage, and from the legal system it presides over. So it must have been the deepest of all his disappointments to realize in the spring of 1796 that the impeachment was not going to be preserved in the proceedings of the House in the way that previous state trials had always been, probably on account of its impenetrable bulk. The defiant letter that Burke writes to the Speaker of the Commons, Henry Addington, on 7 March concludes with a more bitterly understated question: 'Is it not extraordinary, that this Trial, is the first that has not been printed by order of the House? I beg a thousand pardons for this trouble.'[137] Burke's last word to Henry Dundas on the matter is that 'the House of Commons has virtually pleaded guilty by not publishing under its authority, for the first time, the whole of the Trial' – guilty, that is, of false accusation.[138] The final, sad irony of Burke's ethicizing rhetoric, in which the accuser is always so very nearly as much on trial as the accused, is that he dies in the opinion that it has retorted upon his character (and the character of the Commons) with such pernicious effect.

In the Fitzwilliam Museum, Cambridge, there is an unfinished double portrait (*c.*1766) of Burke with his patron, Lord Rockingham, by Joshua Reynolds. Reynolds has begun to paint in Rockingham's face, with its expression of courtly frankness and rather delicate, kindly features. But there is little more than a shadowy sketch of Burke. We can see that he is looking attentively at his master, who places a proprietorial hand upon the jumble of papers that Burke has, presumably, prepared for him. Rockingham is painted seated and at full length, looking genially at the viewer, whereas Burke leans in tense expectation against the writing table, pen in hand – turning for a moment from the work. The portrait was intended as companion to another piece in Rockingham's collection, van Dyck's double portrait (1639–40) of his ancestor the Earl of Strafford with a protégé and Irish adventurer called Sir Philip Mainwaring. Since the Strafford portrait is itself an imitation of Titian's *Georges d'Armagnac, Bishop of Rodi, with his secretary Guillaume Philandrier* (1536–8), there is an extra poignancy about the unfinished state of Reynolds's work – it represents a tradition unachieved. In the earlier pieces Mainwaring and Philandrier are absorbed in a moment of dynamic complicity with their patrons, who are themselves coiled and powerful presences. It is tempting to imagine Reynolds abandoning his imitation because he could not recapture their air of excited supplication in his portrait of Burke, or the glow of destiny in Rockingham. There is, in any case, too much of a contrast between elegant patron and hunched secretary.

Knowing what we do about the shape of Burke's political career, it is tempting to read Reynolds's unfinished canvas as a foreshadowing, a summary in advance of some of its rhetorical themes and preoccupations. It gives us an image of the laboriousness that Burke regarded as his chief qualification for public trust, that 'earnest and anxious perseverance of mind, which, with all its good and all its evil effects, is moulded into my constitution'.[139] Reynolds's hastily sketched details of Burke's figure communicate something of that roughness and rude energy that would become so important to his public persona by the time of the Hastings trial. The double portrait is also a reminder of how important these personal qualities of hard work and unpolished vigour were to Burke, in so far as they let him present his style as a contrast (and a complement) to the manners of the Whig grandees with whom he acted in Parliament. For the Georgian gentleman, leisure and politeness had an unassailable cultural and moral value: they allowed him freedom for the cultivation of sociability, and as such gave him a sort of privileged expertise in what binds society together.[140] Burke never lost an opportunity to point out how different he was to his masters in this respect, and how distinct his character was in the House of Commons: 'what would be left to me, if I myself was the man, who softened, and blended, and diluted, and weakened all the distinguishing colours of my life, so as to leave nothing distinct and determinate in my whole conduct?'[141] Burke's differences from the grandees allowed him to make a claim that is implicit everywhere in his ethicized rhetoric, in his theories of friendship, in his character-drawing and in the personal drama of impeachment. Whereas all politicians should be knowledgeable about the characters of the people they govern ('the temper of the people amongst whom he presides ought . . . to be the first study of the statesman'), Burke claims a supplementary expertise in the characters and dispositions of the politicians themselves. This is, after all, how 'an individual without authority is often able to govern those who are his equals or superiours; by a knowledge of their temper, and by a judicious management of it'.[142] These elements of Burke's ethicized rhetoric are present in his writings and speeches from the earliest years of his career. In his most celebrated work, *Reflections on the Revolution in France*, they are recombined in a new and powerful synthesis.

CHAPTER 5

Reflections on the Revolution in France and the rhetoric of character

In Edmund Burke's most important work, *Reflections on the Revolution in France* (1790), the ethos-driven rhetoric that I have been describing assumes its defining form. More than ever before, Burke's personal assertion of his authority as a writer and thinker is connected in the *Reflections* with his general analysis of what good and bad political deliberation should be. The ethical bias of Burke's rhetoric, and particularly his discriminations between competent and unqualified speakers, has a complex relation to his ideas about the structure of states, and about their position within what he understands to be the divine, natural order of things. Although the art of rhetoric must play a small part in so large a scheme, it plays a central one in the structure of the *Reflections.*

This chapter begins by outlining the most important lesson of political pragmatics that Burke gives in the *Reflections*: that thinking and speaking well about government is a matter of acquiring (and being seen to have acquired) the right sort of knowledge of one's fellow citizens, and of using it to balance their powers and interests in political discussion. Burke holds that citizens have a sort of prescribed property in their public characters, and that a peculiarly refined discretion is required of those who would dispose that property in the state. Next, the chapter turns to other concepts used by Burke to delineate the intellectual processes of good deliberation, particularly the positive terms 'reflection' and 'analogy', and the negative terms 'sophistry' and 'metaphysics'. These terms form part of Burke's larger figurative scheme for distinguishing the discursive wealth of inherited constitutional politics from what he takes to be the discursive meagreness of the radical Enlightenment. This chapter examines how certain key terms in the *Reflections* assert and explain Burke's rhetorical strategies.

The principal difference between the *Reflections* and the texts examined in the previous chapter is that the *Reflections* is a written performance, quite unconnected with the printed transcription of spoken eloquence.

Although Burke continued to speak in Parliament until the close of the Hastings trial in June 1794, the *Reflections* is very much a valediction to his career as an orator. It is haunted by the pride and pomp of Westminster debate. But Burke's anticipations of exile from the legislative scene prompt his most compelling thinking about the business of public argument. He finds himself unwontedly making a written response to spoken provocations: the *Reflections* replies to a sermon delivered by Richard Price on 4 November 1789, later published as *A Discourse on the Love of our Country*, and to the legislative debates reported from the French National Assembly [245].[1] Accordingly, he produces a distinctly literary performance, linguistically dense and closely argued.

And yet in several respects the *Reflections* resembles one of Burke's speeches. It inherits their high informal style, and it goes on for rather too long, propelled forward by the rhythmic alternation of exclamatory eloquence and political information. The *Reflections* is a big book, running to 365 pages of businesslike demy octavo paper in the 1790 first edition. It has no architecture of chapters or sections to guide the reader, and this seems to have been the result of a conscious artistic decision. Burke wanted the *Reflections* to roll forward as a living body of language, unconstrained by the divisions that structure treatises or histories. The physical form of the first edition shows that the book was assembled at intervals, with clear indications of interrupted composition at the start of signature H ([97]: 'Before I proceed further . . .'), signature R ([241]: 'This letter is grown to a great length . . .') and a probable one at the start of signature L ([145]: 'These, my dear Sir, are . . . the sentiments . . .'). Yet these breaks are unmarked even by a blank line between paragraphs, which the compositor might easily have inserted.[2] Burke designed the book as an uninterrupted torrent of eloquence. The structure of the material arises out of its sense alone, as it must do in a spoken oration. The *Reflections* seems often to be glancing backwards to the oratorical event from the world of print.

The gestation of the *Reflections* coincided with its author's turning away from the parliamentary scene. Burke began writing a response to Price's sermon in the last week of January 1790. During a debate over military spending on 9 February he declared himself '*separated in politics*' from Sheridan and Fox by their advocacy of the French Revolution, a declaration that made his retirement from parliamentary business inevitable.[3] Three days later the *Reflections* was advertised as 'in the Press, and speedily to be published'.[4] In the authorized version of his *Speech on Army Estimates* published on 20 February, Burke confessed that he was 'near the end of his natural, probably still nearer to the end of his political career; that he was weak and weary; and wished for rest'.[5] However, the termination of Burke's duties to His Majesty's loyal opposition does not mean retirement from politics, as this seems to suggest – he is only talking about the end of his laborious adversarial vigilance over ministerial policy. On the contrary, Burke is already anticipating how the final evolution of his public career will require a transformation of his rhetorical methods: 'That at his time of life, if he could not do something by some sort of weight of opinion, natural or acquired, it was useless and indecorous to attempt any thing by mere struggle.'[6] This tangled construction appears to dismiss the twenty-five years Burke has spent on the opposition benches as a sequence of pointless contentions – the multiplying negativity of 'not do' and 'useless and indecorous' suggests a final resignation. However, they also form a kind of litotes or ironic understatement, and give a hint of positive purpose. At one level the sentence is a modesty trope, a confession that he lacks the natural influence of rank or office on general opinion, and that it would be indecorous for an old man to proceed without it.[7] But behind the fumbled 'somethings', a new idea is forming. Burke estimates the personal weight that he has acquired, and works out what could still be achieved with it. It may be enough somehow to redirect the force of public opinion, even though Burke cannot pretend to embody that opinion (which he believed the great landed proprietors did), or wrestle against it as he has in the past. This tension between resignation and renewal, and this revaluation of his personal ethos, is at the heart of Burke's rhetoric in 1790.

DESCRIPTION, DELIBERATION, PRESCRIPTION

The estimation of his political weight that Burke makes in February 1790, with all its hesitant self-assurance, is carried over into the opening pages of the *Reflections*. The exordium to the book does something more than confirm the author's rhetorical ethos. In a typically aggressive inversion, Burke folds back that uncertainty about his personal political authority into a sweeping attack on the public character of his chief domestic opponents, the members of the radical societies of London. The point at issue is whether it is appropriate for the London Corresponding Society to communicate, as an institution, directly with the National Assembly of France. To what extent can a private association measure itself against a foreign government?

For one, I should be sorry to be thought, directly or indirectly, concerned in their [the LCS's] proceedings. I certainly take my full share, along with the rest of the world, in my individual and private capacity, in speculating on what has been done, or is doing, on the public stage ... [but] I should think it, at least improper and irregular, for me to open a formal correspondence with the actual government of a foreign nation.[8]

According to Burke, the London radicals are absurdly mistaken in thinking that their common right of assembly puts them in the sphere of correspondence with a national institution. The significance of this error is rhetorical. The radicals' misunderstanding of the ethical weight of their association betrays an ignorance of political form – of what Burke calls in the *Third Letter on a Regicide Peace* (1797) 'decorum in character and order in business'[9] – that makes it impossible to take seriously their political 'speculations' (which they have every right to make): for 'those who quit their proper character', he later comments, 'to assume what does not belong to them, are, for the greater part, ignorant both of the character they leave, and the character they assume' [14]. Burke's earliest surviving response to the Revolution, recorded in a letter to the Irish Patriot leader Lord Charlemont of 9 August 1789, returns repeatedly to the language that we see here of 'Spectators', 'wonderful Spectacle' and 'Speculation' (the Revolution is 'one of the most curious matters of Speculation that ever was exhibited').[10]

The word 'speculation' has a special role in the *Reflections*. Burke wishes, along with so many of his British contemporaries, to be a spectator of the Parisian *événements*, but the urge to see the Revolution yields to a more fundamental impulse, the urge to form conjectures about 'what has been done, or is doing'.[11] The spectator turns towards speculation. The callowness of the London Corresponding Society indicates its liability to the same abuse of speculation that Burke sees in France: that of making political investments, in the wrong places, with misappropriated political credit. As the *Reflections* progresses, speculation comes to stand for the disengagement of metaphysical theories of right from the business of politics: they are 'shallow speculations' and 'ranting speculations'; France is 'at the mercy of untried speculations'.[12] Twice Burke links speculation with 'extravagance' ('extravagant and presumptuous speculation' [54]; 'the dissoluteness of an extravagant speculation' [96]), mingling the Shakespearean sense of extravagance as a wandering out of bounds with its more modern sense of personal profligacy.[13] Public incompetence and intellectual trespass are aspects of the same political character.

In the very act of describing the London radicals Burke is of course designating his own character as a man possessed of the authority his opponents lack. There is much violence in Burke's polemic, but the general discretion with which he handles the public characters of the radicals is an important element to authorial ethos in the *Reflections*. Since the impropriety of the Corresponding Society's correspondence with the French National Assembly gave first provocation, Burke is cautious to make his own address proper and direct.[14] His relationship with the French correspondent to whom the book is addressed is denoted with special care: 'In the first letter I had the honour to write to you, and which at length I send, I wrote neither for nor from any description of men; nor shall I in this. My errors, if any, are my own. My reputation alone is to answer for them' [1]. There is a kind of occupatio at work here, the figure by which a point is mentioned, passed over, but efficiently made by the mentioning: Burke's disavowal is meant to recall how grand his connections have been. The London revolutionists make false claims for the authority of their voluntary associations – and so Burke, the great theorist of modern party connection, will renounce his genuine claims to the dignity of a place in the public trust. Of course his recent break with Fox and the Portland Whigs rather forces his hand in the matter.[15]

Nevertheless, the phrase 'neither for nor from any description of men' conveys a peculiarly refined discretion. Burke insists that he is writing for no *description* of men: for no party, no profession, no religious group; from no cabal of like-minded allies (as he would in *Observations on the Conduct of the Minority*), and from no disembodied tradition of ministerial Whiggism (as he would in *An Appeal from the New to the Old Whigs*).[16] At the same time he makes no affectation of Tory catholicism, and has no pretension to the scientific neutrality of the Scottish sociologists. He claims to be writing from outside faction, and yet he holds that partiality and engagement are essential to all political business. Burke would later say that his only title to the honour of being useful to his country was his knowledge of its laws and interests, but in the *Reflections* it is his Baconian knowledge of the characters of men that authorizes his critical role: 'I speak from the experience I have had', he avers, 'in a pretty extensive and mixed communication with the inhabitants of this kingdom, of all descriptions and ranks.'[17] Burke lays claim to a capacity for social description that implies both immediacy of experience and a critical disinterest in the categories described.

The use of the word 'description' here and above ('I wrote neither for nor from any description of men') to mean 'class or type or person' is characteristically Burkean, and it gives some important indications about the nature of his ethicized rhetoric.[18] In the *Reflections*, it seems 'descriptions' categorize certain professions, confessions or groups of people, without implying that the distinctiveness of such groups has intrinsic social or political meaning.[19] 'The mass of any description of men are but men', Burke writes – descriptions represent real social combinations, without conferring upon their assignation any wider authority [153]. As Burke knew from his study of the abuses of colonial rule in Ireland and India, powerful groups often find it useful to lump subject peoples into a single homogeneous description. Representatives of the Protestant Ascendancy in Ireland, for example, use laws that were designed originally to maintain order amongst a desperate peasantry to stop the Catholic political classes from assembling – the common description of 'Catholic' confounds community leaders and the political classes with starving rioters.[20] This sort of abuse of description is an affront to equity, and Burke is very careful to avoid the imputation of making it. But at the same time he is alert to a corresponding danger: that of leading figures in certain groups claiming a false authority to speak for a whole description of people. Soon after beginning work on the *Reflections*, Burke makes a speech during the debate over the repeal of the Test and Corporation Act on 2 March 1790, in which he makes a sharp distinction between the body of the British dissenting congregations and their leaders, whose recent aggressive use of their electoral influence at the polls he resented deeply.[21] Just as he had refused the direct parliamentary instructions of his Bristol constituents in 1774, he now fears that 'every claim in individuals to publick confidence from *General* service, would be wholly swallowed up' in the demands of particular pressure groups, brought together merely by their common description, rather than any more stable relationship of interest or community.[22] The business of social description draws immediate attention to problems of representation and leadership: what conditions give one person the right to speak on behalf of another, and what relation does that right have to the good of the larger community? Burke's handling of rhetorical ethos in the *Reflections* is circumscribed by his caution over the different abuses of description, over the question of his own social authority as an influential writer, but particularly over his descriptions of the characters of others.

One of Burke's central arguments in the *Reflections* is that the competency of every political system should be judged by the quality of the ethical knowledge that its governors have of the governed, and (by extension) of themselves. This is what he means when he argues that

'In all bodies, those who will lead, must also, in a considerable degree, follow: They must conform their propositions to the taste, talent, and disposition of those whom they wish to conduct.'[23] In other words, the good politician is dedicated to studying and describing the characters of Parliament and of the people it represents, so as to know how to follow them. Burke is so suspicious of the revolutionaries because their leaders really do seem to be *leading* them, rather than knowing and being led by them. The structure of the *Reflections* assumes an analogy of group character between the comparatively obscure London radicals and the newly powerful delegates of the French revolutionary Assembly. The London radicals are tradesmen led by natural historians and dissenting divines, while the French revolutionaries, according to Burke's analysis, are provincial attorneys led by bankers, men of letters and discontented aristocrats. For the analogy to hold, Burke must stress that their common revolutionary character is a product of something more than the neutral social phenomena that are comprehended by description – that the revolutionary characters are the result of a political perversion rather than of a social disaffection. All public actors are known by their description, and yet description alone does not determine political character:

> In France you are now in the crisis of a revolution ... – you cannot see that character of men exactly in the same situation in which we see it in this country. With us it is militant; with you it is triumphant; and you know how it can act when its power is commensurate to its will. I would not be supposed to confine those observations to any description of men, or to comprehend all men of any description within them – No! far from it. I am ... incapable of that injustice. [95]

Burke insists that he is not reducing the revolutionary character to particular social descriptions, and this denial is connected with the earlier claim that he does not write 'for [or] from any description of men'. Indeed, the denial corresponds with a central topic of the *Reflections*: the perceived reluctance of Burke's radical opponents to discriminate between the various 'moral conditions and propensities' found among the citizens of a state [274]. Their failure of self-perception is a symptom of their lack of analytical capacity.

The 'new description of men' known in France as *philosophes* can best be characterized, in Burke's view, by a certain temper that precludes sympathetic knowledge of the characters of others: they are 'so taken up with their theories about the rights of man, that they have totally forgot his nature' [165, 95]. By neglecting the science of social description, the revolutionists have been able 'to confound all sorts of citizens, as well as they could, into one homogeneous mass' [274]. The difficulty that Burke has in recognizing his opponents (they are 'non-descripts' [15] among the genera and species of dissent) is presented, by a transfer of effects, as a symptom of their universalizing indifference to the various characters of citizens. Their lack of ethical knowledge somehow makes it more difficult to perceive them as political characters. Just as showing a good knowledge of character confers character on a speaker, so the failure of the radicals' public ethos betrays the dysfunction in their moral thought. In these terms, the principle of description is basically rhetorical. Burke's descriptions display how refined a political observer he is, and expose the coarseness of his opponents' thinking, all at once. But description has deeper connections in Burke's political thought than this implies.

In the *Reflections* ethical description has an oblique but profound link with Burke's distinctive conception of 'prescription' – that is, the legal prescription of property, a crucial element in his vision of civil society. 'Prescription' and 'description' have common etymological stems in the verb *scribere*, of course, but they also have similar applications respectively in their proper spheres, law and civil science. Both imply not only the writing but the laying down of meaning; both are utterances that fix things and ascertain interpretations. The 'description' of men or women is the pragmatic categorization of a group of persons whose various differences preclude any less arbitrary designation. The 'prescription' of a right of property is a similarly pragmatic judgment about the circumstances of ownership (normally the duration of possession) that weighs against other sorts of claims based on dormant titles, say, or occupancy, or improvements to the property.[24] It is clear from several passages in the *Reflections* that Burke thought of personal character as a kind of property, especially when it relates to profession or rank. Certain descriptions, one might say, are capable of prescription:

> When men are encouraged to go into a certain mode of life by the existing laws, and protected in that mode as in a lawful occupation ... I am sure it is unjust in legislature, by an arbitrary act, to offer a sudden violence to their minds and their feelings; forcibly to degrade them from their state and condition, and to stigmatize with shame and infamy that character and those customs which before had been the measure of their happiness and honour. [230]

Burke believes that prescribed property lies under a general threat from the Revolution, but it is the French state's recent appropriation of the wealth of the established Church that gives a specific pretext for his anxieties. The physiocrats and *encyclopédistes* (especially Turgot) had long been complaining about the Church's right to accumulate vast capital and landholdings under the protection of mortmain, using arguments that Burke the economic reformer could not help but find convincing.[25] But a disproportionately significant part of Burke's objection to the seizure of Church goods is his opposition to the National Assembly's argument (which he frames in incongruously Hobbesian terms) that 'ecclesiastics are fictitious persons, creatures of the state', whose professional *characters* may be dissolved at the pleasure of the state, irrespective of 'what they may suffer in their natural feelings and natural persons, on account of what is done towards them in this their constructive character'.[26] Clergymen held their rights of both rank and property, he avers, under the 'accumulated prescription of a thousand years'. Burke's opponents, particularly James Mackintosh, thought Burke's analogy between personal character and public property a false argumentative move, but they felt its rhetorical force as well, and declined to confront it directly: 'we confine ourselves', writes Mackintosh, 'strictly to [the clergy's] *political* and *collective* character. Mr. Burke, on the contrary, has grounded his eloquent apology purely on their *individual* and *moral character*. This however is totally irrelevant to the question . . .'.[27] But analogy is so important to Burke that he risks compromising the general idea of legal prescription by associating it with this sort of socially determined 'constructive character' in individuals.

Description refers to the social character of individuals and associations in the *Reflections*, but the patterns of thought it establishes radiate outwards into Burke's ideas of the largest forms of government and law. Part of Burke's purpose in the *Reflections* is to explain how citizens play a positive and constitutive role in institutions that they have merely inherited, not created themselves. Thus he describes in Stoic terms the connection between our love of whichever 'little platoon we belong to in society' and an expanding circle of devotion to our government, to 'our country and to mankind' [68]. Burke wants the reader to view these relations not only subjectively (as a chain of sentiments and obligations extending from the individual), but also from an external, analytical perspective. The correspondence of individual characters with the characters of governments and nations looks rather more intricate from this point of view. Burke often uses images of weavings and textiles, of 'politic well-wrought veils' [25], to describe it: the British constitution has 'so coarse a texture', he says in the *Speech on Conciliation*, 'as perfectly to suit the ordinary capacities of those who are to enjoy, and those who are to defend it'.[28] He seems to switch between these perspectives (and metaphors) during an important passage in his speech *On the Reform of the Representation* of

7 May 1782, a speech which anticipates many themes taken up again in the *Reflections*. The analogy between constitutional prescription and human description is especially important here:

> Prescription is the most solid of all titles, not only to property, but, which is to secure that property, to Government. They harmonize with each other, and give mutual aid to one another ... a nation is not an idea only of local extent, and individual momentary aggregation, but it is an idea of continuity, which extends in time as well as in numbers, and in space. And this is a choice not of one day, or one set of people, not a tumultuary and giddy choice; it is a deliberate election of ages and of generations; it is a Constitution made by what is ten thousand times better than choice, it is made by the peculiar circumstances, occasions, tempers, dispositions, and moral, civil, and social habitudes of the people, which disclose themselves only in a long space of time. It is a vestment, which accommodates itself to the body. Nor is prescription of government formed upon blind unmeaning prejudices – for man is a most unwise, and a most wise, being. The individual is foolish. The multitude, for the moment, is foolish, when they act without deliberation; but the species is wise, and when time is given to it, as a species it almost always acts right.[29]

This passage is about the evolution of a constitution through many years of legislative adjustment and debate. The words 'deliberate' and 'deliberation' are central to the theme. But Burke uses them in senses that do not signify immediate rational discussion or choice. Only through history can the nation act with 'deliberation'. The 'deliberate election of ages' involves no decisive weighing up of arguments: it is a ponderous process of impersonal thought, accumulative and unconfined.[30] Although 'deliberate'-ness is impersonal in this usage, it is highly moral. It involves a balancing of human 'tempers, dispositions' and 'habitudes' that itself produces certain kinds of election, and certain modes of social being. This idea helps clarify Burke's designation of personal 'constitutive character' as a kind of property. It is not so much the quality of the suffering caused by the loss of character that Burke is concerned about – although he places an adventitious emotional weight on that consideration. 'Constitutive character' is rather one of several threads of 'habitude', placed alongside the strands of moral and social custom (and of natural characters, dispositions and tempers), and woven against the historical weft 'of ages and of generations'. Obviously, part of the function of these habitudes is to cover, to conceal with modesty the nakedness and usurpation upon which states tend to have been founded. The 'politic well-wrought veil' thrown over the Glorious Revolution by Lord Somers and his colleagues is only a recent adaptation of the 'secret veil' that is 'to be drawn over the beginnings of all governments', as Burke described it during the Hastings trial.[31] The very existence of different social characters is a kind of argument by ethos. It specifies a 'rank productive force of the human mind' that cannot be destroyed and, like the 'force of fixed air in nitre, or the power of steam' in nature, it has an unignorable power [233].

The language that Burke uses to discuss the manifestation of selfhood in political society – the language of 'characters', 'tempers', 'descriptions', 'habitudes' and 'dispositions' – has a peculiar richness and diversity in the *Reflections.* It seems that Burke is searching for general, comprehensive terms with which to talk about the enormous variety of lives and experiences that make up political society, conscious all the while that he must not fall into patterns of thought that abstract or disembody those collected selves. There is a terrific strain in Burke's writing to imagine the accumulated moral momentum of those selfhoods, the weight of human desires, needs, hopes and histories that presses behind them when they are represented in political institutions. Burke claims that his opponents cannot be trusted to represent their own characters realistically, and that this failure of personal ethics is linked to their larger incapacity for deliberating about the characters and interests of others in anything but the most abstracted terms. Burke's ethicizing rhetoric is part of an attempt to exemplify in his own writings the balancing and disposing discretion that is required of politicians who would deal in the human matter of political society. Let us now look in more detail at the rhetorical functionings of Burke's moral language.

RHETORIC AND VERBAL BIAS IN THE 'REFLECTIONS'

In the previous section I dealt with a handful of terms from the opening pages of the *Reflections* – 'speculation', 'prescription' and 'description' – in relation to their deployment in the rest of the book. As everybody who reads the *Reflections* soon realizes, the text is threaded through with these sorts of specially weighted keywords. Burke draws our attention to them by repetition, by direct discussion of their meanings, or by the peculiarities of usage to which he puts them. Several of these keywords – 'prejudice', 'opinion' and 'contract', for example – are widely discussed in Burke criticism, but the general technique of verbal heightening has gone largely unremarked.[32]

These points of linguistic emphasis give the prose of the *Reflections* its peculiar rhetorical texture, and Burke is highly self-conscious about how he uses them. There is a clear correspondence between his critical comments on the keywords of his opponents, for example, and the way that he twists and redeploys several of those keywords for his own purposes. In several cases what begins as a semi-parodic imitation of the revolutionists' language is rapidly absorbed into Burke's own rhetorical repertoire, and made his own. 'Liberty' is the most obvious example of a word he thought had been knocked from its proper place in political discourse.[33] The passage in which he describes his idea of a 'manly, moral, regulated liberty' [7] is answered at the very end of the book by one with a sharper tone:

> Those who know what virtuous liberty is, cannot bear to see it disgraced by incapable heads, on account of their having high-sounding words in their mouths. Grand, swelling sentiments of liberty, I am sure I do not despise ... Neither do I wholly condemn the little arts and devices of popularity. They facilitate the carrying of many points of moment; they keep the people together; they refresh the mind in its exertions; and they diffuse occasional gaiety over the severe brow of moral freedom. Every politician ought to sacrifice to the graces; and to join compliance with reason. But in such an undertaking as that in France, all these subsidiary sentiments and artifices are of little avail. [352]

This passage is very much in the spirit of the Scottish scientists of man – it combines a detached interest in the psychological effect of words on human passions with a warm recognition of their social utility. The first sentence is dominated by a firm moral realism: practical liberty is quite separated from the 'high-sounding words' by which it is invoked (including the word 'liberty' itself, presumably). Burke assumes that his critical treatment of his opponents' language requires qualification, or at least a defensive admission that he is susceptible (both as audience and orator) to such 'little arts and devices of popularity' himself. So the word 'compliance' faces both ways: it combines the obsolete Miltonic sense of the politician's complaisant agreement with other persons, and a more conventional sense of the compliance that the linguistic artifices of politicians coerce from their public.[34] However, Burke's artistic interest in this kind of political language is limited by context. The kinds of sentiment that can be excited by words are entirely 'subsidiary' to the sentiments and opinions that constitute the social fabric.

Burke's British contemporaries were familiar with sloganizing, and with debates about the morality of sloganizing, in political writing. Since the late seventeenth century, British party writers had been fighting over the keywords and party jargon that appeared in their pamphlet literature.[35] But Burke is fascinated by a new quality of weightiness that radical writers have attained with their vocabulary during the eighteenth century. He also senses that the monumentality of the radicals' language makes their discourse unwieldy, and more likely to be used unreflectively. The 'plain meaning of their words', he observes, obliges them to 'equivocations and slippery constructions', since they retain seditious implications of which their users have imperfect control [18]. Even when their language is applied sincerely, he contends, it betrays its derivation from a '*patois* of fraud' [155]. Burke is particularly resentful that the word 'enlightened' must now be 'understood according to the new dictionary, as it always is in your new schools', as referring to religious scepticism [278]. Towards the end of the *Reflections* he punningly adapts a line from Molière, substituting the word *saignare* (draw blood) for *assignats*, and grumbles: 'I suppose they must talk of *assignats*, as no other language would be understood' [339].[36] If the many rhetorical peculiarities of the *Reflections* can be said to have a common underlying purpose, it is that of encircling what Burke thought of as the entrenched linguistic forces of his opponents. The linguistic practice of the *Reflections* is at once meticulous and destructively satirical. Burke's conscientious regard for legislative speech acts, for the 'language of preceding acts' [26], the 'words and even the spirit of the law' [27], for the 'primitive language of the law' [41], is also bound up with a sense of the capacity of such expressions to cut through the 'shell and husk of history' [209].[37] This is what he means when he singles out the 'penetrating style' in which Lord Somers wrote the Declaration of Right for his highest stylistic praise [27]. But the same intricacies of civil life that can only be transfixed by this sort of piercing linguistic energy are themselves the medium and subject matter of the *Reflections*. The 'objects of society are of the greatest possible complexity' [91], and it is Burke's purpose to enact that complexity in his prose – to do otherwise would be, in its way, to write 'under an equivocal description' [6].

Although Burke's treatment of keywords grows out of his critical view of contemporary linguistic practices, many of his most unusual recurring usages are peculiar to the *Reflections*, rather than reappropriated from his opponents. Of these, there are four that have a particular relevance to questions of rhetoric, and particularly to the styles of reasoning then current in public life. Two of them are positive terms – 'reflection' and 'analogy' – and two of them are negative – 'sophistry' and 'metaphysics'. Indeed, the first, most obvious, and most easily missed hint that Burke gives us about the rhetorical nature of his book is contained in its title: the basic structuring principle of the *Reflections* is that of reflection. The word 'reflection' has two contrasting (though occasionally combined) functions in the book. In the first place, the *Reflections* presents itself as a model for the kind of cogitative reflection that is best suited to political questions. By choosing *Reflections* for his title (instead of *Thoughts*, or *An Inquiry*, or *Considerations*) Burke signals that his mode of argumentation will involve a process of thought, rather than a series of isolated acts of intellection.[38] 'Reflections' are thoughts that have been given time to turn in upon themselves. Meditating on the establishment of British liberties in legal statute, for example, Burke describes this policy as 'the result of profound reflection; or rather the happy effect of following nature, which is wisdom without reflection' [47]. The self-correction here ('or rather ...') is itself reflective, and it has a subtle rhetorical effect: that of enacting the evolution of sustained reflection into a 'permanent reason' [27], one that is 'above' particular acts of cogitation. Reflection has the dynamic potential to transform itself from an act of political thought into its own object. As such it is closely linked with other Burkean words that express the historical dimension of ideas and institutions, like 'prejudice', 'opinion' and 'prescription'.

In a second sense, and at a more practical level, the idea of reflection also gives the book's subject matter its basic structure. Reflection refers to the optical phenomena of mirrored images, and is in turn related to Burke's lexicon of puns on illumination: 'this new-sprung modern light' [111], 'this enlightened age' [129], etc. The *Reflections* is organized around a reflective comparison of two nations, Britain and France. The British have always fashioned themselves in the mirror of French manners ('we dress our behaviour in the frippery of France' [104]), and the French political classes have shown a corresponding interest in British constitutional arrangements: 'I hear it is sometimes given out in France, that what is doing among you is after the example of England' [131]. According to Burke's argument, the reflection between Britain and France has become badly distorted of late. The French National Assembly finds its image in 'Certain Societies in London', rather than in the government at Westminster, while the French Revolution of 1789 is compared preposterously with the English dynastic Revolution of 1688 – Burke is astonished 'to find how little you [the French] seem to know of us' [126]. The original plan of the *Reflections* was 'to compare the whole of what you have substituted in the place of what you have destroyed, with the several members of our British constitution' [241]. Burke abandons this mirroring scheme two thirds of the way through the *Reflections*, but the basic idea of the new French constitution as a botched reflection – the 'profane burlesque, and abominable perversion' of a representative assembly – appears often in his polemic [102]. To a great extent Burke anticipates some kind of distortion as an inevitable consequence of political disquisition, especially when ideas, abstractions or principles are in agitation:

These metaphysical rights entering into common life, like rays of light which pierce into a dense medium, are, by the laws of nature, refracted from their straight line. Indeed in the gross and complicated mass of human passions and concerns, the primitive rights of men undergo such a variety of refractions and reflections, that it becomes absurd to talk of them as if they continued in the simplicity of their original direction. [90–1]

In this passage Burke brings the two senses of reflection – cognitive and optical – together to express a principle of political complexity. The 'refractions and reflections' that happen when cogitative thought encounters moral matter are inevitable, but this is not to say that institutions and the opinions that support them cannot perpetuate their image across time. In other passages Burke figures political ideas in terms of biological generation, as a 'stock of inheritance' [36, 37, 45], and this provides him with a metaphorical explanation for why states and constitutions stay looking like themselves through history: 'we have given to our frame of polity the image of a relation in blood' [49], and in that image of the state and its institutions we look for the reflections of certain family resemblances – 'the physiognomy and aspect of a grave legislative body' [102]. It is typical of Burke's descriptive morality that this system of mirroring figures should resolve itself into the idea of family character. From its title onwards, the *Reflections* involves the process of political reasoning with the particularity of ethos.

Another term that is related to Burkean 'reflection' is 'analogy'. It has its own important applications in the text: any future constitutional reforms undertaken by the British Parliament will be, Burke predicts, 'carefully formed upon analogical precedent, authority and example' [45]; 'By adhering in this manner and on those principles to our forefathers', he adds, 'we are guided not by the superstition of antiquarians, but by the spirit of philosophic analogy' [49]. Burke's usage of 'analogy' suggests that he is mindful of the word's application in logic and other technical discourses to the 'just correspondence and symmetry' [48, 295] of two things by proportion, ratio or a similar relation.[39] When he writes in the first instance of 'analogical precedent' he is in fact drawing on the idiom of common law.[40] But the 'philosophic analogy' of the second sentence has broader implications. It concludes the paragraph that begins with Burke's self-correcting reference to 'profound reflection; or rather ... wisdom without reflection', and again it educes a mode of reasoning that corresponds (even in the instant of reflection) with various 'principles' of traditional or extra-rational knowledge.

The way that Burke links together reflection and analogy is not, it must be said, in line with the most rigorous thought of his time.[41] What it does suggest is the continuing influence of Anglican apologetic and anti-Deist polemic on his discursive style, an influence that may be inferred from some interesting parallels between the rhetorical method of the *Reflections* and that of Bishop Joseph Butler's widely read *Analogy of Religion* (1736). Butler asserts the reasonableness of natural and revealed religion by its 'analogy to the experienced constitution of nature'.[42] His proof involves no a priori reasoning, relying instead on the 'weight' of probability to enforce the analogy between what we know in nature and what we cannot know beyond nature: 'It is enough to the present purpose to observe that this general way of arguing is evidently natural, just and conclusive.'[43] However small the probability of the Christian revelation might be, Butler argues, it imposes a 'formal obligation' on us to act 'upon that presumption or low probability, though it be so low as to leave the mind in very great doubt which is the truth'.[44] The distinctive thing about Butler's method is the resolute modesty of its claims, even though they describe a process of moral obligation. He acknowledges that arguments from analogy are far more likely to persuade such readers 'as profess to follow nature, and to be less satisfied with abstract reasonings' than they are to make an impression on those inclined to Deism or scepticism.[45] The method of reasoning in the *Reflections* is characterized, as we shall see, by a similar chastity of method, a similarly exclusive appeal to the weight of modest good sense, and a similar suspicion of abstract reasoning. Burke's text also shows that self-reflexive modesty of method is quite compatible with displays of great linguistic exuberance. Moreover, Burke goes further than Butler in his rejection of logical methods that are ungrounded in experience, induction or analogy.

The great majority of the explicit references to rhetorical theory in the *Reflections* are in fact attacks on non-inductive or non-analogical thinking. The words that Burke applies to these abuses most frequently are 'metaphysics' and 'sophistry'. Although occasionally he combines these terms of abuse and writes about 'mazes of metaphysical sophistry' [29], or about 'the politicians of metaphysics who have opened schools for sophistry' [325], for the most part he has distinct uses for the two words. When Burke writes of 'metaphysics' he is generally describing modes of thought that eschew all questions of correspondence. Metaphysics is unreflective because its reasonings refer only to themselves: they stand 'stripped of every relation, in all the nakedness and solitude of metaphysical abstraction' [7], and when applied to morality or politics they produce a monadic 'simplicity of contrivance' [91]. 'Sophistry', on the other hand, is pernicious because it puts ideas and things into false relations, or entangles them with irrelevancies. Burke flatteringly assumes that his reader is not 'of that sophistical, captious spirit . . . to require, for every general observation or sentiment, an explicit detail of all the correctives and exceptions' [73]; he observes that theories of popular right 'are almost always sophistically confounded' with ideas of power [92]; while the British people, he believes, keep their social sentiments whole and entire, 'unsophisticated by pedantry and infidelity' [128]. Where sophistry mixes incompatible ideas, metaphysics reduces or ignores the inconvenient moral evidence. Sophistry confounds where metaphysics excludes.

Burke is slightly more likely to use sophistry as a term of occasional abuse, or as a criticism of his enemies' use of language: he disparages these 'talking sophisters' [154], these 'sophisters and declaimers' [331], for their 'paltry style of debating' [231]. But Burke also understood the technical aspects of sophistry. As long ago as 1757, in the preface to the second edition of *A Vindication of Natural Society*, Burke had linked Isocrates' orations against the Sophists with his own project of removing the 'Gloss upon ingenious Falsehoods, that dazzles the Imagination, but which neither belongs to, nor becomes the sober Aspect of Truth'.[46] When he identifies dysfunctions in his opponents' logic in the *Reflections*, they generally fall into the first category of the seven non-linguistic fallacies listed in logic textbooks, the fallacy of accident or *secundum quid* – that is, an argument in which qualified conclusions are inferred from absolute or abstract premises.[47] This is what happens when 'metaphysical rights' are applied to the 'complicated mass of human passions and concerns' [91]. Burke does not seem to have remembered much Aristotle from his undergraduate reading, but it is worth noting that, in Book II of the *Rhetoric*, the fallacy of accident is closely associated with sophistic practice.[48] The Sophists gloss over the responsibility of ethical judgment by making simple facts seem absolutely determinative, refusing to qualify them by reference to circumstances, relations and manners. When Burke challenges the National Assembly to distinguish the '*causes*' of civil strife ('pride, ambition, avarice') from their '*pretexts*' ('Religion, morals, laws, prerogatives, privileges') he is making the same sort of logical distinction: 'Wise men will apply their remedies to vices, not to names; to the causes of evil which are permanent, not to the occasional organs by which they act, and the transitory modes in which they appear' [209].

Burke puts a slightly greater weight of meaning on the intellectual vice of metaphysics, probably because it has more immediately prudential consequences than sophistry. As we have seen, he argues that the fundamental topic in political science of which the revolutionaries and their supporters are ignorant is the ethical knowledge of character. Indeed, Burke uses the language of analogical ratio to express the opposition of metaphysics and ethics: 'in proportion as [propositions of the revolutionaries] are metaphysically true, they are morally and politically false' [91]. The ancient legislators, by contrast with their modern emulators in France, bend all their attention to this moral topic:

> They had to do with men, and they were obliged to study human nature ... As the first sort of legislators attended to the different kinds of citizens, and combined them into one commonwealth, the others, the metaphysical and alchemistical legislators, have taken the direct contrary course. They have attempted to confound all sorts of citizens, as well as they could, into one homogeneous mass ... [273, 274]

The cardinal intellectual virtue, according to the *Reflections*, is the capacity for complex moral valuation, and when Burke writes of 'metaphysics' he tends to mean the correspondent intellectual vice of reductiveness. It is significant that Burke's only direct reference to formal logic or rhetoric comes later in this same paragraph.[49] The delegates of the National Assembly reason only about substance and quantity, he continues: 'They might learn from the catechisms of metaphysics that there were eight heads more, in every complex deliberation, which they have never thought of, though these, of all the ten, are the subject on which the skill of man can operate any thing at all' [274]. Burke lists the eight remaining classes of logical predicament (quality, relation, action, passion, position, 'where', 'when', possession) in a punctilious footnote.[50] It all smacks of Scriblerian learned wit – indeed, the metaphysical scale derived from Aristotle had been given full satirical treatment in the *Memoirs of Scriblerus*.[51] But the language with which he describes the predicaments is more revealing: they are 'subjects' for skilful 'operation'. Burke is less concerned with the logical processes of reasoning, it seems, than he is interested in the different kinds of material upon which logic and rhetoric might operate. Since the matter of politics is human, the discovery and organization of that material must involve the particularities of moral character.

The uses to which Burke puts the words 'metaphysics' and 'sophistry' suggest the strength of the anti-rhetorical undercurrent in Burke's late political discourse. However indulgent he is about the orator's little arts and devices of popularity, academic instruction in political eloquence is repugnant to him, especially when that instruction precedes experience. In the *Reflections*, metaphysics and sophistry are proper only to 'the ordinary exercise of boys at school' [93] and to the 'professors of metaphysics' who instruct them [91]. He enjoys recalling how Cicero 'ludicrously describes Cato as endeavouring to act in the commonwealth upon the school paradoxes which exercised the wits of the junior students in the stoic philosophy' [251]. This anti-scholastic and anti-rhetorical theme has roots before 1789 in Burke's horrified depiction of the 'young men (boys almost)' who abuse and exploit the governmental responsibilities of the East India Company.[52] After 1790 it develops a furious polemical intensity: in *A Letter to a Member of the National Assembly* (1791), where it is associated with the National Assembly's interest in Rousseau's educational thought, and again in the *Letter to a Noble Lord* (1796), where Burke hopes finally to 'shut up' orator John Thelwall's London branch of the 'vile illiberal school, this new French academy of the *sans culottes*'.[53]

It is by contrast with this sort of youthful sophistic eloquence that Burke presents his mature rhetorical ethos. His most consistent appeals to his own authority are those he makes to his relative old age, the great length of his parliamentary service and the maturity of his political experience. If asked what made him bold enough to desert his old party allies and to attack the Revolution, he 'should give the same answer Solon was said to have returned to some prince or politician, who questioned him in the like manner: "That his age made him bold"'.[54] The severing of his relationship with Charles James Fox was discussed by both sides as a dispute between pupil and teacher, and Burke was charged with 'the foul crime', as he described it in the *Appeal from the New to the Old Whigs*, 'of teaching a set of maxims to a boy, and afterwards, when these maxims became adult in his mature age, of abandoning both the disciple and doctrine'.[55] Themes of pedagogy and maturity attended Burke through the Revolution controversy from the beginning, but they have a particular importance to the *Reflections*:

> Every man has his own relish. But I think, if I could not attain to the wisdom, I would at least preserve something of the stiff and peremptory dignity of age. These gentlemen deal in regeneration; but at any price I should hardly yield my rigid fibres to be regenerated by them; nor begin, in my grand climacteric, to squall in their new accents, or to stammer, in my second cradle, the elemental sounds of their barbarous metaphysics. [313]

This late passage of the *Reflections* refers back to an earlier one in which Burke talks about duties of solicitude and caution that politicians owe to state institutions, a 'wise prejudice' by which 'we are taught to look with horror on those children of their country who are prompted rashly to hack that aged parent in pieces, and put him into the kettle of magicians, in hopes that by their poisonous weeds, and wild incantations, they may regenerate the parental constitution, and renovate their father's life'.[56] This allusion of Burke's to the story of Medea, and her murderous persuading of the daughters of King Pelias to dice and cook their aged father, is comparable to Thomas Hobbes's witty deployment of the same tale. In *The Elements of Law* Hobbes likens Medea's evil counsel to the 'eloquence of ambitious men' in republican states, and the chopping of Pelias to the division of the body politic into factions.[57] With Burke's Medea the original act of persuasion has already given way to the magician's stammering squalls and garbled incantations. Our attention is drawn from the murderers to the mangled corpse of Pelias. Hobbes's farce of stupidity and eloquence is personalized and made tragic by Burke – it is Burke himself who must be renewed. The assumed link here between personal and political maturity has been made before: 'We procure reverence to our civil institutions', Burke suggests, 'on the principle upon which nature teaches us to revere individual men: on account of their age; and on account of those from whom they are descended' [51].[58] Since the British constitution is itself self-renewing, and really 'never old, or middle-aged, or young', Burke's own old age becomes, movingly, the complement of its continuing life [48]. Cicero's essay on old age, *De senectute*, is quoted three times during the last hundred pages of the *Reflections*, and it seems to have been at the back of Burke's mind as he completed the book.[59] The third quotation follows a brief rhapsody on the extraordinary political vices ('no common folly, no vulgar incapacity') required to overthrow a state: '*Cedo qui vestram rempublicam tantam amististis tam cito*', it runs, 'how lost you, pray, your mighty state so soon?' Burke leaves his readers to remember the punchline: '*proveniebant oratores novi, stulti adulescentuli*' ('new orators arose, foolish young men').[60]

DISCURSIVE MEAGRENESS

The kinds of dysfunctional political rhetoric deprecated in the *Reflections* as sophistry and metaphysics are associated largely with the characters of the radical leaders in Paris and London. For the most part they are the intellectual vices of an educated elite, and their faults are those of disengagement from the everyday matter of politics. But they are related to another theme in Burke's critical discourse that deals more generally with the rhetorical culture of the revolutionists. The purpose of this theme is to represent that culture as socially debased, imaginatively narrow and conceptually meagre. When writing in this critical mode, Burke figures the arguments of his opponents as dried goods ranged in warehouses, as the chirrupings of desiccated insects, and as the topics of dusty pedants. We do not see Burke at his most sympathetic when he uses these satirical themes, but they are an unignorable source of rhetorical exuberance in the *Reflections.*

The most vigorously satirical passages of the *Reflections* concerned with the style and rhetoric of his opponents are directed, as we have seen, against Richard Price's *Discourse on the Love of our Country*, which gave Burke his original provocation to write about the Revolution. But much of the curious detail of Burke's satire refers to a book that Price had published some seventeen years earlier, titled *Observations on Reversionary Payments* (1772, 9th edn 1776). In addition to his distinguished career as a political writer and divine, Price had enjoyed great success with this collection of essays on life assurance, annuities and the public debt. When Burke refers to 'the calculating divine' [15] or to the coming age of 'sophisters, œconomists, and calculators' [115], it is this modest, practical book that he is deprecating.[61] Burke often attacked statesmen whose competence in law or finance he thought compromised their liberal capacity as legislators to balance and dispose the various interests of the state, and by the same principle he counted Price's knowledge of 'political arithmetic' among his disqualifications as a commentator on state affairs. He subscribed to the common gentlemanly assumption that habits of close, orderly thinking are inimical to liberal political action, and to some extent he accepted that his own party role as a 'man of business' disqualified him from office at the cabinet level.[62] But here the theme takes on a redundant satirical energy that far exceeds its purpose as a point of public decorum. If Price's auditors, writes Burke,

> should find nothing to satisfy their pious fancies in the old staple of the national church, or in all the rich variety to be found in the well-assorted warehouses of the dissenting congregations, Dr. Price advises them to improve upon non-conformity; and to set up, each of them, a separate meeting-house upon his own particular principles . . . I doubt whether religion would reap all the benefits which the calculating divine computes from this 'great company of great preachers'. It would certainly be a valuable addition of non-descripts to the ample collection of known classes, genera and species, which at present beautify the *hortus siccus* of dissent. [14–16]

The phrase 'well-assorted warehouses' indulges in the polite scandal that non-conformist congregations sometimes met in places of business. Burke transforms this silly slander into an extraordinarily productive theme, as he had done once before, in February 1787, when he compared Pitt's ministry to 'scraps stolen from a great merchant's warehouse, to furnish out a pedlar's box'.[63] The orderly divisions of the warehouse become figures for schismatic subdivision, the 'spreading of contradiction' on a principle of infinite opposition. They represent congregation without community. Burke makes them correspond unexpectedly with the divisions of Linnaean taxonomy. The dry tidiness of the warehouse is superimposed upon images of desiccated specimens, ordered into their 'classes, genera and species' for the botanist's *hortus siccus*.[64] The dignity of Price, Priestley and their associates as scientists is degraded into a function of trade.

This is little more than an opportunistic insult, but the charges become serious when Burke moves on to Price's statement of the main tenet of radical Whiggism, that since 1688 the English monarchy has owed the security of the Crown to the direct assent of the people. He accuses Price of dressing up seditious principles with a nugatory loyalty: 'For the present it would operate as a theory, pickled in the preserving juices of pulpit eloquence, and laid by for future use. *Condo et compono quae mox depromere possim*' [18].[65] The Horatian tag speaks of the storing of wisdom for use throughout a lifetime: Burke applies it ironically to Price's planting of revolutionary maxims in his sermon. When he talks of pickling here he means in part the spurious effect of permanence that print lends to oratory. Combined with the earlier metaphors of warehouses and scientific collections, the image of 'preserving juices' suggests a morbid rhetorical copiousness, a scheme for the invention and disposition of dead topics. This whole system of insults is further complicated, of course, by the irony of describing a progressive like Price in terms of conservation.[66] Burke returns to this conceit of a preservative eloquence in one of the most heightened passages of the *Reflections*, where he renounces the influence of enlightened *philosophisme*: 'We have not been drawn and trussed, in order that we may be filled, like stuffed birds in a museum, with chaff and rags, and paltry, blurred shreds of paper about the rights of man. We preserve the whole of our feelings still native and entire, unsophisticated by pedantry and infidelity' [128]. Having mentioned the preservative properties of storehouses, scientific collections, pulpit eloquence and pickles, Burke turns at last to taxidermy, completing a scheme of wit that is truly Scriblerian in its urge for degradation. The logic of the conceit is extravagantly over-fulfilled: shredded pages of pamphlets on natural rights are the final preservative ingredient, the wadding for a stuffed ideology. It is an image which completes Burke's earlier association of the radical discourse with fugitive print media, while introducing a grim metaphor for moral evisceration.[67]

These figures of preservation and taxidermy have a peculiar correspondence with the famous image of grasshoppers at the end of the previous paragraph:

> Because half a dozen grasshoppers under a fern make the field ring with their importunate chink, whilst thousands of great cattle, reposed beneath the shadow of the British oak, chew the cud and are silent, pray do not imagine, that those who make the noise are the only inhabitants of the field; that, of course, they are many in number; or that, after all, they are other than the little shrivelled, meagre, hopping, though loud and troublesome insects of the hour. [126–7]

The shrivelled, desiccated body of the grasshopper adds another aspect to Burke's figuration of the London radicals.[68] As before, a touch of rural jollity belies many sombre associations. The silence of the cattle anticipates the hour at which 'the silent tomb shall have imposed its law on our pert loquacity' [128]. Somewhere in the back of Burke's mind are the anacreontic grasshoppers of seventeenth-century verse, laughing at the efforts of poets to rest and to contemplate – although here their chink is merely petulant and cruel.[69] Another association is with a maxim or riddle referred to by Aristotle in the *Rhetoric* (and referred to by Burke's friend Thomas Leland in his *Dissertations of Human Eloquence*): the lyric poet Stesichorus 'said to the Locrians, that they ought not to be insolent, lest their grasshoppers should be forced to chirp from the ground' – that is, if their orators did not cease making bellicose speeches, their crops and trees would wither away.[70] An indeterminate threat of pestilential profusion hangs over the pastoral scene – how did the thousands of cattle come to outnumber the grasshoppers, insects proverbially associated with multitude and famine?[71] Of course the shadow of the shambles is in the background too. The passage anticipates Burke's bovine imagery in *A Letter to a Noble Lord* (1796), where the dim-witted Duke of Bedford is pictured as a fattened bullock, his hide marked into cuts by his radical associates: 'alive as he is, and thinking no harm in the world, he is divided into rumps, and sirloins, and briskets'.[72] At the pitch of his eloquence Burke describes a country in which eloquence has no audience, and a national character in which 'cold sluggishness' [127] is both a practical defence and a terrible vulnerability. The image of the grasshopper, like the metaphors of desiccation and artificial preservation, is used by Burke to describe the textual character of his opponents' discourse: the claim of Price's text to record a moment of oratorical immediacy, and the briny, sterile quality of that speech in its printed form. Similarly, it is the shortness of the grasshopper's life that Burke opposes to the permanence of the herds of cattle reposing beneath the British oak. Finally, there is an important ethical dimension to his criticism – there is, Burke implies, no beating heart behind Price's sermon. Burke is demanding (and missing) a quality of incarnation in his opponent's prose, a palpable connection between the character of the author and the character of his argument, a sense of its relation to the real commerce of the nation, and to a community's habits of contemplation. The satirical themes through which Burke enforces his demands are a crucial component of the book's rhetorical self-reflexivity, and of his positive vision of an ethicized political discourse.

DISCURSIVE WEALTH

Commentary on rhetoric in the *Reflections* is not confined to Burke's system of metaphors for the intellectual meagreness of his opponents. His positive models for argument and expression in politics are, as one would expect, presented in comparatively muted terms, but they draw more deeply on modern rhetorical thought. They also have their own rhetorical peculiarities. When Burke describes good political discourse he uses three closely related categories: first, he writes about the process of inventing arguments in terms of calculation or of a 'computing principle'; second, he discusses the embodiment of those arguments in maxims; and third, he describes how maxims are redeployed by people of 'light and leading' in political society through systems of moral prejudice. These categories of invention, expression and application seem to have sprung from an austere impulse to reject all traces of intellectual glamour from political argument. But when one examines them closely, Burke's three strategies for sound political argumentation are possessed of their own peculiar energy.

There is an intense aggressiveness in the way Burke reappropriates certain elements of radical polemic and turns them to his own purposes. The figurative language with which he condemns the style of his opponents is almost indistinguishable from the terms in which he adumbrates his models for good discourse: calculations and commonplaces can be either impoverishments of thought or manifestations of intellectual discipline and consistency; prejudices represent either the coarsening of opinion or signal its readiness for deployment in debate. It is from the fineness of these distinctions that Burke turns his most striking rhetorical schemes. Some of his earliest critical comments, published in the 1757 preface to *A Vindication of Natural Society*, seem particularly relevant to these perverse aspects of his late polemical rhetoric. Writing about the evasive style of Bolingbroke, Burke speculates on the psychological process that often makes paradoxical opinions more persuasive to a 'common Auditory' than conclusive arguments:

> When Men find that something can be said in favour of what, on the very Proposal, they have thought utterly indefensible, they grow doubtful of their own Reason; they are thrown into a sort of pleasing Surprize; they run along with the Speaker, charmed to find such a plentiful Harvest of Reasoning, where all seemed barren and unpromising . . . There is a sort of Gloss upon ingenious Falsehoods, that dazzles the Imagination, but which neither belongs to, nor becomes the sober Aspect of Truth.[73]

Burke claims to have written the *Vindication* as a parodic satire on this sort of plausible, deceitful writing. But the preface suggests that his real interest is in the psychological process by which such imaginary impressions 'subsist and produce their Effect, even after the Understanding has been satisfied of their unsubstantial Nature'. In the *Reflections* we see a similar combination of satire and absorption in his rhetoric. Calculations, commonplaces and prejudices all wear the sober face of truth, and Burke's discussion of them, though ingenious, is not exactly glossy or dazzling. But the unanticipated sentiments and apparently indefensible proposals with which Burke vexes these categories are apt to provoke his readers out of any doubtfulness they may have had of 'their own Reason'. Burke aims to instil in his reader an invigorated, uncomplacent confidence in customary forms of political reasoning.

The argumentative perversity of the *Reflections* is especially evident in the metaphors of calculation that he uses when discussing the invention of political arguments. As we have seen, Burke deplores the coming of the age of 'sophisters, economists and calculators', and complains bitterly about their moral and conceptual indigence. But in an earlier passage of the *Reflections* the idea of calculation is crucial to his description of sound political council:

> The rights of men in governments are their advantages; and these are often in balances between differences of good; in compromises sometimes between good and evil, and sometimes, between evil and evil. Political reason is a computing principle; adding, subtracting, multiplying, and dividing, morally and not metaphysically or mathematically, true moral denominations. [92]

It is not easy to understand what Burke means here by politicians computing 'metaphysically or mathematically' until one has read on in the *Reflections* to the much later discussion of the National Assembly's arrangements for widening the franchise and rationalizing regional elections. The new democratic system will 'reduce men to loose counters merely for the sake of simple telling', Burke predicts, 'and not to figures whose power is to arise from their place in the table' [274]. Neither is the exact meaning of 'true moral denominations' perfectly clear. Burke might have referred his readers to a passage in Cicero's *De officiis* which must surely be in the back of his mind here. We should habituate ourselves to recognizing the different obligations that are owed to different people, writes Cicero, 'in order to become good calculators of moral duty [*boni ratiocinatores officiorum*], able by adding and subtracting to strike a balance correctly and find just how much is due to each individual'.[74] So Burke's 'moral denominations' are the different political weights of different men, which he (like all but the most radical of his contemporaries) measured in terms of property, and to a lesser extent in terms of office, experience and ability. There is something elusive about Burke's language in this passage, but his decision to keep the phrase 'true moral denominations' as open-ended as possible has an important purpose. The denominations might refer to individuals and 'descriptions' of individuals, but they might equally mean their 'advantages', their institutions or their actions. 'The rights of men are in a sort of *middle*', Burke argues, between the extremes of metaphysical and moral truth, and it is this that makes them 'incapable of definition, but not impossible to be discerned' [92] – they can be perceived, but not described. Burke resists the urge to impose a rhetorical resolution upon 'moral denominations' such as rights, because he understands that their irresolution gives them more power. It is perhaps the apparent reductiveness and impersonality of calculation that prompts Burke to use it in so profoundly moral a context.

The idea that duties can be 'calculated' is an instance of a common figure in eighteenth-century writing, the description of political argument in terms of financial accountancy.[75] It was a favourite metaphor of Hobbes, who described reasoning in *Leviathan* as 'nothing but *Reckoning* (that is, Adding and Subtracting) of the Consequences of generall names agreed upon, for the *marking* and *signifying* of our thoughts'.[76] Just as a sensible manager, says Hobbes, will 'fetch' his own sums 'from the first Items in every Reckoning' rather than trusting the accounts of his deputies, so the good reasoner will avoid absurdity by establishing his own 'generall Rules, called *Theorems*, or *Aphorismes* ... whereof one may be added unto, or subtracted from another'.[77] The figure was much relished by the Scriblerians, and particularly by Jonathan Swift, who used it in *The Sentiments of a Church-of-England Man* for the wonderfully un-Hobbesian purpose of recommending deference to the common opinions of people 'whose Wisdom, and Goodness' one trusts: 'According to *Hobbes*'s Comparison of *Reasoning* with *casting up Accounts*; whoever finds a mistake in the *Sum total*, must allow himself out; although, after repeated Tryals, he may not see in which Article he hath misreckoned.'[78] Whenever Swift introduces a proverb with the phrase 'it is an uncontroulable maxim that . . .', as he often does, he draws on this metaphor of accountancy – or of 'political numbers', as late Stuart satirists often called it.[79] The word 'control' first appears in English as a derivative of the Anglo-French *contreroller*, which means to check accounts by comparison with a 'counter-roll' or duplicate.[80] Like Hobbes, Swift assumes that the basic units of opinion thus totted up are '*Theorems*, or *Aphorisms*', and that 'maxims' are derived from the sum of such reckonings. Burke's language of computation and the 'balances' of moral reasoning corresponds with Swift's figures of reasoning and accountancy. On a larger scale again, it corresponds with his fundamental conception of the 'government of reciprocal controul' [200] as exemplified by the British system: 'a monarchy directed by laws, controlled and balanced by the great hereditary wealth and hereditary dignity of a nation; and both again controlled by a judicious check from the reason and feeling of the people at large acting by a suitable and permanent organ' [184].

Burke's language of computation in the *Reflections* differs from Swift's, however, because Burke is more ambiguous than Swift in his use of the word 'maxim' – by which he means the basic linguistic unit or counter of 'calculation'. When Burke turns from the establishment of the National Assembly to its legislative function, for example, he describes

> a body in its constitution with every possible power, and no possible external controul. We see a body without fundamental laws, without established maxims, without respected rules of proceeding, which nothing can keep firm to any system whatsoever. [286]

The missing 'established maxims' here should have a 'controuling' legislative force of their own. Burke presumably has in mind the sort of jurisprudential maxims associated with the *regulae iuris* of Roman law, upon which he would draw more directly in the *First Letter on a Regicide Peace*.[81] In his *Commentaries* William Blackstone described the English common law as a collection of interdependent maxims and customs: 'the authority of these maxims rests entirely upon general reception and usage; and the only method of proving, that this or that maxim is a rule of the common law, is by showing that it hath always been the custom to observe it'.[82] A basic principle of jurisprudence is that no court can 'controul the maxims of common law' on any general grounds, only in respect to personal and particular inconveniencies.[83] It is typical of Burke's rather generous conception of the law, however, that this technical jurisprudential sense of the word 'maxim' is hard to distinguish in the *Reflections* from the common sense of maxims as personal formulations of political principle, the sort of units into which Burkean 'prejudice' might divide. The maxims of the revolutionaries have no controlling authority: they are 'unwarrantable maxim[s]' [31], 'mischievious maxims' [37], 'dark suspicious maxims' [55], 'grim and bloody maxims' [116] and 'odious maxims' [120].

With characteristic versatility, Burke also refers positively to 'our old settled maxim[s]', 'established maxims', 'the maxims of our forefathers'.[84] But it is in the form of the text that the 'calculating' principle of discourse is most conspicuous. Obviously enough, the *Reflections* can be read as an archive of political aphorisms, a storehouse of new-minted maxims that also represents a sample of 'the general bank and capitol of nations, and of ages' [129]. But at a more dynamic level, the very structure of Burke's prose demonstrates the practical function of good moral calculation using maxims. By 'maxims' in this instance I mean those pithy sentences in the *Reflections* that give strong articulation to a general principle, that are syntactically independent (unconnected by pronoun or preposition) from their neighbouring sentences, and that have a rhetorical character of authority that is meant to elevate them above the ordinary flow of Burke's writing. If one goes through the *Reflections* looking for sentences that fulfil these criteria, it is readily apparent what sort of structural functions they serve. A very high proportion of them are isocolonic in form, using a two-part structure that hinges around some verbal repetition or adjustment of sense. In terms of meaning, they tend to involve analogies of history, reversals of viewpoint and mirrorings of thought. They are part of Burke's rhetoric of 'reflection'. This is especially the case with maxims positioned at the start of paragraphs: 'A state without some means of change is without the means of its conservation' [29]; 'People will not look forward to posterity, who never look backward to their ancestors' [47–8]; 'If civil society be the offspring of convention, that convention must be its law' [87]; 'To make us love our country, our country ought to be lovely' [116]. At the beginning of a passage these isocolonic maxims refract the reader's perspective, and urge a doubling of attention. Indeed, many of Burke's maxims are concerned with the disruption of complacency, or with agitated social exchanges: 'Flattery corrupts both the receiver and the giver' [9]; 'In all bodies, those who will lead, must also, in a considerable degree, follow' [59]; 'He that wrestles with us strengthens our nerves and sharpens our skill. Our antagonist is our helper' [246]; 'Political arrangement, as it is a work for social ends, is to be only wrought by social means. There mind must conspire with mind' [248–9].[85] Once again, these maxims are all concerned with models for effective political thought, not as systems of logic, but as scenes of intellectual entanglement. They serve to shatter the 'solitude of metaphysical abstraction' [7], and to precipitate the mind of the reader into a close engagement (often figured as a social engagement) with what Burke presents as moral fact.

Calculations and maxims are closely related to a third category of medium for political wisdom, that of 'prejudice'. As we have seen, Burke's language in the *Reflections* often works by a double process of estrangement and recognition: he designs his topics to strike the sympathetic reader as strange, or repugnant, or more appropriate to his opponents, and then to transform themselves almost immediately into what feel like familiar maxims. The most conspicuous example of this technique involves his use of the word 'prejudice':

> You see, Sir, that in this enlightened age I am bold enough to confess, that we are generally men of untaught feelings; that instead of casting away all our old prejudices, we cherish them to a very considerable degree, and, to take more shame to ourselves, we cherish them because they are prejudices . . . Many of our men of speculation, instead of exploding general prejudices, employ their sagacity to discover the latent wisdom which prevails in them. If they find what they seek, and they seldom fail, they think it more wise to continue the prejudice, with the reason involved, than to cast away the coat of prejudice, and to leave nothing but the naked reason; because prejudice, with its reason, has a motive to give action to that reason, and an affection which will give it permanence. Prejudice is of ready application in the emergency; it previously engages the mind in a steady course of wisdom and virtue, and does not leave the man hesitating in the moment of decision, skeptical, puzzled, and unresolved. Prejudice renders a man's virtue his habit; and not a series of unconnected acts. Through just prejudice, his duty becomes a part of his nature. [129–30]

From the start of the passage Burke acknowledges that he is doing something counter-intuitive, perhaps even shameful, with the received idea of prejudice, a word which had long been a shibboleth among the enlightened.[86] Prejudice would include, for instance, the sort of general charges against 'descriptions of men' that are much reprobated in the *Reflections.* In fact Burke rather exaggerates the originality of his attempt to rehabilitate prejudice, to present it as part of the livery of virtue. The same rhetorical move is made by James Beattie in a book that Burke greatly admired, *An Essay on the Nature and Immutability of Truth* (1770), in which a variety of moral prejudices are 'avowed' in the name of common sense.[87] Long before that, the negative senses of prejudice had been tossed about in Swift's satire as examples of Whiggish cant.[88] On the other hand, Joseph Addison wrote with Whiggish sympathy in *The Spectator* about the 'honest prejudices' of an Englishman: 'We may perhaps forget the Arguments which occasioned our Conviction', Addison comments in one of the Saturday sermons, 'but we ought to remember the strength they had with us, and therefore still to retain the Conviction which they once produced ... nor is it possible to act otherwise, given the Weakness and Limitation of our Intellectual Faculties.'[89] This mood of latitudinarian indulgence is recaptured by Burke, who gives it a distinctive note of urgency.

The originality of Burke's treatment lies in his presentation of prejudice as a complement to political reason.[90] Whenever Burke writes about prejudice, reason is almost always mentioned in an adjacent sentence.[91] Prejudice is 'involved' with reason rather than opposed to it, and this is an idea that Burke brings to life in the above passage with an extended metaphor of cloaking: the 'coat of prejudice' is not cast away, it becomes man's 'habit'. Once more the sprightliness of Burke's imagery belies its sombre biblical associations. The coat of prejudice evidently corresponds with Christ's coat 'without seam, woven from the top throughout', for which the Roman soldiers cast lots during the crucifixion – itself a common image for the unity of the Christian Church and Gospel.[92] The association of reason and prejudice with clothing seems to have been woven deeply into Burke's thought – the phrase 'naked reason' is not a common expression in eighteenth-century literature, but he uses it twice in the 1759 introduction to the *Philosophical Enquiry* to signify the opposite of cultivated 'taste'.[93] In the *Reflections* reason in its naked state is inert and impermanent. Burke is particularly interested in how prejudice allows him to represent the continuity of institutional forms as an analogy for thought itself. There is a telling correspondence between the idea of prejudice as 'a motive to give action to that reason, and an affection which will give it permanence' and his descriptions elsewhere in the *Reflections* of British civil society as 'a permanent body composed of transitory parts' [48], its institutions designed to give 'a body to opinion, and permanence to fugitive esteem' [205]. Prejudice is another means by which arguments can form themselves into a sort of living body.

The figures of calculation, maxim and prejudice with which Burke describes the exchange and circulation of political wisdom share a peculiar rhetorical characteristic. In each case he has chosen a rather impersonal, unattractive figure (derived respectively from economics, law and 'common sense' philosophy) that seems to distance the process of civil reasoning from the individual. The disjunction between impersonal metaphor and personal application gives a pointedness to their rhetorical function: for calculations and maxims, according to Burke, are the proper media for ethical information about human personalities, descriptions and opinions. Calculations, maxims and prejudices have such an important place in the rhetoric of the *Reflections* because, like the keywords 'metaphysics', 'sophistry' and 'analogy', they are at once part of Burke's critical analysis of the language of his polemical opponents, and crucial to the constructions of good political discourse that explain his own linguistic practice. The wisdom that is developed and stored in calculations and maxims is of the kind that Burke identifies with his political peers: the *Reflections* also claims to imitate it and exemplify it. Burke always writes in cautiously generalized terms about the relationship between his own opinions and those of the 'the men of England, the men, I mean, of light and leading in England' [150] for whom and to whom he writes. These persons are identified as 'not the least learned and reflecting part of this kingdom' (the periphrastic trope here is litotes). 'They who are included in this description', he adds mysteriously, 'form their opinions on such grounds as such persons ought to form them' [145]. He finds their opinions 'so worked into my mind, that I am unable to distinguish what I have learned from others from the results of my own meditation' [147]. In each of these cases Burke is talking about his former colleagues among the ranks of parliamentarians, courtiers and peers, but he is careful not to confine his classification of the British civil leadership to the denizens of Westminster and St James's. The distinction between the active political classes and the more general educated readership that made the *Reflections* a bestseller is politely blurred. Burke's discreet imprecision feeds into his principled reluctance to mark out 'descriptions of men'. It also allows him to describe an interfusion of opinions between the political nation, the author and his readership that appears to have nothing to do with coercion or direct persuasion, because it is so gradual, and finally so similar to self-reflection.

The *Reflections* has the reputation of being the most powerful expression of Burke's eloquence and, as we have seen, it has much to say on its own account about the business of political deliberation and persuasion.

So what general statements does it allow us to make about Burke's rhetorical art? This is a question that cannot be answered by cataloguing the local figures and effects that sharpen the book's polemical edges. Burke's idea of good political speaking is not defined by its capacity to attain the external ends of persuasion. Neither is it determined by purely artistic criteria, such as whether it manifests the best available means of persuasion in any given case. The final measure of political speech in the *Reflections* is whether or not it produces good government – which in Burke's understanding is government that balances the conflicting powers and interests contained by the state in an harmonious whole.

Burke's own example suggests that he thought the best speakers should evoke and reflect that harmony in their deliberations. But on a more general level he imagines the sphere of political speech as a scene of personal contention, with each participant constantly calculating the weight of opinion and influence an individual speaker might represent against the strength of his arguments. The orators of the National Assembly, being a group of untried and innovating statesmen, are attended to much for their reason, 'but not at all to their authority' [242]. Other deliberators, people of experienced 'light and leading', are listened to on account of their 'purchase' on the human material of the state [150, 232]. Thinking and speaking well about government, Burke proposes, is a matter of having the right sort of knowledge about one's fellow citizens, and the right sort of life within the community. This is what he means when he argues that 'In all bodies, those who will lead, must also, in a considerable degree, follow: They must conform their propositions to the taste, talent, and disposition of those whom they wish to conduct.'[94] One must have attained a recognized public character in order to join the conversation, and one must also display an understanding of how the various kinds of public character, with their respective dignities and duties, fit together in any given society. The rhetoric of the *Reflections*, by which I mean its basic persuasive strategy, turns on Burke's personal claim to have attained that character and that knowledge. But the really substantial achievement of the book is that it creates an intellectual context of arguments in which that claim itself becomes meaningful.

The teenaged William Hazlitt won the admiration of Coleridge with a witty observation about Burke: that the sense and candour of anyone belonging to the 'democratic' party could be tested by asking them whether they judged Burke to be a great man.[95] The aptness of this remark is that it articulates a principle of political generosity, and of intelligent realism about the common imperfectability of human characters, works and institutions, that informs every page of the *Reflections*. Hazlitt pretends to be talking critically about the experience of reading Burke, but really he is showing how well he has conned the lesson of Burke's rhetoric. When Burke answers the radicals' petitions on behalf of the wretched of the earth, of the poor and the oppressed, with a pathetic apostrophe to the fallen Queen of France, and with hymns of pity to 'the distresses of the miserable great', he is taking a reckless, provocative, but strictly consistent line on the morality of political deliberation [151]. The apparently unbalanced enthusiasm of Burke's most heightened writing extorts a special openness of mind from the reader. Burke returns the compliment of a liberal reading by refusing to believe that the reader is 'of that uncandid dulness, as to require, for every general observation or sentiment, an explicit detail of all the correctives and exceptions, which reason will presume to be included in all the general propositions which come from reasonable men' [73]. Even the most extravagant aspects of its rhetoric, so brilliantly dissected by his radical opponents Wollstonecraft, Paine, Godwin and Mackintosh, play their part in Burke's larger ethico-political scheme.

Burke is an orator, not a rhetorical theorist, and the artfulness behind his eloquence is not of the kind that can be reduced to an orderly system. But it does encourage us – perhaps more interestingly – to consider the position of that art within his wider political vision. The predominant conceptual mood of the *Reflections* is classical and harmonious. The language of balance, compromise, comparison, reflection, combination, reconciliation, deliberation and moderation runs through all of the most general statements about government that appear in its pages. For Burke, the state in its ideal form represents these equitable qualities in each of its temporal, material and moral dimensions: the state is 'a permanent body composed of transitory parts' [48], a 'choice of inheritance' [49], a 'reciprocal struggle of discordant powers' [51], a 'proud submission' [113]. These paradoxes are animated by a common figure of power meeting mass, of liberty encountering obligation. Burke's conception of good deliberation is instinct with this idea of poised energy. 'To form a *free government*', he believes, 'is to temper together these opposite elements of liberty and restraint in one consistent work' [353]. The verb 'to temper' is an attractive one for Burke because it implies not only the practical arts of the metallurgist or engineer, but also the moral harmony of the philosopher: the opposed and conflicting interests of the old European constitutions 'produce *temperaments*, preventing the sore evil of harsh, crude, unqualified reformations' [51]. To speak of the temperament of a state is to apply the language of personal ethics to the objects of government, as Burke is often inclined to do: 'steady and independent minds, when they have an object of so serious a concern as government under their contemplation . . . will judge of human institutions as they do of human characters. They will sort out the good from the evil, which is mixed in mortal institutions as it is in mortal men' [187]. The best politicians will be judged by their knowledge of their country's laws and histories. They must also show a capacity for imagining its future: 'to proceed with a presiding principle, and a prolific energy', Burke writes, 'is to me the criterion of profound wisdom' [250]. In each of these moderating, self-reconciling statements Burke locates the effective political mind in the middle of contending energies, as he did in his sketch on the 'true lawgiver' at [248–9]: generous in sensibility, intuitive by temperament, but by experience deliberate in both thought and speech. This is the ethical core of Burke's rhetoric in the *Reflections*.

CHAPTER 6

Burke, Rousseau and the purchase of eloquence

By the middle of February 1790, Burke had written enough of the *Reflections* for the work in progress to be worth circulating among his friends. Composition seems to have been interrupted during spring and early summer, however, by parliamentary business. Burke's return to serious work on his manuscript, probably after the dissolution of Parliament on 11 June 1790, is duly recorded on page 241 (signature R) of the first edition: 'This letter is grown to a great length', he admits, 'though it is indeed short with regard to the infinite extent of the subject. Various avocations have from time to time called my mind from the subject.' These lines begin a notably distinct section of the *Reflections*, a two-thousand-word recapitulation of the themes covered in Burke's earlier drafts. This recapitulation will be the focus of my final chapter. Whereas the first two thirds of the *Reflections* are concerned with the political morality of the National Assembly, with the 'arrogance of their pretensions' and with the presumption of their British admirers, the final third, writes Burke, will be concerned more specifically with their measures: 'They must take it for granted that we attend much to their reason', Burke warns, 'but not at all to their authority' [242]. In rhetorical terms, we might say that the first two thirds criticize the varieties of revolutionary character, while the final section of the *Reflections* sets out to deal with their proposals, and, more generally, with the capacity of the National Assembly for good deliberation and legislative pragmatism.

During the twelve pages of the recapitulation, however, Burke makes it clear that he will not consider the reasoning of the revolutionaries as something absolutely distinct from their characters: logos remains a subordinate function of ethos, as it has been throughout the *Reflections*. In these transitional pages Burke describes a slightly different rhetorical problem. What happens when the ethos of the statesman is defined exclusively by his eloquence (as opposed to when the statesman's eloquence is a product of his character, as Burke claims it is in his own case)? Burke does not underestimate the abilities of his French opponents as speakers and political thinkers:

I am convinced that there are men of considerable parts among the popular leaders in the national assembly. Some of them display eloquence in their speeches and their writings. This cannot be without powerful and cultivated talents. But eloquence may exist without a proportionable degree of wisdom. When I speak of ability, I am obliged to distinguish . . . Their purpose everywhere seems to have been to evade and slip aside from difficulty . . . Difficulty is a severe instructor, set over us by the supreme ordinance of a parental Guardian and Legislator, who knows us better than we know ourselves, as he loves us better, too. *Pater ipse colendi haud facilem esse viam voluit.* He that wrestles with us strengthens our nerves and sharpens our skill. Our antagonist is our helper. This amicable conflict with difficulty obliges us to an intimate acquaintance with our object, and compels us to consider it in all its relations.[1]

This passage brings together a series of themes from earlier parts of the *Reflections*. France's rejection of the conventional path to reform in 1789 has already proved that 'difficulty is good for man' [54]. The idea of revolution as a political energy that is at once intense and evasive is familiar from Burke's frequent references to his opponents' 'equivocation' ('equivocal description' [6], 'equivocations and slippery constructions' [18]). 'Equivocation' is one of several terms from the technical lexicon of logical fallacy that takes on an ethical meaning in the *Reflections*. Similarly, the theme of eloquence and instruction repeats Burke's habitual association of the revolutionaries with academic sophistry: 'I have nothing to say to the clumsy subtlety of their political metaphysics. Let them be their amusement in the schools' [86]. Most significantly, the ascription here of political difficulty to a providential dispensation ('supreme ordinance of a parental Guardian') has been anticipated in the earlier passages on 'prejudice': 'He who gave our nature to be perfected by our virtue, willed also the necessary means of its perfection. He willed therefore the state' [146]. One feature that distinguishes the recapitulation is a shifting quality in Burke's prose that seems to enact the 'difficulty' he describes. In the phrase 'He that wrestles with us strengthens our nerves', the reader cannot tell for sure what the pronoun 'He' refers to: it could be the 'Guardian and Legislator' himself; or 'Difficulty', the severe instructor; or any antagonist we might happen to encounter in public debate. The idea of 'amicable conflict' brings a further touch of paradox to the passage, not least because it recalls so incongruously Shaftesbury's well-known remark in the *Characteristicks* on the relationship between politeness, liberty and wit: 'We polish one another, and rub off our Corners and rough Sides by a sort of *amicable Collision*.'[2] The 'amicable conflict' demanded by Burke differs from Shaftesbury's 'amicable collision' because it is less a principle of liberty than one of necessity, of unwilled conflict and salutary antagonism. Burke also compels the reader to pin down his sense in a Protean embrace. We see here the characteristic (and sometimes backfiring) audacity of his rhetorical strategy for the *Reflections* – to attack 'sophistry' and 'equivocation' in a prose that is itself perilously turbulent.

Burke doubts whether the 'powerful and cultivated' eloquence of the National Assembly reveals any unusual depth of personality in its members. He is deeply interested, however, both in the way that its members speak about moral character, and also in what their speeches about public character reveal of their ethical principles. The 'lazy but restless disposition' that turns them aside from difficulty also confines them to 'the most common arts' of political jobbery: 'Trace them through all their artifices, frauds, and violences, you can find nothing at all that is new. They follow precedents and examples with the punctilious exactness of a pleader' [244]. Burke's irony here is that the new French politicians, those 'propagators of all novelties' [167], are incapable of original thought. Eloquence is notoriously an art that can be learned from rules and precedents, and so it is particularly fitting that they should practise it well. Their whole moral system has been acquired at second hand:

> Your legislators seem to have taken their opinions of all professions, ranks, and offices, from the declamations and buffooneries of satirists; who would themselves be astonished if they were held to the letter of their own descriptions. By listening only to these, your leaders regard all things only on the side of their vices and faults, and view those vices and faults under every colour of exaggeration . . . As to the rest, the paradoxes of eloquent writers, brought forth purely as a sport of fancy, to try their talents, to rouze attention, and excite surprize, are taken up by these gentlemen, not in the spirit of the original authors, as means of cultivating their taste and improving their style. These paradoxes become with them serious grounds of action, upon which they proceed in regulating the most important concerns of the state. [250, 251]

Although they want 'nerves' for the strenuous wrestlings of state, the revolutionaries are well trained in Shaftesburian cultural gymnastics, and in the exercise of taste. The 'eloquent writer' that Burke has in mind here is not Shaftesbury, however, but a French author in whose writings he had long been interested, Jean-Jacques Rousseau.[3] The last two pages of the recapitulation are a direct attack on Rousseau, to whom Burke seems also to refer when he writes of the 'declamations and buffooneries of satirists'. In the works that brought him fame in England during the 1750s and 1760s, Rousseau presented himself as a man who used paradox to goad his readers out of their prejudices: 'It is the very aversion they have to things common and usual', he wrote in the *Lettre à d'Alembert*, 'that sometimes makes them return to things the most simple.'[4] Rousseau is the original on whom the revolutionists model their eloquence and from whom they copy (absurdly) their supposed singularity. In the process of imitation, his peculiarities have become conventions.

Burke's assault on Rousseau marks a crucial point in the *Reflections*, and it deserves closer attention than it has received.[5] The attack is positioned at the climax of the recapitulation, and, as we shall see, it ties together some key themes to which Burke wanted to return in July 1790: the historicity of 'prescription'; the problem of 'facility' in politics; and the proper character of the 'legislator'. Since the *First Discourse* brought him fame in 1750, Rousseau had been known for a cultivated eloquence that he dedicated to the destruction of eloquence – and, indeed, to the destruction of cultivation itself.[6] As such, he was a precedent (albeit a problematic one) for Burke's presentation of the leading revolutionaries as a class of men whose capacity for political barbarism was a function of their cultural sophistication. The spectacle of a public figure like Burke attacking a thinker of Rousseau's stature is bound to attract notice. But Burke makes doubly sure of his reader's curiosity by involving David Hume in the dispute as well, quoting the Scotsman as the source of a personal anecdote about Rousseau's ill-fated retreat to England in 1766.[7] Another indication of the significance of the passage to the *Reflections*, and to Burke's thought about the Revolution more generally, is that he repeats the attack within a few months in *A Letter to a Member of the National Assembly* (1791). This second assault against Rousseau is a major paratext for the *Reflections*, because it shows us Burke in the process of rethinking the earlier passage, and of readjusting its polemical balance. In the *Reflections* Burke suggests that the political morality of the revolutionaries, with its dedication to principles of social and institutional renewal, is an accidental product of Rousseau's rhetorical innovations, and particularly of his search for 'the marvelous in life, in manners, in characters'. In the *Letter*, by contrast, it is political morality that precedes and determines Rousseauian eloquence: for 'Rousseau is a moralist, or he is nothing.'[8]

The strategic importance of these attacks on Rousseau is obvious, but it is harder to determine the extent of Burke's intellectual investment in them. How much of Rousseau's work had Burke actually read? To what extent did he rely on the common slanders against Rousseau, so often repeated in magazines and libels – about his vanity, his paranoia, his *gouvernante*, his madness – for ammunition? As the considerable influence of Rousseau's thought on the French National Assembly became clear during 1790, Burke confessed the dullness of his initial response to the citizen of Geneva: 'I have read long since the *Social Contract*', he wrote to a correspondent (possibly Thomas Paine) in January 1790; 'It has left very few traces upon my mind. I thought it a performance of little or no merit; and little did I conceive, that it should ever make revolutions, and give law to nations.'[9] Burke's uncandid readings in the *Letter to a Noble Lord* of Rousseau's *Julie, ou la nouvelle Héloïse* (a fable designed to encourage gallantry between teachers and pupils) and of his *Confessions* (a self-celebration of certain 'obscure and vulgar vices') suggest that he did not become a deep student of their author's writings during the following year. Is Burke's attack on Rousseau anything more than an ill-informed display of hostility against a writer whom his opponents happened to admire?

THE MARVELLOUS IN MORALS AND POLITICS

One reason for looking beyond the petulance of Burke's attack on Rousseau is that the former's aggression appears to conceal a degree of self-identification with the latter, especially with regard to their common skill as writers. Above all, Burke sees Rousseau's writings as the model for the public discourse of the revolutionaries: 'him they study; him they meditate; him they turn over in all the time they can spare from the laborious mischief of the day, or the debauches of the night'.[10] Burke cannot deny the effectiveness of that discourse and, as a politician distinguished above all by his eloquence and literary ability, it is natural that he should take a professional interest in its workings. Burke seems to identify with Rousseau's deftness as a rhetorician. What strikes Burke most forcibly about the eloquence of the National Assembly is that it inherits from Rousseau an instinct for novelty, for 'the marvellous in life, in manners, in characters, and in extraordinary situations, giving rise to new and unlooked-for strokes in politics and morals' [252]. Burke also observes that the originality of Rousseau's style is more effective among French readers than it is among the British: 'perhaps a secret charm in the language may have its share in this extraordinary difference'.[11] Burke shows that he has understood the technical innovation represented by Rousseau's style, while suggesting that it preys upon a certain modernistic parochialism that he identifies in French national culture.[12]

By implication, Burke encourages his reader to consider what peculiarities of rhetorical style help his own writing to succeed with British readers, where Rousseau's leaves them cold.

Another point of apparent identification between Burke and Rousseau is the perceived oral quality of their prose styles. The connection between Burke's eloquence as a parliamentary orator and the compelling brilliance of his printed writings is one that his admirers dwelt upon from the very start of his public career. This sort of connection between oratorical facility and literary effect was also common in criticism of Rousseau, although Rousseau himself thought that writing inhibited the expressiveness of the spoken word.[13] In the very first public notice of Rousseau's writing in England, William Bowyer junior's anonymous preface to his 1751 translation of the *First Discourse*, that work is 'owned to be one of the finest modern pieces of oratory, and of so dangerous a persuasion, that if the author, instead of giving it in writing, had pronounced it with all the force which the fluency of tongue and the grace of action usually add to such orations in publick, I should tremble for all the libraries in Europe'.[14] Most significantly of all, other participants in the Revolution controversy saw points of correspondence between Burke and Rousseau, and Burke was aware that they were being discussed. A pamphlet appeared in January 1791 entitled *A Comparison of the Opinions of Mr. Burke and Monsr Rousseau*, in which a general analogy between their eloquent styles develops into an essay on the similarities between the *Reflections* and Rousseau's *Considerations on the Government of Poland*.[15] The unknown author sent a copy to Burke, who replied evasively – doubtless conscious that his intensified attack on Rousseau in *A Letter to a Member of the National Assembly* would be published the following day in Paris, on 27 January 1791 (the first English edition would not appear until 12 May).[16] Later that year James Mackintosh would write in *Vindiciae Gallicae* that, while a cold Scot like David Hume might be excused for misunderstanding Rousseau's waywardness, Edmund Burke ought to have sympathized with him, since they resemble one another so closely in their passionate temper.[17] It is likely that the currency of these comparisons encouraged Burke to turn upon Rousseau in his own anti-revolutionary polemics.

These circumstances suggest that Burke's attack on Rousseau might have more contextual depth than is at first apparent given the flippant tone of aggression in which it is couched. But documentary evidence that Burke made any sort of satisfactory engagement with Rousseau's writings is hard to come by. During his editorship of *The Annual Register* Burke had published reviews of two works by Rousseau – the *Lettre à d'Alembert*

(1758, English trans. 1759) on the morality of the stage, and William Kenrick's translation of *Emilius and Sophia: or, a New System of Education* (1762) – both of which make conventional criticisms of Rousseau's tendency to paradox.[18] It is unclear whether or not Burke himself wrote these reviews, although the presence in his library catalogues only of his kinsman Thomas Nugent's rival 1763 translation of *Émile*, and the absence of the *Lettre à d'Alembert*, does not encourage the assumption.[19] We might cautiously infer that Burke retained a casual memory of *Émile* and the *Lettre à d'Alembert* in 1790. But beyond that, only the primary texts of the *Reflections* and *A Letter to a Member of the National Assembly* remain as valid evidence for how Burke read and thought about Rousseau. The problem of Burke's engagement with Rousseau is fundamentally a literary one.

The comments on Rousseau in the *Reflections* are briefer and much less aggressive than those in *A Letter to a Member of the National Assembly*. His line in the *Reflections* is that the revolutionists of Paris have misunderstood the satirical and experimental spirit in which Rousseau wrote, and have mistaken his paradoxical morality for a practicable code of politics: 'these paradoxes become with them serious grounds for action, upon which they proceed in regulating the most important concerns of the state' [251]. Once again, Burke's sphere of reference is basically literary and rhetorical:

> Mr. Hume told me, that he had from Rousseau himself the secret of his principles of composition. That acute, though eccentric, observer had perceived, that to strike and interest the public, the marvellous must be produced; that the marvellous of the heathen mythology had long since lost its effect; that giants, magicians, fairies, and heroes of romance which succeeded, had exhausted the portion of credulity which belonged to their age; that now nothing was left to a writer but that species of the marvellous, which might still be produced, and with as great an effect as ever, though in another way; that is, the marvellous in life, in manners, in characters, and in extraordinary situations, giving rise to new and unlooked-for strokes in politics and morals. [251–2]

This anecdote does not ring true. One principle that remained constant throughout Rousseau's writings was that their author had 'consecrated his life to truth' – *vitam impendere vero*. This is the Juvenalian 'motto' to which he refers in *La Nouvelle Héloïse*, the *Lettre à d'Alembert* and occasionally throughout the major works.[20] His books are a testament to that singular act of devotion: 'I may deceive myself', he warned his readers in the *Lettre à d'Alembert*, 'but I do not deceive you willingly; beware of my errors and not my bad faith.'[21] It is morally implausible that Rousseau should have confessed to Hume, a philosopher whose good opinion he valued (at least while they were on speaking terms), that his whole authorial strategy was an imposition on the credulity of his readers. Neither is it consistent with Rousseau's most direct statement about the effectiveness of his eloquent style (which he links directly with the Juvenalian motto): 'Did I have some true talent for writing?' he wonders in his second autobiographical letter to Malesherbes; 'I do not know. A lively persuasion [*vive persuasion*] has always taken the place of eloquence for me, and I have always written in a cowardly manner and badly when I was not strongly persuaded.'[22] The declaration is striking because 'lively persuasion' is such an ambiguous formulation. Is the object of this 'persuasion' Rousseau's readership (which might otherwise expect conventional 'eloquence'), or Rousseau himself? If the latter, has there been a process of self-persuasion that preceded the act of writing, or has the persuasion come to him as a gift from some other source, human or divine – is his own persuadedness a kind of grace? This ambiguity suggests that Rousseau prefers the origins of his eloquence to remain occult: what matters is that it is 'lively', brave and vigorous. The description in Burke's anecdote of a fantastic style meanly stripped of its fabulousness is thoroughly un-Rousseauian.

So what is the origin of Burke's anecdote about Rousseau?[23] One striking thing about the story is that it reflects obliquely on an aspect of Rousseau's writings that made him somewhat self-conscious: their novelistic tendency towards becoming a 'philosophical romance [*Roman de Philosophie*]', as he sometimes called it.[24] At the crisis of Émile's well-planned meeting with his future wife Sophie, the author declares that it does not matter to him if his readers think the episode romantic: 'A fair romance [*assez beau roman*] it is indeed, the romance of human nature. If it is to be found only in this writing, is that my fault?'[25] Elsewhere in Book v of *Émile*, Rousseau says that the romantic maxims ('ces maximes romanesques') he has been maintaining – that true love is chaste, selfless and ideal – only became ridiculous at a certain historical moment.[26] Previously, their truth to human nature had been generally accepted. So, in the most general terms, Rousseau presents *Émile* as a throwback to the sexual morality of chivalric romance, rather than as a manifesto of post-romantic innovation. Like Burke in the *Reflections*, Rousseau is conscious of the historicity of that 'mixed system of opinion and sentiment [which] had its origin in the ancient chivalry' [113]. The difference is that where Burke believes that it has only recently been destroyed by the *événements* of 1789, Rousseau thinks that it perished somewhat earlier. But Burke's anecdote only seems to skirt around these very Rousseauian topics of genre, sexual morality and the philosophical potential of novelistic realism. It is with the more narrowly rhetorical instrumentality of 'romance' that Burke is concerned, with its capacity to create 'new and unlooked-for' effects of wonder and surprise in the reader. Again, Rousseau anticipated the charge that *Julie, ou la nouvelle Héloïse* represented (in an *esprit romanesque*) human morality pushed to unrecognizable extremes, in his second dialogue-preface to that work: 'Who is daring enough to assign exact limits to nature, and assert: Here is as far as men can go, and no further?' asks R. 'With such fine reasoning', replies N, 'unheard-of Monsters, Giants, Pygmies, fantasies of all kinds, anything could be specifically included in nature ... I repeat, in Tableaux of humankind, Man must be recognizable to everyone.' R's reply is that one must distinguish superficial variations from what is essential to (and fundamentally noble in) the human species.[27] As such, the charge of 'romance' goes to the heart of Rousseau's moral thought, and of his psychological method.

There is a passage on novel-writing in Rousseau's *Confessions* that addresses these themes much more directly, but still within the contextual frame of romantic fantasy. It is worth speculating on whether Burke knew it, because it deals with the technical innovations of Samuel Richardson's novels (which Burke admired), and with Rousseau's claim that *La Nouvelle Héloïse* outdoes *Clarissa* in its psychological intensity. Dismissing the variety of character that Diderot had praised in *Clarissa*, Rousseau suggests that Richardson, in common with 'les plus insipides romanciers', is in fact forced to multiply characters and episodes due to the poverty of his ideas:

> It is easy to wake up attention by incessantly presenting both unknown events and new faces which pass like the figures of the magic lantern: but it is certainly more difficult always to maintain this attention on the same objects and without miraculous adventures [*sans aventures merveilleuses*], and, everything being equal, the simplicity of the subject adds to the beauty of the work. Richardson's novels – superior in so many other things – cannot enter into comparison with mine on that score. It is dead, nevertheless, I know it, and I know the cause; but it will rise from the dead.[28]

This passage, like Burke's anecdote, is structured around a comparison between an old, facile, 'magical' way of awakening the attention of one's readership, and an original, Rousseauian method of doing so. The challenge here, as both Rousseau and Burke understand, is that one must *both* 'strike *and* interest the public' [251, my emphasis]: an audience must be aroused and then absorbed, and neither 'aventures merveilleuses' nor 'the marvellous of the heathen mythology' can do so with the power and simplicity at which Rousseau aims. The correspondence between this passage in the *Confessions* and Burke's anecdote in the *Reflections* about Rousseau's cynical deployment of 'the marvellous in life, in manners, in characters' is not quite close enough, perhaps, to support a positive identification between the two. But we know from *A Letter to a Member of the National Assembly* that Burke had at least a passing acquaintance with the *Confessions*, and there is evidence that Rousseau's remarks on Richardson were of particular interest to his British readers.[29] When Capel Lofft answered Burke's attack on Rousseau in the second edition of his *Remarks on the Letter of the Rt. Hon. Edmund Burke* (1791), he carefully compared the simple sublimity of Julie's death with the elaborate and self-regarding heroism of Clarissa.[30]

On the balance of evidence, it seems likely that Burke fabricated the anecdote that he attributed to Hume. Moreover, Burke's fabrication seems to involve an aggressive redeployment of a passage in Rousseau's own writings, where he professes to reject the facility of romance. Whether or not this passage of the *Confessions* had indeed lodged itself in Burke's memory, his intention is clear: to impute to Rousseau a reliance on the rhetoric of the marvellous that Rousseau himself has disclaimed – *La Nouvelle Héloïse* absorbs its reader, Rousseau insists, *without* the aid of the wonderful. Burke's strategy here is finely critical, unflinchingly negative and somewhat devious. Also, it is connected to a larger and more significant point. Burke shows that Rousseau has taken away from romance the only part that he thought really useful: its foundation in an originally chivalric code of social and sexual restraint, upon which the whole European morality of politeness, civility and *honnêteté* depends. To see the extent of critical engagement that Burke's strategy requires, one must follow Rousseau's argument about the attention-holding qualities of his writing a little further.

TO PERSUADE WITHOUT CONVINCING

Burke's case against Rousseau in the *Reflections* is that the Genevan is a *romancier*, a satirist and a pedlar of moral eccentricities. The force of these accusations is to undermine the positive association of Rousseau with a morality of transparency, sincerity and authenticity, and thus with a mode of political debate that aspires to what his most prominent disciple, Maximilien Robespierre, calls 'the eloquence of the heart without which one cannot succeed in persuading'.[31] Moreover, those revolutionists who deploy Rousseau's ideas in the realm of practical politics are making a category error, Burke argues, based on an absurd misapprehension of literary genre. When Burke extends his critique in *A Letter to a Member of the National Assembly*, however, there is more at stake than simple misreading. Statues have been raised to Rousseau, and his works commended to the public by the state itself.[32] In this heightened ethical context, Rousseau's personal character has become the matter in dispute. For Rousseau is a moralist, says Burke, or he is nothing, and he demands that Rousseau's life be read as part of the moral and political text. Indeed, this is no more than Rousseau had himself implied in *Émile*, when describing the moral experience his hero must finally acquire: 'society must be studied by means of men and men by means of society. Those who want to treat morals and politics separately will never understand anything of either of the two.'[33] Once again, the question raised by Burke's handling of these themes is this: has he grasped them intuitively from limited information? Or has he read far enough into Rousseau's works to see how the authorial subject is constituted in their pages?

In the paragraph of Book XI of the *Confessions* that follows the remarks about Richardson, Rousseau reports some stories of the effects that his novel *Julie* has had upon its public. Of particular interest to Rousseau is the recurring assumption among its readers that Julie must have had a real original, a woman whom the author himself had loved and (by implication) seduced: 'it is certain I wrote this novel in the most burning ecstasies', Rousseau admits, 'but they were wrong when they thought that real objects were needed to produce them; they were far from conceiving to what extent I can catch fire [*je puis m'enflammer*] from imaginary beings'.[34] Rousseau had established this policy of ambiguity in the second dialogue-preface to *Julie*, where N decides that some of the letters are so poorly written that they must be real. R refuses to confirm or deny this inference: 'to declare that one wishes to keep truth unspoken [*veut taire*] is still to honour it. You would have an easier time with a man who was willing to lie.'[35] The point that Rousseau is making here is that the absorption of his best readers has a natural connection with their assumption of the author's personal involvement. These readers have put themselves successfully in the places of the characters represented (to borrow Rousseau's language from the *Lettre à d'Alembert*). This process of identification, as Rousseau conceives it, depends on the general truth of the emotions depicted, rather than upon their historical reality.[36] Rousseau regards this process of emotional generalization or distancing as salutary, and he contrasts it implicitly with the dangerous, contagious, more immediately passionate sympathy that caused Julie's fatal transgression with Saint-Preux: 'I felt myself troubled by his transports, his sighs oppressed my heart', she writes to her cousin Claire; 'I shared his torments, thinking I was merely being compassionate ... Love alone might have spared me; O my Cousin, it was pity [*la pitié*] that undid me.'[37] The uncertainty of his readers about the biographical truth of *Julie* limits their responses to the novel to the degree of tenderness and sympathy, rather than pitching them over into the realm of truly tormenting pity.

By the time Edmund Burke returns to his critique in *A Letter to a Member of the National Assembly*, he has decided that the moral universe of *Julie* is – despite Rousseau's relatively cautious moral psychology – very much more pernicious than he allowed it to be in the *Reflections*. Burke's strategy in this renewed polemic is to take Rousseau's delicate psychology of sympathetic identification, with its subtle connections to the personal history of the author himself, and to conflate it – not without some ingenuity – with Rousseau's more general thinking about education. By consecrating Rousseau as a hero to the Revolution, the French National Assembly encourages every young man of parts to behave like Saint-Preux:

> They systematically corrupt a very corruptible race, (for some time a growing nuisance amongst you) a set of pert, petulant, literators, to whom, instead of their proper, but severe, unostentatious duties, they assign the brilliant part of men of wit and pleasure. They call on the rising generation in France, to take sympathy in the adventures and fortunes, and they endeavour to engage their sensibility on the side of pedagogues, who betray the most awful family trusts, and vitiate their female pupils.[38]

The purpose of this unlikely project is 'to destroy the gentlemen of France', says Burke – by which he means every vestige of social authority of the *ancien régime*.[39] Rousseau is important to the revolutionists, Burke deduces, because his writings (*Julie* especially) have a unique potential to 'form the character of the age' – and they do so not positively, but negatively. To the National Assembly, Rousseau's writings are useful because they are the opposite of ethical: 'no revolution whatsoever *in their disposition* [that of the revolutionists] is to be expected', Burke warns, and they do not intend to alter anybody else's dispositions either. The distinctive effect of Rousseau's writings is that they 'regulate the human will and action' in a way that is somehow anti-moral. Rather than restraining all forms of 'pride, petulance and self-conceit', the National Assembly learns (from *Émile*, one imagines) how to 'artificially foment these evil dispositions, and even form them into springs and actions'. The revolutionists 'find dispositions in the mind . . . for the purposes of such a state as theirs' among 'writers indulgent to the peculiarities of their own complexion'.[40] One would expect the Revolution to be accompanied by a universal moral transformation. Burke's counter-intuitional view of the Rousseauists is that they have triumphed by changing nothing. This reading is all the more plausible, perhaps, because it feels like a Rousseauian paradox.

A Letter to a Member of the National Assembly distorts several aspects of Rousseau's thought. What is even more striking than the distortions, however, is the knowledge of that thought displayed by Burke as he turns it to his own purposes. To begin with, Burke has grasped the basic Rousseauian principle of negative education.[41] Negative education involves not only a tenderness on the instructor's part towards the natural self-love of children (that 'primitive, innate passion, anterior to every other') – which is what Burke has in mind, at least partly, when he describes Rousseau as 'the great professor and founder of *the philosophy of vanity*'.[42] Negative education also involves a fine perspicacity on the part of the instructor with regard to the particular lineaments that primitive passion has left upon the character of the pupil: 'each mind has its own form [*sa forme propre*], according to which it needs to be governed', writes Rousseau in *Émile*; 'the success of one's care depends on governing it by this form and not by another'.[43] The great exemplar of the penetrating eye required to trace such forms of personality is the godlike Wolmar, who portrays himself in *Julie* as a man almost devoid of character, except for his love of order, his pain at the suffering of others and his passion for observation: 'I like to read what is in men's hearts', Julie reports him saying; 'as my own little deludes me [*le mien me fait peu d'illusion*], as I observe composedly [*de sang-froid*] and disinterestedly, and as long experience has given me some sagacity, I scarcely err in my judgments.'[44] It is clear from *A Letter to a Member of the National Assembly* that Burke sees the followers of Rousseau in France not as enthusiasts attracted to the cult of his personality – in the manner of Germaine de Staël or (to take the most relevant British example) Capel Lofft – but as an altogether cooler, more clear-eyed class of statesman.[45] They have more in common with Wolmar than with Rousseau himself.

Burke's explanation for the National Assembly's elevation of Rousseau to the rank of secular saint is that they have identified a special use for his thought. In Rousseau's own terms, they plan to use him as a tool for overcoming the inconvenient distance and opacity that civil society puts between one citizen and another.[46] By turning the rising generation of France into so many versions of Saint-Preux – 'vain', impulsive, isolated – they can turn themselves into all-seeing Wolmars or legislators. After all, as Émile will discover, 'the more [men in civil society] disguise themselves the better one knows them'.[47] It is in this light, albeit from a different perspective, that Burke shows his Parisian correspondent Menonville in *A Letter to a Member of the National Assembly* how 'statesmen, like your present rulers, exist by every thing which is spurious, fictitious and false' in their citizens; 'by every thing which takes man from his house, and sets him on a stage, which makes him up an artificial creature, with painted theatric sentiments, fit to be seen by the glare of candlelight, and formed to be contemplated at a due distance'.[48] It is not the members of the National Assembly, but their audience, the citizenry of France, that is placed upon a stage and made unfamiliar with itself. Throughout his career Burke has argued that in order to speak well about politics one must acquire (and be seen to have acquired) the right sort of knowledge about the characters of one's fellow citizens. Good deliberation and eloquence are the expression of such knowledge. The debates of the National Assembly are flawed deliberations because they substitute an artificial, self-fulfilling romance of political identity for the complex ethical knowledge of the true statesman.

As ever with Burke, ethics and rhetoric are never far apart in his reading of Rousseau. Another of his arguments in *A Letter to a Member of the National Assembly* is that one cannot attribute the effectiveness of Rousseau's writing to a conventional, well-rounded eloquence. Burke sees that Rousseau attracts disciples even though his books are not artistically complete in the way prescribed by Ciceronian rhetoric: they are not as reasoned as they are passionate, as pithy as they are fluent, as cultivated as they are spontaneous. On the contrary, Rousseau is effective because of a certain poverty or lopsidedness in his discourse:

> We certainly perceive, and to a degree we feel, in this writer, a style glowing, animated, enthusiastic; at the same time we find it lax, diffuse, and not in the best taste of composition; all the members of the piece being pretty equally laboured and expanded, without any due selection or subordination of parts. He is generally too much on the stretch, and his manner has little variety. We cannot rest upon any of his works, though they contain observations which occasionally discover a considerable insight into human nature. But his doctrines, on the whole, are so inapplicable to real life and manners, that we never dream of drawing from them any rule for laws or conduct . . .[49]

Part of the point here is that these stylistic vices are all to the purpose. There is something in the lax fluency of Rousseau's prose that disarms the reader. The very 'weakness of language proves strength of feeling', as Rousseau himself suggests in the second preface to *Julie* – an effect that he attributes to our perception that real passion cannot imagine anyone distrusting it, and therefore does not try to persuade.[50] Burke perhaps feels the power of this effect, but he is also keen to account for what has been lost through such an acquisition.

To do so, Burke falls back on the neoclassical discourse of taste: 'a moral taste is not of force to turn vice into virtue', he argues; 'but it recommends virtue with something like the blandishments of pleasure; and it infinitely abates the evils of vice. Rousseau, a writer of great force and vivacity, is totally destitute of taste in any sense of the word.'[51] The connection between stylistic and 'moral' taste here is a conventional one, and has a deep context within Burke's own writings. But again, does it have any real intellectual purchase upon Rousseau's thought? Thirty years earlier, when writing in his 'Introduction on Taste' to the second edition of the *Philosophical Enquiry*, Burke had attempted to identify the basic, universal principles of physiology upon which to base his psychology of aesthetic response. Rousseau, in his important statement on taste in Book IV of *Émile*, argues, on the contrary, that any such search for the origin of sensation is undermined by local geographical and cultural variations in our most simple experiences of taste. Moreover, taste has no true connection with our simple, driving physiological experiences: 'taste is exercised only in regard to things which are neutral [*les choses indifférentes*]', Rousseau says, 'or which are at most of interest and entertainment, and not in regard to those things connected with our needs. To judge the latter, taste is not necessary. Appetite alone suffices.'[52]

The distinction here between the two writers' conceptions of taste – Burke's Lockean search for first psychological principles, versus Rousseau's cautious socialization of taste – foreshadows a more fundamental conflict between their political ideas. In the *Reflections* Burke shows how artistic precepts for the construction of poems can be applied to the construction of states [115]. States, like poems, should be pleasure-giving in their loveliness, an idea Burke illustrates with an Horatian epigram: 'It is not enough for poems to have beauty: they must have charm, and lead the hearer's soul where they will.'[53] In his criticism of Rousseau, Burke turns around his earlier analogy between style and politics. He draws an implied correspondence between Rousseau's failure to select or to subordinate the 'members' of his texts, and the geometrical equality of representation designated in the new French constitution ('the most unequal of all measures in the distribution of men' [255]). One of the ways by which a well-made constitution secures the love of its citizens is through its outward beauty, says Burke – through its maturity, its traditions, its institutional ornaments. The disciples of Rousseau, guided by a paradoxical morality, have no conception of this socializing principle: 'their minds are not only unfurnished with patterns of the fair and good, but by habit they come to take no delight in the contemplation of those things. By hating vices too much, they come to love men too little' [251]. This may not be a particularly faithful reading of Rousseau, but it does suggest what sort of connections and inferences Burke is making within the Rousseauian text, and how carefully he is reading argument against style. It indicates once more how closely questions of rhetoric are bound up with Burke's thinking about the psychological underpinnings of civil life.

When Burke writes that Rousseau is 'totally destitute of taste', either moral or artistic, he assumes that the power and vivacity of Rousseau's writing is in some sense basic, sensual, uncultivated. In the terms of Burke's 'Introduction on Taste', Rousseau's eloquence belongs to the realm of the passions, and not to the realm of judgment, evaluation or reason: 'So far as the imagination and the passions are concerned, I believe it true, that the reason is little consulted', Burke writes in 1759; 'but where disposition, where decorum, where congruity are concerned, in short wherever the best Taste differs from the worst, I am convinced that the understanding operates and nothing else' (*PE*, 26). Transferring these terms to the context of the 1790s, Burke is arguing that the poverty of Rousseau's eloquence is that it acts upon one's heart and imagination, without that action having any true correspondence to the moral arguments that it is enforcing. The shallow powerfulness of Rousseau's style should itself be cause for the reader's suspicion, even before one has attended to the ideas that it is supporting. This assertion of Burke's about Rousseau's lack of taste is interesting because, once again, there are several passages in Rousseau's writings that appear to anticipate it – passages in which the most powerful eloquence is associated with the most primitive performance. The strongest model of eloquence found in Rousseau's writings is that of the Legislator's occult persuasiveness in the *Social Contract*. This model has been the focus of much recent scholarship on Rousseau and rhetoric.[54] For a nascent people to be turned into citizens, Rousseau says in Book II, Chapter 7 of the *Social Contract*, neither violence nor reasoning is useful: the Legislator 'must of necessity have recourse to an authority of a different order, which might be able to rally without violence and to persuade without convincing [*entraîner sans violence et persuader sans convaincre*]'.[55] The Legislator secures the attention of his people by using a melodious, half-articulate, emotional language, saturated with symbols that appeal to each of the senses – a language which 'penetrates to man's inmost being [*jusqu'à l'intérieur de l'homme*], and affects his will no less than his actions'.[56]

Several modern critics of Rousseau's rhetoric have assumed that this idea of a transformative, fatherland-founding eloquence has some correspondence with Rousseau's conception of his own eloquent style, or at least with his view of what true, citizenly oratory could be.[57] It is doubtful, however, that Rousseau thought of this as a relevant model for modern statesmen, or as a useful account of the felicity of his own style. When Rousseau describes more carefully the force of such primitive eloquence in the *Essay on the Origin of Languages*, he pauses again on its neglect of 'grammatical analogy in favor of euphony ... it would persuade without convincing and depict without arguing [*elle persuaderoit sans convaincre et peindroit sans raisonner*]'.[58] But he also insists that these effects are only available within geographical and historical limits – to the early speakers of southern and oriental languages. The nearest equivalent available to Europeans is the silence of '*une matinée à l'anglaise*', spent with a true friend.[59] Where the climate is hot and the land is lush, however, languages are the product of pleasure rather than of need. Their 'seductive accents [*accent séducteur*]' are really an evolved system of gesture.[60] It is true that the youthful Émile is capable of a similar kind of charismatic eloquence, a 'warmth which shines forth in his glance, which is sensed in his speech, which is visible in his actions'.[61] But then Émile is an adolescent, and a sort of refugee from the golden age to boot. In general, modern northern languages such as French and English are formed through necessity and industry: they are characterized by Rousseau as 'muted [*sourdes*], crude, articulated, shrill, monotone, clear by dint of their words [*à force de mots*] rather than of good construction'.[62] It is impossible for peoples to speak such weak languages and to remain free, because it is physically impossible for orators to address popular assemblies while speaking them – the words simply have no resonance in the open air, on the field or in the marketplace. Such is the language that Rousseau writes in himself – such are the natural constraints on his own eloquent style.

For all its powerful negativity, Burke's attack on Rousseau does have a positive corollary: it distinguishes a truly practicable style of political intelligence from Rousseau's exercises in paradoxical morality, without failing to appreciate the brilliance of those exercises. Rousseau had himself insisted on the difference between his eloquent, self-persuaded style and the truly penetrating rhetoric of the legislators, teachers and heroes whose actions he depicts in his major works. Although Rousseau tried on the legislator's mantle when discussing the constitutions of Poland and Corsica, he understood that he lacked the rare and necessary distinction of personal authority required to fulfil that role – and he lacked their peculiar intensity of eloquence as well. As he confesses in the 'Sixth Walk' of the *Rêveries*, his extreme independence of temperament unsuits him to society, and unsuits him especially to the quality of servility required by those who wish to command.[63] Burke and Rousseau are both psychologists and both moralists in their approach to the art of rhetoric. Burke's approach to the art is always practical and political. Rousseau's eloquent style, on the other hand, derives its power from a more wild and elusive principle – as Burke sensed, it is much more difficult to account for by reference to his own reflections upon its workings. Burke acknowledges the predominance of Rousseau's style, but he also predicts the limits of its efficacy. It is too coarse to operate upon the objects of moral taste, and too unlovely to achieve 'that union of minds which alone can produce all the good we aim at' [249].

Burke sets about isolating a principle of intellectual stamina and strength that he can contrast with the argumentative facility or 'genius' of Rousseau and the French orators. He frames this principle in language that describes political intelligence as a cultivated disposition: he writes of 'parts', 'minds', 'powerful and cultivated talents', 'wisdom' and 'ability'. The word 'mind' is especially important in the *Reflections* during the recapitulation and attack on Rousseau: Burke writes of 'a comprehensive and disposing mind', of 'a vigorous mind, [and] steady persevering attention', of how 'mind must conspire with mind', of 'that union of minds', 'the minds and affairs of men', and 'the aid of more minds than one age can furnish'.[64] Burke is describing a style of mind here, much as humanist rhetoricians like George Puttenham thought of literary style as 'the image of man [*mentis character*], for man is but his minde, and as his minde is tempered and qualified, so are his speches and language at large'.[65] Although by this definition Burke's 'mind' is an individuating, characteristic faculty, he puts a defining emphasis on its social tendency – and this emphasis carries an implicit rebuke to Rousseau. At the heart of the recapitulation is Burke's statement of his idea of a 'perfect legislator', and here once again the contrast with Rousseau's legislators is implied throughout:

The true lawgiver ought to have a heart full of sensibility. He ought to love and respect his kind, and to fear himself. It may be allowed to his temperament to catch his ultimate object with an intuitive glance; but his movements towards it ought to be deliberate. Political arrangement, as it is a work for social ends, is to be wrought only by social means. There mind must conspire with mind. Time is required to produce that union of minds which is all the good we aim at. [248–9]

There are three levels of political character in this sketch. As a feeling individual, Burke's legislator is sentimentally responsive to immediate human objects of sympathy. As a thinker, the legislator can grasp the final ends of political action as a matter of intuition. But between these extremes of individual emotion and holistic apprehension, there is the social, slowly reconciling, temperament-producing sphere of practical deliberation. The verb 'conspire' brings this passage to life, adding a dash of dark colour to the innocent talk of social ends. It defines a quality that is missing from Rousseau's eloquence, suggesting instead a political intimacy so close that these legislators breathe together, transforming even intuition and inspiration into a process of mutuality.[66] In the first section of this chapter I mentioned Burke's use of the word 'deliberate' in his speech on representation of 1782. Here once more, its mediating position opens up more than one meaning. As a participial adjective it designates the 'firm but cautious and deliberate spirit' [2] of the Revolution Whigs defended by Burke at the very opening of the *Reflections*. But it also retains its verbal character, implying something like 'characterized by true deliberation' – as opposed to the 'compelled appearance of deliberation' [100] or 'farce of deliberation' [102] practised in the National Assembly. This shading between deliberateness and deliberation goes to the heart of Burke's conception of the good political mind. On the one hand, he expects it to be sluggish, cautious and steady – since deliberation (according to the maxim of Quintilian) is always concerned with doubtful questions.[67] On the other, it should be capable of a certain freedom of movement, and even of a celerity comparable to intuition. Like prejudice, it is of 'ready application in an emergency' [130].

When Burke writes about deliberation he often describes the subject of discussion as a substantial thing, as matter to be grappled and grasped. 'A politician', he insists, 'to do great things, looks for a *power*, what our workmen call a *purchase*; and if he finds that power, in politics as in mechanics he cannot be at a loss to apply it' [232]. This conceptualization of thought in terms of its hold or traction forms a contrast with the slipperiness and evasion of which Burke accuses Rousseau and the orators of the National Assembly. It also draws the reader's attention towards the 'subject' that is being clenched. According to Burke, the good politician gets his purchase on the moral matter of the state, which he takes to be the characters of people and of the institutions into which they are organized.

Personal character is the material upon which statecraft operates, and it is absurd to imagine that even the greatest political ingenuity can mould or form this human matter. As Burke had told Rockingham in 1774, 'we have not the making of men, but must take them as we find them'.[68] 'Wisdom cannot create materials', he rejoins in the *Reflections*; 'they are the gifts of nature or of chance; her pride is in their use' [232].[69] The political culture of Rousseau and the revolutionaries seeks to alter the moral constitution of the state, Burke claims, so as to fit the instrumental ends of their deliberations more efficiently. Whether or not this is an accurate assessment, it allows Burke to define the positive and practical ends of his own rhetoric of character.

Conclusion

In the introduction to this book I mentioned some of the problems of method that make analysing Burke's rhetoric such a complicated task. Should a study of Burke's rhetoric take in the full record of his parliamentary oratory, or focus on his printed publications? Should it look to the classical and humanistic theory of rhetoric as context for his art, or to contemporary seventeenth- and eighteenth-century criticism as a more valid set of intellectual sources? Should we investigate the reception history of Burke's writings and speeches for evidence of how they actually worked as persuasive compositions, or should we concentrate on internal evidence of his rhetorical strategies drawn from the texts themselves?

With each of these three sets of alternatives I have chosen to emphasize the second problem, while keeping an attentive eye on the first. This is because it is these second problems that allow us to get at the fundamental artistic coherence of Burke's rhetoric. Most readers will understand, after only a cursory perusal of, say, the *Reflections on the Revolution in France*, what people mean when they talk about 'Burke's rhetoric', however innocent they may be of the technical discourse of rhetoricians. Obviously enough, the phrase glances at the political context in which Burke's writings were published and his speeches made, and it acknowledges a more or less straightforward design to persuade. But principally the term 'rhetoric' takes in all those qualities of linguistic intensity and argumentative dynamism that Burke's contemporaries found so extraordinary, and that still impress many of his readers today. It involves a sense – gathered perhaps from knowledge of Burke's career, or perhaps caught at by a well-tuned ear – that these literary qualities have some sort of connection with the author's capacity for spontaneous eloquence, and with his development of that capacity through long practice in senatorial oratory. When we talk about Burke's rhetoric we are discussing artistic principles inferred (since he made no systematic statement on the subject) from the ways in which this very literary politician went about speaking, deliberating and writing. This may be only a part of what the early modern schoolmen and some eighteenth-century instructors of elocution meant by 'rhetoric', but it is comprehended within systematic assessments of the art that were current during the seventeenth and eighteenth centuries, as we saw at the start of the book.

In the preceding pages I have described what is most distinctive and coherent about Burke's rhetoric, as understood in this relatively informal sense. The 'body' of Burke's rhetoric (to use Aristotle's metaphor) is ethical. If rhetoric is the art of finding the best available means of persuasion in any given deliberative situation, Burke believes that the proper approach to those means is through the display of good political character, as manifested above all in real knowledge of the characters of those to whom (and of whom, and for whom) one speaks. In other words, when Burke wants to prove a point he is less concerned with moving the passions of his audience, or with convincing them by an immaculate train of logic, than he is with appealing to their moral characters and dispositions. Of course this is not to say that the proofs of pathos and logos have no place in Burke's ethicized rhetoric. Burke thought that all wise legislators share a basic goal. Regarding the citizens on whose behalf they are working, they aim 'at improving instincts into morals, and at grafting the virtues onto the stock of the natural affections'.[1] They find out ways of taking citizens' natural passions and inclinations towards civil life, and of turning them into something more permanent and reasoned: into moralities, into principles, into institutions. This process is greatly facilitated by certain intermediating forms of socialization, or of second nature: by manners ('manners are what vex or sooth, corrupt or purify, exalt or debase, barbarize or refine us, by a constant, steady, uniform, insensible operation, like that of the air we breathe in. They give their whole form and colour to our lives'), and, of course, by habits and prejudices ('prejudice renders a man's virtue his habit; and not a series of unconnected acts. Through just prejudice, his duty becomes a part of his nature').[2]

Virtue and morality, as the refinements of our sociable passions and second natures, are more than adequate ends for the ethical lives of most people. But in the realm of politics, Burke thinks, there is scope to improve those instincts much further. 'The principles of true politicks are those of morality enlarged', he writes in 1771, 'and I neither now do or ever will admit of any other.'[3] The phrase 'morality enlarged' does not refer to ethical metaphysics, or to what he calls elsewhere the 'eternal and immutable rules of morality': Burke is making an analogy here between personal morality and public virtue.[4] When he puts the business of public deliberation in its largest context, he thinks of it as a sort of completion of human nature. Passions and instincts improve into morality, and then morality is fulfilled in political reasoning.[5] 'For man is by nature reasonable', Burke writes in 1791, 'and he is never perfectly in his natural state, but when he is placed where reason may be best cultivated, and most predominates' – the 'where' here refers, of course, to the political state, which he describes in the *Reflections* as 'the necessary means of [our nature's] perfection'.[6] So the business of political deliberation in state institutions offers a unique opportunity for certain privileged people to reconcile their most basic passional instincts with their most exalted potential for reason. The rhetorical language in which that business is conducted will appeal necessarily both to pathos and to logos.[7] But for Burke it is the middle terms of ethos that reconcile and control those discursive extremes of passion and rationality. Instinct is perfected in morality, and morality perfects itself in the rational form of the laws and duties that sustain the state.

It is important to consider Burke's rhetoric in terms of his political thought, because if one concentrates exclusively on his persuasive strategies in specific writings or speeches, the problem of their repeated practical failure becomes obtrusive, and tends to distract attention from more significant coherences. A signal instance of the powerlessness of opposition is the episode of 9 May 1770, when Burke moved a despairingly simple resolution in the House, that 'disorders have of late prevailed' in America.[8] The resolution was put to the previous question (the 'previous question' always being whether the question should be asked at all) so as to avoid the need to vote on it. 'I fear', Burke later complained, 'that ere long, our rights, freedom, spirit, nay the House itself, will vanish in a previous question.'[9] As we have seen, for all his vaunted eloquence Burke was not very good at winning the hearts or minds of voters. Some of Burke's readers have found arguments for using his political failures to dismiss his achievements as a statesman.[10] But most literary readers will be alert to the more interesting paradox that his failures produce: on the one hand, Burke's rhetoric throughout his career is evidently the product of a strenuous and unceasing struggle to find the best available means of persuasion; on the other, the reader is often aware that the immediate practical end of winning votes is not always important to him. The question put to him by Richard Brinsley Sheridan in 1778 – how can Burke take such pains over his speeches, 'knowing with certainty that it could produce no effect?' – really is the crucial one.[11] Burke answers plausibly that he is more interested in effecting small improvements to the general opinions of Parliament, and that in any case he enjoys making an oratorical coup for its own sake, or for that of his reputation. But it is easy to infer how much more he might have said.

Although Burke describes the state as a providential means for bringing humans up towards perfection, he never confuses ultimate human perfectibility with the perfectibility of political institutions:

> There is, by the essential fundamental constitution of things, a radical infirmity in all human contrivances; and the weakness is so often attached to the very perfection of our political mechanism, that some defect in it – something that stops short of its principle, something that controls, that mitigates, that moderates it – becomes a necessary corrective.[12]

So the standard of perfectibility in political deliberation, as in all other things moral and political, is adjusted merely to the 'fallible and feeble contrivances of our reason' – whereas the final perfectibility of humans themselves is measured by a standard natural, rational and divine.[13] Burke's relative indifference to the immediate consequences of his rhetoric is characteristic of a more general doubt that he has about the direction of political actions towards 'perfect' ends: 'The *means* to any end being first in order', he tells Charles-Jean-François Depont, 'are *immediate* in their good or their evil; they are always, in a manner, *certainties.* The *end* is doubly problematical; first, whether it is to be attained; then, whether, supposing it attained, we obtain the true object we sought for.'[14] Burke is writing here about the broadest principles of political action, but the point is applicable to his art of rhetoric and to his local argumentative strategies as well. It is a distraction to worry too much about the particular ends of persuasion, because the nature of national politics makes it so very difficult to bring strangers over to your own point of view. And even when an opponent does confess himself convinced, there is every chance that he will have misunderstood the content of the argument. If you can secure the validity of your argumentative 'means', on the other hand – and especially if those means are given the permanency of a published, celebrated text – their immediate effects (as opposed to their final ends) become to an extent durable and certain. In order for the 'means' to be plausible they must of course move vigorously, as though towards a real end of persuasion. But the final attainment of that end is not a necessary criterion of effectiveness, however exhausting or dispiriting the personal failure may be. Burke can expect a large proportion of the readership for any one of his tracts to be unpersuaded by his specific proposals, while anticipating that a good part of that large proportion will find themselves moved by his language, or impressed by the authority of his counsel, or obliged to adopt his language and ideas when they turn to deliberate on the same questions themselves. These are the sorts of effect that Burke's rhetoric is designed to create, and they are consistent with his larger vision of politics.

The apparent failure of Burke's rhetoric to attain its persuasive ends relates to another problem in my account of its function. As we have seen in the last three chapters, there is a conflict between his repeated professions about the duty of statesmen to follow the opinions of the people they represent, and his violent resistance to the attempts of electors to issue parliamentary instructions to MPs on particular issues. Once again, Burke's habits of defiance seem to be at variance with the arts of attentiveness to (and complicity with) public opinion that he identifies as essential to the good deliberator. In *Thoughts on the Present Discontents* Burke had made explicit the connection between personal ethos and public opinion. We are dependent for both of them on an uncontrollable popular decision: 'I have nothing to do here with the abstract value of the voice of the people. But as long as reputation, the most precious possession of every individual, and as long as opinion, the great support of the State, depend entirely upon that voice, it can never be considered as a thing of little consequence either to individuals or to Government.'[15] Again, Burke holds that the rights of government over a people cannot be 'safely exercised', as he tells his Bristol electors in 1777, 'without regard to the general opinion of those to be governed':

> The general opinion is the vehicle, and organ of legislative omnipotence . . . In effect, to follow, not to force the publick inclination; to give a direction, a form, a technical dress and a specific sanction, to the general sense of the community, is the true end of legislature . . . it [is] our duty, in all soberness, to conform our Government to the character and circumstances of the several people who compose this mighty and strangely diversified mass.[16]

As we have seen, Burke thinks that the validity of any given political deliberation can be judged by how it proves the deliberator's knowledge of the 'character and circumstances' of the people he represents. And yet the *Letter to the Sheriffs of Bristol*, from which this passage is taken, is a document of Burke's contempt for the cruel hostility of British public opinion towards the American revolutionists of 1776. This consciousness of how deeply his conciliatory hopes differed from the general opinion of the electorate leads ultimately to the despairing defiance of his speech previous to the Bristol election of September 1780: 'I did not obey your instructions: No. I conformed to the instructions of truth and nature, and maintained your interest, against your opinions, with a constancy that became me.'[17] In a letter to the Duke of Portland sent three days before this speech, Burke writes of how much he would rather, 'innocently and obscurely, mix with them [his constituents], with the utter ruin of all my hopes, (which hopes are my all) than betray them by learning lessons from them. They are naturally proud, tyrannical, and ignorant; bad scholars and worse masters.'[18]

The disparity between Burke's professions of popular opinion, and his resistance to that opinion in its most direct manifestation, reveals something more than a conflict between optimistic rhetoric and defeated realism, I think. It also tells us something crucial about the relatively limited scope of Burke's rhetoric, for all its expanding sphere of international engagement. There is always the temptation to think of his parliamentary failures as a precondition for his larger literary success: the thought of the indifference of the Commons adds a relish to the retired reader's subsequent assent. But Burke's ethicized rhetoric is inseparably tangled with the business of representing the opinions and characters of the political nation in Parliament. All the same, it makes no artistic sense to think of Burke's rhetoric as having been addressed directly to that political nation. The parliamentary setting is indispensable, because it is only through the representative (one might almost say, imaginary) medium of the House of Commons that the deliberative independence of statesmen (their independence as characters) can be reconciled with their duty of reflecting the opinions of a passionate, unreflective political nation. This is why Burke's public character as an MP remains so important even in an avowedly extra-parliamentary text like the *Reflections*.

Edmund Burke's rhetoric refines and reinvigorates an ancient art by obliging those who read and hear him to justify their principles of political deliberation against a theory of government. It is this critical cast in his rhetoric that makes it so original, and that ensures its continued readability two-and-a-half centuries after the works of his oratorical rivals – Pitts elder and younger, Fox, Sheridan – translated so disappointingly from debating chamber to press. The question of how politicians should find a power or purchase on the minds of nations gave Burke a great political theme. It also allowed him to move beyond the common conception of rhetoric as a language technology for producing persuasion, towards a more comprehensive and artistic model for writing and speaking on civil matters.

Where Burke's rhetoric seems most brilliant and progressive, however, the ethical ideas that energize it seem, on their own terms, somewhat less sophisticated than one would expect. For somebody who wrote and talked so much about character, it is interesting (although perhaps unsurprising, given his conventionally Augustan moral principles) that one finds no hint of thought about how human personalities can change, or what the best conditions for their flourishing might be. There is no timetable for the process of human perfectibility. Burke's theory of character is immediately social and political, and it seems likely that John Stuart Mill's Humboldtian rule of ethical development would have been quite incomprehensible to him, had he somehow been able to anticipate it: 'Where, not the person's own character, but the traditions or customs of other people are the rule of conduct, there is wanting one of the principal ingredients of human happiness, and quite the chief ingredient of individual and social progress.'[19] It is the 'other people' here that Burke would have found hardest to imagine – his idea of custom did not extend to the possibility that people of other traditions and practices might intrude into the kind of deliberations where social progress is on the agenda in any sort of legitimate or practical way.

There is little purpose in using the expansive generosity of Burke's sympathies with Britain's colonial subjects as a defence against the charge of failed imagination here. But it is arguable that Burke's conception of character is lighter and more other-directed, more pragmatically impressionistic than that of Mill or Coleridge. In his student notebook Burke writes:

> Say they, moral Precepts when graced with the advantages of Eloquence, invite the inattentive, and by being mixed with something pleasurable, make a deeper Impression. It is true they do so; but in fact the great Powers of Eloquence ... and the great Benefits that result from them, are not in giving Precepts but in creating Habits ... for it is the Bias the Mind takes that gives direction to our Lives; and not any Rules or Maxims of Morals and Behaviour.[20]

Burke cannot be thinking of eloquence as an action of limited and local persuasion. For it to take on a habit-creating and life-directing power it must be a long-term study – '*abeunt studia in mores*', he wrote of the American colonists, one's common pursuits pass over into character – and it must be an object of study.[21] The habits must themselves be dynamic and responsive, not constraining in the way that Mill saw them. This is the possibility that animates Burke's highly literary, highly ethicized rhetoric.

Notes

INTRODUCTION: BURKE, RHETORIC AND ETHICS

1 Wordsworth to William Matthews, 17 June 1791, in Wordsworth, *Letters*, 62.
2 Roe, *Wordsworth and Coleridge*, 28–31.
3 Wordsworth, *Fourteen-Book Prelude*, IX.97, p. 182.
4 *Ibid.*, VII.499–511, pp. 150–1.
5 For Burke as the 'dinner-bell', driving younger MPs to supper when he rose to speak, see Bryant, 'Contemporary Reception', 272–3.
6 Burke, *Reflections* [96]. I have adopted the convention established by F.P. Lock of making references in square brackets, e.g., [46], to the pagination of the 1790 first edition as given by Clark, though always using the text as established in his Stanford edition.
7 Wordsworth, *Fourteen-Book Prelude*, V.498–9, p. 107.
8 See McFarland, *Heritage of Rousseau*, 66; cf. Wu, *Wordsworth's Reading*, 119–20; but cf. also Voisine, *Rousseau en Angleterre*, 479; Mitchell argues in his article 'Influence' that Wordsworth worked hard to suppress any possible parallels between himself and Rousseau in the 1805 *Prelude*.
9 Burke, *Reflections* [251–2].
10 See Chandler, *Wordsworth's Second Nature*, 15–30; for Rousseauian echoes here, see Dart, *Rousseau*, 163–70.
11 Wordsworth, *Fourteen-Book Prelude*, V.497, p. 107; cf. the 'dark | Inscrutable workmanship' of I.341–2, p. 37.
12 Alexander Pope, 'Epistle to a Lady', line 2 (all references to Pope are to the *Twickenham Edition*; for echoes of the line through the eighteenth century, see Nussbaum, *Brink of All We Hate*, 2, 49–50; cf. Mill, *On Liberty*, 67.
13 Smiles, *Self-Help*, 7, 28; for context here, see Collini, 'Character'.
14 Mill, *On Liberty*, 69; Collini, 'Character', 37–8.
15 Burke, *Reflections* [75].
16 On the study of rhetoric as comprehensive strategy (rather than semiotic system or material trace), see Ong, *Presence of the Word*, 214–22; Struever's theory of rhetoric as 'a permanent subjective mental mode', *Language of History*, esp. 155; Lanham, *Motives of Eloquence*, 1–35; and William J. Kennedy, *Rhetorical Norms*, 8–14.
17 See Burke to Boswell, 20 July 1791, in Boswell, *Correspondence*, 162–3.

18 Sheridan's question has a similar form to the bitter remark he later made to Samuel Rogers: 'When posterity read the speeches of Burke, they will hardly be able to believe that during his life-time he was not considered as a first-rate speaker, not even as a second-rate one' (Dyce, *Table-Talk of Samuel Rogers*, 67). For Goldsmith on the political ineffectiveness of Burke's eloquence, see 'The Haunch of Venison, a Poetical Epistle to Lord Clare', lines 69–72, and 'Retaliation', lines 29–42, in Gray, Collins and Goldsmith, *Poems*, 701, 748–9.

19 Boswell, *Life of Johnson*, vol. III, 233–4.

20 *WS*, vol. II, 299.

21 For the opposition's dominance in debate during Burke's career, see P. D. G. Thomas, *House of Commons*, 240–2.

22 In this respect Burke's view of oratory resembles that of the Earl of Chesterfield: cf. Chesterfield, *Letters*, vol. IV, 1442–3, 1461, 1700, etc.

23 *Letter to a Noble Lord*, *WS*, vol. IX, 182. For Burke on vanity and eloquence, see *Letter to a Member of the National Assembly*, *WS*, vol. VIII, 311–14.

24 Burke, *Appeal*, 32.

25 It is not a function of Burke's ethicized rhetoric to take the next logical step, however, and distinguish individual readers within these particular audiences, for which see Ong, 'Writer's Audience'.

26 Aristotle, *Rhetoric*, I.i.11 (1355a3–19), I.ii.2–3 and 8–11 (1355b35–1356a13 and 1356b1–25), II.xx.1–9 (1393a23–1394a8). For the meaning of *pistis*, see Grimaldi, *Aristotle's Rhetoric*, 58 ff.; in *De Institutio oratoria*, V.x.8, Quintilian is reluctant to translate *pistis*, 'quod etiam si propria interpretatione dicere fidem possumus, apertius tamen probationem interpretabimur' ('a term which, although the literal rendering is "a warrant of credibility", we shall make clearer sense of if we call it "proof"').

27 Aristotle, *Rhetoric*, I.viii.5–6 (1366a2–17); II.i.2–3 (1377b20–8); II.vi.14–18 (1384a21–35). For the dominance of ethos, see Garver, *Aristotle's Rhetoric*, 142–54; for a contextual account, see Christopher Carey, 'Rhetorical Means', 406–11.

28 Aristotle, *Rhetoric*, III.xvii.7–8 (1418a9–20).

29 *Ibid.*, I.ii.4 (1356a6–8) (trans. Freese).

30 Aristotle, *Nichomachean Ethics*, I.xiii.20 (1103a7–10) (trans. Rackham); see Striker, 'Emotions in Context'.

31 Aristotle, *Rhetoric*, II.i.3–4 (1377b24–33).

32 *Speech at Bristol Previous to Election* (1780), *WS*, vol. III, 626.

33 Burke, *Reflections* [73–4].

34 Burke makes the same pun in *Appeal*, 130, again while discussing aristocracy: 'The state of civil society which necessarily generates this aristocracy is a state of Nature, and much more truly so than a savage and incoherent mode of life. For man is by nature reasonable; and he is never perfectly in his natural state, but when he is placed where reason may be best cultivated.' Once again, his use of the word 'reasonable' is lexically strained, apparently meaning 'capable of reason' (as the compilers of the *OED* have noticed: see quotations for 'reasonable', 1a.); in the *Speech on Conciliation* he trusts the Commons will

not 'reject a reasonable proposition, because it had nothing but reason to recommend it' (*WS*, vol. III, 108).

35 *WS*, vol. II, 194.

36 *WS*, vol. III, 130, with echo of Matthew 26.73: 'Surely thou also art *one* of them; for thy speech bewrayeth thee.'

37 *Letter to the Sheriffs of Bristol* (1777), *WS*, vol. III, 315.

38 *WS*, vol. II, 252.

39 *WS*, vol. III, 491, 493, with echoes of Genesis 17.1 (cf. Psalms 85.13 and Luke 24.15 ff.)

40 Burke, *Reflections* [59].

41 Burney, 16 February 1788, *Journals and Letters*, vol. III, 448–9; see Bolton, 'Imperial Sensibilities'.

42 Boswell, *Private Papers*, vol. VI, 83; cf. vol. XIII, 220.

43 Wraxall, *Historical Memoirs*, vol. II, 36.

44 *Corr.*, vol. I, 241; and cf. 243.

45 *Ibid.*, 243. Although dated later, this letter must have preceded the one quoted in n.44 above.

46 For the classic contemporary statement of these themes, see Samuel Johnson's *Rambler*, in *Yale Works*, esp. vol. III, 13, 74–80, 169, 216 ff.; vol. IV, 258–64; vol. V, 13–17.

47 Flood to Lord Charlemont, in Charlemont, *Manuscripts and Correspondence*, 391; William Hazlitt made similar comments on Burke's speeches, in 'On the Difference between Writing and Speaking', *Complete Works*, vol. XII, 268–9, 275–6.

48 In *Observations on the Conduct of the Minority* Burke wrote that Fox's speeches were always done justice by the press (*WS*, vol. IX, 448).

49 For a comparative analysis, see *EB*, vol. II, 116–17.

50 See Christopher Reid, 'Foiling the Rival'.

51 Sheridan's speech of 7 February 1787 was printed as *The Genuine Speech of Mr. Sheridan . . .* (1787), and also as *The Speech of R.B. Sheridan, Esq. . .* (1787). Both transcriptions ran to second editions.

52 Anecdote passed down to the Burke editor Bliss Perry, and recorded by Bryant, 'Contemporary Reception', 274.

53 Wollstonecraft, *Rights of Men*, 61, 5.

54 See esp. *Report on the Lords' Journals* (1794), *WS*, vol. VII, 122–31.

55 Paine, *Rights of Man*, 59; Mackintosh, *Vindiciae Gallicae*, 7.

56 *Political Correspondence*, 72–3.

57 See, for example, Cicero, *De oratore*, I.xxxii.146; Augustine adds that good orators practise the rules thus observed because they are eloquent, but not in order to become eloquent (*On Christian Teaching*, IV.iii.11–12, p. 103), a point much emphasized by Arnauld and Nicole in *Logic*, III.xvii.183. For a contemporary discussion of artistic categories, see James Harris, *Three Treatises*, 15–17.

58 For Quintilian's early scepticism about naturalness in rhetoric, see *Institutio oratoria*, XII.x.40–4.

59 The phrase is used by Cicero (*Pro Archia*, 3, 16), and applied by the humanists to their reformed university syllabuses, as described by Kristeller, *Renaissance Thought*, 9–11, 19–21, 92–119.
60 For Burke on 'second nature', see *WS*, vol. VII, 540; cf. Canavan, *Political Reason*, 63.
61 *WS*, vol. III, 547.
62 Burke, *Appeal*, 130; for similar commonplaces, cf. Browne, *Religio Medici*, 16: 'Art is the perfection of Nature'; and Hobbes, *Leviathan*, 9: 'Nature (the Art whereby God hath made and governes the World)'.
63 See, for example, *WS*, vol. II, 279: 'The people, by their representatives and grandees, were entrusted with a deliberative power in making laws; the King with the control of his negative.'
64 For Isocrates, see *WS*, vol. I, 134; for Tacitus, *WS*, vol. IX, 163, and *Corr.*, vol. VII, 99; for Quintilian, *WS*, vol. III, 242, where Burke also mentions some modern writers on rhetoric: Fénelon, Rollin, Fordyce and Chesterfield.
65 Weinberg, 'Translations and Commentaries'; Cronk, *Classical Sublime*; Lamb, 'Sublime'.
66 Canter, 'Impeachments'; Browning, 'Origin', esp. 60–4; Carnall, 'Modern Cicero'.
67 Burke, *WS*, vol. III, 157; Hampsher-Monk, 'Rhetoric and Opinion'; Lock, 'Rhetoric and Representation'; and Bruyn, 'Uses of Eloquence'.
68 Hampsher-Monk, 'Rhetoric and Opinion', 461.
69 In 1770 Burke described opinion (along with character) as 'the great support of the State', *WS*, vol. II, 252; cf. *Address to the King* (1777), *WS*, vol. III, 263; Burke's thought on character is an emotionalized development of the view, explored by Adam Smith and David Hume (and conventional before then), that opinion is the foundation of government; see Haakonssen, *Science*, 131–2.
70 In the *Fourth Letter on a Regicide Peace* (1795) Burke wrote of 'the spirit of our Laws, or that of our own dispositions, which are stronger than Laws', *WS*, vol. IX, 110.
71 Hampsher-Monk, 'Rhetoric and Opinion', 464.
72 Lock, 'Rhetoric and Representation', 25.
73 The debate over the relevance of the concept of the sublime to Burke's later writings is perhaps more open than Lock acknowledges: the coherence hypothesis first laid out by Wood, 'Aesthetic Dimension', is refined by (among others) David Jules Law, *Rhetoric of Empiricism*, 131–64; and Lamb, 'Sublime', 403–6.
74 Paulson, *Representations of Revolution*, 71, 67; Weiskel, *Romantic Sublime*, 97–9.
75 Samuel Johnson, *Rambler* no. 49, in *Yale Works*, vol. III, 265.
76 For the fragmentation of rhetoric after the late seventeenth century, see Vickers, 'Royal Society'; for the complexities of Locke's attack on and reabsorption of rhetoric, see Walker, *Locke*, 112–27.
77 The Oxford edition of *Aristotelous technes rhetorikes biblia tria* (1759) appears as item 15 in Burke's printed library catalogue; there is no evidence that Burke

kept up his undergraduate Greek, however: see *Corr.*, vol. VI, 36, and the diffident footnote regarding his knowledge of Aristotle's *Politics*, in *Reflections* [186].

78 See, for example, *Note-Book*, 86–7: 'perhaps the mind can do more in sudden starts than in an even progression'; for rhetoric and system, see Ong, *Ramus.*

79 *LRBL*, 25; for the integrating turn in rhetorical studies, see Bitzer, 'Rhetorical Situation', and White, *Human Discourse.*

80 The best summary of these problems is in Christopher Reid, *Edmund Burke*, 118–36.

81 The editors of the Clarendon *Writings and Speeches of Edmund Burke* have identified about thirty Commons speeches for which we have both reports or transcriptions of the speech as it was delivered and manuscript notes or drafts prepared to help their delivery; there are a very few cases (e.g., *Speech on the Use of Indians*, 6 February 1778, *WS*, vol. III, 354) in which Burke supplied the periodical press with a copy of his speech.

82 Todd, *Bibliography*, 24, 25, 31, 33, 44, 46, 47, 52.

83 *Ibid.*, 18–23, 35–40, 30; the Hastings speeches include the articles of impeachment (48), the reports to the Select Committee on India (41), the 1792 *Speech in Westminster Hall* (61) and the speech in answer to observations on the managers of the Hastings trial (64).

84 This category is represented by the nine speeches printed from MS fragments by Laurence and King in *Works . . . of Edmund Burke*, vol. V, 321–423, which include *On the Reform of the Representation in the House of Commons, 7 May 1782* (387–98); Todd comments: 'Even in the exceptional texts, as available in the revised *Works*, there is the constant danger of further revision by the executors' (*Bibliography*, 233).

85 See *WS*, vol. II, 359, 368, 381; 370, 377; Burke's second speech on conciliation with the colonies, of 16 November 1775, was worked up, presumably with a view to publishing it as a companion piece to its more successful twin (*WS*, vol. III, 183 ff.).

86 *Corr.*, vol. II, 178; see also vol. II, 532, vol. IV, 394, vol. V, 254, 296, vol. VI, 97; cf. Malone to Burke, 16 December 1792, *Corr.*, vol. VII, 323–4.

87 *Third Letter on a Regicide Peace*, *WS*, vol. IX, 354.

88 One contemporary assessment of Burke's elocution is *Review of the Parliamentary Conduct of . . . Charles James Fox and . . . Edmund Burke* (1789), which in fact covers the issue in a single sentence: 'Mr. Burke's voice is manly, clear, and mellow, his manner animated, and action not ungraceful' (77).

89 Christopher Reid, 'Speaking Candidly', and 'Character Construction'; Wilkinson, 'Politics and Topography'; and see also articles on Parliament and print culture by Jason Peacey, Michael Harris, James E. Bradley and Ian Harris in a special issue of *Parliamentary History*, 26 (2007).

90 The History of Parliament Trust has archived photocopies and transcripts from the parliamentary diaries of Henry Cavendish (MS in British Library,

1768–74), Matthew Brickdale (Bristol University Library, 1770–4) and James Harris (Hampshire Record Office, Malmesbury Papers, 1781–6), as well as the reports made by James Watt and George Onslow for the Duke of Newcastle, and by James Harris and others for the Hardwicke family.

91 See Burke to Archbishop Markham, post 9 November 1771: 'After stating by an Aposeopesis, the force of which mode of speech no one better understands than our Lordship ...' (*Corr.*, vol. II, 260); see also *WS*, vol. III, 139; Burke's tumultuous speech on the atrocities at Rangpur on 18 February 1788 ended in physical collapse; several ladies (including the actress Sarah Siddons) fainted on the same day; Sheridan later sank into Burke's arms at the end of a fourteen-hour speech on 13 June; Hastings complained that the managers had turned a grave parliamentary trial into a theatrical entertainment: see Hastings to Thompson, 17 July 1788, in *Harper's Monthly Magazine*, quoted in *EB*, vol. II, 190.

92 See Gray and Hindson, 'French Revolution as Drama'; and Russell, 'Burke's Dagger'.

93 *Parliamentary History of England*, vol. XXX, 189.

94 Robinson, *Edmund Burke*, 162–6; see Bruyn, 'Political Quixote'.

95 Robinson, *Edmund Burke*, 133, 137, 146, 149, 155, 157, 163, 164, 166, 172.

96 Ralph Broome, in *Letters from Simpkin*, I, draws attention to Burke's peculiarly aggressive way of nodding his head as he spoke.

97 *WS*, vol. II, 301, vol. III, 152, vol. VIII, 296; *Reflections* [37, 59].

98 *On the Reform of the Representation*, in *Works of Edmund Burke*, vol. V, 387–99, at 394; the tag, which is from the *Astronomica* of Manilius ('reason is never deceived, nor ever deceives'), seems to have been a shibboleth for radical Enlightenment writers earlier in the century.

99 'Several Scattered Hints Concerning Philosophy and Learning', *Note-Book*, 84.

1 THE ETHICAL TURN IN EARLY MODERN RHETORIC, 1600–1760

1 Bacon, *Advancement of Learning*, 148, 127, 133–4; for Bacon's realist treatment of ethics and psychology, see Dean, 'Civil History-Writing'; and on Bacon's 'psychology of discovery', see Wallace, *Nature of Man*.

2 Bacon, *Advancement of Learning*, 147.

3 Bacon, 'Translation of *De Augmentis*', in Works, vol. V, 21; see Nadel, 'History as Psychology', esp. 283–6; and Jardine, *Discovery*, 151–6.

4 Bacon, *Advancement of Learning*, 149.

5 *Ibid.*, 150.

6 Vickers shows that Bacon's idea of the mechanics of rhetoric (and of the imagination in particular) is drawn from Aristotelian and Galenic faculty psychology, in 'Bacon and Rhetoric', 213–22; the point I make here is more general.

7 Aristotle, *Rhetoric*, II.i.4 (1377b28–1378a29).

8 Rainolds, *Oxford Lectures*, 68.

9 Bacon, *Advancement of Learning*, 127, 148.
10 *Ibid.*, 177.
11 Bacon, 'Translation of *De augmentis*', *Works*, vol. v, 22.
12 Bacon, *Advancement of Learning*, 168.
13 The *locus classicus* is Montaigne, *Essais*, i.xxxviii ('Comme Nous Pleurons et Rions d'une Mesme Chose'), vol. i, 383: 'Et tout ainsi qu'en nos corps ils disent qu'il y a une assemblée de diverses humeurs, desquelles celle-là est maîstresse qui commande le plus ordinairement en nous, selon nos complexions: aussi en nos âmes' ('Even as there is said to be a variety of humours assembled in our bodies, the dominant one being that which normally prevails according to our complexion, so too in our souls', trans. Screech, 263); although this is later developed into his idea of the *forme maistresse*, as discussed by Screech, *Montaigne and Melancholy*, 100–6; cf. Pope, *An Essay on Man*, ii.123–44, and *Epistle to Cobham*, lines 174–209.
14 Bacon, *Advancement of Learning*, 145; Puttenham, *Arte of English Poesie*, 64.
15 Crane, 'Relation'.
16 See the 'Explanatory Notes' to Vickers's edition of *The Essays*, 161, 163–4, 167, 211–12.
17 Bacon, *Essayes Civill and Morall*, 170; cf. Aristotle, *Rhetoric*, ii.i.9, where the emotion of anger is used as the example for this sort of tripartite division.
18 A recent exception is Gross, *Secret History of Emotion*, esp. 39–43.
19 See esp. Howell's survey of the early modern period in *British Logic and Rhetoric*; or, on a larger scale, Conley, *European Tradition*, 151 ff.; Fumaroli (ed.), *Histoire de la rhétorique*, represents an alternative to the totalizing survey, as discussed previously by Fumaroli in *Âge de l'éloquence*, 16.
20 Aristotle, *Rhetoric*, i.ii.7 (1356a25); i.i.1 (1354a1).
21 *Ibid.*, i.i.3 (1354a15).
22 *Ibid.*, iii.xvii.7–8 (1418a9–21).
23 *Ibid.*, ii.xxi.16 (1395b12–13); i.ii.4 (1356a8–10).
24 *Ibid.*, i.ii.4 (1356a13). Ethos controls rhetorical logos because enthymemes are built up from commonplace maxims (*gnome*), and it is by the appropriate use of maxims that the orator connects with the moral sense of a community: 'Such speeches have an ethos in which the moral purpose [*prohairesis*, or choice] is clear', he writes. 'And this is the effect of all maxims, because he who uses them in a general manner declares his moral preferences, so if the maxims are good, they also make the speaker seem of good character', ii.xxi.2 (1394a26–8); ii.xxi.16 (1395b14–17); cf. *Poetics*, xv (1454a16–26). Ethos controls pathos in so far as the knowledge of human passions and habits required by the orator for persuading by pathos is a subset of the knowledge needed for persuading by ethos, *Rhetoric*, ii.xii.2 (1388b31). For a popular eighteenth-century discussion of maxims, see Fuller, *Gnomologia*, A4^{v}–A5^{r}.
25 Aristotle, *Rhetoric*, ii.i.7 (1378a15–19).
26 *Ibid.*, iii.vii.6 (1408a26); cf. *Poetics*, xv (1454a21).
27 Aristotle, *Rhetoric*, ii.xii.2 (1388b34–5); iii.vii.7 (1408a30–1).
28 *Ibid.*, iii.vii.4 (1408a20).

29 Quintilian, *Institutio oratoria*, VI.ii.8–19, 9; see Wisse, *Ethos and Pathos*, 222–49.
30 Cicero, *De oratore*, II.xxix.128, xliii.182–3 for *conciliare*; for *ingenium* (or *natura*), I.xxv.113–15, xxxii.146; see Enos and Schnakenberg, 'Helenic Ethos', where the Ciceronian terms *prudentia*, *diligentia* and *dignitas* are also discussed.
31 Cicero, *De oratore*, II.xliii.184; this element is missing from the discussion of *notatio* in *Rhetorica ad Herennium*, IV.L.63–li.65.
32 Quintilian, *Institutio oratoria*, VI.ii.8, 17: 'cum hos imitamur ex his ducimus orationem'; Skinner reads this passage out of context in *Reason and Rhetoric*, 128, assuming that it refers only to the orator's own character.
33 Quintilian, *Institutio oratoria*, VI.ii.9–10; see George Kennedy, *Art of Rhetoric*, 222–3.
34 Seneca, *Epistulae morales*, XCV.65–6 (trans. Gummere, vol. III): 'hanc Posidonius *ethologian* vocat, quidam *characterismon* appellant, signa cuiusque virtutis ac vitii et notas reddentem, quibus inter se similia discriminentur. Haec res eandem vim habet quam praecipere.'
35 For the ancients, see Quintilian, *Institutio oratoria*, IX.ii.30 ff., XII.x.60–2; for a wide-ranging account, see Alexander, 'Prosopopoeia'.
36 Shakespeare, *Julius Caesar*, III.i.72–3, III.ii.228–30.
37 Quintilian, *Institutio oratoria*, IV.i.63–70, IV.ii.106–7, IX.ii.38–40; Alexander ('Prosopopoeia', 99, 263 n.7) cites Aphthonius' *Progymnasmata* (1572) as the fullest discussion of *ethopoeia*.
38 The discussion of what Bacon calls 'the seueral characters & tempers of mens Natures and dispositions' also happens under the descriptions of 'knowledge of the world', 'the knowledge of men', 'reading men and manners'; in this chapter I treat these terms as more or less interchangeable.
39 Fumaroli, *Âge de l'éloquence*, 678: '[la description] peut s'accompagner d'une sorte de bande sonore qui donne une voix aux choses ou aux personnages décrits: interrogation, dialogisme, prosopopée'; for *enargeia*, see Quintilian, *Institutio oratoria*, IV.ii.63–6, IX.ii.40; and Cave, *Cornucopian Text*, 27–34, 130–4.
40 Fumaroli, *Âge de l'éloquence*, esp. 257–391.
41 Le Moyne, *Peintures morales*, discussed by Fumaroli, *Âge de l'éloquence*, 379–91.
42 For Vossius and Aristotelian rhetoric, see Laurens, 'Vossius', 508.
43 Various anomalies in the text have persuaded Hobbes scholars such as Karl Schuhmann and Quentin Skinner that the attribution of the *Briefe* (as opposed to the manuscript Latin paraphrase now among the Chatsworth muniments, which is in Hobbes's hand) is wrong; see Skinner, *Visions of Politics*, vol. III, 4, 43–4.
44 See Rapin, *Critical Works*, vol. II, 43 (cf. Preface, vol. II, [ii]); Lawson, among others, makes the same point in his *Lectures Concerning Oratory*, 46.
45 Locke, 'Mr Locke's Extemporè Advice &c.', in *Some Thoughts Concerning Education*, 325, where Locke mentions 'Satyrical writings also, such as

Juvenal, and Persius, and above all Horace, tho they paint the Deformities of Men, yet thereby they teach us to know them'; for dating of this transcript to 1703, see Cranston, *John Locke*, 460.

46 Locke, *Some Thoughts Concerning Education*, 262; Locke means domestic European tourism, not the sort of travel that is mentioned most frequently in the *Essay*, travel to strange and remote nations, for which see Daniel Carey, 'Locke's Anthropology'.

47 Locke owned editions of La Bruyère from 1689 (4th edn) and 1696 (9th and final authoritative edn); see Harrison and Laslett (eds.), *Library of John Locke*, item 505.

48 For the larger philosophical context, see Thiel, 'Personal Identity'.

49 Locke, *Essay*, II.xxvii.18, 26.

50 Cicero, *De officiis*, I.xxx.107–xxxiii.116. Hobbes had drawn upon the same source in 'Of Persons, Authors, and things Personated', *Leviathan*, 111–15; see Skinner on Hobbes's revisions to this chapter, in *Visions of Politics*, vol. III, 177–208, esp. 188–94.

51 Locke, *Essay*, II.xxvii.20; see Winkler, 'Personal Identity'.

52 For 'punctual' selfhood, see Taylor, *Sources of the Self*, 159–76; cf. Seigel, *Idea of the Self*, 88–110, esp. 92–3.

53 See Seneca, *Controversiae*, IX.i.13; Quintilian, *Institutio oratoria*, X.i.101; both are discussed by La Mothe Le Vayer in his chapter on Sallust, in *Anciens et principaus historiens*, 214–15.

54 Thucydides, *Peloponnesian Warre*, A3^{r}, probably with Tacitus in mind; Thucydides was so eloquent that he might have been a great demagogue, Hobbes tells us, but he chose to displace his eloquence away from the democratic sphere (where he feared it would be corrupted to 'dangerous and desperate enterprizes') into literature; cf. Rapin, *Comparison de Thucydide et de Tite Live* (1681), in *Critical Works*, vol. I, 237.

55 Quintilian, *Institutio oratoria*, IX.iv.16–18; an important French example is J.-L. Guez de Balzac, 'Entretien XXVI: De l'utilité de l'histoire aux gens de court', discussed by Beugnot, 'Précellence'; see also Lafond, 'Esthétique'.

56 Thucydides, *Peloponnesian Warre*, a4^{v}; curiously, this passage from Hobbes is plagiarized by Davenant and inserted into his translation of La Mothe Le Vayer's *Notitia historicorum* (Oxford, 1678), 20.

57 Cf. Rapin, *Critical Works*, vol. I, 236: Thucydides' aphoristic style captures 'the most imperceptible *Movements* of the secretest Passions that set Mankind on work . . . 'Twas through the Shrewdness of his *View*, that he stor'd his Mind with those grand Maxims of the *publick Good*, and all those *political* Considerations wherewith his *History* abounds.'

58 Sallust, *Bellum Catalinarium*, V.3

59 Hobbes, *Elements of Law*, 169.

60 See Skinner, *Reason and Rhetoric*, 287–90.

61 Saint-Évremond, *Œuvres*, vol. II, 65 ('Observations sur Saluste et sur Tacite'): 'on rencontre peu souvent ensemble une connoissance delicate des hommes, et une profonde intelligence des affaires'; vol. I, 163–4

('Sur Sénèque, Plutarque, et Pétrone'): 'se qui lui semble se dementir'. Saint-Évremond's praise of Sallust's 'alieni appetens, sui profusus' is later attacked by Warburton (*Enquiry*, 95–6) who (like Hobbes) thinks Sallust's paradoxes are really just moral commonplaces.

62 Saint-Évremond, *Œuvres*, vol. II, 61: 'le genie des hommes des affaires viennent aprés naturellement par les actions peu recherchées de ces mesmes personnes qu'il a dépeintes'.

63 Hobbes, *Elements of Law*, 50–9. The classic account of its Aristotelian roots is in Strauss, *Political Philosophy of Hobbes*, 30–43; cf. Tilmouth, *Passion's Triumph*, 221–30.

64 As many commentators point out, the equivalent catalogue in Chapter 6 of *Leviathan* is less radically egotistical: see Hobbes, *Leviathan*, 37–46; cf. Raphael, Hobbes, 41–7.

65 Cureau de la Chambre, *Characters of the Passions*, 'a Necessary Advertisement', A3[v]; another popular example is Le Noble, *L'École du monde* (1695), translated by Abel Boyer as *The Art of Prudent Behaviour* (1701), 'Dialogue I: Of the Knowledge of Men'.

66 Cureau de la Chambre, *L'Art de connoistre les hommes*, vol. I, 5–12.

67 Hume, *Treatise*, 348–9, 411–12; see McIntyre, 'Character', 194–5.

68 Pierre Charron, *Œuvres*, vol. I, 67: 'soufleurer tous les fols & seditieux de l'ame, qui sont les passions'; Senault, *De l'usage des passions*, 138: 'Elles s'elevent sans nostre congé, et par l'impression qu'elles font sur le visage, elles apprennent à nos ennemis tout qui se passe dans nostre coeur.' Similar metaphors in Francis Bacon's *Advancement of Learning* (1605), Thomas Wright's *The Passions of the Mind in General* (1604) and others are quoted by James, *Passion and Action*, 11.

69 For Charron, men differ from men only in terms of the natural (though modifiable) effects of temper and capacity, and of the artifical effects of profession, rank and fortune (*Œuvres*, vol. I, 160).

70 Reynolds, *Treatise*, 42, 41.

71 *Ibid.*, 42.

72 *Ibid.*, 31, 43.

73 *Ibid.*, 234–6, at 235.

74 *Ibid.*, 235–6.

75 Senault, *De l'usage des passions*, 146: 'avec ces artifices innocens ils formerent les Villes, ils gouvernerent les Republiques, et commanderent long-temps aux Monarques, car ils estudioient leurs indications, et les manioient avec tant d'adresse, que la Monarchie fust denenuë enslave de l'Eloquence'.

76 The most important examples are Joseph Hall's *Characters of Vertues and Vices* (1608), the collection assembled by Sir Thomas Overbury's literary circle under the title *A Wife . . . Whereunto are added many Witty Characters* (1614), and the characters of Samuel Butler published in *Genuine Remains in Verse and Prose* (1759); see McCabe, 'Refining Theophrastus'; and Smeed, *Theophrastan 'Character'*, esp. 1–81.

77 Flecknoe, *Choicest Epigrams*, vol. II, A3[r].

78 In the 1668 first edition there are only 12 portraits among 420 *remarques*; by the final eighth edition of 1694, 130 of the 1,120 *remarques* are portraits; see Gally, 'Characteristic-Writings', 80; for La Bruyère and Rochefoucauld, see Mourges, *Two French Moralists*, 114; and Jaouën, *De l'art plaire*, 32.
79 La Bruyère, *Les Caractères*, 447 ('De l'Homme' 147): 'Les hommes n'ont point de caractères, ou s'ils en ont, c'est celui de n'en avoir aucun qui soit suivi, qui ne se démente point, et où ils soient reconnaissables … Ils ont des passions contraires, et des faibles qui se contredisent: il leur coûte moins de joindre les extrémités, que d'avoir une conduite dont une partie naisse de l'autre.'
80 *Ibid.*, 398 ('De l'Homme' 4): 'Inquiétude d'esprit, inégalité d'humeur, inconstance de cœur, incertitude de conduite. Tous vices de l'âme, mais différents, et qui avec tout le rapport qui paraît entre eux, ne se supposent pas toujours l'un l'autre dans un même sujet.'
81 Ménalque became a particular favourite among La Bruyère's most engaged British readers, the circle of wits associated with Joseph Addison while he was publishing *The Spectator* (1711–14). Other British readers of La Bruyère complained that his character portraits lack 'a strict Relation and Correspondence' with some recognizable human type, and that their inconsistencies are improbable: see Gally, 'Critical Essay', 66–70; and [Thomas Wharton], *Adventurer*, no. XLIX, vol. I, 292.
82 See, for example, La Bruyère, *Caractères*, 397, 409, 425, 428 ('De l'Homme' 3, 18, 84, 91).
83 *Ibid.*, 446 ('Des Jugements' 34): 'Combien d'art pour rentrer dans la nature, combien de temps, de règles, d'attention et de travail pour danser avec la même liberté et la même grâce que l'on sait marcher; pour chanter comme on parle; parler et s'exprimer comme l'on pense; jeter autant de force, de vivacité, de passion et de persuasion dans un discours étudié et que l'on prononce dans le public, qu'on en a quelquefois naturellement et sans préparation dans les entretiens les plus familiers.'
84 See *ibid.*, 452 ('Des Jugements' 10): 'l'esprit de singularité, s'il pouvait avoir ses bornes, et ne pas aller trop loin, approcherait fort de la droite raison et d'une conduite régulière'; for *honnêteté* see 470 ('Des Jugements' 55) and (with regard to speech) 257 ('Des Jugements' 32).
85 Addison, *Freeholder*, 194–5.
86 Thucydides, *Peloponnesian Warre*, a4^{v}.
87 Saint-Évremond, 'Sur les historiens françois', *Oeuvres*, vol. III, 69–95, at 82: 'autant que nous pouvons l'estre, à chaque terme d'un style coupé et d'une construction variée, de peur que l'esprit ne vint à se dissiper en des considerations trop vagues'.
88 Rapin, *Critical Works*, vol. I, 236.
89 Molesworth, *Account of Denmark*, Preface, C2^{r}; the resemblance to Locke is noticed by Robbins, *Commonwealthman*, 96; for a distinctly Aristotelian French example, see Montesquieu, *De l'esprit des lois*, IV.13, *Œuvres complètes*, 561: a wise legislator should lead men's spirits 'par des maximes de philosophie, de morale et de religion, assorties à ces caractères'.

90 *PW*, vol. IV, 12; Ned Ward is the obvious object of Swift's complaints, as the remark about '*Trips, Spies, Amusements*' and '*The Humour of the Age*' suggests: see Ward's *Trip to Jamaica* (1698) and *Trip to New-England* (1699), and his periodicals, including the *London Spy* (1702) and *The Weekly Comedy: or, The Humours of the Age* (1707–8); another example is Tom Brown, *Amusements Serious and Comical* (1700); but Swift may also be thinking of two of the more 'polite', 'maxim'-driven works of this kind: Dykes, *Moral Reflexions* (1708) and Mapletoft, *Select Collection of Proverbs* (1710).

91 See Swift, *Thoughts on Various Subjects*, *PW*, vol. I, 241–5, vol. IV, 243–54; and 'Verses on the Death of Dr. Swift', *Complete Poems*, 485–98.

92 Ong, *Ramus*, 277–9, 288–92; but see the sceptical treatment of Ong's account in Feingold, 'English Ramism'.

93 Quintilian, *Institutio oratoria*, VI.ii.9, 19. Aristotle was not excluded, however, from the proverbial association of rhetoric with emulation and self-advancement: the story of his taking up rhetoric as an aggression against the over-refined Isocrates – Aristotle felt it was a disgrace to remain silent and let such a declaimer speak – was dwelt upon during the seventeenth and eighteenth centuries by (among others) Bacon, *Advancement of Learning*, 127; Fénelon, *Dialogues on Eloquence*, 117; and Lawson, *Lectures Concerning Oratory*, 48; all are variations on Cicero, *De oratore*, III.xxxv.141.

94 Augustine, *On Christian Teaching*, IV.xxvii.59–xxxi.64, at xxx.63, 168; see Murphy, *Rhetoric in the Middle Ages*, 47–65, 285–92.

95 Cicero, *Orator*, XXI.69–70 and 71–2 for the ethical dimension.

96 Auerbach, *Literary Language*, 39–50, at 43.

97 See Fumaroli, *Âge de l'éloquence*, 279–98 (esp. 294 on character and style), 354–79; Stephen F. Campbell, 'Nicolas Caussin'; Gross, 'Caussin's Passion', 106 ff.

98 Caussin, *Eloquentia*, Book XIV, 'Theorhetor, sive de maiestate sacrae eloquentiae', discussed by Stephen F. Campbell, 'Nicolas Caussin', 66–7.

99 For Glanvill, see *An Essay Concerning Preaching* (1678), II, 20–3, 86–94; for Lamy and ethos, see Declerque, 'Rhétorique classique', 684–5, 691–2; for Pascal, see *Pensées*, 1135 (187 [437]): 'Les discours d'humilité sont matière d'orgueil aux gens glorieux et d'humilité aux humbles'; for Fénelon, see *Dialogues sur l'éloquence*, in *Œuvres*, vol. I, 21–2.

100 Shaftesbury, *Characteristicks*, III.i.2, vol. I, 188.

101 *Ibid.*, III.i.3, vol. I, 194.

102 *Ibid.*

103 Shaftesbury, *Philosophical Regimen*, 192, in the section on 'character'.

104 Shaftesbury, *Characteristicks*, III.i.2, vol. I, 189.

105 On Smith's engagement with Shaftesbury, see Vivienne Brown, 'Dialogic Experience', esp. 239–46; Rivers describes Smith's attitude to Shaftesbury as 'contemptuous', in *Reason, Grace and Sentiment*, vol. II, 260, 304–5; for Shaftesburian aspects of the impartial spectator, see David Marshall, 'Adam Smith', 598–9, 612 n.14.

106 *LRBL*, 56.
107 *Ibid.*
108 *Ibid.*
109 Shaftesbury attempts to clarify his concept of the perfect character in the fifth 'Miscellany': 'Were a Man to form himself by one single Pattern or Original, however perfect; he would himself be a mere *Copy*. But whilst he draws from various Models, he is *original, natural*, and *unaffected*' (*Characteristicks*, vol. III, 262).
110 Cf. *TMS*, 330, on casuistry as the grammar of morals; see Rhodes, *Power of Eloquence*, 8–12; and Skinner, *Reason and Rhetoric*, 91.
111 See *LRBL*, 40, 55 for similar formulations.
112 *Ibid.*, 40.
113 *Ibid.*, 34.
114 *Ibid.*, 79; for Clarendon and Burnet, see David Nichol Smith, 'The Essay on Character', in David Nichol Smith (ed.), *Characters*, xxx–xlvii.
115 *LRBL*, 81.
116 *Ibid.*, 82.
117 But cf. *Ibid.*, 40: 'it is not in the middle point between these two characters that an agreeable one is to be found'.
118 *Ibid.*, 34.
119 *TMS*, III.iii.4, p. 137.
120 This one is not present in the draft of 1759 and must have been written at the very last moment before publication of the first editon; see *TMS*, 34–46 and n.*j* on 136.
121 For 'wonder' in Smith's thought, see opening of 'The History of Astronomy', *Essays on Philosophical Subjects*, 33 ff.
122 *TMS*, VII.iii.3, pp. 328–9.
123 *Ibid.*, I.iii.1, p. 48; this passage was greatly amplified in 1790 by the passages in VI.iii that deal with pride, magnanimity and vanity; see Hanley, *Adam Smith*, 132–74.
124 *TMS*, I.i.4, p. 22.
125 *Ibid.*, II.i.5, p. 74.
126 *Ibid.*, III.i.5, p. 113.
127 *Ibid.*, 114.
128 For Burke and Smith, see the former's letter to the latter on reading *The Theory of Moral Sentiments*, 10 September 1759, *Corr.*, vol. I, 129–30; see also *EB*, vol. I, 186–7, vol. II, 52–4.

2 RHETORIC IN IRELAND, 1693–1765

1 For example, Court, *Institutionalizing*, 17–38; Crawford, *Devolving*, 16–44; Crawford (ed.), *Scottish Invention*.
2 They are, however, contemporary with Kames, *Elements of Criticism* (1762).
3 Miller, 'Formation', 266–7, and 'College English Studies', 52; cf. Moss, 'Discordant Consensus'.

4 See, for example, O'Brien, 'Grattan Mystique'; cf. Connolly, *Religion, Law and Power*, 85–97.
5 *LRBL*, 38.
6 Leland, *Dissertation*, 84; Hurd, *Letter*, 19; Leland complained of this move in the second edition of the *Dissertation* (Dublin, 1765), 200.
7 Sprat, *History*, 113; see Vickers, 'Royal Society'.
8 Locke, *Essay*, III.x.34, p. 508, following the 1690 reading.
9 William Molyneux to Locke, 22 December 1792, in Locke, *Familiar Letters*, 17; Locke was brought onto the Trinity curriculum by St George Ashe, Jonathan Swift's tutor and friend: see Berman, 'Enlightenment', 149.
10 Swift, *Gulliver's Travels*, *PW*, vol. XI, 185–6; for Swift's rhetoric and the new science, see Price, *Swift's Rhetorical Art*, 1–35.
11 Faulkner's anecdote (in the preface to the 1763 edition of Swift's *Works*) of the Dean's habit of reading his writings aloud to servants, 'which, if they did not comprehend, he would alter and amend' (*PW*, vol. XIII, 202–3), is predated by Laetitia Pilkington's story of him adopting the same practice with her as a joke: see Pilkington, *Memoirs*, vol. I, 61; cf. Thomas Sheridan, *Jonathan Swift*, 239–40.
12 But for Sprat on simplicity of style, see 'An Account of the Life and Writings', in Cowley, *Works*, b1^{v}–b2^{r}.
13 Swift, 'To a Lady', lines 147–8, in *Complete Poems*, 518.
14 Swift, *A Letter to a Young Gentleman*, *PW*, vol. IX, 65.
15 Price, *Swift's Rhetorical Art*; Lock, *Swift's Tory Politics*; Phiddian, *Swift's Parody*.
16 Swift, *Thoughts on Various Subjects*, *PW*, vol. IV, 246; cf. the fourth and seventh aphorisms, *PW*, vol. I, 240.
17 Pascal, *Pensées*, 513 (*4*), 576; Parish, 'Port-Royal'; for the wider context, see Declerque, 'Rhétorique classique'.
18 Pascal, *Pensées*, 512 (*1*), 513 (*4*); see Brody, 'Platonisme', 8.
19 Swift, *Letter to a Young Gentleman*, *PW*, vol. IX, 69.
20 Swift, *Tale of a Tub*, 279.
21 See Monk, 'Pride'.
22 *PW*, vol. I, 241.
23 Cicero, *De oratore*, II.xlv.189.
24 Swift, *Tale of a Tub*, 61, 56.
25 *Ibid.*, 60, 232.
26 *PW*, vol. XI, 273, 279–80.
27 Swift, *Correspondence*, vol. II, 303–4.
28 *PW*, vol. X, 86.
29 *Ibid.*, vol. XII, 159.
30 Swift, *Complete Poems*, 420.
31 *PW*, vol. IV, 252.
32 See 'On the Irish Club', in Swift, *Complete Poems*, 409–10; and Swift to Sheridan, 30 September 1735, *Correspondence*, vol. IV, 398: 'The Club meets this Week, and I determine to leave the Town as soon as possible, for I am

not able to live within the Air of such Animals'; cf. *ibid.*, 397, 417, 427, 447, 449, 459.

33 Swift, *Complete Poems*, 551–2.
34 Swift, *Tale of a Tub*, 173, and *PW*, vol. XII, 157–8.
35 *PW*, vol. IV, 251; Swift adds this aphorism to his collection in 1735.
36 Swift, *Memoirs Relating to that Change*, *PW*, vol. VIII, 123.
37 Swift, *Swift vs. Mainwaring*, 35.
38 Swift placed Molesworth in an Old Whig tradition that included 'Mr. *Locke*, Mr. *Molineaux*, Colonel *Sidney*, and other dangerous Authors' (*PW*, vol. X, 86); for this Irish strand of the commonwealthsman tradition, see Robbins, *Commonwealthman*, 87–94, 130–71.
39 Molesworth, *Account of Denmark*, $B8^{v}$–C^{r}; cf. Locke, *Concerning Education*, 244; for Molesworth on education, see Robbins, *Commonwealthman*, 96–7.
40 Molesworth, *Account of Denmark*, $B4^{r-v}$; cf. *Ibid.*, 233–5 on the decline of Danish learning.
41 Molesworth, *Considerations*, 28–9.
42 See Swift, *A Letter to a Young Clergyman* (dated 1719/20), *PW*, vol. IX, 79–80, and *A Vindication of Carteret*, *PW*, vol. XII, 161.
43 See esp. Swift, *Arguments Against Enlarging the Power of the Bishops* (1723), *PW*, vol. IX, 59; Molesworth is mentioned often in Swift's early correspondence as an extreme enemy of the Tory cause: see *Correspondence*, vol. I, 129, 425, vol. II, 4–5.
44 Toland, *State-Anatomy*, 70–7, and 'Letter', 9–10; Tindal, 'Power', 235–7; see Gascoigne, 'Church and State', 408–9.
45 Stewart, 'John Smith'; see also Michael Brown, *Francis Hutcheson*, 99–122.
46 See the edition of Arbuckle's *Dublin Weekly Journal* essays, *Hibernicus's Letters*, vol. II, 85–93 (no. 65, on false eloquence), and 155–62 (no. 73, on education).
47 For Madden, see Robbins, *Commonwealthman*, 152–4.
48 Madden, *Reflections*, 76–85, esp. 78–9; cf. Madden's earlier Proposal.
49 Madden, *Reflections*, 79.
50 Chesterfield to Madden, 15 April 1749, in Chesterfield, *Letters*, vol. IV, 1329 (no. 1632).
51 Chesterfield to his son, 18 March 1751, *ibid.*, esp. vol. VI, 1700.
52 This query does not appear at all in the 1735 first edition of *The Querist*, and Berkeley only added the sentence quoted above to Query no. 203 (which itself appeared for the first time in the 1751 second edition, p. 22) in *Miscellany*, 140–1.
53 *Corr.*, vol. I, 90; see *EB*, vol. I, 63n.
54 Molyneux, *Case of Ireland*, 113, 150–1.
55 *Ibid.*, 166–8.
56 See Connolly, 'Precedent and Principle', 135–9, 156.
57 For the significance of the 1719 Declaratory Act to the Irish Patriots, see McNally, *Parties*, 180–6.

58 Swift, *Drapier's Letters*, no.3, *PW*, vol. x, 31; cf. vol. x, 62, Swift's classic statement on Irish constitutional independence; for his listlessness in April 1720, see Swift to Charles Ford, *Correspondence*, vol. II. 342–3.
59 *Letter of a Member of the House of Commons in Ireland*, 13.
60 [Toland], *Reasons most Humbly Offer'd*, 12, 23, 25; cf. Molyneux, *Case of Ireland*, 127: 'It has ever been acknowledged that the Kingdom of Ireland is inseparably annex'd to the Imperial Crown of England. The Obligation that our Legislature lies under by Poyning's Act makes this Tye between the two Kingdoms indissoluble.'
61 *EB*, vol. I, 54–8.
62 Thomas Sheridan, *British Education*, 158; see Goring, *Rhetoric of Sensibility*, 91–113.
63 Thomas Sheridan, *British Education*, xxii–xxiv.
64 Thomas Sheridan, *Oration*, 19–20; it may be that by speaking Swift is referring to the smoothing away of Irish accents, which he thought made English people anticipate 'nothing but bulls, blunders, and follies' (*On Barbarous Denominations in Ireland*, appendix 'h', *PW*, vol. IV, 281); elocution was the focus of Sheridan's rhetoric by 1762.
65 Swift, *Letter to a Young Gentleman*, *PW*, vol. IX, 65; cf. the classic statement of this point in Eachard, *Grounds & Occasions*, 33–4.
66 Thomas Sheridan, *British Education*, 17–18.
67 *Ibid.*, 245–7, 267, quoting Swift, *PW*, vol. IV, 14–15: 'if it were not for the *Bible* and *Common-Prayer-Book* in the vulgar Tongue, we should hardly be able to understand any thing that was written among us an hundred years ago: For these Books being perpetually read in Churches, have proved a kind of Standard for Language'.
68 Thomas Sheridan, *British Education*, 47–8, 58, 73, 84.
69 *Ibid.*, 85
70 *Ibid.*, 92–3.
71 *Ibid.*, 86.
72 Sheldon, 'Hibernian Academy', 25.
73 *Second Oration*, 5; cf. Swift, *Gulliver's Travels*, III.v, *PW*, vol. XI, 180: 'There was a most ingenious Architect who had contrived a new Method for building Houses, by beginning at the Roof, and working downwards to the Foundation; which he justified to me by the like Practice of those two prudent insects the Bee and the Spider.' See the same anonymous author's *Address to the Hibernian Society*, esp. 4–11, for a further attack on Sheridan's oratory.
74 *Proceedings of the Hibernian Society*, 5, 15.
75 Flood's name appears in the *Proceedings*; see Kelly, *Henry Flood*, 35–7; Charlemont appears at later committee meetings; for Leland's dominance of the Academy and later attacks on the propriety of his motives in Faulkner's *Dublin Journal*, see Sheldon, 'Hibernian Academy', 27–30.
76 The minutes of the 'Academy' (TCD MSS Mun/Soc/Hist/81) are reproduced in Samuels, *Early Life*, 226–95.

77 Clark, 'Progymnasmata'; *EB*, vol. I, 39, refers to a schedule of oral disputations at Trinity from 1743–4 (TCD MSS Mun v/27 (1), 94a), but doubts that Burke would have participated in such exercises.
78 *Corr.*, vol. I, 2; see *EB*, vol. I, 24.
79 In Robert Barclay's *Apology for the Quakers* (1678; Burke owned the 5th edn, 1703), general classical learning is deemed 'necessary', but logic and philosophy are treated cautiously as 'the root of all contention and debate' (308–12).
80 Locke, *Concerning Education*, 243; Thomas Farnaby's *Troposchematologia* (1668) went through Dublin editions in 1735, 1750 and 1753.
81 *Corr.*, vol. I, 28 (and 4, 7–9, 21).
82 Burgersdicii, *Institutionum logicarum*, II.xi.200–5 ('De Inductione, Enthymeme & Exemplo'), xvi.214–27 ('De Inventione argumentarum dialecticorum, sive de locis & regulis topicis'), xxviii.289–96 ('De Methodo').
83 Jean Le Clerc's *Logica, sive, ars ratiocinandi* (London edition, 1692) is also mentioned on the 1736 tutor's list, although we have no direct evidence of Burke studying it; Le Clerc's treatment of the rhetorical proofs is brief (see IV.i.6, p. 149; IV.vii.9, pp. 167–8).
84 Locke, *Concerning Education*, 241; for Locke's hatred of disputation, see Walmsley, 'Dispute and Conversation', 381.
85 TDC MSS Mun v/27 (1), 6; quoted in McDowell and Webb, *Trinity College Dublin*, 45–9.
86 A list of texts for the humanities from 1743 survives in TCD MSS Mun v/27 (1), 90b.
87 See Gascoigne, *Cambridge*, 142–84; and Feingold, 'Aristotle'.
88 Burke's son Richard and his 'kinsman' William Burke were both Christ Church men; Quarrie, 'Christ Church Collections Books', 499. Answers on Aristotle's rhetoric became popular after the publication of a student edition in 1759, edited anonymously by William Holwell, a 'student' of Christ Church; when Gilbert Elliot (later Lord Minto, a close political ally of Burke) came up to Christ Church in 1768, he was told by the Dean, William Markham (an erstwhile patron of Burke), 'only classical and historical knowledge could make an able statesman' (Elliot, *Life and Letters*, vol. I, 38).
89 See M.L. Clarke, 'Classical Studies'.
90 Waterland, *Advice to a Young Student*, 16–17; Waterland refers to *M.T. Ciceronis orationes omnes perpetuis notis logicis*, ed. Thomas Freigius, 3 vols. (Basel, 1583); for discussion, see Stewart, 'Curriculum', 102, with remarks on the displacement of Burgersdijk as the source of 'Terms of Art' between the 1710 MS and the 1755 Oxford edition.
91 Waterland's dismissal of topical analysis corresponds with Arnauld and Nicole's attack on the practice, in *Logic*, 181–4.
92 Lawson, *Lectures Concerning Oratory*, 21, 23.
93 *Ibid.*, 22–3.
94 *Ibid.*, Dedication, x–xi.

95 Howell (*British Logic and Rhetoric*, 617) avers incorrectly that Lawson's lectures are the only surviving printed documents connected with the teaching of rhetoric at Trinity from 1724 to 1800.
96 Leland, *Dissertation*, 101.
97 Warburton, *Doctrine of Grace*, vol. I, 69–70, 75.
98 Leland, *Dissertation*, 77.
99 Here Leland responds to Middleton, *Gift of Tongues.*
100 Leland, *Dissertation*, 98.
101 *Ibid.*, 6–8, and esp. 45–7; cf. *PE*, 163–72.
102 Leland, *Dissertation*, 3, 69–77; cf. *PE*, 22–3.
103 Leland, *Dissertation*, 58–68, using Bishop Huet as representative of the rejected opinion; the *querelle* between Boileau and Huet is discussed by Kames, *Elements of Criticism*, vol. I, 301–2.
104 Leland, *Dissertation*, 45–7; cf. Warburton, *Doctrine of Grace*, vol. I, 70.
105 For Berkeley and Burke, see Berman, *Berkeley*, 126–34.
106 *EB*, vol. I, 202; Brooke, 'Hamilton'.
107 Caldwell, *Debates*, vol. I, 31, 36; Kelly, *Henry Flood*, 84–91.
108 Connolly, *Religion, Law and Power*, 85–97, esp. 92; Kelly, *Prelude to Union*, 38–9.
109 Caldwell, *Debates*, 504.
110 There are, however, a few manuscript accounts of Irish debates from before the 1760s, such as Sir Richard Cox's 'Irish politicks or an historical record of proceedings of the House of Commons of Ireland in the year, 1737' (TCD MS, 586.4); see also Hayton, 'Irish Parliamentary Diary', and, for reporting in the Irish parliament, 'Introduction', esp. 20–1.
111 P.D.G. Thomas, 'Authorship'; the 1768–74 parliamentary diary of Henry Cavendish is at the British Library, Egerton MSS 215–263, 3711; see Christopher Reid, *Edmund Burke*, 109–16.
112 Caldwell, *Debates*, v–vii.
113 Lawrence Parson's MS biography of Flood (Birr Castle, Co. Offaly, Rosse Papers, C/12/1), quoted by Kelly, *Henry Flood*, 80.
114 *Corr.*, vol. I, 191–4, 195–8.
115 *Ibid.* vol. I, 195 (and vol. VIII, 257); vol. II, 332; vol. II, 22.
116 Charlemont, *Manuscripts and Correspondence*, vol. I, 27–8; Kelly, *Henry Flood*, 110–15.
117 *Corr.*, vol. I, 194.
118 See Burke's article on Pitt in *Annual Register for 1761*, 45–7.
119 *Corr.*, vol. I, 191, 194.
120 Pery congratulated the nation 'upon the Honour and Advantages it has derived from his [Swift's] Genius and Public Spirit' on 4 February 1764 (Caldwell, *Debates*, vol. I, 678); Charles Lucas, *Appeal*, 15; see Connolly, 'Precedent and Principle', 130, 140; and Hill, *Patriots*, 83–91; for doubts, see Mahoney, *Jonathan Swift*, 46–65.
121 *Annual Register for 1758*, 'Characters', 257.
122 *PW*, vol. VIII, 134.
123 *Ibid.*, 144.

124 For 'refinement', see *ibid.*, 143, 151, 161.
125 *Ibid.*, 139.
126 *Ibid.*, 158.
127 For a more Catholic conception of Burke's Irish identity, see Gibbons, *Burke and Ireland*, and essays by Michael Brown and Nathan Wallace in Donlan, *Burke's Irish Identities.*
128 Samuels, *Early Life*, 275–6.
129 See McCabe, 'Refining Theophrastus'; Smeed, *Theophrastan 'Character'*, 1–8; for the characters by Clarendon, Burnet and their contemporaries, see David Nichol Smith (ed.), *Characters*; collections of characters after La Bruyère, such as John Dunton's *History of Living Men* (1702), John Macky's *Memoirs of the Secret Services* (1733) and Lord Chesterfield's *Characters* (1778) mark the decline of the genre.
130 *Note-Book*, 104, 114.
131 *Ibid.*, 108.

3 THE EPICUREAN AESTHETICS OF THE 'PHILOSOPHICAL ENQUIRY'

1 *Corr.*, vol. I, 241, vol. VIII, 364–5 and n.7.
2 The most suggestive attempt is Wood, 'Aesthetic Dimension'; see also Wilkins, *Problem*, 119–51; and Chandler, *Wordsworth's Second Nature*, 64–77.
3 Strauss, *Natural Right*, 315; cf. Frisch, 'Burke on Theory', and Canavan, *Political Reason*, 28–53; see also Lenzner, 'Strauss's Three Burkes', 370–6.
4 Strauss, *Natural Right*, 312.
5 See Furniss, *Aesthetic Ideology*, 31; Hampsher-Monk, 'Rhetoric and Opinion'; and O'Donnell, 'Irish Oratory'.
6 See Cronk, *Classical Sublime*, esp. 172–5; see also Brody, *Boileau and Longinus.*
7 The original account of the *Philosophical Enquiry* as a de-rhetoricized treatise is Monk, *Sublime*, 84–100, esp. 92–4; see also Paulson, *Representations of Revolution*, 71: 'I must distinguish the sublime in which Burke himself is participating [in the *Reflections*] from the sublime as a rhetorician's tool.'
8 See, for example, Bentley, 'Matter and Motion' (Bentley's second Boyle Lecture, delivered 4 April 1692), 15: 'the very Life, and vital Motion, and the formal Essence and Nature of Man, is wholly owing to the Power of God; and … the Consideration of ourselves, of our own Souls and Bodies, doth directly and nearly conduct us to the Acknowledgment of his Existence'.
9 For example, *PE*, 12 ('digest'), 13 ('principles, by which the imagination is affected'), 31 ('every instrument that works upon the mind'); cf. *Reflections* [232]: 'A politician, to do great things, looks for a *power*, what our workmen call a *purchase*.'
10 George Campbell, *Philosophy of Rhetoric*, vii; Priestley, *Oratory and Criticism*, 72.
11 I have borrowed the term 'extrinsic' from Taylor's discussion of the Shaftesbury–Locke contention, in *Sources of the Self*, 248–65, at 253–4.
12 Quintilian, *Institutio oratoria*, IV.ii.63–6, IX.ii.40; see Cave, *Cornucopian Text*, 27–34, 130–4; and Galyon, 'Puttenham's Enargeia'; it may be

significant that Burke's friend Leland (*Dissertation*, 1–8, at 8) attributed the argument that poetry only ever conveys ideas, not visual impressions, to Le Clerc's *Epistolae*, II.15.

13 *PE*, V.vi.173, quoting Horace, *De arte poetica*, line 111: 'with the tongue for interpreter, [Nature] proclaims the emotions of the soul'.

14 See Declerque, 'Rhétorique classique', 701–2: 'Le rayonnement irrésistible de la grande âme est une incontestable promotion de l'*ethos*, qui vient compenser le discrédit du *pathos*, et réintègre ce dernier dans une rhétorique du ravissement et de l'admiration'; see also Rapin's treatise *Du grand ou du sublime*.

15 Longinus, *On the Sublime*, 12.4–5, 14.1–2, 34.1–4; Burke's friend Leland, a fellow at Trinity College, Dublin, provides good examples of the prevailing eighteenth-century admiration for Demosthenes, in *Dissertation*, 69–76, at 73, and in Demosthenes, *Orations*, trans. Leland, xix ff., a copy of which was in Burke's library (item 162).

16 Other examples are at lines 139 ff., 250 ff.; see Brink, *Horace*, 184–94, at 192.

17 Cf. Lucretius, *De rerum natura*, V.1056 ff.; for earlier commentators making this connection, see Brink, *Horace*, 188; Horace's 'interprete lingua' at l. 111 is also Lucretian: see *De rerum natura*, VI.1149: 'atque animi interpres manabat lingua cruore'.

18 *De arte poetica*, lines 309–22, at 309–11; Shaftesbury, *Characteristicks*, III.i.3, vol. I, 190–209, at 192, 195, 205–6; Shaftesbury added another layer of figuration here by interpreting 'Socraticae chartae' as 'Sea-Cards' or maritime maps charting the ocean of human nature.

19 *PE*, 1 (Preface to first edition); but there is a partial concession that sublimity and beauty can be mixed at III.xxvii.124.

20 Shaftesbury, *Characteristicks*, vol. II, 29; see Nicolson, *Mountain Gloom*, 299–300, 358–9; and Bullard, 'Meaning'.

21 Cicero, *De officiis*, I.iv.14; Thomas Cockman's scholarly translation of 1699 does not translate *honestum*, and highlights the passage (Cicero, *Tully's Offices*, 9 ff.).

22 Cicero, *De finibus*, II.xiv.45–7; referred to by Shaftesbury in *Characteristicks*, III.182n.

23 Cicero, *De finibus*, II.i.1–II.xxxv.119; see Stokes, 'Cicero', 150–1.

24 For 'deformity', see *PE*, III.v.103; cf. Shaftesbury, *Characteristicks*, vol. I, 207 on the poet who 'marks the *Sublime* of Sentiments and Action, and distinguishes the *Beautiful* from the *Deform'd*, *the Amiable* from *the Odious*'.

25 Shaftesbury, *Characteristicks*, vol. II, 105, 284; cf. vol. I, 336: 'If he has no Eye, or Ear, for these *interiour Numbers*; 'tis not likely he shou'd be able to judg better of that *exteriour Proportion* and *Symmetry* of Composition, which constitutes a legitimate Piece'; see also vol. I, 136, 139, 277, 353, vol. II, 388–427, vol. III, 182–5. Burke attributes the predominance of 'proportion' in aesthetic discourse to a combination of pride in human works, false reasoning about the figures of animals, and 'the Platonic theory of fitness and aptitude' (*PE*, III.iv.101) – perhaps another reference to Shaftesburian idealism.

26 Addison *et al.*, *Spectator*, no. 144 (21 June 1712), vol. III, 538; cf. Pope, in Spence, *Anecdotes*, 40: 'That which is not just in buildings, is disagreeable to the eye; as a greater upon a slighter, &c. This [Pope] called "the reasoning of the eye".'
27 Burke identifies the *je-ne-sais-quoi* with the quality of 'grace', in *PE*, III.xxii.119; see Marin, 'On the Sublime'; Scholar, *Je-ne-sais-quoi*, 43–59, 196–9; and Cronk, *Classical Sublime*, 108–9.
28 *PE*, II.v.64–8, I.xiii.45, II.iii.58–60.
29 Swift, *Tale of a Tub*, 174.
30 Harth, *Swift*, 132–41; cf. Quehan, 'Lucretius'.
31 Swift's reference to '*Films* and *Images*' also has a direct Epicurean source: the *simulacra* of Lucretius, *De rerum natura*, IV.30–53.
32 See, for example, Swift, *Examiner*, no. 19 (14 December 1710), *PW*, vol. III, 37; cf. *PW*, vol. VI, 130.
33 Temple, *Works*, vol. I, 172; cf. Epicurus' 'Letter to Herodotus', in Diogenes Laertius, *Lives of Eminent Philosophers*, X.78 (trans. Hicks, vol. II, 607), quoted by Wilson, *Epicureanism*, 34.
34 *PE*, I.xix.52; cf. II.v.68.
35 For summaries of the Epicurean inheritance in late seventeenth-century thought, see Wilson, *Epicureanism*, 1–38; and the essays by Margaret Osler, Lisa Sarasohn, J.J. Macintosh and Thomas Lennon, in Osler (ed.), *Atoms*.
36 For Epicureanism in the new sciences, see Meinel, 'Atomism'; for a survey, see Johnson and Wilson, 'Lucretius'.
37 For Epicurus in the temple, see Barbour, *English Epicures*, 75–111.
38 Burke's only reference to the Christian revelation is in *PE*, III.v.70.
39 See Saint-Évremond, 'Reflexions sur la doctrine d'Epicure', in *Œuvres*, vol. VI, 42, but cf. 'Sur la morale d'Epicure', esp. vol. V, 4 (the 'Reflexions' are in fact by the satirist Jean-François Sarasin).
40 Mandeville, Fable, vol. I, 147–8, quoting (as I mention below) Virgil, *Eclogues*, II.65, 'each is led on by his own pleasure' (cf. Lucretius, *De rerum natura*, II.257–8); for Mandeville's use of Epicurus to 'discomfort his readers', see Hundert, *Enlightenment's Fable*, 47.
41 Hume, *Essays*, 138 (a 1742 footnote expanded for the third edition of 1748); for the essays as a group, see Jones, '"Art" and "Moderation"', 172–9; M.A. Stewart, 'Stoic Legacy', 276–88; for a contemporary comment, see Kames, who thought that 'to interweave characters with reasoning' as these essays do 'requires the perfection of genius, taste and judgment' (*Elements of Criticism*, vol. II, 152).
42 Hume, *Essays*, 139.
43 Lucretius, *De rerum natura*, I.76–7, repeated at I.595–6, V.89–90, VI.65–6: 'finita potestas denique cuique | quanam sit ratione atque alte terminus haerens'; the discussion of permanent characteristics is at III.294–336 (lines 307 and 309 quoted above); but pleasure is also subject to the contingency of the atomic swerve at II.251–62, which accounts for human free will.
44 Hume, *Essays*, 141, with a footnote to *De rerum natura*, II.172, 'dux vitae dia voluptas'.

45 For a recent account, see Osler, 'Gassendi'.
46 Dennis to Shackleton, March 1758, Beinecke Library, Yale University, Osborn Files 10.213.
47 *PE*, I.xiii.44, I.xvii.50–1.
48 Locke, *Reasonableness of Christianity*, 287–9.
49 Locke, *Essay*, II.xxi.29–38, at 33.
50 For Locke's hedonism, see Aaron, *John Locke*, 257; Drisgol, 'Influence of Gassendi'; and Darwall, *British Moralists*, 149–75.
51 Locke, *Essay*, II.xxi.35, 47; for Locke on free will and determinism, see James A. Harris, *Liberty and Necessity*, 22–40.
52 Hutcheson, Essay, 24.
53 *Ibid.*, 28.
54 See the distinction between love and desire at *PE*, III.i.91, for example.
55 The most formidable arguments against his theory of the moral sense were, as he recognized, the rationalist objections put to him in correspondence by Gilbert Burnet (junior), which had received their fullest statement in Samuel Clarke's 1704 Boyle Lectures on *The Being and Attributes of God*; for Hutcheson's later capitulation towards the rationalism of Clarke, see Rivers, *Reason, Grace and Sentiment*, vol. II, 212–15.
56 Hutcheson, *Essay*, 22, 29, 134.
57 Archibald Campbell, *Enquiry into the Original of Moral Virtue* (1733), xiii–xiv, quoted by Rivers, *Reason, Grace and Sentiment*, vol. II, 179.
58 Shaftesbury, *Characteristicks*, vol. I, 117–19, where Lucretian quietism and naturalism are distinguished from Hobbesian and libertine hedonism; Hutcheson is more subtle in his identification of Hobbes with the 'old *Epicureans*' (*Essay*, 134–5), and John Clarke with a more specious, mitigated Epicureanism; for 'Epicureans of the better sort', see Hutcheson's friend Arbuckle in *Hibernicus's Letters*, vol. I, 381, originally printed as Letter 45, *Dublin Weekly Journal*, 4 February 1725/6; for 'Epicurean in his senses', see Warburton on Pliny, *Divine Legation*, vol. I, 329; for Shaftesbury and Epicureanism, see Badelon, 'Épicureanisme'.
59 John Clarke, *Foundation of Morality*, 31–2.
60 John Clarke was certainly being read in Cambridge: he is cited approvingly by Edmund Law's close friend Waterland, in *Nature*, 16–17.
61 For general discussion of the group, see Gascoigne, *Cambridge*, 126–30. See also Rivers, *Reason, Grace and Sentiment*, vol. II, 203–4; and Young, *Religion*, 99–112.
62 Law became a fellow of Christ's College in 1727, Gay a fellow of Sidney Sussex College in 1724; for other associates of the Law circle, see Stephens, 'Edmund Law'; Gay is particularly important to the account of Enlightenment psychology in Spadafora, *Idea of Progress*, 138–66.
63 Jenyns matriculated at St John's College in 1722, Hartley was elected MA at Jesus College in 1729, Rutherforth a fellow of St John's in 1733 and John Brown BA at St John's in 1735; for the influence of the circle outside Cambridge, see Hudson, *Samuel Johnson*, 66–85.

64 In the printed catalogue of 1813, Brown's *Essays* is item 36, and Hartley's *Observations* item 265; Burke also owned Thomas Johnson's edition of Pufendorf, *De officio hominis & civis* (1737), item 456; Rutherforth, *System of Natural Philosophy* (1744), item 550, and Jenyns, *Miscellaneous Pieces* (1747), item 281, including the *Free Inquiry into the Nature and Origin of Evil* (1757), which reiterates the Christian Epicureanism of Gay and Brown.
65 For the distinctiveness of the English Enlightenment, see J.G.A. Pocock, 'Post-Puritan England', 91, 106, and 'Clergy and Commerce'.
66 Locke, *Essay*, II.xxi.42–3, xxviii.8.
67 Rutherforth, *Essay*, 209.
68 John Brown, *Essays*, 159; cf. Edmund Law, 'Nature', lv; Gay, 'Preliminary Dissertation', xxiii, xxviii, xxxii–xxxviii; and Thomas Johnson, *Essay*, 3–4, 31–46.
69 *PE*, I, III.viii.114; see also III.xxvii.124.
70 Shaftesbury, *Characteristicks*, vol. II, 29.
71 John Brown, *Essays*, 116–17.
72 Locke, *Essay*, III.xi.15–17, pp. 516–17; for John Brown's Lockeanism, see his letter to William Gilpin, 12 February 1741/2, Bod. MSS Eng. Misc. c. 389, fol. 59^{v}: 'Pray is Mr. Locke in any credit at Oxford? If it be not quite heterodox to be suspected of having any correspondence with him, (once, I know, it was) I shou'd think that an hour or two every day might be spent with him to as much Advantage as with the said Burgesdicius' – the latter a Dutch logician also much resented by the young Burke (*Corr.*, vol. I, 7–9).
73 Wecter, 'Burke's Theory', 171 n.14; *PE*, 'Editor's Introduction', xxxiv; cf. Hamm, 'Burke and Metaphysics', 209.
74 Burke's attitude to the association of ideas is in fact similar to that of Locke and that of Hutcheson, both of whom regret it as a source of childish prejudice and extravagant opinion, but Burke is impatient with the tendentious narratives with which Locke illustrates the process by which these prejudices arise; see *PE*, IV.ii.130–1, 143; cf. Locke, *Essay*, II.xxxiii.10.
75 Hartley, *Observations*, vol. I, 360–1.
76 *Ibid.*
77 *Ibid.*, vol. I, 348.
78 *PE*, IV.i.129; note that Burke actually dislikes the term 'æther'.
79 With a punctilious footnote at I.iii.34 he reminds the reader that Locke, by contrast, viewed pain and pleasure as mutually exclusive, and yet linked by a sort of causal contiguity, so that the removal of pain is itself a source of pleasure, and vice versa.
80 For a similar idiom, cf. *Corr.*, vol. I, 78–9, 'a melting tenderness tinged with sorrow'.
81 Epicurus, *Epikouros Menoikei Charein.*
82 Charleton, 'Apologie for Epicurus', *Epicurus's Morals*, v.i.xi, p. 22.
83 *Ibid.*, 26, corresponding with Epicurus, '*Epikouros Menoikei Charein*', lines 129.5–130.5.

84 *De rerum natura*, III.28–30, according to the Loeb text (trans. Rouse), not *PE*.
85 For the common milieu of Longinus and Lucretius, see Porter, 'Poetics of the Void'.
86 Lucretius, *De rerum natura*, VI.655.
87 Dryden, 'Lucretius: Beginning of the Second Book', lines 1–4, 24–7, *Poems*, vol. II, 312–14, translating *De rerum natura*, II.1–4, 20–4.
88 As Hammond notes, line 25 is Dryden's addition (or rather transferral from *De rerum natura*, I.76–7); for the reading of 'nullas' (rather than the conventional 'multas') in *De rerum natura*, II.22, see Hammond, 'Integrity', 6–9.
89 For a Cambridge Epicurean on the absurdity of describing infinity in terms of human mensuration, see Law, *Enquiry*, 95–129; for Burke on the illusion of infinity, see *PE*, II.viii.73; for Lucretius on optical illusions and simulacra, see *De rerum natura*, esp. IV.33–469.
90 On Lucretius and the scientific sublime, see Porter, 'Lucretius and the Sublime', 169–72.
91 For the perception of light, cf. *De rerum natura*, III.359–69 and IV.324–468 with *PE*, II.xiv.79–81; for rough and smooth, cf. *De rerum natura*, II.381–443 with *PE*, III.xiv.114, xxiv.120–1, IV.xx.151.
92 *PE*, V.vi.172, quoting *De rerum natura*, I.62–7: 'When man's life lay for all to see foully grovelling upon the ground, crushed beneath the weight of Superstition, which displayed her head from the regions of heaven, lowering over mortals with horrible aspect . . .'.
93 Hume, *Natural History*, 91 n.'c'; cf. Cudworth, *Intellectual System*, vol. II, 84; and Stillingfleet, *Origines Sacrae*, 365.
94 For a visual assessment of the image by a critic sometimes posited as an influence on Burke (see *PE*, lxix–lxx), see Spence, who compares it with similar classical images of Ceres (*Polymetis*, 103–4).

4 EPISODES IN THE EVOLUTION OF BURKE'S ELOQUENCE

1 *WS*, vol. III, 116.
2 *Ibid.*, 166; cf. vol. III, 110 for the same idiom.
3 *WS*, vol. V, 488.
4 Burke's colonial politics have received a great deal of attention since the publication of P.J. Marshall's edition of the writings and speeches on Indian affairs; see, for example, Whelan, *Edmund Burke and India*; Mehta, *Liberalism and Empire*, 39–44, 153–86; and Pitts, *Turn to Empire*, 59–100; for a sceptical response to liberal admiration of Burke's imperial politics, see Vanech, 'Painful Homecoming'.
5 *Corr.*, vol. VII, 438.
6 *WS*, vol. V, 539–40.
7 *Corr.*, vol. VIII, 256.
8 *WS*, vol. IX, 160; for Burke using the same formulation two decades previously, in April 1770, see *Corr.*, vol. II, 128.

9 On the varieties of '*new* men', see *Corr.*, vol. VII, 53.
10 *Corr.*, vol. V, 471.
11 *Speech on Address*, 26 May 1767, *WS*, vol. II, 73.
12 *WS*, vol. II, 213.
13 *WS*, vol. II, 318.
14 Burke to William Baker, 1 October 1771, *Corr.*, vol. II, 243.
15 Mandeville, *Fable*, vol. I, 341–3; Samuel Johnson, *Rambler*, no. 28, *Yale Works*, vol. I, 155, and 'Life of Pope', *Lives of the Poets*, vol. IV, 58–9; cf. *Rambler*, no. 13, *Yale Works*, vol. i., 71, on Sarah Churchill, Queen Anne and friendship.
16 Hume, *Essays*, 63; cf. 'On the Independency of Parliament', *Essays*, 43.
17 *WS*, vol. II, 320; the passage anticipates a famous Horatian statement in the *Reflections* [116]: 'To make us love our country, our country ought to be lovely.'
18 Burke to William Markham, post 9 November 1711, *Corr.*, vol. II, 263.
19 *WS*, vol. II, 316.
20 *Ibid.*; cf. Cicero, *De amicitia*, X.33: 'nam vel ut non idem expediret incidere saepe, vet ut de re publica non idem sentiretur'; for contemporary commentary on a similar passage in *De amicitia*, VI.20, see William Melmoth's notes in Cicero, *Cato and Laelius*, vol. II, 217–22.
21 See Bolingbroke, *A Dissertation upon Parties*, in *Political Writings*, 7.
22 See esp. *Ibid.*, 'Letter VII: 29 December 1733', 55–65; for Bolingbroke on the politics of friendship, see 'Letter X: 26 January 1734', 88–97, at 89.
23 *WS*, vol. II, 317; cf. 314: 'When men are not acquainted with each other's principles, nor experienced in each other's talents, nor at all practised in their mutual habitudes and dispositions by joint efforts in business . . .'.
24 Unlike Aristotle (see *Rhetoric*, II.iv.3), Cicero makes no prescriptions about friendship in his rhetorics, even during the discussion of means by which good will is secured (*De oratore*, II.xliii.182 ff.); but see *De oratore*, II. xvii.72, where Antonius speaks feelingly of how difficult it is to turn hatred into benevolence.
25 *De officiis*, I.xvii.55–7: 'quam morum similitudo bonorum'.
26 Cicero, *De amicitia*, VIII.27: 'quasi lumen aliquod probitatis at virtutis perspicere videamur'; VII.23: 'quod bonam spem praelucet in posterum'.
27 Cicero, *De officiis*, II.ix.31: 'quibus rebus pariuntur a singulis, eisdem fere a multitudine'.
28 Tacitus, *Dialogus de oratoribus*, V.4: 'qua parere simul et tueri amicitiias, asciscere necessitudines, complecti provincias possit'.
29 *WS*, vol. II, 316–17. For the historiography of Addison and the Junto, see Horn, 'Addison's *Campaign*'.
30 Burke enhances the prozeugmatic structure here (the verb 'they believed' supplying three subordinate clauses) with anadiplosis, the chain-like duplication of the last term in one clause into the first term of the next: it is a

highly schematized passage; cf. *Speech at the Conclusion of the Poll* (1774), *WS*, vol. III, 65: 'easy gradations of acquaintance, friendship, and esteem'.

31 Addison, *Miscellaneous Works*, vol. I, 68; for the politics of Sarah Churchill's friendship with Anne, see her *Account of the Conduct*, cited by Tindall, *Continuation of Mr Rapin*, vol. I, 535n.: 'A friend was what she most coveted . . .'.

32 Swift, *Correspondence*, vol. II. 277, 299, vol. III, 98.

33 Swift makes this point in *Examiner*, no. 31 (1 March 1711), *Swift vs. Mainwaring*, 273.

34 Hume, *Essays*, 3–8, at 6–8.

35 Addison *et al.*, *Spectator*, vol. I, 289; this paradox may have its source in Shaftesbury's 'Essay on Wit and Humour', *Characteristicks*, vol. I, 112, where friendship becomes a natural control on the turbulence of 'generous Spirits'.

36 *Corr.*, vol. II, 282.

37 *WS*, vol. II, 291, for example.

38 *WS*, vol. III, 314–15; cf. *Letter to Sir Hercules Langrishe*, *WS*, vol. IX, 629: 'Virtual representation is that in which there is a communion of interests, and a sympathy in feelings and desires between those who act in the name of any description of people, and the people in whose name they act, though the trustees are not actually chosen by them.'

39 *WS*, vol. II, 292; for oratory in this function, see Arthur Onslow's comment: 'This constitutional check upon power, by the house of commons, is one of the most beneficial advantages the people receive by frequent parliaments . . . [A majority] is not a sufficient security for doing wrong; and I have known the smallest minority there, by the freedom of speech only, keep the ablest and boldest ministers in awe' (note to Burnet, *History*, vol. V, 278).

40 *WS*, vol. II, 291–2.

41 Cf. *Letters of Junius*, 110: 'now it seems we have no better rule to live by than the temporary discretion and fluctuating integrity of the House of Commons'; for a general statement on the temporary constitution of legislatures, see Rutherforth, *Institutes*, vol. II, 243.

42 *WS*, vol. II, 453; see Shebbeare's sarcasms on this passage, in *Answer*, 192.

43 *WS*, vol. III, 109; for the quantum of mind-changing that *was* allowed members, see P. D. G. Thomas, *House of Commons*, 200–2.

44 *WS*, vol. II, 452; there are also shorter characters of George Grenville, Rockingham and Henry Seymour Conway.

45 *Ibid.*

46 Burke to Rockingham, post 6 November 1769, *Corr.*, vol. II, 109; the relevant passages in both *Thoughts* and *American Taxation* share a language of vastness, merit and political friendship.

47 *WS*, vol. II, 264.

48 *WS*, vol. II, 450; cf. the comment of Burke's one-time patron (and great opponent of Pitt) the Earl of Egmont, in *Faction Detected*, 164–5: the true patriot 'will neither be fettered by general Maxims, nor tied to any

chimerical System, but will be governed by Times and Circumstances'; see Brewer, *Party Ideology*, 99.

49 Elizabeth Montagu to the Earl of Bath, 21 October 1762, Huntington Library, Montagu Papers, 4547, quoted by Black, *Pitt the Elder*, 226.

50 Cf. *WS*, vol. II, 141; and Waldegrave, *Memoirs and Speeches*, 184, on Pitt's 1756 triumph over Newcastle: 'The whole system of the House of Commons was at once entirely changed ... Pitt standing without a rival, no orator to oppose him, who had courage even to look him in the face.'

51 *WS*, vol. II, 319; cf. speech on the civil list, 28 February 1769, Cavendish, *Debates*, 269–77, at 276: 'The maxim of "*Not Men But Measures*" is an insignificant maxim'; for an account of the association of the maxim with Walpole, see Brewer, *Party Ideology*, 68–71.

52 *WS*, vol. II, 451.

53 James Harris, Parliamentary Diary, 24 November 1763, quoted by Black, *Pitt the Elder*, 247.

54 For Shandean aspects of Pitt, see Lamb, 'Sterne', 223 ff.

55 For Pitt and Townshend, see Namier and Brooke, *Charles Townshend*, 41–53, 146–60.

56 For a more severe account of Townshend's disloyalty, see his biographer Namier, 'Charles Townshend', vol. III, 540: 'it is doubtful if he felt affection for anyone ... poverty of heart accounts for his life's failure'.

57 *WS*, vol. II, 452.

58 Cf. William Burke to Edmund Burke, post 4 September 1767, *Corr.*, vol. II, 327: Townshend 'could never argue from a real sense of right or wrong'.

59 Walpole, *Memoirs*, vol. II, 47; cf. William Burke, *Corr.*, vol. II, 326: Townshend proves that 'it would be dangerous to a Man's principles, to accustom himself to a display of parts in saying the best things He could on both sides of a question'.

60 *Corr.*, vol. V, 338.

61 *WS*, vol. II, 453.

62 For example, the undated letter of Townshend's among Buccleuch MSS, quoted by Namier, 'Charles Townshend', vol. III, 539; cf. Namier and Brooke, *Charles Townshend*, 184–6.

63 *WS*, vol. II, 455.

64 See *EB*, vol. II, 13–15.

65 *Mr. Edmund Burke's Speeches at Bristol, and at the Conclusion of the Poll* (1774); the first edition, printed for J. Wilkie, may have been unauthorized, since Burke's printer James Dodsley quickly brought out a second; see Todd, *Bibliography*, items 22, 23.

66 Todd, *Bibliography*, items 24, 25.

67 Burke was immediately imitated, however, by his fellow Rockinghamite Hartley (the younger), *Speech and Motions*.

68 P. D. G. Thomas, 'Beginning'; Bullard, 'Parliamentary Rhetoric'.

69 Cromartie, 'Printing'.

70 Burke might have found an account of the publication of Cicero's oratory in Middleton, *History*, vol. I, 216; Cicero preserved his speeches for pedagogical reasons: see Leeman, 'Technique', 198–9.
71 *Corr.*, vol. VIII, 253.
72 See Elofson, *Rockingham Connection*, 11–35.
73 Other examples of grandees' men include Grenville's secretary and Burke's ally in the petitioning movement Thomas Whately, Bedford's dependant Richard Rigby, and Lord Townshend's secretary John Courteney; see Christie, *British 'non-elite' MPs*, 97 ff.; and Namier and Brook (eds.), *History of Parliament*, vol. II, 'Members A–J'.
74 Namier, *Structure of Politics*, 88–91; on the 'political fiction' that all MPs are equal, 'whether they represent counties or boroughs', see P.D.G. Thomas, *House of Commons*, 211.
75 Burke, *Army Estimates*, 32; on Burke's ultimate lack of parliamentary authority, see, for example, Wraxall, *Historical Memoirs*, vol. II, 277.
76 *WS*, vol. III, 162.
77 *Ibid.*, 108; for both Pitt's and Townshend's influence as 'dazzling' in *American Taxation*, see *WS*, vol. II, 431, 441.
78 *WS*, vol. III, 107–8; Burke's use of the word 'disreputably' here is the earliest recorded instance in the *OED*.
79 *Ibid.*, 116.
80 *Ibid.*, 118; cf. 'depreciated, sunk, wasted' (119).
81 *Ibid.*, 133.
82 *Ibid.*, 145.
83 *Ibid.*, 147; on 28 April 1774 Thomas Townshend complains of encountering Burke 'armed to the teeth with precedents' (P. D. G. Thomas, *House of Commons*, 9).
84 As the Clarendon editors note, 'wise beyond what is written' is from 1 Corinthians 4.6; 'form of sound words' from 2 Timothy 1.13; cf. 'genuine simplicity of heart is an healing and cementing principle', etc. (*ibid.*, 109) – another montage of homiletic idioms for modest effect.
85 See Hume, *Essays*, 35–6 (and the important passage relegated to 606–7) for the basic pragmatic argument against instruction; see Cannon, *Parliamentary Reform*, 65–6.
86 *WS*, vol. III, 68–9; for Burke and the Rockinghamites on reform, see Cannon, *Parliamentary Reform*, 75–84.
87 *WS*, vol. III, 591–2 (quoting Northampton: Northamptonshire Record Office, Fitzwilliam MSS, A.xxxi.18, 19).
88 *Ibid.*, 634.
89 *Reflections* [242]: 'They must take it for granted that we attend much to their reason, but not at all to their authority.'
90 *WS*, vol. III, 624; cf. Burke on Henry Dundas's refusal to release papers on the Arcot debt: 'The whole tenor of the right honourable gentleman's argument is consonant to the nature of his policy.'

91 But see Burke to Richard Champion, 26 June 1777, *Corr.*, vol. III, 46: 'I could not have believed how very little the local constituents attend to the general public line of their member.'

92 *WS*, vol. VI, 47–65.

93 *Ibid.*, 125 ff.; P.J. Marshall, *Impeachment*, 88–179.

94 For Burke's writings on India as central evidence for his theory of civil society, see Ahmed, 'Theater'; for the Indian trials as theatre, see, for example, Bolton, 'Imperial Sensibilities'; for Burke's 'Indianism' as a source of ideas for his European politics, see Agnani, 'Jacobinism'.

95 For important discussion of the validity of a person's 'general fame' as grounds for impeachment, see the debate during the trial of Strafford, *Parliamentary or Constitutional History*, vol. VI, 435–9; cf. Hatsell, *Precedents*, 103–4.

96 *WS*, vol. V, 457; but see Blackstone, *Commentaries*, vol. IV, 256 on impeachment as 'prosecution of the known and established law, [which] has frequently been put in practice'.

97 See *Thoughts*, *WS*, vol. II, 294: 'Impeachment, that great guardian of the purity of the constitution, is in danger of being lost, even to the idea of it'; for impeachment as a manifestation of anger, see his impulse to impeach North in 1779, *WS*, vol. III, 445–7, 454–63.

98 *WS*, vol. VI, 272; see Blackstone, *Commentaries*, vol. IV, 258 on the function of the Lords as extraordinary tribunal in impeachments.

99 See, for example, South in his sermon 'On the General Resurrection', *Sermons*, vol. IV, 235–8; the *OED* notes similar usages in Seldon, Hale and Cudworth.

100 *WS*, vol. VII, 141, 133; for legal implications of the printing, see Perceval, *Review*, 91–6.

101 For the state trials and reports as sources of evidence propositions, see Macnair, *Law of Proof*, 19.

102 *WS*, vol. VI, 57 (17 February 1786).

103 *WS*, vol. VII, 79.

104 Burke to Henry Addington, 7 March 1796, *Corr.*, vol. VIII, 405; cf. Philip Francis in 1805 recalling his part in the impeachment of Hastings: 'I was tried, and *he* was acquitted' (*Parliamentary History of England*, vol. VI, 394).

105 *WS*, vol. VI, 275–6; Burke uses the same military metaphor in *Thoughts*, *WS*, vol. II, 287: 'the array of riot, and the discipline of confusion'.

106 See Hatsell, *Precedents*, 211–12, 253, for debates about the permanency of that role during the impeachment of Strafford and Hastings, relative to the continuance of impeachments across parliaments; see also Perceval, *Review*, 101–8.

107 *WS*, vol. VI, 291.

108 Burke to Philip Francis, 10 December 1785, *Corr.*, vol. V, 242–3.

109 *WS*, vol. VI, 271.

110 Burke to Philip Francis, 23 December 1785, *Corr.*, vol. V, 245.

111 This was a much-contested point in 1709: see Sacheverell, *Tryal*, 448–9: the Lords present on 10 March found that precise words should be specified in the indictment, but their opinions were overruled in the upper house itself on 14 March; see Hatsell, *Precedents*, 282–3.
112 *WS*, vol. VII, 122.
113 *Corr.*, vol. V, 242.
114 *WS*, vol. VII, 89.
115 *WS*, vol. VI, 271–2.
116 *WS*, vol. VII, 240.
117 Cf. *Reflections* [113]: 'It is gone, that sensibility of principle, that chastity of honour, which felt a stain like a wound, which inspired courage whilst it mitigated ferocity, which ennobled whatever it touched, and under which vice itself lost half its evil, by losing all its grossness'; and *First Letter on a Regicide Peace* (1796), *WS*, vol. IX, 242.
118 *WS*, vol. VIII, 312–19; see Bullard, 'Figure of Enlightenment'.
119 Burke's notorious inability to control his tendency to personal abuse in Parliament is followed in *EB*, vol. II, esp. 13, 175–6, 197.
120 *WS*, vol. VII, 232; *EB*, vol. II, 230 discusses a speech made in May 1789 in which Burke talks of Hastings's evasive statements as turning on a comparable rhetorical figure called the *painche* or screw, which he defines as 'a puzzled and a studied involution in a period, in order to prevent the discovery of truth'.
121 *WS*, vol. VII, 241–4, at 244.
122 *Ibid.*, 245; for Burke's most violent language, see his notorious accusation of 'murder ... by the hand of Sir Elijah Impey' against Hastings on 13 March 1789, and censure of Burke on 4 May (*EB*, vol. II, 224–8); cf. Sacheverell, *Tryal*, 150; and Hatsell, *Precedents*, 280.
123 *WS*, vol. VII, 242, 243; indignation is indeed an emotion much played upon by Macclesfield's prosecutors, and especially by the manager Sir John Rushout, in Macclesfield, *Tryal*, 87, 89; for the notorious harshness of the trial, see John Campbell, *Lord Chancellors*, vol. IV, 501–66, at 555.
124 *WS*, vol. VII, 131 (quoting Foster, *Report*, 376); cf. *ibid.*, 141–51 on impeachment.
125 *WS*, vol. V, 382 (my emphasis).
126 *Ibid.*, 403–4.
127 *TMS*, 16–26, 27 and esp. 48; see McKenna, *Adam Smith*, 73–132.
128 *WS*, vol. V, 519–20.
129 *WS*, vol. VII, 91 (23 December 1790).
130 *Ibid.*, 237. Burke's standard of proper submission seems to have been set by Lord Bacon's humble behaviour, recorded in *Complete Collection of State-Trials*, vol. I, 360–1; cf. Hatsell, *Precedents*, 100, 203.
131 *WS*, vol. VI, 277–8, 393; for the peculiar appropriateness of impeachment to prosecution of people of great character, see Blackstone, *Commentaries*, vol. IV, 260–1.
132 Burke to Philip Francis, 10 December 1785, *Corr.*, vol. V, 243.

133 *Speech on the Nabob of Arcot's Debts*, *WS*, vol. v, 502.
134 See Hatsell, *Precedents*, 281–2n., an account largely favourable to Burke's position; cf. Sacheverell, *Tryal*, 328.
135 *WS*, vol. vii, 142.
136 *Ibid.*, 92.
137 *Corr.*, vol. viii, 405; see 417 for the results of French Laurence's unavailing attempts to set the business of publication in motion.
138 *Corr.*, vol. viii, 439.
139 *Speech on Economical Reform*, *WS*, vol. iii, 547.
140 See Phillipson, 'Culture and Society'; cf. Klein, *Shaftesbury*, 123–53.
141 *Speech at Bristol Previous to the Election*, *WS*, vol. iii, 630.
142 *Thoughts on the Present Discontents*, *WS*, vol. ii, 252.

5 'REFLECTIONS ON THE REVOLUTION IN FRANCE' AND THE RHETORIC OF CHARACTER

1 The best account of Burke's knowledge of the *Procès-verbal de l'Assemblée nationale* (Paris, 1789–), the *Assemblée nationale, ou Courier françois*, and other sources for the National Assembly debates is in Clark's introduction to his edition of the *Reflections*, 48–9; see, for example, his account of a speech by de la Tour du Pin on 4 June 1790 [305].
2 This conjecture about the composition of the text is supported by remarks in Todd, *Bibliography*, item 53a; indeed, Burke reportedly 'blotted, rewrote, printed, cancelled, [and] reprinted' his proofs so often that not a page of the original composition survived intact (M'Cormick, *Memoirs*, 339, apparently reproducing the anecdote of Burke's then-secretary, William Thomas Swift); Thomas Paine, recently returned from Paris to refute Burke's forthcoming pamphlet, reported to a correspondent that the proof had been revised 'six, seven, and one nine times!' (*Complete Writings*, vol. ii, 1300–2).
3 *Parliamentary History of England*, vol. xxviii, 373.
4 *EB*, vol. ii, 254; the notice appeared in *The World*, 13 February 1790.
5 Burke, *Army Estimates*, 31–2; Burke had sketched out this sentence as early as 10 July 1789 in a letter to the Earl of Charlemont, *Corr.*, vol. vi, 1.
6 Burke, *Army Estimates*, 32.
7 Cf. Burke to William Windham, *c.*24 January 1789, *Corr.*, vol. v, 437, referring to his anxious 'solicitude relative to the present state of affairs, which ... is certainly less suitable to my time of life, in which all emotions are less allowed ...'.
8 *Reflections* [5–6]; cf. *Corr.*, vol. vi, 97: 'what have I to do with France?'
9 *WS*, vol. vii, 334, in a passage on state etiquette.
10 *Corr.*, vol. vi, 10–11; see also 26, 36, 37, 51.
11 The urge to witness the Revolution was felt by several of Burke's acquaintances, including his protégé William Windham (*Corr.*, vol. vi, 20–2), and by the many authors of eye-witness journals; see Blakemore, *Crisis in Representation.*

12 [76, 94, 244]. For an early statement on how speculation must be completed by practice, cf. Burke, *Note-Book*, 81: 'The end of learning is not knowledge but virtue; the end of all speculation should be practice of one sort or another.'
13 *OED*, 'extravagant', A1 (*Hamlet*, I.i.154) and A7 (*Spectator*, no. 243 ¶8).
14 Indeed, Depont's references to 'l'authorité de la Societé de la Revolution d'Angleterre' (*Corr.*, vol. VI, 59) may have first provoked Burke.
15 *EB*, vol. II, 369–75.
16 Cf. [126].
17 [126]; *WS*, vol. IX, 160; cf. vol. VI, 403: 'My Lords, permit me for one moment to drop my representative character here, and to speak to your Lordships only as a man of much experience in the world, and conversant with the affairs and with the characters of men . . .'.
18 *OED*, 'description', 3b; Burke's usage in *Thoughts on the Present Discontents*, *WS*, vol. II, 295, 'general descriptions of men', predates the earliest *OED* citation by eleven years; it is a word he often uses to describe the Dissenters, for example when discussing Joseph Priestley's leadership and their electoral influence in a letter to Fox, 9 September 1789: 'it would be something to neutralize the acid of that sharp and eager description of men' (*Corr.*, vol. VI, 15); two important discussions of Burkean 'description' focusing on his defence of minority interests are Williams, 'Burkean "Descriptions"'; and Pitts, *Turn to Empire*, 59–100, esp. 89.
19 Burke also writes of 'descriptions of law . . . describing the persons' to benefit from an inheritance [28]; in a later passage Burke seems to be using 'description' to mean the opposite of 'prescription', a right conceived of as original rather than historical [223].
20 Cf. *Letter to Sir Hercules Langrishe* (1792), *WS*, vol. IX, 602–3; and *Letter to Lord Kenmare* (1782), *WS*, vol. IX, 572.
21 Cf. *Remarks on the Policy of the Allies* (1793), *WS*, vol. VIII, 496: 'Everything like lumping men in masses, and of forming tables of proscription, ought to be avoided.'
22 For Burke's famous statement against instructions from constituencies, see *Speech at the Conclusion of the Poll* (1774), *WS*, vol. III, 69: a representative's 'unbiassed opinion, his mature judgement, his enlightened conscience, he ought not to sacrifice to you'; see Burke to Portland, *Corr.*, vol. IV, 274; and *Speech at Bristol Previous to Election* (1780), *WS*, vol. III, 632.
23 [59]; cf. Burke, *Appeal*, 180–1.
24 Paul Lucas, 'Doctrine of Prescription'.
25 See Jack A. Clarke, 'Turgot's Critique ', 502–5; and Crook, 'Citizen Bishops'.
26 [271]; cf. Hobbes, *Leviathan*, 111–15.
27 Mackintosh, *Vindiciae Gallicae*, 46.
28 *WS*, vol. III, 318.
29 Burke, *Works and Correspondence*, vol. VI, 130; cf. Pocock, 'Ancient Constitution', 227, where a curious emphasis is placed on an abbreviated citation of the third sentence here.

30 See examples from Bacon and Hall in *OED*, *adj.* 2.
31 *WS*, vol. v, 316–17.
32 For Burke on 'contract', see O'Gorman, *Edmund Burke*, 13, 17, 114–16; for 'opinion', see Hampsher-Monk, 'Rhetoric and Opinion', 473–84; for 'prejudice', see Wilkins, *Problem*, 108–13.
33 See also Burke to Depont, November 1789, *Corr.*, vol. vi, 42: 'of all the loose Terms in the world Liberty is the most indefinite'.
34 See *OED*, 'compliance'.
35 See Knights, *Representation*, 279–305; and Ashcraft, 'Language'.
36 See Molière, *Le Malade imaginaire* (1673), troisième intermède, 358: 'Mais, si maladia | Opiniatria | Non vult se guarire, | Quid illi facere? . . . Clysterium donare, | Postea seignare, | Ensuita purgare, | Reseignare, repurgare, et reclysterizare.'
37 For Burke on legal language, see also *Thoughts on the Present Discontents*, *WS*, vol. ii, 300, and *Speech on American Taxation*, *WS*, vol. ii, 427.
38 For a discussion of the philosophical discourse of reflection in Locke, see David Jules Law, *Rhetoric of Empiricism*, 51–92.
39 Burke's logic textbook at Trinity College, Dublin, Burgersdijck's *Institutionum logicarum* (1626), covers relations of analogy ('convenientia analogica') in i.xx.8, 91–2; for Burke's impatience with Burgersdijck, see *EB*, vol. i, 37.
40 See, for example, Burke's *First Letter on a Regicide Peace*, *WS*, vol. ix, 247–8, on the 'conformity and analogy' between the laws of the European nations; see Hale, *History*, 70.
41 Thomas Reid, for example, opposed 'reflection' and 'analogy' in *An Inquiry into the Human Mind* (1764), 503–8, esp. 508: 'The old [pre-Cartesian] philosophy seems to have been purely analogical: the new is more derived from reflection, but still with a very considerable mixture of the old analogical notions.'
42 Joseph Butler, *Analogy of Religion*, 278; the *Analogy* does not appear in Burke's library catalogue, but the many texts in which he could have found its method epitomized include Beattie, *Essay on the Nature and Immutability of Truth* (1770), 128–32.
43 Joseph Butler, *Analogy of Religion*, 4.
44 *Ibid.*, 287, 10.
45 *Ibid.*, 288; the attraction of natural scientists to analogical reasoning is discussed by Cheyne, 'Philosophical Conjectures'.
46 *WS*, vol. i, 134–5, referring to Isocrates, *Antidosis*, 15–16.
47 Aristotle, *Sophistici elenchi*, 167a1–20; discussed by Burgersdijck in *Institutionum logicarum*, ii.xxvii.1–15, pp. 284–9; see Engel, *With Good Reason*, 133–6.
48 Aristotle, *Rhetoric*, ii.xxiv.10; see Garver, *Aristotle's Rhetoric*, 168, 183; for Burke's comparative 'ignorance of Greek', see *EB*, vol. ii, 43.
49 Cf. Burke, *Appeal*, 19: 'These exceptions and modifications are not made by the process of logick, but by the rules of prudence.'
50 Burke had listed the categories once before, in the manuscript 'Plan for Arguing' that he transcribed into his notebook of the early 1750s. He places

them under the heading of deliberative arguments on principles of convenience (rather than justice): 'I think something in the way of Categories of great Use . . . these serve to class our Ideas' (*Note-Book*, 45–9, at 48).

51 *Memoirs of Scriblerus*, 120; cf. Watts, *Logick*, 37.

52 See *Speech on Fox's India Bill*, *WS*, vol. v, 402: 'Animated with all the avarice of age, and all the impetuousity of youth'; cf. *WS*, vol. vi, 283.

53 *WS*, vol. vii, 312; vol. viii, 163; cf. Thelwall, *Sober Reflections*, 4.

54 Burke, *Army Estimates*, 5 February 1790, *Parliamentary History of England*, 353.

55 Burke, *Appeal*, 28.

56 [331]; note the similarities between Burke's version of the Ovidian tale of Medea and the daughters of Pelias, and that of Richard Allestree in *Christian Piety*, 379, during a discussion of Satan's use of zealous people, 'whom he seems to have deluded in the same manner, that Medea is said to have done the daughters of Peleas, whom she perswaded to hack their aged Father in pieces, in hope that by her Magick, he should not only recover life but youth: so these rend and tear their Mother the Church out of a hope, no less delusive, of restoring her pristine beauty and vigor; how far the Event parallels it also, the dying state of Christianity does too sadly testifie'.

57 Hobbes, *Elements of Law*, 193; for similar references in Hobbes's *De cive*, see Skinner, *Reason and Rhetoric*, 174, 290.

58 The aphorism sounds Ciceronian, and recalls the discussion of special laws of duty in *De officiis*, i.xli.149, but also reflects a more modern commonplace sense that age and quality are the first characteristics to secure reverence (see, for example, Hobbes, *Behemoth*, 231).

59 The first citation is at [278], quoting *De senectute*, vii.25 on old age husbanding goods for the next generation (cf. *Army Estimates*, 32, quoting Ovid's 'turpe senex miles', as Burke does again in *Corr.*, vol. viii, 364; Rousseau uses the same tag in *Lettre à d'Alembert*); the second is at [312–13], quoting *De senectute*, xxiii.83 on preserving the 'stiffness' of old age.

60 [331]; Cicero, *De senectute*, vi.20.

61 See D. O. Thomas, 'Richard Price'.

62 For Burke's exclusion from the cabinet in 1782, see *EB*, vol. i, 503–4.

63 *Parliamentary History of England*, vol. xxvi, 358 (based on a report in *The Public Advertiser*, 6 February 1787); for an example, see Graves, *Spiritual Quixote*, vol. ii, 236, where Wildgoose and Captain Johnson attend a Methodist service conducted by a tradesman 'in an upper room, over his warehouse in the garden'.

64 The Birch translation of Bayle's *Dictionary* records that the first *hortus siccus* ordered on generic principles was made by Caesalpinus (Bayle, *General Dictionary*, vol. iv, 3–4).

65 Horace, *Epistles*, i.i: 'What right, what true, what fit we justly call, | Let this be all my care – for this is All: | To lay this harvest up, and hoard with haste | What ev'ry day will want, and most, the last' (Pope, iv.279–80); the tag's urgent sincerity clashes with Burke's theme of deceit.

66 For Burke's earlier language of desiccation in *Speech on Conciliation* ('mysterious virtue of wax and parchment', 'dry husks of oppressed indigence'), see *WS*, vol. III, 120, 129, 163.
67 Cf. Burke, *Appeal*, 197 on radical commonplaces: 'the rotten stuff, worn out in the service of delusion and sedition in all ages, and which being newly furbished up, patched, and varnished, serves well enough'.
68 In Oliver Goldsmith's fascinating little essay on grasshoppers in *History of the Earth*, vol. VII, 331–40, the female insect simply dries up after she has laid her eggs; he also mentions that grasshoppers are like cattle in so far as they have multiple stomachs for ruminative digestion.
69 See Marvell's 'Upon Appleton House', stanza xlvii, *Poems*, 277; and Cowley's 'The Grasshopper', no. 34 of the 'Anacreonta', *Poems*, 37.
70 Aristotle, *Rhetoric*, II.xxi.8; cf. Leland, *Dissertation*, 79 on rude sublimity; for an earlier example of Burke's insect imagery, see *American Taxation*, *WS*, vol. II, 448: 'in vain hopes that when their maggots had taken wing, their importunate buzzing might sound something like the public voice'.
71 See, for example, Judges 6.5 on the Midianite campaign against Israel: 'For they came up with their cattle and their tents, and they came as grasshoppers for multitude; *for* both they and their camels were without number: and they entered into the land and destroyed it.'
72 *WS*, vol. IX, 180; cf. 177, where the Duke's estates are 'fitted for nothing but to fatten bullocks, and to produce grain for beer, still more to stupify the dull English understanding'.
73 *WS*, vol. I, 134–5.
74 This allusion has gone unrecognized by Burke's editors: see Cicero, *De officiis*, I.xviii.61: 'ut boni ratiocinatores officiorum esse possimus et addendo deducendoque videre, quae reliqui summa fiat, ex quo, quantum cuique debeatur, intellegas'.
75 For background to the 'new form of social knowledge' involved with political arithmetic, see Brewer, *Sinews of Power*, 223–30.
76 Hobbes, *Leviathan*, 32.
77 *Ibid.*, 32–3; cf. Skinner, *Reason and Rhetoric*, 347.
78 Swift, *PW*, vol. II, 15; since Swift is discussing Jacobitism in this passage, there may be irony in the Hobbes reference; see Arbuthnot, *Proposals*, 8; *Memoirs of Scriblerus*, 118.
79 See, for example, Arthur Mainwaring, *The Medley*, no. 11 (11 December 1710), in Swift, *Swift vs. Mainwaring*, 88, for witty analogy with poetic and mathematical numbers: 'the Political Numbers come so little short of either one or the other, that even Law and Reason submit and fall down before them'; this appears to be an imitation of Swift's 'Oratorical Machines' and mystical numbers in *Tale of a Tub*, 'Introduction', 57–8.
80 *OED*, 'control', *v.*; see Swift, *Contests and Dissensions*, *PW*, vol. I, 200, *Advice to the October Club*, *PW*, vol. VI, 78, 'Introduction' to *Polite and Ingenious Conversation*, *PW*, vol. IV, 120 (cf. *Hints Towards an Essay*, vol. IV, 87), and the title of *Maxims Controlled in Ireland*, *PW*, vol. XII, 129–38.

81 *WS*, vol. IX, 251: 'for there is a sort of presumption against novelty, drawn out of a deed of consideration of human nature and human affairs; and the maxim of jurisprudence is well laid down, *Vestus pro lege semper habetur* [ancient custom is always considered law]'; see Bacon, 'Maxims', 35–108; and Stein, *Regulae Iuris*, 170–4.
82 Blackstone, *Commentaries*, vol. I, 67–8.
83 See Lord Cowper's ruling in Chancery, recorded by Robert Lucas, *Modern Reports*, vol. X, 1.
84 [149, 286]; *WS*, vol. III, 330.
85 Conversely, several maxims in the *Reflections* are concerned with pride, isolation and failure of self-knowledge: examples can found at [14], [68] and [70].
86 See Burke to Adrien-Jean-François Duport, post 29 March 1790, *Corr.*, vol. VI, 109; for the classic British Enlightenment attack on prejudice, see Toland, 'Origin', esp. 1–18; the best scholarly summary of the intellectual background to Burke's idea of prejudice is in Paul Lucas, 'Doctrine of Prescription', 61.
87 Beattie, *Essay*, 6, 411–13; cf. 235, 369 on 'philosophical prejudice'.
88 Swift, *Thoughts on Various Subjects*, *PW*, vol. I, 243: 'Some Men, under the notions of weeding out Prejudices; eradicate Religion, Virtue, and common Honesty'; see also *Tale of a Tub*, 161, and *Gulliver's Travels*, *PW*, vol. XI, 133.
89 Addison *et al.*, *Spectator*, no. 465, vol. IV, 142; see also vol. III, 18: 'if I am told I am acted by Prejudice, I am sure it is an honest Prejudice, it is a Prejudice that arises from the love of my Country, and therefore such a one as I shall always indulge'; also vol. III, 437; Chesterfield echoed Addison's tolerance of prejudice both in his unpublished correspondence (9 February 1749, *Letters*, vol. IV, 1307) and in one of the essays that he wrote for *The World*, no. 112 (20 February 1755).
90 Cf. Canavan, *Political Reason*, 74–80.
91 See [136] ('not a prejudice destitute of reason') and [242].
92 John 19.23–4; for the importance of this passage to the Church Fathers and to Swift's *Tale of a Tub*, see Quehen, 'Cyprian'; cf [255]: 'But if . . . we should uncover our nakedness by throwing off that Christian religion which has hitherto been our boast and comfort . . .'.
93 *PE*, 25, 27.
94 *Reflections* [59]; cf. *Appeal*, 180–1 on the compromised power of party leaders.
95 Hazlitt, 'My First Acquaintance with Poets', *Complete Works*, vol. XVII, 111; cf. the same remark in 'The Character of Mr. Burke', vol. VII, 305.

6 BURKE, ROUSSEAU AND THE PURCHASE OF ELOQUENCE

1 [245–6], quoting Virgil, *Georgics*, I.121–2: 'God himself has willed that the farmer's path should not be easy'; the passage on eloquence and wisdom recalls Sallust on Catiline, *Bellum Catalinarium*, V.3: 'eloquentiae satis, sapientiae parum' – J. C. D. Clark recognizes the allusion in *Reflections*, 338, n.556; Burke referred to character-writing in Sallust's Catiline, in *PE*, 111.

x.111; cf. Hobbes, *De corpore politico*, 11.viii.13, p. 87; for discussion, see Skinner, *Reason and Rhetoric*, 289.

2 Shaftesbury, *Characteristicks*, vol. 1, 64.

3 For Burke's earliest interest in Rousseau, see Ian Harris, 'Rousseau and Burke'; and Bullard, 'Figure of Emancipation', in Susan Manning and Peter France (eds.), *Enlightenment and Emancipation* (Lewisburg: Bucknell University Press, 2006), 44–62.

4 Rousseau, *Letter to d'Alembert*, 17; the *Letter* was reviewed in Burke's *Annual Register for the Year 1759*, 479.

5 But see Stanlis, 'Burke'; and Ritchie, 'Desire and Sympathy'; older studies stressing the similarities between Burke and Rousseau include Osborn, *Rousseau and Burke*; and Cameron, *Social Thought*.

6 See France, *Rhetoric and Truth*, 249–52.

7 The best historical account of the retreat is still Pottle, 'Part Played'.

8 *WS*, vol. VIII, 317, 313.

9 Burke to unknown, *c.*17 January 1790, *Corr.*, vol. VI, 81; Burke later uses the same form of words to dismiss another conjecturing political thinker, in *Reflections* [187]: 'I do not often quote Bolingbroke, nor have his works, in general, left any permanent impression on my mind.'

10 *WS*, vol. VIII, 312.

11 *Ibid.*, 318; in the French translation that was the first published edition of the *Letter to a Member of the National Assembly*, the translator Menonville gave the first sentence here as 'une charme qui nous échappe dans son langage', and the last as 'trop generalement manièré et lèché' (67) – with an implication of artificiality that is not there in Burke's English.

12 It is possible, however, that Burke has inherited some of these criticisms from his friend Hugh Blair, a copy of whose *Lectures* he has in his library; in Lecture 37 Blair condemns the unnatural events, tediousness and immorality of *Julie*, while acknowledging its power and tenderness (vol. II, 309).

13 Rousseau, *Discourses*, 260 (*OC*, vol. V, 388: 'elle substitue l'exactitude à l'expression').

14 Rousseau, *Discourse which Carried the Præmium*, ii–iii; the attribution of the preface to Bowyer is made by Nichols, *Literary Anecdotes*, vol. II, 225–7.

15 *Comparison of the Opinions of Mr. Burke*, 1–4, 20–55.

16 Burke to unknown, 26 January 1791, *Corr.*, vol. VI, 214–16; François Menonville, the recipient and translator of *Lettre de M. Burke a un membre de l'Assemblée nationale de France*, sent copies to Burke that same day; see Todd, *Bibliography*, 166–8.

17 Mackintosh, *Vindiciae Gallicae*, 207–8.

18 The *Letter* was reviewed in Burke's *Annual Register for the Year 1759*, 479: a list of Rousseau's faults is headed by 'a tendency to paradox, which is always the bane of solid learning, and threatens now to destroy it'; Rousseau's most famous paradox, the idea in *Emile* that education is about losing time, not gaining it, is quoted in a review of William Kenrick's translation in *Annual Register for the Year 1762*, 227; Burke also excerpted or referred to Rousseau's works in the *Annual Registers* for 1762 (158–9, the parallel between Christ and

Socrates from *Émile*; 208–10, Voltaire's 'prophetic' satire on Rousseau) and 1763 (5–8, an extract from Rousseau's autobiographical letter to Christophe de Beaumont; 86, a news report on the prosecution of *Lettre à d'Alembert* in Geneva).

19 A 1764 edition of Kenrick's translation of *Eloisa: or, a Series of Original Letters* does appear in the MS catalogue (fol. 24r); an Amsterdam edition of *Émile, ou De l'éducation* (1762) and the Nugent translation of *Emilius; or, An Essay on Education* appear in both MS (fol. 4r) and printed (p. 469) catalogues; Thomas Nugent was probably related to Burke's father-in-law, Dr Christopher Nugent, whom he mentions in his will ('Thomas Nugent', *Oxford Dictionary of National Biography*).

20 The tag is from Juvenal, *Satires*, IV.91; see Rousseau, *Julie, or the New Héloïse*, *CW*, vol. VI, 20 (*OC*, vol. II, 27): 'No, Monsieur, I shall not put my motto on this book; but that does not mean I shall give it up'; cf. also the opening of the 'profession de foi du vicaire Savoyard' in *Emile*, 266 (*OC*, vol. IV, 565–6): 'I do not want to argue with you or even convince you [*tenter de vous convaincre*]. It is enough for me to reveal to you what I think in the simplicity of my heart.'

21 *CW*, vol. X, 348 (*OC*, vol. V, 120); this corresponds closely with the passage in *Emile*, Book IV, 260 (*OC*, vol. IV, 558) in which he alludes to the motto: 'Readers, do not fear from me precautions unworthy [*indignes*] of a friend of the truth. I shall never forget my motto [*mon devise*]. But it is only too permissible for me to distrust my judgments'; cf. also his *Lettres de la montagne*, *OC*, vol. III, 686: 'je prie les lecteurs de vouloir bien mettre à part mon beau style, et d'examiner seulement si je raisonne bien ou mal'.

22 Rousseau to Malesherbes, 12 January 1762, *CW*, vol. V, 576 (*OC*, vol. I, 1136); cf. the 'Fragment biographique', *OC*, vol. I, 1113: 'c'est un grand avantage pour bien parler que de dire toujours ce qu'on pense, la bonne foi set de rhétorique, l'honneteté de talent et rien n'est plus semblable à l'éloquence que le ton d'un h[omme] fortement persuadé'; the letter to Malesherbes was referred to by Capel Lofft as evidence of the quality of Rousseau's sincerity, in *Remarks on the Letter of the Rt. Hon. Edmund Burke*, 81.

23 It perhaps owes something to Samuel Johnson's view of Rousseau, that 'a man who talks nonsense so well, must know that he is talking nonsense' (30 September 1769, Boswell, *Life of Johnson*, vol. II, 74).

24 Rousseau, *Discourses*, 11 (*OC*, vol. III, 11).

25 Rousseau, *Emile*, 416 (*OC*, vol. IV, 777).

26 *Ibid.*, 391 (*OC*, vol. IV, 743).

27 Rousseau, 'Second Preface', *CW*, vol. VI, 7–8 (*OC*, vol. II, 10–11).

28 *CW*, vol. V, 457 (*OC*, vol. I, 547). Cf. Richardson, *Selected Letters*, 41: 'I am introducing a new species of writing which might possibly turn young people into a course of reading different from the pomp and parade of romance writing, and dismissing the improbable and the marvellous, with which novels generally abound, might tend to promote the cause of religion and virtue'; see Munro, 'Richardson, Marivaux'.

29 John Nichols, for example, in *Literary Anecdotes*, alludes to this passage: 'Richardson has often been compared to Rousseau, and Rousseau was one of his professed admirers ... but the esteem was not reciprocal' (vol. IV, 598).

30 Lofft, *Remarks on the Letter of the Rt. Hon. Edmund Burke*, 177–9; Lofft commented on the sublimity of *La Nouvelle Héloïse* again in *Remarks on the Letter of Mr. Burke to a Member of the National Assembly*, 45–6.
31 Quoted by Hunt, 'Rhetoric of Revolution', 88–9; see also Dart, *Rousseau*, 43–75.
32 The political apotheosis of Rousseau had in fact begun before the publication of the *Reflections*: the position of honour given to his bust and a copy of the *Social Contract* was reported in *Le Moniteur*, no. 174 (23 June 1790), vol. IV, 691, col. 1; the statue was decreed on 21 December 1790, and the campaign for the removal of his remains from Ermenonville to the Panthéon began soon afterwards; see McNeil, 'Cult of Rousseau', 204.
33 Rousseau, *Emile*, 235 (*OC*, vol. I, 672).
34 *CW*, vol. V, 458 (*OC*, vol. I, 548).
35 *CW*, vol. VI, 20 (*OC*, vol. II, 28).
36 *CW*, vol. X, 264 (*OC*, vol. V, 18), where Rousseau remarks on the inevitable failure of Sophocles on the modern French stage: 'we would be unable to put ourselves in the places of men who are totally dissimilar to us [*qui ne nous ressemblent point*]'.
37 *CW*, vol. VI, 78–9 (*OC*, vol. II, 96); I am following here Nicholas Paige's argument about Rousseau's distinction between distanced commiseration and contagious propagation of passion, in 'Rousseau's Readers', 142–5.
38 *WS*, vol. VIII, 316.
39 *Ibid.*, 318.
40 *Ibid.*, 311, 312, 313.
41 Shklar, *Men and Citizens*, 148–150; see *Emile*, 93 (*OC*, vol. IV, 323) for Rousseau's basic discussion of the concept.
42 *WS*, vol. VIII, 313.
43 *Emile*, 94 (*OC*, vol. IV, 324).
44 *CW*, vol. VI, 403 (*OC*, vol. II, 491).
45 See de Staël, *Lettres*, esp. 37 on the 'bon Jean-Jacques'; see Lofft, *Remarks on the Letter of Mr. Burke to a Member of the National Assembly*, 170 on Rosseau's impenetrability to those not dispositionally sensitive to his work; see also McNeil, 'Cult of Rousseau', 200.
46 For the mutual opacity of men in civil society in the *First Discourse*, see Starobinsky, *Jean-Jacques Rousseau*, 13–40.
47 Rousseau, *Emile*, 237 (*OC*, vol. IV, 526).
48 *WS*, vol. VIII, 315; Menonville's French translation is less focused on the problem of authenticity: 'l'existence des hommes d'état, de la trempe de vos maîtres actuels, ne peut se soutenir qu'à l'aide des maximes inconséquentes, barbares, fallacieuses' (Burke, *Lettre*, 59).
49 *WS*, vol. VIII, 318.
50 *CW*, vol. VI, 10 (*OC*, vol. II, 13).
51 *WS*, vol. VIII, 317.
52 Rousseau, *Emile*, 340 (*OC*, vol. IV, 671).

53 Horace, *De arte poetica*, 99–100 (trans. Fairclough): 'Non satis est pulchra esse poemata, dulcia sunt.'

54 For example, Starobinsky, 'Rousseau et l'éloquence'; France, 'Lumières, politesse, énergie', 992–3, where he argues that in depicting Émile's warm eloquence Rousseau is describing his own; and most recently Garsten, *Saving Persuasion*, 55–83, who reads Rousseau's rhetoric as a tool for achieving the complete internalization of the Hobbesian sovereign, and thus the end of civic eloquence.

55 Rousseau, *Social Contract*, 71 (*OC*, vol. III, 383).

56 *Ibid.*, 13 ('Political economy') (*OC*, vol. III, 251); for the imitative (rather than philosophical) nature of Rousseauian musical rhetoric, see Kelly, *'To persuade'*, 329.

57 See n.54 above; an exception is Baczko, 'La cité et ses langages', 93, who argues that Rousseau restricts the Legislator's eloquence to moments of foundation and crisis; another is Starobinsky, 'Eloquence and Liberty', 205, who also emphasizes the historical dimension.

58 Rousseau, *Discourses*, 256 (*OC*, vol. V, 383).

59 *CW*, vol. VI, 456 (*OC*, vol. II, 557–8).

60 Rousseau, *Discourses*, 267–78, 279 (*OC*, vol. V, 395–408, 409).

61 Rousseau, *Emile*, 252 (*OC*, vol. IV, 547).

62 Rousseau, *Discourses*, 280 (*OC*, vol. V, 409).

63 *CW*, vol. VIII, 56 (*OC*, vol. VI, 1059); in the last pages of the *Confessions* Rousseau is on the point of seeking refuge in Corsica: 'however, in order to live peacefully, I would renounce the labour of legislation' (*CW*, vol. V, 545; *OC*, vol. I, 650); cf. Dillon, *Historical and Critical Memoirs*, 294, on how indifferent a politician Rousseau would have been, despite being capable of producing the *Social Contract*.

64 [245, 247, 249]. These usages of the word 'mind' refer back to the paragaph at [233–4] that begins: 'There are moments in the fortune of states when particular men are called to make improvements by great mental exertion.'

65 Puttenham, *Arte of English Poesie*, 123–4; see also Ben Jonson's note on 'ingeniorum discrimina' in *Timber*, 562–4; and Charleton, *Two Discourses*, 1–144.

66 For a similar punning usage, see Shaftesbury, *Characteristicks*, vol. I, 112: 'The *close Sympathy* and *conspiring Virtue*'.

67 Quintilian, *Institutio oratoria*, III.vii.25: 'Omnis enim deliberatio de dubiis est.'

68 25 September 1774, *Corr.*, vol. III, 46; cf. Burke to Sir Gilbert Elliot, 22 September 1793, *Corr.*, vol. VII, 434: 'No politician can make a Situation. His skill consists in well playing the Game dealt him by fortune; and following the indications given by nature, times, and circumstances.'

69 This becomes an increasingly urgent theme in Burke's later French pamphlets: 'I must see the things; I must see the men ... Plans must be made for men. We cannot think of making men, and building nature to our designs' (*WS*, vol. VIII, 326).

CONCLUSION

1 Burke, *First Letter on a Regicide Peace*, *WS*, vol. IX, 243.
2 *Ibid.*, 242; *Reflections* [130].
3 Burke to William Markham, post 9 November 1771, *Corr.*, vol. II, 282.
4 Cf. Canavan, *Political Reason*, 18, where he quotes the 'immutable rules' phrase from a transcription of Burke's speech at the impeachment of Hastings, 7 May 1789; see *WS*, vol. VII, 60–5.
5 Cf. *Speech at the Conclusion of the Poll* (1774), *WS*, vol. III, 68–9.
6 Burke, *Appeal*, 130; *Reflections* [146].
7 See *Letter to a Noble Lord*, *WS*, vol. IX, 171: 'under the direction of reason, instinct is always in the right'.
8 *WS*, vol. II, 332; *Journal of the House of Commons*, vol. XXXII, 969–70.
9 *Parliamentary History of England*, vol. XVIII, 835–6; for 'previous question', see P. D. G. Thomas, *House of Commons*, 178–82, quoting Burke at 180.
10 Esp. Namier, 'Character of Burke'; see the exchange between Alan Ryan and Conor Cruise O'Brien on Burke and the Namierites, 28 January 1993, *New York Review of Books*, 40.3.
11 Boswell, *Life of Johnson*, vol. III, 233.
12 Burke to Charles-Jean-François Depont, November 1789, *Corr.*, vol. VI, 48.
13 *Reflections* [49].
14 Burke to Charles-Jean-François Depont, November 1789, *Corr.*, vol. VI, 48.
15 *WS*, vol. II, 252.
16 *Letter to the Sheriffs of Bristol*, *WS*, vol. III, 314–16.
17 *WS*, vol. III, 634.
18 Burke to Portland, 3 September 1780, *Corr.*, vol. IV, 274; cf. *WS*, vol. III, 662: 'I had . . . much rather pass the remainder of my life hidden in the recesses of the deepest obscurity . . . than to be placed on the most splendid throne in the universe, tantalized with a denial of the practice of all which can make the greatest situation other than the greatest curse.'
19 Mill, *On Liberty*, 63.
20 Burke, *Note-Book*, 88.
21 *Speech on Conciliation*, *WS*, vol. III, 124, quoting Ovid, *Herodias*, XV.53.

Bibliography

This bibliography notes primary sources that are mentioned in the two surviving catalogues of Edmund Burke's library. The first is a printed sale catalogue, *Catalogue of the Library of the late Right Hon. Edmund Burke* (1833). The second is an earlier manuscript shelf list in the Bodleian Library, Oxford, *Catalogue of a library of Books late the property of the R. Hon. Ed Burke dc'd, August 17th 1813* (Bod. MS Eng Misc d. 722). I have made these notes in square brackets after the relevant entries. Where the edition in the catalogues differs from the edition I have used, I have noted the date of publication from the catalogue. Then I give the entry number from the printed catalogue, followed by a semi-colon, followed by the page number, page side (recto or verso) and entry number from the manuscript catalogue.

PRIMARY SOURCES

Addison, Joseph, *The Freeholder*, ed. James Leheny (Oxford: Clarendon Press, 1979)

Miscellaneous Works in Verse and Prose, ed. Thomas Tickell, 3 vols. (London, 1736)

et al., *The Spectator*, ed. Donald F. Bond, 5 vols. (Oxford: Clarendon Press, 1965) [1757: 499; 23^{v}/8]

An Address to the Hibernian Society, with a Plan of Education (Dublin, 1758)

The Adventurer, 2 vols. (London, 1753) [1762: 487; 23^{v}/16]

Allestree, Richard, *The Causes of the Decay of Christian Piety* (London, 1667) [*Works*, 1695: 661; 5^{v}/10]

Arbuckle, James, *Hibernicus's Letters*, 2nd edn, 2 vols. (London, 1734; 1st edn 1729)

Arbuthnot, John, *Proposals for Printing . . . a Treatise of the Art of Political Lying*, in Conal Condren, *Satire, Lies and Politics: The Case of Dr. Arbuthnot* (Basingstoke: Macmillan, 1997)

Aristotle, *Aristotelous technēs rhētorikēs biblia tria*, ed. G. Holwell, (Oxford, 1759) [15; 14^{v}/9]

The 'Art' of Rhetoric, trans. J. H. Freese, Loeb Classical Library (London: Heinemann; Cambridge, MA: Harvard University Press, 1959)

Nichomachean Ethics, trans. H. Rackham, Loeb Classical Library (London: Heinemann; New York: G.P. Putnam's Sons, 1926)

Arnauld, Antoine and Pierre Nicole, *Logic or the Art of Thinking (1662–83)*, ed. Jill Vance Buroker (Cambridge University Press, 1996)

Augustine of Hippo, *On Christian Teaching*, trans. R. P. H. Green (Oxford University Press, 1997)

Saint Augustine of the Citie of God: With the Learned Comments of J.L. Vives (London, 1620) [176; 36r/3]

Bacon, Francis, *The Advancement of Learning*, ed. Michael Kiernan, The Oxford Francis Bacon 4 (Oxford: Clarendon Press, 2000)

The Essayes or Counsels, Civill and Morall, ed. Michael Kiernan, The Oxford Francis Bacon 15 (Oxford: Clarendon Press, 1985)

The Essays, ed. Brian Vickers (Oxford University Press, 1999)

'The Maxims of the Law', in *Law Tracts* (London, 1737), 35–108

The Works of Francis Bacon, ed. James Spedding *et al.*, 7 vols. (London, 1858) [1753: 186; 6v/14]

Barclay, Robert (the elder) *An Apology for the True Christian Divinity, as the same is held forth ... by the people, called ... Quakers* (1678) [1703: 36; 24v/13]

Bayle, Pierre, *A General Dictionary, Historical and Critical*, ed. Thomas Birch *et al.*, 10 vols. (London, 1734)

Pensées diverses sur la comète (The Hague, 1727)

Beattie, James, *An Essay on the Nature and Immutability of Truth* (Edinburgh, 1770) [1776: 125; 33v/14]

Dissertations Moral and Critical (London, 1783) [125; 33v/15]

Bentley, Richard, 'Matter and Motion Cannot Think, or, A Confutation of Atheism from the Faculties of the Soul', in *A Defence of Natural and Revealed Religion: Being a Collection of the Sermons Preached at the Lecture Founded by the Honourable Robert Boyle, Esq.*, 3 vols. (London, 1739), vol. 1, 12–22

Berkeley, George, *Alciphron: or, the Minute Philosopher*, 2 vols. (London, 1732)

A Miscellany, Containing Several Tracts on Various Subjects, (Dublin, 1752)

Blackstone, William, *Commentaries on the Law of England*, 4 vols. (Oxford, 1765–9) [1770: 118; 24r/7]

Blair, Hugh, *Lectures on Rhetoric and Belles Lettres* (1783) [124; 34r/3]

Boileau-Despréaux, Nicholas, *Oeuvres diverses du sieur D*** avec le Traité du sublime ou du merveilleux dans le discours* (Paris, 1674) [–; 10r/4]

Bolingbroke, first Viscount (Henry Saint-John), *Bolingbroke: Political Writings*, ed. David Armitage (Cambridge University Press, 1997) [1754: 123; 33r/10]

Boswell, James, *Boswell's Life of Johnson*, ed. George Birkbeck Hill, 6 vols. (Oxford: Clarendon Press, 1887)

The Correspondence of James Boswell with David Garrick, Edmund Burke, and Edmund Malone, ed. Thomas W. Copeland *et al.* (London: Heinemann, 1986)

The Letters of James Boswell, ed. Chauncey Brewster Tinker, 2 vols. (Oxford: Clarendon Press, 1924)

Private Papers of James Boswell from Malahide Castle, ed. Geoffrey Scott, 18 vols. (Mount Vernon: Rudge, 1928–34)

Bouhours, Dominique, *The Arts of Logicke and Rhetorick, Illustrated by Examples Taken out of the Best Authors*, trans. John Oldmixon (London, 1728)

Broome, Ralph, *Letters from Simpkin the Second, to his Dear Brother in Wales* (London, 1789)

Brown, John, *Essays on the Characteristics* (London, 1751) [1755: 33; 25^{v}/12]

An Estimate of the Manners and Principles of the Times (London, 1757) [33; 21^{v}/8]

Brown, Tom, *Amusements Serious and Comical, Calculated for the Meridian of London* (London, 1700)

Browne, Sir Thomas, *Religio Medici and Other Works*, ed. L. C. Martin (Oxford: Clarendon Press, 1964) [1686: 191; 6^{v}/10]

Burgersdicii, Fr., *Institutionum logicarum libri duo* (Cambridge, 1637)

Burke, Edmund, *An Appeal from the New to the Old Whigs* (London, 1791)

The Correspondence of Edmund Burke, ed. Thomas W. Copeland, 10 vols. (Cambridge University Press, 1958–78)

Lettre de M. Burke à un membre de L'Assemblée nationale de France, trans. Francois-Louis Thibault de Menonville (Paris, 1791)

A Note-Book of Edmund Burke: Poems, Characters, Essays and Other Sketches in the Hands of Edmund and William Burke now Printed for the First Time in their Entirety and Edited, ed. H. V. F. Somerset (Cambridge University Press, 1957)

A Philosophical Enquiry into the Origin of our Ideas of the Sublime and Beautiful, ed. J. T. Boulton (London: Routledge, 1958)

Reflections on the Revolution in France: A Critical Edition, ed. J. C. D. Clark (Stanford University Press, 2001) [numbers in square brackets referring to the pagination of the 1790 1st edn]

Substance of the Speech ... on the Army Estimates (London, 1790)

The Works and Correspondence of the Right Honourable Edmund Burke, new edn, 8 vols. (London: Rivington, 1852)

The Works ... of Edmund Burke, ed. W. King and F. Laurence, 8 vols. (London, 1792–1827)

The Writings and Speeches of Edmund Burke, gen. ed. Paul Langford, 9 vols. (Oxford: Clarendon Press, 1981–2000)

Burnet, Gilbert, *Bisoph Burnet's History of his own Time*, ed. M. J. Routh, 6 vols. (Oxford: Clarendon Press, 1823) [1724–34: 189; 35^{v}/5]

Burney, Frances, *The Journals and Letters of Fanny Burney (Madame d'Arblay)*, ed. Joyce Hemlow *et al.*, 12 vols. (Oxford: Clarendon Press, 1972–84)

Butler, Joseph, *The Analogy of Religion, Natural and Revealed, to the Constitution and Course of Nature* (London, 1736)

Butler, Samuel, *The Genuine Remains in Verse and Prose of Mr. Samuel Butler*, ed. R. Thyer, 2 vols. (London, 1759)

Caldwell, James, *Debates Relative to the Affairs of Ireland in the Years 1763 and 1764*, 2 vols. (London, 1766)
Campbell, George, *The Philosophy of Rhetoric* (London, 1776)
Campbell, Lord John, *Lives of the Lord Chancellors*, 4th edn, 10 vols. (London, 1856–7)
Caussin, Nicolas, *Eloquentia sacrae et humanae parallela*, 2nd edn (Cologne, 1626)
Cavendish, Sir Henry, *Debates of the House of Commons*, ed. J. Wright, 2 vols. (London, 1841–3)
Charlemont, first Earl of (James Caulfeild), *Historical Manuscripts Commission, 13th Report, Appendix, Part VIII: The Manuscripts and Correspondence of James, First Earl of Charlemont*, 2 vols. (London: HMSO, 1891–4), vol. II: *1784–1799*
Charleton, Walter, *Epicurus's Morals* (London, 1656)
Two Discourses: I. Concerning the Different Wits of Men: II. Of the Mysterie of Vintners, 2nd edn (London, 1675)
Charron, Pierre, *Œuvres*, 2 vols. (Geneva: Slatkine Reprints, 1970)
Chesterfield, fourth Earl of (Philip Dormer Stanhope), *Characters of Eminent Personages of his own Time* (London, 1778)
The Letters of Philip Dormer Stanhope, 4th Earl of Chesterfield, ed. Bonamy Dobrée, 6 vols. (London: King's Printers, 1932)
Cheyne, George, 'Philosophical Conjectures', in *An Essay on Regimen, together with Five Discourses* (London, 1740), 193–236
Cicero, Marcus Tullius, *Cato and Laelius*, trans. William Melmoth, 2 vols. (London, 1777)
Tully's Offices in English, trans. T. Cockman, 3rd edn (London, 1714)
Clarke, John, *The Foundation of Morality in Theory and Practice* (London, 1726)
A Comparison of the Opinions of Mr. Burke and Monsr. Rousseau on Government Reform, and Strictures on the Answers to Mr. Burke (London, 1790)
A Complete Collection of State-Trials, and Proceedings for High Treason, 2nd edn, 6 vols. (London, 1730)
Cowley, Abraham, *Poems* (London, 1656)
The Works of Mr. Abraham Cowley, ed. Thomas Sprat (London, 1668) [208; 6^r/11]
Cudworth, Ralph, *The True Intellectual System of the Universe*, ed. Thomas Birch, 2 vols. (1678; 2nd edn 1743)
Cureau de la Chambre, Marin, *L'Art de connoistre les hommes*, 2 vols. (Paris, 1659–69)
The Characters of the Passions, trans. John Holden (London, 1649)
de Staël, Germaine, *Lettres sur les écrits et caractère de J.J. Rousseau* (Paris, 1788)
Demosthenes, *The Orations of Demosthenes, Delivered on Occasions of Public Deliberation*, trans. Thomas Leland (London, 1771) [162; 13^r/6]
Dillon, Sir John Talbot, *Historical and Critical Memoirs of the General Revolution in France* (London, 1790)

Diogenes Laertius, *Lives of Eminent Philosophers*, trans. R. D. Hicks, 2 vols., Loeb Classical Library (London: Heinemann; Cambridge, MA: Harvard University Press, 1931–8)

Dryden, John, *The Miscellaneous Works of John Dryden, Esq.; Containing all his Original Poems, Tales, and Translations*, ed. Samuel Derrick, 4 vols. (London, 1760) [99; 21^{v}/18]

The Poems of John Dryden, ed. Paul Hammond *et al.*, 5 vols. (London: Longman, 1995–2005)

Dunton, John, *The History of Living Men: or, Characters of the Royal Family, the Ministers of State, and the Principal Natives of the Three Kingdoms* (London, 1702)

Dyce, Samuel, *Recollections of the Table-Talk of Samuel Rogers* (New Southgate: H.A. Rogers, 1887)

Dykes, Oswald, *Moral Reflexions upon Select English Proverbs: Familiarly Accommodated to the Humour and Manners of the Present Age* (London, 1708)

Eachard, John, *The Grounds & Occasions of the Contempt of the Clergy and Religion*, 8th edn (London, 1672; 1st edn 1670)

Egmont, second Earl of (John Perceval), *Faction Detected, by the Evidence of Facts*, 3rd edn (Dublin, 1743)

Elliot, Sir Gilbert, *The Life and Letters of Sir Gilbert Elliot*, ed. Countess of Minto, 3 vols. (London: Longmans, Green, 1874)

Elyot, Sir Thomas, *The Book Named the Governor* (London, 1531)

Epicurus, *Epikouros Menoikei Charein*, in *Epicurus: The Extant Remains*, ed. Cyril Bailey (Oxford: Clarendon Press, 1926), 80–93

Fénelon, François de la Mothe, *Dialogues on Eloquence,* trans. W. S. Howell (Princeton University Press, 1951)

Œuvres, ed. Jacques le Brun, 2 vols. (Paris: Gallimard, 1983)

Ferguson, Adam, *An Essay on the History of Civil Society* (Edinburgh, 1767) [138; 33^{v}/10]

Flecknoe, Richard, *A Collection of the Choicest Epigrams and Characters of Richard Flecknoe*, 2 vols. (London, 1673)

Fordyce, David, *Dialogues Concerning Education*, 2 vols. (London, 1745) [103; 28^{v}/3]

Theodorus: A Dialogue Concerning the Art of Preaching, 3rd edn (London, 1755)

Foster, Sir Michael, *A Report on some Proceedings on the Commission of Oyer and Terminer* (Oxford, 1762)

Fuller, Thomas, *Gnomologia: Adagies and Proverbs* (London, 1732)

Gally, Henry, 'A Critical Essay on Characteristic-Writings', in *Moral Characters of Theophrastus* (London, 1725)

Gay, John, 'Preliminary Dissertation Concerning the Fundamental Principle of Virtue or Morality', in William King, *An Essay on the Origin of Evil*, ed. Edmund Law, expanded and corrected 4th edn (Cambridge, 1758; 1st edn 1731)

Glanvill, Joseph, *An Essay Concerning Preaching: Written for the Direction of a Young Divine* (London, 1678)

A Seasonable Defence of Preaching: And the Plain Way of It (London, 1678)

Goldsmith, Oliver, *A History of the Earth, and Animated Nature*, 8 vols. (London, 1774)
Graves, Richard, *The Spiritual Quixote: A Comic Romance*, 3 vols. (London, 1773)
Gray, Thomas, William Collins and Oliver Goldsmith, *The Poems of Gray, Collins and Goldsmith*, ed. Roger Lonsdale (Harlow: Longman, 1969)
Hale, Matthew, *The History and Analysis of the Common Law of England* (London, 1713)
Hall, Joseph, *Characters of Vertues and Vices* (London, 1608)
Harris, James, *Three Treatises. The first Concerning Art. The Second Concerning Music, Painting, and Poetry. The Third Concerning Happiness* (London, 1744) [269; 29^{r}/3]
Hartley, David, *Observations on Man, his Frame, his Duty, and his Expectations*, 2 vols. (London, 1749) [265; 22^{v}/4]
Hartley, David (the younger), *Speech and Motions Made in the House of Commons* (London, 1775)
Hatsell, John, *Precedents of Proceedings in the House of Commons*, vol. IV: *Relating to Conference, and Impeachment* (London, 1796)
Hazlitt, William, *The Complete Works*, ed. P. P. Howe, 21 vols. (London: Dent, 1930–4)
Hill, John, *A Review of the Works of the Royal Society of London*, 2nd edn (London, 1780)
Hobbes, Thomas, *Behemoth*, in *The English Works of Thomas Hobbes of Malmesbury*, ed. Sir William Molesworth, 11 vols. (London: John Bohn, 1839), vol. VI
De corpore politico, in *The Moral and Political Works of Thomas Hobbes* (London, 1750)
The Elements of Law, Natural and Politic, ed. J. C. A. Gaskin (Oxford University Press, 1994)
Leviathan, ed. Richard Tuck (Cambridge University Press, 1991)
Horace, *Satires, Epistles and Ars poetica*, trans. H. Rushton Fairclough, Loeb Classical Library (London: Heinemann; Cambridge, MA: Harvard University Press, 1929)
Hume, David, *Enquiries Concerning Human Understanding, and Concerning the Principles of Morals*, ed. L. A. Selby-Bigge, 3rd edn, rev. P.H. Nidditch (Oxford: Clarendon Press, 1975)
Essays, Moral, Political and Literary, ed. Eugene R. Miller (Indianapolis: Liberty Fund, 1985)
The History of England, from the Invasion of Julius Cæsar to the Revolution in 1688, 2 vols. (London, 1762) [335; 33^{r}/17]
The Natural History of Religion, in *Four Dissertations* (London, 1757)
A Treatise of Human Nature, ed. L. A. Selby-Bigge, 2nd edn (Oxford University Press, 1978)
Hurd, Richard, *A Letter to the Rev. Dr. Thomas Leland, Fellow of Trinity College, Dublin: In which his Late Dissertation on the Principles of Human Eloquence is Criticized* (London, 1764) [1765: 260; 23^{v}/4]

Hutcheson, Francis, *An Essay on the Nature and Conduct of the Passions* (London, 1728)
An Inquiry into the Original of our Ideas of Beauty and Virtue, ed. Wolfgang Leidhold (Indianapolis: Liberty Fund, 2004)
A System of Moral Philosophy, in Three Books, 2 vols. (London, 1755) [339; 34r/1]
Jackson, John, *A Defense of Human Liberty* (London, 1725)
Jenyns, Soame, *Miscellaneous Pieces*, 2 vols. (London, 1747) [1761: 281; 21r/6]
Johnson, Samuel, *The Lives of the Poets*, ed. Roger Lonsdale, 4 vols. (Oxford: Clarendon Press, 2006)
The Yale Edition of the Works of Samuel Johnson, ed. J. H. Middendorf *et al.*, 24 vols. (New Haven, CT: Yale University Press, 1958–)
Johnson, Thomas, *An Essay on Moral Obligation: With a View towards Settling the Controversy, Concerning Moral and Positive Duties* (London, 1731)
Jonson, Ben, *Timber*, in *English Renaissance Literary Criticism*, ed. Brian Vickers (Oxford: Clarendon Press, 1999)
Kames, Lord (Henry Home), *The Elements of Criticism*, 3 vols. (Edinburgh, 1762) [1765: 261; –]
La Bruyère, Jean de, *Les Caractères*, ed. Marc Escola (Paris: Champion, 1999)
La Mothe Le Vayer, François de, *Des anciens et principaus historiens, grecs et latins* (Paris, 1646)
Notitia historicorum selectorum, or, Animadversions upon the Antient and Famous Greek and Latin Histories, trans. William Davenant (Oxford, 1678)
Lamy, Bernard, *La Rhétorique ou l'art de parler*, ed. Christine Noille-Clauzade (Paris: Champion, 1998)
Law, Edmund, *An Enquiry into the Ideas of Space, Time, Immensity and Eternity* (Cambridge, 1734)
'The Nature and Obligations of Man, as a Sensible and Rational Being', in William King, *An Essay on the Origin of Evil*, ed. Edmund Law, expanded and corrected 4th edn (Cambridge, 1758; 1st edn 1731)
Lawson, John, *Lectures Concerning Oratory, Delivered at Trinity College, Dublin* (Dublin, 1758)
Le Clerc, Jean, *Epistolae criticae et ecclesiasticae, in quibus ostenditur usus artis criticae* (Amsterdam, 1700)
Logica, sive, ars ratiocinandi (London, 1692)
Le Grand, Antoine, *An Entire Body of Philosophy According to the Principles of the Famous Renate Des Cartes* (1694)
Le Moyne, Pierre, *Peintures morales: ou Les passions sont representées par tableaux, par characteres, & par questions nouvelles & curieuses*, 2 vols. (Paris, 1640–3)
Le Noble, Eustache, *The Art of Prudent Behaviour, in a Father's Advice to his Son*, trans. Abel Boyer (London, 1701)
Leland, Thomas, *A Dissertation on the Principles of Human Eloquence* (London, 1764; 2nd edn 1765)
A Letter of a Member of the House of Commons in Ireland to a Gentleman of the Long Robe in England (London, 1720)
The Letters of Junius, ed. John Cannon (Oxford: Clarendon Press, 1978)

Locke, John, *An Essay Concerning Human Understanding*, ed. Peter Nidditch (Oxford: Clarendon Press, 1975) [1751: 413; $31^{v}/3$]

The Reasonableness of Christianity as Delivered in the Scriptures (London, 1695)

Some Familiar Letters between Mr. Locke and Several of his Friends (London, 1708)

Some Thoughts Concerning Education, ed. John W. Yolton and Jean S. Yolton (Oxford: Clarendon Press, 1989)

Lofft, Capel, *Remarks on the Letter of Mr. Burke, to a Member of the National Assembly* (London, 1791)

Remarks on the Letter of the Rt. Hon. Edmund Burke, 2nd edn, with additions (London, 1791)

Longinus, *Dionysiou Longinou peri hypsous hypomnēma: Dionysii Longini de sublimitate commentarius*, ed. Zachary Pearce (London, 1743) [302; $37^{r}/1$]

Lucas, Charles, *An Appeal to the Commons and Citizens of London* (London, 1756)

Lucas, Robert, *Modern Reports, or Cases in Law and Equity*, 10 vols. (London, 1736)

Lucretius, *De rerum natura*, trans. W. H. D. Rouse, 3rd edn, Loeb Classical Library (London: Heinemann; Cambridge, MA: Harvard University Press, 1937)

Macclesfield, first Earl of (Thomas Parker), *The Tryal of Thomas Earl of Macclesfield, in the House of Peers, for High Crimes and Misdemeanors* (London, 1725) [647; –]

Mackintosh, James, *Vindiciae Gallicae*, ed. Donald Winch (Indianapolis: Liberty Fund, 2006)

Macky, John, *Memoirs of the Secret Services of John Macky, Esq.* (London, 1733)

Madden, Samuel, *Proposal for the General Encouragement of Learning in Dublin-College* (Dublin, 1731)

Reflections and Resolutions Proper for the Gentlemen of Ireland (Dublin, 1738)

Mandeville, Bernard, *The Fable of the Bees, or Private Vices, Publick Benefits*, ed. F. B. Kaye, 2 vols. (Oxford: Clarendon Press, 1924) [1732: 309; $23^{r}/8$]

Mapletoft, John, *A Select Collection of Proverbs … Morally Adapted to the Humours of the Age* (London, 1710)

Marvell, Andrew, *The Poems of Andrew Marvell*, ed. Nigel Smith (London: Longman, 2003)

M'Cormick, Charles, *Memoirs of the Right Honourable Edmund Burke* (London, 1797)

Memoirs of the Extraordinary Life, Works and Discoveries of Martinus Scriblerus, ed. Charles Kerby-Miller (Oxford University Press, 1988)

Middleton, Conyers, *An Essay on the Gift of Tongues*, in *Miscellaneous Works*, 4 vols. (London, 1752), vol. II, 79–103 [360; $34^{v}/2$]

History of the Life of Marcus Tullius Cicero (1741; 5th edn 1755)

Mill, John Stuart, *On Liberty and Other Essays*, ed. John Gray (Oxford University Press, 1991)

Milton, John, *Paradise Lost. A Poem, in Twelve Books*, ed. Thomas Newton, 2 vols. [361; 33^{r}/12]
Molesworth, Robert, first Viscount, *An Account of Denmark, as it was in the Year 1692* (London, 1694) [318; 25^{r}/8]
Some Considerations for the Promoting of Agriculture, and Employing the Poor (Dublin, 1723)
Molière, Jean-Baptiste, *Le Malade imaginaire*, in *Œuvres complètes*, 8 vols. (Paris, 1825), vol. VIII [1760–70: 303; 37^{r}/7]
Molyneux, William, *The Case of Ireland's being Bound by Acts of Parliament in England, Stated* (Dublin, 1698)
Le Moniteur (Réimpression de l'ancien Moniteur) (Paris: Henri Plon, 1860)
Montaigne, Michel de, *The Complete Essays*, ed. and trans. M. A. Screech, (London: Allen Lane, 1991)
Essais, ed. André Tournon, 3 vols (Paris: Imprimerie nationale, 1998)
Les Essais de Michel Seigneur de Montaigne, ed. Pierre Coste, 3 vols. (London, 1724) [308; 10^{v}/1]
Montesquieu, Baron de (Charles de Secondat), *Œuvres complètes*, ed. Danile Oster (Paris: Éditions du Seuil, 1964) [1757: 307; 3^{r}/10]
Nichols, John, *Literary Anecdotes of the Eighteenth Century*, 6 vols. (London, 1812)
Overbury, Sir Thomas, *A Wife Now the Widow of Sir Thomas Overburie … Whereunto are Added Many Witty Characters, and Conceyted Newes; Written by Himselfe, and Other Learned Gentlemen his Friendes* (London, 1614)
Paine, Thomas, *Complete Writings*, ed. P. S. Foner, 2 vols. (New York: Citadel Press, 1945)
The Rights of Man (Part I, 1790), in *Political Writings*, ed. Bruce Kuklick (Cambridge University Press, 1989)
Parliamentary or Constitutional History of England, 24 vols. (London, 1751–6)
The Parliamentary History of England from the Norman Conquest in 1066 to the Year 1803, ed. W. Cobbett, 36 vols. (London, 1806–20)
Pascal, Blaise, *Pensées*, in *Œuvres complètes*, ed. Jacques Chevalier (Paris: Gallimard, 1954)
Perceval, Spencer, *A Review of the Arguments in Favor of the Continuance of Impeachments* (London, 1791)
Pilkington, Laetitia, *Memoirs of Mrs. Laetitia Pilkington*, 3 vols. (London, 1748)
Political Correspondence: or Letters to a Country Gentleman, Retired from Parliament (London, 1793)
Pope, Alexander, *The Twickenham Edition of the Poems of Alexander Pope*, ed. John Butt *et al.*, 11 vols. (London: Methuen, 1939–69) [1760: 449; 21^{v}/16]
Priestley, Joseph, *A Course of Lectures on Oratory and Criticism* (London, 1777)
The History and Present State of Discoveries Relating to Vision, Light, and Colours, 2 vols. (London, 1773) [547; 33^{v}/12]
The Proceedings of the Hibernian Society (Dublin, 1758)
Pufendorf, Samuel, *De officio hominis & civis*, ed. Thomas Johnson (Cambridge, 1737) [456; 26^{r}/6]

Puttenham, George, *The Arte of English Poesie Contrived into Three Bookes* (London, 1589)

Rainolds, John, *John Rainolds's Oxford Lectures on Aristotle's Rhetoric*, ed. L. D. Green (Newark: University of Delaware Press, 1986)

Rapin, René, *Du grand ou du sublime dans les moeures et dans les différentes conditions des hommes* (Amsterdam, 1786)

The Whole Critical Works, trans. Basil Kennet *et al.*, 2 vols. (London, 1706)

Reid, Thomas, *An Inquiry into the Human Mind* (Edinburgh, 1764)

Retz, Cardinal de (Jean François Paul de Gondi), *Memoires de Monsieur le Cardinal de Retz* (Amsterdam, 1717) [306; 3^r/18]

A Review of the Parliamentary Conduct of the Right Hon. Charles James Fox and the Right Hon. Edmund Burke; and a Parallel Drawn between their Different Modes of Elocution (London, 1789)

Reynolds, Edward, *A Treatise of the Passions and Faculties of the Soule of Man* (London, 1640)

Rousseau, Jean-Jacques, *The Collected Writings of Rousseau*, gen. ed. Roger Masters and Christopher Kelly, 13 vols. (Hanover, NH: University Press of New England for Dartmouth College, 1990–)

The Discourses and Other Early Political Writings, ed. and trans. Victor Gourevitch (Cambridge University Press, 1997)

The Discourse which Carried the Præmium at the Academy at Dijon (London, 1751)

Emile, or on Education, trans. Allan Bloom (New York: Basic Books, 1979)

A Letter from M. Rousseau ... to M. d'Alambert, trans. William Kenrick (London, 1759)

Œuvres complètes, ed. B. Gagnebin and M. Raymond, Bibliothèque de la Pléiade, 5 vols. (Paris: Gallimard, 1959–95)

The Social Contract and Other Later Political Writings, ed. and trans. Victor Gourevitch (Cambridge University Press, 1997)

Rutherforth, Thomas, *An Essay on the Nature and Obligations of Virtue* (Cambridge, 1744)

Institutes of Natural Law, 2 vols. (Cambridge, 1754–6)

System of Natural Philosophy, 2 vols. (Cambridge, 1744) [550; 34^r/2]

Sacheverell, Henry, *The Tryal of Dr. Henry Sacheverell, before the House of Peers, for High Crimes and Misdemeanors* (London, 1710) [647; 6^r/7]

Saint-Évremond, Charles de, *Œuvres en prose*, ed. René Ternois, 4 vols. (Paris: Didier, 1965) [1725: 471; –]

A Second Oration to the Hibernian Society (Dublin, 1758)

Senault, Jean-François, *De l'usage des passions*, ed. Christine Frémont (Paris: Fayard, 1987)

Seneca, *Ad Lucilium epistulae morales*, trans. Richard M. Gummere, 3 vols., Loeb Classical Library (London: Heinemann; Cambridge, MA: Harvard University Press, 1917–25)

Shaftesbury, third Earl of (Anthony Ashley Cooper), *Characteristicks of Men, Manners, Opinions, Times*, 2nd edn, 3 vols. (London, 1714; 1st edn 1711) [1727: 483; 28^r/13]

Complete Works, Selected Letters, and Posthumous Writings, vol. II, *Band 5: Chartæ Socraticæ: Design of a Socratick History*, ed. Wolfram Benda, Christine Jackson-Holzberg, Friedrich A. Ühlein and Erwin Wolff (Stuttgart: Frommann-Holzboog, 2007)

Letters from the Right Honourable the Late Earl of Shaftesbury, to Robert Molesworth, Esq., ed. John Toland (London, 1721)

The Life, Unpublished Letters, and Philosophical Regimen of Anthony, Earl of Shaftesbury, ed. Benjamin Rand (London, 1900)

Shebbeare, John, *An Answer to the Printed Speech of Edmund Burke* (London, 1776)

Sheridan, Richard Brinsley, *The Genuine Speech of Mr. Sheridan, Delivered in the House of Commons ... Against Warren Hastings ... for Extortion, Perfidy, and Cruelty, to the Princesses ... of Oude* (London, 1787)

The Speech of R.B. Sheridan, Esq ... Reported by a Member of the House of Commons (London, 1787)

Sheridan, Thomas, *British Education: or, the Source of the Disorders of Great Britain* (London, 1756)

The Life of the Rev. Dr. Jonathan Swift (London, 1784)

An Oration Pronounced before a Numerous Body of the Nobility and Gentry (Dublin, 1757)

Smiles, Samuel, *Self-Help: With Illustrations of Character, Conduct, and Perseverance*, ed. Peter W. Sinnema (Oxford University Press, 2002)

Smith, Adam, *Essays on Philosophical Subjects*, ed. W. P. D. Wightman and J. C. Bryce (Oxford: Clarendon Press, 1980)

Lectures on Rhetoric and Belles Lettres, ed. J. C. Bryce (Oxford: Clarendon Press, 1983)

The Theory of Moral Sentiments, ed. D. D. Raphael and A. L. Macfie (Oxford University Press, 1979)

Smith, David Nichol (ed.), *Characters from the Histories and Memoirs of the Seventeenth Century* (Oxford: Clarendon Press, 1918)

South, Robert, *Sermons Preached upon Several Occasions*, 6 vols. (London, 1737)

Spence, Joseph, *Anecdotes, Observations and Characters of Men*, ed. Samuel Weller Singer (London: Centaur Press, 1964)

Polymetis: or, an Enquiry Concerning the Agreement between the Works of the Roman Poets, and the Remains of the Antient Artists, corrected 2nd edn (1755; 1st edn 1747) [1747: 618; 30^{v}/21]

Sprat, Thomas, *The History of the Royal-Society of London* (London, 1667)

Stillingfleet, Edward, *Origines Sacrae: or, A Rational Account of the Grounds of Christian Faith* (London, 1662)

Strictures on the Letter of the Right Hon. Mr. Burke, on the Revolution in France (London, 1791)

Swift, Jonathan, *The Complete Poems*, ed. Pat Rogers (Harmondsworth: Penguin, 1983)

Correspondence, ed. Harold Williams, 5 vols. (Oxford: Clarendon Press, 1963–5)

The Prose Works of Jonathan Swift, ed. Herbert Davis, 16 vols. (Oxford: Blackwell, 1939–74)

Swift vs. Mainwaring: The Examiner and the Medley, ed. Frank H. Ellis (Oxford: Clarendon Press, 1985)

A Tale of a Tub, ed. A. C. Guthkelch and D. Nichol Smith, 2nd edn (Oxford: Clarendon Press, 1958; 1st edn 1920)

The Works of Jonathan Swift, D.D. Dean of St. Patrick's, Dublin, 6 vols. (London, 1765) [554; $33^r/13$]

Temple, Sir William, *The Works of Sir William Temple, Bart.*, 2 vols. (London, 1720) [1750: 649; $6^r/13$]

Thelwall, John, *Sober Reflections upon the Seditious and Inflammatory Letter of Edmund Burke to a Noble Lord* (London, 1796)

Thucydides, *Eight Bookes of the Peloponnesian Warre*, trans. Thomas Hobbes (London, 1629)

Tindal, Matthew, 'Of the Power of the Magistrate, and the Rights of Mankind', in *Four Discourses* (London, 1709)

Tindall, Nicholas, *The Continuation of Mr Rapin de Thoyras's History of England*, 2 vols. (1751)

Toland, John, 'A Letter Concerning the Roman Education', in *A Collection of Several Pieces of Mr. John Toland, 2 vols.* (London, 1726), vol. II, 1–12

'The Origin and Force of Prejudice', in *Letters to Serena* (London, 1704)

Reasons Most Humbly Offer'd to the Honble House of Commons . . . (London, 1720)

The State-Anatomy of Great Britain (London, 1717)

Trenchard, John and Thomas Gordon, *Cato's Letters: or, Essays on Liberty, Civil and Religious, and Other Important Subjects*, ed. Ronald Hamowy (Indianapolis: Liberty Fund, 1995) [1733: –; $24^r/2$]

Waldegrave, James, second Earl, *Memoirs and Speeches*, ed. J. C. D. Clark (Cambridge University Press, 2002)

Walpole, Horace, *Memoirs of the Reign of King George II*, ed. Henry Fox, 3 vols. (London, 1847)

Warburton, William, *A Critical and Philosophical Enquiry into the Causes of Prodigies and Miracles, as Related by Historians. With an Essay towards Restoring a Method and Purity in History* (London, 1727)

The Divine Legation of Moses, 2 vols., corrected 3rd edn (1742–58; 1st edn 1737–41)

The Doctrine of Grace: or, the Office and Operations of the Holy Spirit Vindicated from the Insults of Infidelity, and the Abuses of Fanaticism, 2 vols. (London, 1763)

Waterland, Daniel, *Advice to a Young Student. With a Method of Study* (1755)

The Nature, Obligation, and Efficacy of the Christian Sacraments, Considered (London, 1730)

Watts, Isaac, *Logick: or, The Right Use of Reason in the Enquiry after Truth* (London, 1725)

Wollstonecraft, Mary, *A Vindication of the Rights of Men*, in *Political Writings*, ed. Janet Todd (Oxford University Press, 1993)

Wordsworth, William, *The Fourteen-Book Prelude*, ed. W. J. B. Owen (Ithaca, NY: Cornell University Press, 1985)

The Letters of William and Dorothy Wordsworth, ed. Ernest de Selincourt, 2nd edn, 8 vols. (Oxford: Clarendon Press, 1967–93), vol. 1: *The Early Years, 1787–1805*, rev. Chester L. Shaver

Selected Prose, ed. John O. Hayden (Harmondsworth: Penguin, 1988)

Wraxall, Sir Nathaniel, *Historical Memoirs of My Own Time: Part the First: from 1772 to 1780; Part the Second: from 1781 to 1784*, 2nd edn, 2 vols. (London: Cadell and Davies, 1815)

SECONDARY SOURCES

Aaron, Richard I., *John Locke*, 3rd edn (Oxford: Clarendon Press, 1971; 1st edn 1937)

Agnani, Sunil, 'Jacobinism in India, Indianism in English Parliament: Fearing the Enlightenment and Colonial Modernity with Edmund Burke', *Cultural Critique*, **68** (2008), 131–62

Ahmed, Siraj, 'The Theater of the Civilized Self: Edmund Burke and the East India Trials', *Representations*, **78** (2002), 28–55

Alexander, Gavin, 'Prosopopoeia: The Speaking Figure', in Sylvia Adamson *et al.* (eds.), *Renaissance Figures of Speech* (Cambridge University Press, 2007), 97–112

Ashcraft, Richard, 'The Language of Political Conflict in Restoration Literature', in *Politics as Reflected in Literature: Papers Presented at a Clark Library Seminar, 24 January 1987* (Los Angeles: Clark Memorial Library, University of California, 1989), 1–28

Auerbach, Erich, *Literary Language and its Public in Late Latin Antiquity*, trans. Ralph Manheim (London: Routledge, 1965)

Baczko, Bronislaw, 'La cité et ses langages', in R. A. Leigh (ed.), *Rousseau After Two Hundred Years* (Cambridge University Press, 1992), 87–108

Badelon, Françoise, 'L'épicureanisme selon Shaftesbury', *Dix-huitième siècle*, 35, 'L'épicureanisme de Lumières: numéro spécial' (2003), 141–55

Barbour, Reid, *English Epicures and Stoics: Ancient Legacies in Early Stuart Culture* (Amherst: University of Massachusetts Press, 1998)

Berman, David, *Berkeley and Irish Philosophy* (London: Continuum, 2005)

'Enlightenment and Counter-Enlightenment in Irish Philosophy', *Archiv für Geschichte der Philosophie*, **64** (1982), 148–65

Beugnot, Bernard, 'La précellence du style moyen', in Fumaroli (ed.), *Histoire de la rhétorique*, 439–599

Bitzer, Lloyd F., 'The Rhetorical Situation', *Philosophy and Rhetoric*, **1** (1968), 1–14

Black, Jeremy, *Pitt the Elder* (Cambridge University Press, 1992)

Blakemore, Steven, *Crisis in Representation: Thomas Paine, Mary Wollstonecraft, Helen Maria Williams, and the Rewriting of the French Revolution*

(Madison: Fairleigh Dickinson University Press; London: Associated University Presses, 1997)

Bolton, Betsy, 'Imperial Sensibilities, Colonial Ambivalence: Edmund Burke and Fanny Burney', *ELH*, **72** (2005), 871–99

Brewer, John, *Party Ideology and Popular Politics at the Accession of George III* (Cambridge University Press, 1982)

The Sinews of Power: War, Money and the English State, 1688–1783 (Cambridge, MA: Harvard University Press, 1988)

Brink, C. O., *Horace on Poetry*, 3 vols. (Cambridge University Press, 1971), vol. II: *The 'Ars poetica'*

Brody, Jules, *Boileau and Longinus* (Geneva: Droz, 1958)

'Platonisme et classicisme', in *Lectures classiques* (Charlottesville: Rookwood Press, 1996)

Brooke, John, 'William Gerard Hamilton', in Namier and Brooke (eds.), *History of Parliament*

Brown, Michael, *Francis Hutcheson in Dublin, 1719–1730* (Dublin: Four Courts Press, 2002)

Brown, Vivienne, 'The Dialogic Experience of Conscience: Adam Smith and the Voices of Stoicism', *Eighteenth-Century Studies*, **26** (1992–3), 233–60

Browning, Reed, 'The Origin of Burke's Ideas Revisited', *Eighteenth-Century Studies*, **18** (1984), 57–71

Bruyn, Frans de, 'Burke and the Uses of Eloquence: Political Prose in the 1770s and 1780s', in John Richetti (ed.), *The Cambridge History of English Literature, 1660–1780* (Cambridge University Press, 2005), 768–93

'Edmund Burke the Political Quixote: Romance, Chivalry, and the Political Imagination', *Eighteenth-Century Fiction*, **16** (2004), 695–733

Bryant, Donald Cross, 'The Contemporary Reception of Edmund Burke's Speaking', in Raymond F. Howes (ed.), *Historical Studies of Rhetoric and Rhetoricians* (Ithaca, NY: Cornell University Press, 1961), 271–93

Bullard, Paddy, 'The Figure of Emancipation: Paradox, Rhetoric and the Enlightenments of Rousseau and Burke', in Susan Manning and Peter France (eds.), *Enlightenment and Emancipation* (Lewisburg, PA: Bucknell University Press, 2007), 44–62

'The Meaning of the "Sublime and Beautiful": Shaftesburian Contexts and Rhetorical Issues in Edmund Burke's Philosophical Enquiry', *Review of English Studies*, n.s. 56.224 (2005), 169–91

'Parliamentary Rhetoric, Enlightenment and the Politics of Secrecy: The Printer's Crisis of March 1771', *History of European Ideas*, **31** (2005), 313–25

Cameron, David, *The Social Thought of Rousseau and Burke: A Comparative Study* (University of Toronto Press, 1973)

Campbell, Stephen F., 'Nicolas Caussin's "Spirituality of Communication": A meeting of divine and human speech', *Renaissance Quarterly*, **46** (1993), 44–70

Canavan, Francis, *The Political Reason of Edmund Burke* (Durham, NC: Duke University Press, 1960)

Cannon, John, *Parliamentary Reform, 1640–1832* (Cambridge University Press, 1973)

Canter, H. V., 'The Impeachments of Verres and Hastings: Cicero and Burke', *Classical Journal*, **9** (1913–14), 199–211

Carey, Christopher, 'Rhetorical Means of Persuasion', in Amélie Oksenberg Rorty (ed.), *Essays on Aristotle's 'Rhetoric'* (Berkeley: University of California Press, 1996), 399–415

Carey, Daniel, 'Locke's Anthropology: Travel, Innateness, and the Exercise of Reason', *The Seventeenth Century*, **19** (2004), 260–85

Carnall, Geoffrey, 'Burke as Modern Cicero', in Geoffrey Carnall and Colin Nicholson (eds.), *The Impeachment of Warren Hastings* (Edinburgh University Press, 1989)

Cave, Terence, *The Cornucopian Text* (Oxford: Clarendon Press, 1979)

Chandler, James K., *Wordsworth's Second Nature: A Study of the Poetry and Politics* (University of Chicago Press, 1984)

Christie, Ian R., *British 'Non-Elite' MPs, 1715–1820* (Oxford: Clarendon Press, 1995)

Clark, Donald L., 'The Rise and Fall of Progymnasmata in Sixteenth and Seventeenth Century Grammar Schools', *Speech Monographs*, **19** (1952), 258–63

Clarke, Jack A., 'Turgot's Critique of Perpetual Endowments', *French Historical Studies*, **3** (1964), 495–506

Clarke, M. L., 'Classical Studies', in L. S. Sutherland and L. G. Mitchell (eds.), *The History of the University of Oxford*, vol. 5: *The Eighteenth Century* (Oxford: Clarendon Press, 1986), 513–33

Collini, Stefan, 'The Idea of "Character" in Victorian Political Thought', *Transactions of the Royal Historical Society*, 5th series, **35** (1985), 29–50

Conley, Thomas M., *Rhetoric in the European Tradition* (University of Chicago Press, 1990)

Connolly, S. J., 'Precedent and Principle: The Patriots and their Critics', in S. J. Connolly (ed.), *Political Ideas in Eighteenth-Century Ireland* (Dublin: Four Courts Press, 2000), 130–58

Religion, Law and Power: The Making of Protestant Ireland, 1660–1760 (Oxford University Press, 1992)

Court, Franklin E., *Institutionalizing English Literature: The Culture and Politics of Literary Study, 1750–1900* (Stanford University Press, 1992)

Crane, Ronald S., 'The Relation of Bacon's *Essays* to his Program for the Advancement of Learning' (1923), in Brian Vickers (ed.), *Essential Articles for the Study of Fancis Bacon* (London: Sidgwick & Jackson, 1968), 272–92

Cranston, Maurice, *John Locke: A Biography* (London: Longmans, 1957)

Crawford, Robert, *Devolving English Literature*, 2nd edn (Edinburgh University Press, 2000; 1st edn 1992)

(ed.), *The Scottish Invention of English Literature* (Cambridge University Press, 1998)

Cromartie, A. D. T., 'The Printing of Parliamentary Speeches, November 1640–July 1642', *Historical Journal*, **33** (1990), 23–44

Cronk, Nicholas, *The Classical Sublime: French Neoclassicism and the Language of Literature* (Charlottesville: Rookwood Press, 2002)

Crook, Malcolm, 'Citizen Bishops: Episcopal Elections in the French Revolution', *Historical Journal*, **43** (2000), 955–97

Dart, Gregory, *Rousseau, Robespierre and English Romanticism* (Cambridge University Press, 1999)

Darwall, Stephen L., *The British Moralists and the Internal 'Ought', 1640–1740* (Cambridge University Press, 1995)

Davison, Jenny, *Hypocrisy and the Politics of Politeness: Manners and Morals from Locke to Austen* (Cambridge University Press, 2004)

Dean, L. F., 'Sir Francis Bacon's Theory of Civil History-Writing', *ELH*, **8** (1941), 161–83

Declerque, Gilles, 'La rhétorique classique entre évidence et sublime', in Fumaroli (ed.), *Histoire de la rhétorique*, 629–706

Donlan, Seán Patrick (ed.), *Edmund Burke's Irish Identities* (Dublin: Irish Academic Press, 2006)

Drisgol, Edward A., 'The Influence of Gassendi on Locke's Hedonism', *International Philosophical Quarterly*, **12** (1972), 87–110

Elofson, W. M., *The Rockingham Connection and the Second Founding of the Whig Party* (Montreal: McGill-Queen's University Press, 1996)

Engel, S. Morris, *With Good Reason: An Introduction to Informal Fallacies*, 4th edn (New York: St Martin's Press, 1994)

Enos, Richard Leo and Karen Rossi Schnakenberg, 'Cicero Latinizes Hellenic Ethos', in James S. Baldwin and Tita French Baumlin (eds.), *Ethos: New Essays in Rhetorical and Critical Theory* (Dallas: Southern Methodist University Press, 1994), 191–209

Feingold, Mordechai, 'Aristotle and the English Universities in the Seventeenth Century: A Revaluation', in Helga Robinson-Hammerstein (ed.), *European Universities in the Age of Reformation and Counter Reformation* (Dublin: Four Courts Press, 1998), 135–48

'English Ramism: A Reinterpretation', in Mordechai Feingold, Joseph S. Freedman and Wolfgang Rother (eds.), *The Influence of Petrus Ramus* (Basel: Schwabe, 2001), 127–76

France, Peter, 'Lumières, politesse, énergie', in Fumaroli (ed.), *Histoire de la rhétorique*, 945–99

Rhetoric and Truth in France: Descartes to Diderot (Oxford: Clarendon Press, 1972)

Frisch, Morton J., 'Burke on Theory', *Cambridge Journal*, **7** (1954), 292–7

Fumaroli, Marc, *L'Âge de l'éloquence: rhétorique et 'res literaria' de la Renaissance au seuil de l'époque classique* (Geneva: Droz, 1980)

(ed.), *Histoire de la rhétorique dans l'Europe moderne, 1450–1950* (Paris: Presses Universitaires de France, 1999)

Furniss, Tom, *Edmund Burke's Aesthetic Ideology: Language, Gender and Political Economy in Revolution* (Cambridge University Press, 1993)

Galyon, Linda, 'Puttenham's Enargeia and Energeia: New Twists for Old Terms', *Philological Quarterly*, **60** (1981), 29–40

Garsten, Bryan, *Saving Persuasion: A Defense of Rhetoric and Judgment* (Cambridge, MA: Harvard University Press, 2006)

Garver, Eugene, *Aristotle's Rhetoric: An Art of Character* (University of Chicago Press, 1994)

Gascoigne, John, *Cambridge in the Age of Enlightenment: Science, Religion and Politics from the Restoration to the French Revolution* (Cambridge University Press, 1988)

'Church and State Allied: The Failure of Parliamentary Reform of the Universities, 1688–1800', in A. C. Beier *et al.* (eds.), *The First Modern Society: Essays in English History in Honour of Lawrence Stone* (Cambridge University Press, 1989), 401–29

Gibbons, Luke, *Edmund Burke and Ireland: Aesthetics, Politics and the Colonial Sublime* (Cambridge University Press, 2003)

Goring, Paul, *The Rhetoric of Sensibility in Eighteenth-Century Culture* (Cambridge University Press, 2005)

Gray, Tim and Paul Hindson, 'Edmund Burke and the French Revolution as Drama', *History of European Ideas*, **14** (1992), 203–11

Grimaldi, William, *Studies in the Philosophy of Aristotle's Rhetoric* (Wiesbaden: Franz Steiner Verlag, 1972)

Gross, Daniel M., 'Caussin's Passion and the New History of Rhetoric', *Rhetorica*, **21** (2003), 89–112

The Secret History of Emotion: From Aristotle's Rhetoric to Modern Brain Science (University of Chicago Press, 2006)

Haakonssen, Knud, *The Science of a Legislator: The Natural Jurisprudence of David Hume and Adam Smith* (Cambridge University Press, 1981)

Hamm, Victor, 'Burke and Metaphysics', in Anton C. Pegis (ed.), *Essays in Modern Scholasticism* (Westminster, MD: Newman, 1944), 206–21

Hammond, Paul, 'The Integrity of Dryden's Lucretius', *Modern Language Review*, **78** (1983), 1–23

Hampsher-Monk, Iain, 'Rhetoric and Opinion in the Politics of Edmund Burke', *History of Political Thought*, **9** (1988), 455–84

Hanley, Ryan Patrick, *Adam Smith and the Character of Virtue* (Cambridge University Press, 2009)

Harris, Ian, 'Rousseau and Burke', in Stuart Brown (ed.), *British Philosophy and the Age of Enlightenment* (London: Routledge, 1996), 354–73

Harris, James A., *Of Liberty and Necessity: The Free Will Debate in Eighteenth-Century British Philosophy* (Oxford: Clarendon Press, 2005)

Harrison, John and Peter Laslett (eds.), *The Library of John Locke* (Oxford Bibliographical Society, 1965)

Harth, Philip, *Swift and Anglican Rationalism: The Religious Background of 'A Tale of a Tub'* (University of Chicago Press, 1961)

Hayton, David, 'Introduction', *The Irish Parliament in the Long Eighteenth Century: The Long Apprenticeship*, special issue of *Parliamentary History*, **20** (2001), 1–25

'An Irish Parliamentary Diary from the Reign of Queen Anne', *Analecta Hibernica*, **30** (1982), 88–149

Hill, Jacqueline, *From Patriots to Unionists: Dublin Civic Politics and Irish Protestant Patriotism, 1660–1840* (Oxford: Clarendon Press, 1997)

Horn, Robert D., 'Addison's *Campaign* and Macaulay', *PMLA*, 63 (1948), 886–902

Howell, W. S., *Eighteenth-Century British Logic and Rhetoric* (Princeton University Press, 1971)

Hudson, Nicholas, *Samuel Johnson and Eighteenth-Century Thought* (Oxford: Clarendon Press, 1988)

Hundert, E. J., *The Enlightenment's Fable: Bernard Mandeville and the Discovery of Society* (Cambridge University Press, 1994)

Hunt, Lynn, 'The Rhetoric of Revolution in France', *History Workshop Journal*, **15** (1983), 78–94

James, Susan, *Passion and Action: The Emotions in Seventeenth-Century Philosophy* (Oxford: Clarendon Press, 1997)

Jaouën, Françoise, *De l'art plaire en petits morceaux: Pascal, La Rochefoucauld, La Bruyère* (Saint-Denis: Presses Universitaires de Vincennes, 1996)

Jardine, Lisa, *Francis Bacon: Discovery and the Art of Discourse* (Cambridge University Press, 1974)

Johnson, Monte and Catherine Wilson, 'Lucretius and the History of Science', in Stuart Gillespie and Philip Hardie (eds.), *The Cambridge Companion to Lucretius* (Cambridge University Press, 2007), 131–48

Jones, Peter, ' "Art" and "Moderation" in Hume's Essays', in David Fate Norton (ed.), *McGill Hume Studies* (San Diego: Austin Hill Press, 1979), 161–80

Kelly, Christopher, ' "To persuade without convincing": The Melodious Language of Rousseau's Legislator', *American Journal of Political Science*, **31** (1987), 321–35

Kelly, James, *Henry Flood: Patriots and Politics in Eighteenth-Century Ireland* (Dublin: Four Courts Press, 1998)

Prelude to Union: Anglo-Irish Politics in the 1780s (Cork University Press, 1992)

Kennedy, George, *The Art of Rhetoric in the Roman World* (Princeton University Press, 1972)

Kennedy, William J., *Rhetorical Norms in Renaissance Literature* (New Haven, CT: Yale University Press, 1978)

Klein, Laurence E., *Shaftesbury and the Culture of Politeness* (Cambridge University Press, 1994)

Knights, Mark, *Representation and Misrepresentation in Later Stuart Britain: Partisanship and Political Culture* (Oxford University Press, 2005)

Kristeller, Paul Oskar, *Renaissance Thought: The Classic, Scholastic, and Humanistic Strains* (New York: Harper and Brothers, 1961)

Lafond, Jean, 'L'esthétique du *dire moderno* dans l'historiographie de P. Mathieu et de ses émulateurs', in *Mélanges à la mémoire de Franco Simone: France et Italie dans la culture européenne* (Geneva: Slatkine, 1981), 135–48

Lamb, Jonathan, 'Sterne and Irregular Oratory', in *Laurence Sterne's 'Tristram Shandy': A Casebook* (Oxford University Press, 2006), 213–39

'The Sublime', in H. B. Nisbet and Claude Rawson (eds.), *The Cambridge History of Literary Criticism*, vol. IV: *The Eighteenth Century* (Cambridge University Press, 1997), 394–416

Lanham, Richard A., *The Motives of Eloquence: Literary Rhetoric in the Renaissance* (New Haven, CT: Yale University Press, 1976)

Laurens, Pierre, 'Vossius et le réaménagement de l'édifice rhétorique', in Fumaroli (ed.), *Histoire de la rhétorique*, 499–516

Law, David Jules, *The Rhetoric of Empiricism: Language and Perception from Locke to I.A. Richards* (Ithaca, NY: Cornell University Press, 1993)

Leeman, A. D., 'The Technique of Persuasion in Cicero's *Pro Murena*', in S. T. Stroh (ed.), *Éloquence et rhétorique chez Cicéron* (Geneva: Hardt, 1982)

Lennon, Thomas M., 'Did Bayle Read St. Evremond?', *Journal of the History of Ideas*, **63** (2002), 225–37

Lenzner, Steven J., 'Strauss's Three Burkes: The Problem of Edmund Burke in Natural Right and History', *Political Theory*, **19** (1991), 364–90

Lock, F. P., *Edmund Burke*, 2 vols. (Oxford: Clarendon Press, 1998–2006)

'Rhetoric and Representation in Burke's *Reflections*', in John Whale (ed.), *Edmund Burke's Reflections on the Revolution in France: New Interdisciplinary Essays* (Manchester University Press, 2000), 18–39

Swift's Tory Politics (London: Duckworth, 1983)

Lucas, Paul, 'On Edmund Burke's Doctrine of Prescription; or, An Appeal from the New to the Old Lawyers', *Historical Journal*, **11** (1968), 35–63

Macnair, Michael, *The Law of Proof in Early-Modern Equity* (Berlin: Duncker & Humblot, 1999)

Mahoney, Robert, *Jonathan Swift: The Irish Identity* (New Haven, CT: Yale University Press, 1995)

Marin, Louis, 'On the Sublime, Infinity, *Je ne sais quoi*', in D. Hollier (ed.), *A New History of French Literature* (Cambridge, MA: Harvard University Press, 1989), 340–5

Marshall, David, 'Adam Smith and the Theatricality of Moral Sentiments', *Critical Inquiry*, **10** (1984), 592–613

Marshall, P. J., *The Impeachment of Warren Hastings* (Oxford University Press, 1965)

McCabe, Richard A., 'Refining Theophrastus: Ethical Concerns and Moral Paragons in the English Character Book', *Hermathena*, **169** (1995), 33–50

McDowell, R. B. and D. A. Webb, *Trinity College Dublin, 1592–1952: An Academic History*, 2nd edn (Trinity College Dublin Press, 2004)

McFarland, Thomas, *Romanticism and the Heritage of Rousseau* (Oxford: Clarendon Press, 1995)

McIntyre, Jane L., 'Character: A Humean Account', *History of Philosophy Quarterly*, **7** (1990), 193–206

McKenna, Stephen J., *Adam Smith: The Rhetoric of Propriety* (Albany: State University of New York Press, 2006)

McNally, Patrick, *Parties, Patriots and Undertakers: Parliamentary Politics in Early Hanoverian Ireland* (Dublin: Four Courts Press, 1997)

McNeil, Gordon H., 'The Cult of Rousseau and the French Revolution', *Journal of the History of Ideas*, **6** (1945), 197–212

Mehta, Uday S., *Liberalism and Empire: A Study of Nineteenth-Century British Liberal Thought* (University of Chicago Press, 1999)
Meinel, Christopher, 'Early Seventeenth-Century Atomism: Theory, Epistemology, and the Insufficiency of Experiment', *Isis*, **79** (1988), 68–103
Michael, Fred S. and Emily Michael, 'Gassendi's Modified Epicureanism and British Moral Philosophy', *History of European Ideas*, **21** (1995), 743–61
Miller, Thomas P., 'The Formation of College English', *Rhetoric Society Quarterly*, **20** (1990), 261–86
'Where did College English Studies Come From?', *Rhetoric Review*, 8 (1990), 50–69
Mitchell, W. J. T., 'Influence, Autobiography, and Literary History: Rousseau's *Confessions* and Wordsworth's *Prelude*', *ELH*, **57** (1990), 643–64
Monk, Samuel Holt, 'The Pride of Lemuel Gulliver', *Sewanee Review*, **63** (1955), 48–71
The Sublime: A Study of Critical Theories in XVIII-Century England, 2nd edn (Ann Arbor: University of Michigan Press, 1960)
Moss, Jean Dietz, '"Discordant Consensus": Old and New Rhetoric at Trinity College, Dublin', *Rhetorica*, **14** (1996), 383–441
Mourges, Odette de, *Two French Moralists: La Rochefoucauld and La Bruyère* (Cambridge University Press, 1978)
Munro, James S., 'Richardson, Marivaux, and the French Romance Tradition', *Modern Language Review*, **70** (1975), 752–9.
Murphy, James J., *Rhetoric in the Middle Ages: A History of the Rhetorical Theory from Saint Augustine to the Renaissance* (Berkeley; London: University of California Press, 1974; repr. Tempe: Arizona Center for Medieval and Renaissance Studies, 2001)
Nadel, George H., 'History as Psychology in Francis Bacon's Theory of History', *History and Theory*, **5** (1966), 275–87
Namier, Lewis, 'The Character of Burke', *The Spectator* (19 December 1958), 895–6
'Charles Townshend', in Namier and Brooke (eds.), *History of Parliament*
The Structure of Politics at the Accession of George III, 2nd edn (London: Macmillan, 1960)
and John Brooke, *Charles Townshend* (London: Macmillan, 1964)
(eds.), *History of Parliament: The Commons, 1754–1790*, 3 vols. (London: HMSO, 1964)
Nicolson, Marjorie Hope, *Mountain Gloom and Mountain Glory: The Development of the Aesthetics of the Infinite* (Seattle: University of Washington Press, 1997)
Nussbaum, Felicity, *The Brink of All We Hate: English Satires on Women, 1660–1750* (Lexington: University Press of Kentucky, 1984)
O'Brien, Gerard, 'The Grattan Mystique', *Eighteenth-Century Ireland*, **1** (1986), 177–94
O'Donnell, Katherine, 'Burke and the School of Irish Oratory', *Studies in Burke and His Time*, **21** (2007), 72–89
O'Gorman, Frank, *Edmund Burke: His Political Philosophy* (London: Routledge, 2004)

Ong, Walter J., *The Presence of the Word: Some Prolegomena for Cultural and Religious History* (New Haven, CT: Yale University Press, 1967)
Ramus, Method and the Decay of Dialogue (Cambridge, MA: Harvard University Press, 1958)
'The Writer's Audience is Always a Fiction', *PMLA*, **90** (1975), 9–21
Osborn, Annie Marion, *Rousseau and Burke* (London: Oxford University Press, 1940)
Osler, Margaret J., 'Gassendi on Fortune, Fate and Divination', in Osler (ed.), *Atoms, Pneuma, and Tranquillity*, 155–74
(ed.), *Atoms, Pneuma, and Tranquillity: Epicurean and Stoic Themes in European Thought* (Cambridge University Press, 1991)
Paige, Nicholas, 'Rousseau's Readers Revisited: The Aesthetics of *La Nouvelle Héloïse*', *Eighteenth-Century Studies*, **42** (2008), 131–54
Parish, Richard, 'Port-Royal and Jansenism', in Glyn P. Norton (ed.), *The Cambridge History of Literary Criticism*, vol. III: *The Renaissance* (Cambridge University Press, 1999), 475–84
Paulson, Ronald, *Representations of Revolution (1789–1820)* (New Haven, CT: Yale University Press, 1983)
Petersen, E., '"The Communication of the Dead": Notes on the *Studia Humanitatis* and the Nature of Humanist Philology', in A. C. Dionisotti *et al.* (eds.), *The Uses of Greek and Latin: Historical Essays* (London: Warburg Institute, 1988), 57–69
Phiddian, Robert, *Swift's Parody* (Cambridge University Press, 1995)
Phillipson, Nicholas, 'Culture and Society in the Eighteenth-Century Province: The Case of Edinburgh', in Laurence Stone (ed.), *The University and Society*, 2 vols. (Princeton University Press, 1974), vol. II, 407–48
Pitts, Jennifer, *A Turn to Empire: The Rise of Imperial Liberalism in Britain and France* (Princeton University Press, 2005)
Pocock, J. G. A, 'Burke and the Ancient Constitution', in *Politics, Language and Time: Essays on Political Thought and History* (London: Methuen, 1971), 202–31
'Clergy and Commerce: The Conservative Enlightenment in England', in Lester G. Crocker *et al.*, *L'Eta dei Lumi: studi storici sul Settecento Europeo in onore di Franco Venturi* (Naples: Joveni, 1985), 525–62
'Post-Puritan England and the Problem of Enlightenment', in Perez Zagorin (ed.), *Culture and Politics: From Puritanism to the Enlightenment* (Berkeley: University of California Press, 1980)
Porter, James I., 'Lucretius and the Poetics of the Void', in A. Monet (ed.), *Le jardin romain: épicurisme et poésie à Rome: mélanges offerts à Mayotte Bollack* (Villeneuve d'Ascq: Presses de l'Université Charles-de-Gaulle, 2003), 197–226
'Lucretius and the Sublime', in Stuart Gillespie and Philip Hardie (eds.), *The Cambridge Companion to Lucretius* (Cambridge University Press, 2007), 167–84
Pottle, F. A., 'The Part Played by Horace Walpole and James Boswell in the Quarrel between Hume and Rousseau', *Philological Quarterly*, **4** (1925), 351–63

Price, Martin, *Swift's Rhetorical Art: A Study in Structure and Meaning* (New Haven, CT: Yale University Press, 1953)

Quarrie, P., 'The Christ Church Collections Books', in L. S. Sutherland and L. G. Mitchell (eds.), *The History of the University of Oxford*, vol. 5: *The Eighteenth Century* (Oxford: Clarendon Press, 1986), 493–511

Quehan, A. H. de, 'Lucretius and Swift's *Tale of a Tub*', *University of Toronto Quarterly*, **63** (1993), 287–307

'Cyprian and Swift's Coats', *Notes and Queries*, 39.237 (1992), 37–8

Raphael, D. D., *Hobbes: Morals and Politics* (London: Routledge, 2004)

Reid, Christopher, 'Character Construction in the Eighteenth-Century House of Commons: Evidence from the Cavendish Diary (1768–74)', *Rhetorica*, **22** (2004), 375–99

Edmund Burke and the Practice of Political Writing (Dublin: Gill and Macmillan, 1985)

'Foiling the Rival: Argument and Identity in Sheridan's Speeches', in James Marwood and David Crane (eds.), *Sheridan Studies* (Cambridge University Press, 1995), 114–30

'Speaking Candidly: Rhetoric, Politics, and the Meanings of Candour in the later Eighteenth Century', *British Journal for Eighteenth-Century Studies*, **28** (2005), 67–82

Rhodes, Neil, *The Power of Eloquence in English Renaissance Literature* (New York; London: Harvester Wheatsheaf, 1992)

Richardson, Samuel, *Selected Letters of Samuel Richardson*, ed. John Carroll (Oxford: Clarendon Press, 1964)

Ritchie, Daniel E., 'Desire and Sympathy, Passion and Providence: The Moral Imaginations of Burke and Rousseau', in Steven Blakemore (ed.), *Burke and the French Revolution: Bicentennial Essays* (Athens: University of Georgia Press, 1992), 120–43

Rivers, Isabel, *Reason, Grace and Sentiment: A Study of the Language of Religion and Ethics in England, 1660–1780*, 2 vols. (Cambridge University Press, 1991–2000)

Robbins, Caroline, *The Eighteenth-Century Commonwealthman* (Cambridge, MA: Harvard University Press, 1959; repr. 1968)

Robinson, Nicholas K., *Edmund Burke: A Life in Caricature* (New Haven, CT: Yale University Press, 1996)

Roe, Nicholas, *Wordsworth and Coleridge: The Radical Years* (Oxford: Clarendon Press, 1988)

Russell, Gillian, 'Burke's Dagger: Theatricality, Politics and Print Culture in the 1790s', *British Journal for Eighteenth-Century Studies*, **20** (1997), 1–16

Russell, Paul, *Freedom and Moral Sentiment: Hume's way of Naturalizing Responsibility* (Oxford University Press, 2002)

Samuels, Arthur P. I., *The Early Life, Correspondence and Writings of the Rt. Hon. Edmund Burke, LL.D.: With a Transcript of the Minute Book of the Debating "Club" Founded by him in the Trinity College, Dublin* (Cambridge University Press, 1923)

Scholar, Richard, *The Je-ne-sais-quoi in Early Modern Europe: Encounters with a Certain Something* (Oxford University Press, 2005)

Screech, M. A., *Montaigne and Melancholy: The Wisdom of the Essays*, new edn (London: Duckworth, 2000)

Seigel, Jerrold, *The Idea of the Self: Thought and Experience in Western Europe Since the Seventeenth Century* (Cambridge University Press, 2005)

Sheldon, Esther K., 'The Hibernian Academy: An Eighteenth-Century Group Experiment in Modern Education', *Long Room*, **11** (1975), 23–31

Shklar, Judith, *Men and Citizens: Rousseau's Social Theory* (Cambridge University Press, 1969)

Skinner, Quentin, 'Paradiastole: Redescribing the Vices and Virtues', in Sylvia Adamson *et al.* (eds.), *Renaissance Figures of Speech* (Cambridge University Press, 2007), 149–66

Reason and Rhetoric in the Philosophy of Hobbes (Cambridge University Press, 1996)

Visions of Politics, 3 vols. (Cambridge University Press, 2002)

Smeed, J. W., *The Theophrastan 'Character': The History of a Literary Genre* (Oxford: Clarendon Press, 1985)

Spadafora, David, *The Idea of Progress in Eighteenth-Century Britain* (New Haven, CT: Yale University Press, 1990)

Stanlis, Peter J., 'Burke and the Sensibility of Rousseau', *Thought*, **36** (1961), 246–76

Starobinsky, Jean, 'Eloquence and Liberty', *Journal of the History of Ideas*, **38** (1977), 195–210

Jean-Jacques Rousseau: la transparence et l'obstacle (Paris: Gallimard, 1971)

'Rousseau et l'éloquence', in R. A. Leigh (ed.), *Rousseau after Two Hundred Years* (Cambridge University Press, 1982), 185–205

Stein, Peter, *Regulae Iuris: From Juristic Rules to Legal Maxims* (Edinburgh University Press, 1966)

Stephens, John, 'Edmund Law and his Circle at Cambridge', in G. A. J. Rogers and Sylvana Tomaselli (eds.), *The Philosophical Canon in the Seventeenth and Eighteenth Centuries* (Rochester University Press, 1996), 163–73

Stewart, M. A., 'Curriculum in Britain, Ireland and the Colonies', in Knud Haakonssen (ed.), *The Cambridge History of Eighteenth-Century Philosophy*, 2 vols. (Cambridge University Press, 2006), vol. 1, 97–120

'John Smith and the Molesworth Circle', *Eighteenth-Century Ireland*, 2 (1987), 89–102

'The Stoic Legacy in the Early Scottish Enlightenment', in Osler (ed.), *Atoms, Pneuma, and Tranquillity*, 273–96

Stokes, M. C., 'Cicero on Epicurean Pleasures', in J. G. F. Powell (ed.), *Cicero the Philosopher: Twelve Papers* (Oxford University Press, 1995), 145–70

Strauss, Leo, *Natural Right and History* (University of Chicago Press, 1953)

The Political Philosophy of Hobbes: Its Basis and Genesis, trans. Elsa M. Sinclair (University of Chicago Press, 1952)

Striker, Gisela, 'Emotions in Context: Aristotle's Treatment of the Passions in the *Rhetoric* and his Moral Psychology', in Amélie Oksenberg Rorty (ed.), *Essays on Aristotle's 'Rhetoric'* (Berkeley: University of California Press, 1996), 286–302

Struever, Nancy S., *The Language of History in the Renaissance: Rhetoric and Historical Consciousness in Florentine Humanism* (Princeton University Press, 1970)

Suleri, Sara, *The Rhetoric of English India* (University of Chicago Press, 1992)

Taylor, Charles, *Sources of the Self: The Making of Modern Identity* (Cambridge University Press, 1989)

Thiel, Udo, 'Personal Identity', in *The Cambridge History of Seventeenth-Century Philosophy*, ed. Daniel Garber and Michael Ayers, 2 vols. (Cambridge University Press, 1998), vol. 1, 868–912

Thomas, D. O., 'Richard Price and Edmund Burke: The Duty to Participate in Government', *Philosophy*, **34** (1959), 308–22

Thomas, P. D. G., 'The Authorship of the Manuscript Irish Parliamentary Diary (1776–89) in the Library of Congress', *English Historical Review*, **77** (1962), 94–5

'The Beginning of Parliamentary Reporting in Newspapers, 1768–1774', *English Historical Review*, **74** (1959), 623–36

The House of Commons in the Eighteenth Century (Oxford: Clarendon Press, 1971)

Tilmouth, Christopher, *Passion's Triumph over Reason: A History of the Moral Imagination from Spenser to Rochester* (Oxford University Press, 2007)

Todd, William B., *A Bibliography of Edmund Burke* (London: Hart-Davis, 1964)

Vanech, William, 'Painful Homecoming: Reflections on Burke and India', *Bulletin of Research in the Humanities*, **82** (1979), 175–84

Vickers, Brian, 'Bacon and Rhetoric', in Markku Peltonen (ed.), *The Cambridge Companion to Bacon* (Cambridge University Press, 1996), 200–31

'The Royal Society and English Prose Style: A Reassessment', in Brian Vickers and Nancy S. Struever, *Rhetoric and the Pursuit of Truth*, intro. Thomas F. Wright (Los Angeles: William Andrews Clark Memorial Library, 1985), 1–76

Voisine, Jacques, *J.-J. Rousseau en Angleterre à l'époque romantique: les écrits autobiographiques et la légende* (Paris: Didier, 1956)

Walker, William, *Locke, Literary Criticism, and Philosophy* (Cambridge University Press, 1994)

Wallace, Karl R., *Francis Bacon on the Nature of Man: The Faculties of Man's Soul* (Urbana: University of Illinois Press, 1967)

Walmsley, Peter, 'Dispute and Conversation: Probability and the Rhetoric of Natural Philosophy in Locke's *Essay*', *Journal of the History of Ideas*, **54** (1993), 381–94

Wecter, Dixon, 'Burke's Theory of Words, Images and Emotions', *PMLA*, **55** (1940), 167–81

Weinberg, Bernard, 'Translations and Commentaries of Longinus, *On the Sublime*, to 1660: A Bibliography', *Modern Philology*, **47** (1950), 145–51

Weiskel, Thomas, *The Romantic Sublime: Studies in the Structure and Psychology of Transcendence* (Baltimore, MD: Johns Hopkins University Press, 1976)

Whelan, Frederick G., *Edmund Burke and India: Political Morality and Empire* (University of Pittsburgh Press, 1996)

White, Eugene F., *The Context of Human Discourse: A Configural Criticism of Rhetoric* (Columbia: University of South Carolina Press, 1992)

Wilkins, Burleigh Taylor, *The Problem of Burke's Political Philosophy* (Oxford: Clarendon Press, 1967)

Wilkinson, Clare, 'Politics and Topography in the Old House of Commons, 1783–1835', *Parliamentary History*, **21** (2002), 141–65

Williams, Melissa S., 'Burkean "Descriptions" and Political Representation: A Reappraisal', *Canadian Journal of Political Science*, **29** (1996), 23–45

Wilson, Catherine, *Epicureanism at the Origins of Modernity* (Oxford University Press, 2008)

Winkler, Kenneth P., 'Locke on Personal Identity', *Journal of the History of Philosophy*, **29** (1991), 201–26

Wisse, Jakob, *Ethos and Pathos from Aristotle to Cicero* (Amsterdam: Hakkert, 1989)

Wood, Neal, 'The Aesthetic Dimension of Burke's Political Thought', *Journal of British Studies*, **4** (1964), 41–64

Wu, Duncan, *Wordsworth's Reading, 1770–1799* (Cambridge University Press, 1993)

Young, Brian, *Religion and Enlightenment in Eighteenth-Century England: Theological Debate from Locke to Burke* (Oxford University Press, 1998)

Index